HORRIBLE PRETTINESS

Cultural Studies of

the United States

Alan Trachtenberg

editor

ROBERT C. ALLEN

HORRIBLE

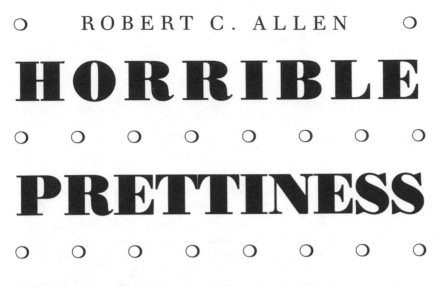

PRETTINESS

BURLESQUE AND AMERICAN CULTURE

The University of North Carolina Press   Chapel Hill and London

The publication of this work was made possible in part through a grant from the Division of Research Programs of the National Endowment for the Humanities, an independent federal agency whose mission is to award grants to support education, scholarship, media programming, libraries, and museums, in order to bring the results of cultural activities to a broad, general public.

Library of Congress Cataloging-in-Publication Data
Allen, Robert Clyde, 1950–
    Horrible prettiness : burlesque and American culture / Robert C. Allen.
        p.   cm. — (Cultural studies of the United States)
    Includes bibliographical references and index.
    ISBN 0-8078-1960-3 (alk. paper). — ISBN 0-8078-4316-4 (pbk.: alk. paper)
        1. Burlesque (Theater)—United States—History.   2. United States—Popular culture—19th century.   3. United States—Popular culture—20th century.   I. Title.   II. Series.
PN1948.U6A45   1991
792.7'0973—dc20   90-48608
                                                                                    CIP

Manufactured in the United States of America
95 94 93 92 91   5 4 3 2 1

Contents

○   ○   ○   ○   ○   ○   ○   ○   ○   ○   ○   ○

Illustrations

Foreword

○   ○   ○   ○   ○   ○   ○   ○   ○   ○   ○   ○

Among the hazards of submitting popular entertainments to scholarly study are the twin dangers of holding the subject in too low or too high a regard. Because topics like burlesque, or the television soap operas about which Robert Allen has written so knowingly in a previous book, still seem exotic and transgressive in academic settings, scholars are often tempted to cover themselves in elaborate apologies, by defensive condescension or over-celebration of their "low" subject matter. One of the many virtues immediately apparent in Allen's new book on burlesque is the author's total confidence in his subject, his respect for burlesque as a demanding and significant popular art form, one that invites imaginative participation by the scholar and rewards detailed historical attention and close formal analysis. The book represents its popular subject as a significant historical subject in its own right, not restricted to the segregated field of "popular culture," a category that often serves to quarantine the transgressive and routinize the scandalous. There is no special pleading in *Horrible Prettiness*, only a subtle, richly documented, and provocative argument with ramifications far beyond its explicit subject.

A critical history of American burlesque, its flowering in the late-middle nineteenth century, its decline into seamy quasi-pornographic theater for almost exclusively male audiences, and its final shabby demise (and collapse into a nostalgia-ridden trope) in the mid-twentieth century, Robert Allen's book provides a major investigation of the role of commercial popular culture in American urban society. What it shows about burlesque sheds light on modern popular forms in general. Allen reveals the subversive character of early burlesque, its calculated efforts to wring a wildly ironic humor by playing off against "high" cultural values, particularly regarding women. Half the book treats the original burlesque troupe of the Englishwoman Lydia Thompson, which stormed American cities starting in 1869. Initially dominated by women writers and producers as well as performers, burlesque took wicked fun in reversing roles, shattering polite expectations, brazenly challenging notions of the approved ways women might display their bodies and speak in public. Then, as American society in the later Gilded Age underwent increasing professionalization and cultural stratification, men took over. Controlled now by male theatrical proprietors and impresarios and booking agents, the once-sparkling wit, daring eroticism, and shuddering assault on all forms of respectability of original burlesque devolved into an increasingly disreputable vehicle for display of the voiceless female body in stylized erotic gyrating motion, starting with the cooch dance in the 1890s and the shimmy and striptease dances of the early twentieth century. Speech was taken from women performers, and sexuality in the debased form of the stylized erotic dance was separated from the insubordination that had given early burlesque its threatening electrical charge. Denied their voice and the chance to talk back, and placed onstage by profiteering male handlers as forbidden objects of gazing male audiences, female performers lost their power to unsettle and subvert.

In rich detail *Horrible Prettiness* traces and interprets this transformation by placing it in relation to social, demographic, and cultural changes in post–Civil War and early twentieth-century America. It shows the intertwined cultural valences of class distinction and gender role and how hierarchies in the form of gender stereotypes ignore class boundaries. We see how displays of the female body in other media (legitimate theater, photography, and early cinema especially) provided a cultural setting in which burlesque became increasingly the very definition of the "low." Cultural definitions of "low" and "high," the book argues throughout, project broader conceptions of power, of domination and subordination, of the cultural process of "ordination" as such. Early burlesque attacked the stereotype of the independent woman as a "low other" and through its inversions onstage enacted alternative values; it *reordinated* according to implicitly freer, unrepressed, and thus oppositional standards of value. The threat of cultural inversion and reordination, Allen argues provocatively, helps explain the devolution of burlesque into illicit salacious sexuality, with a strong working-class aura. It was a way of controlling by quarantine a potential contagion.

The book is partly a narrative history, fascinating in its accounts of performance styles, scripts, costumes, music and dance, of commercial and legal arrangements, and of the furor of conflicted response in the popular and genteel press. Allen shows how burlesque developed by assimilating elements of earlier commercial theater in America and other entertainment forms that arose during the antebellum years of rapid urbanization, such as dime museums, concert saloons, minstrel shows, and circuses. He shows, too, in a brilliant concluding chapter on the twentieth century, how the original vitality of burlesque survived and reappeared in the figure of the "unruly woman" into which Sophie Tucker and Mae West breathed new creative life. Treating these women of extraordinary (and extraordinarily subverting) talent in proximity with the Ziegfeld *Follies* and other bowdlerized and defanged revisions of original burlesque, Allen extends the range of his study beyond burlesque itself into the domain of the female popular performer as such.

An original chronicle of popular cultural history, the book makes its most powerful mark as an interpretation. The *legibility* of burlesque, what performances *meant* to its predominantly female performers and its predominantly male audiences – this is the core of Allen's study. The question of meaning focuses Allen's reconstructions of essentially ephemeral artifacts, that is, live performances before an audience. Never losing sight of the "irreducible complexity of burlesque" embodied in the irrecoverable chemic elements of performance like gesture, color, inflection, rapport between performers and audience, Allen argues at once for the necessity of interpretation and for its final limits. Burlesque survives in Allen's book as a living experience richer than anything the historian can say about it. Yet only the act of interpretation brings that surfeit of irrecoverable meaning into play. The book provides a much-needed demonstration of how a scholarly work on a popular theme can avoid the hazard of overkill. Allen explains only as much as necessary.

Horrible Prettiness turns an important corner in recent cultural studies, for it shows how entertainment subjects can at once give pleasure and serve the serious interests of cultural history and criticism. The book brings its more or less ephemeral subject of entertainment performances to a par, as a subject of critical and historical interest, with the closed and determinant written texts of traditional literary or theatrical subjects. It shows that the ephemerality of improvised performance can indeed be captured and reconstructed into significant cultural texts without depleting the special meanings that attach to improvisatory performance itself. And most memorably, in its analysis of the social dynamics that shaped the meaning of popular entertainment forms, *Horrible Prettiness* gives us a prime lesson in the dialectical reading of cultural texts. The book recovers a lost but revealing component of American cultural life and teaches a way of listening to and watching the popular voices, images, and moving bodies of contemporary life.

Alan Trachtenberg

Acknowledgments

○ ○ ○ ○ ○ ○ ○ ○ ○ ○ ○ ○

A number of institutions and individuals provided invaluable assistance to me during the research and writing of this book. Among the former are the libraries and archives I consulted, especially the Harvard Theatre Collection; the Performing Arts Collection of the New York Public Library; and the Manuscripts, Prints and Photographs, and Motion Pictures divisions of the Library of Congress. In this regard, special thanks go to Patrick Loughney, archivist, scholar, and gentleman of the Motion Pictures Division, for his masterful guidance through the Library of Congress's vast but, to the outsider, largely hidden wealth of popular cultural treasures. A grant from the Research Council of the University of North Carolina at Chapel Hill supported travel to these archives, and a grant from the College of Arts and Sciences' Publication, Performance, and Exhibition Fund aided with the reproduction of illustrations.

A year at the National Humanities Center, supported by a fellowship from the American Council of Learned Societies and research leave from the University of North Carolina at Chapel Hill, gave me the time to think about what I wanted this book to be. The center's amazing library staff enabled me to follow out connections between burlesque and other aspects of American culture, and other fellows served as helpful sounding boards for some of my ideas as this project gradually took shape. If, as people around here are fond of saying, the Chapel Hill area is the "southern part of heaven," then the National Humanities Center is heaven's cloister.

Any scholarly project that takes four years to gestate almost inevitably is shaped by the comments, insights, and ideas of colleagues and friends. That is certainly the case with this book. I was greatly aided in the revision of the manuscript by the insightful critiques and helpful xvi ○ *Acknowledgments*

suggestions of Alan Trachtenberg, Peter Buckley, and Kathy Peiss. Professor Buckley also generously shared with me his own important work in this area and put me on the trail of several important, fugitive sources. Over the past several years I have learned much – about gender representation, the study of culture, ballet, and lobsters – from discussions with Jane Desmond, John Fiske, and Jane Gaines. I have given presentations drawn from the book in several forums: at Yale University, the University of Wisconsin–Madison, the University of Akron, and Rhodes College. Comments and questions from faculty and students helped to sharpen my thinking and strengthen my arguments.

On a more personal level, my wife Allison not only persevered but also actively supported me during the long process of seeing this book to completion. Finally, in a strange way, some of the credit for this book goes to my mother. She is the least likely person I know to have given birth to a burlesque scholar, but had it not been for her hard work, encouragement, and example, I would not have become a scholar at all.

HORRIBLE PRETTINESS

1

○　○　○　○　○　○　○　○

A Chronicle of Lydia Thompson's

First Season in America

DRAMATIS PERSONAE

MARS – commander-in-chief, as Ma's usually are. THE NINE
MUSES, including POLLY HYMNIA. Those Thessalians who
would be these aliens if they weren't natives; dreadful Demo-
crats, members of several secret societies who demand the right
of free speaking in a state of free-dumb. Crowd of Red Repub-
licans, unread republicans, avengers, scavengers, Greeks,
sneaks, and female furies.

– Ixion

○ ○ ○ ○ ○ ○ ○ ○ ○ ○ ○ ○ ○ ○ ○ ○

On February 8, 1868, the following classified advertisement appeared in the *New York Clipper*, America's principal theatrical trade paper:

> Miss Lydia Thompson, the Celebrated Burlesque, will arrive in New York in August or September. Applications for engagements to be made to Mr. Alex. Henderson, Prince of Wales' Theatre, Liverpool.

To the theater managers, actors, and aficionados who constituted the primary readership of the *Clipper*, this notice was not the first they had read of Lydia Thompson and certainly not the first they had heard of burlesque. But the ad was confirmation of reports circulated over the past eighteen months that the talk of the London theater scene would be coming to the United States.

Her debut in New York had already been arranged: in the summer of 1866 George Wood, owner of several Manhattan theaters, had asked Thompson to appear at his 1,302-seat Broadway Theater near Broome Street in lower Manhattan. But before she received the invitation, Thompson had already signed to appear at the Prince of Wales Theater in London. Success there, at the Drury Lane, and especially in the winter and spring of 1868 at the Strand delayed her accepting Wood's offer until the summer of that year. In the meantime, Wood had purchased Banvard's Museum and Theater farther uptown on the west side of Broadway near Thirtieth Street and decided on Thompson and her company as the bill to open the refurbished theater (reportedly at a cost of $30,000) in the fall of 1868. The renovated museum would boast a theater seating over 2,200 and, beneath it, an 800-seat lecture room for the display of "living curiosities."[1] The idea of combining a "museum" of living and inanimate curiosities with a theater was not original to George Wood. P. T. Barnum, who served as adviser to Wood on the "natural history" side of his operation and who was scheduled to give

3

The playbill for *Ixion*.
(Billy Rose Theatre Collection, New York Public Library)

the inaugural address on the facility's opening, twenty years before had begun the practice of presenting "highly moral and instructive domestic dramas" at his American Museum.[2]

When she made her first of several trips to America in August 1868, Lydia Thompson was thirty-two and had been on the stage for sixteen years. Her Quaker father died when she was three, but her mother remarried a fairly well-to-do businessman, enabling Thompson to take dancing lessons from one of the most popular teachers in London. An apt pupil, Thompson was just about to leave for further training in Italy when her stepfather's business failure necessitated her putting her dancing talents to professional use. Her first parts were in pantomimes and extravaganzas. In 1854 a Spanish dancer, billed as the most accomplished in Europe, played London. Thompson, then at the St. James Theater, proved that she could match her step for step, making Thompson something of a national cultural hero and a popular sensation.

On the basis of her success at the St. James, Thompson toured Europe and Russia for three years – the tour coming to a premature conclusion in August 1859 with the death of her mother. Over the next five years Thompson starred in a series of successful extravaganzas in London. She married a prosperous businessman and, in May 1864, gave birth to a daughter. With the death of her husband in a riding accident in June, however, Thompson once again found herself in financial straits. She accepted the offer of Alexander Henderson, manager of the Theater Royal Birkenhead (across the river from Liverpool), to star in F. C. Burnand's burlesque, *Ixion; or, The Man at the Wheel.* After two seasons in Liverpool, she returned to London. Henderson went with her, and they were married in February 1868. That summer Thompson and her new husband-*cum*-manager left London for America on the steamship *City of Antwerp*, flush with her most recent success in William Brough's *Field of the Cloth of Gold* at the Strand Theater. She brought with her four other performers who had already achieved considerable renown as burlesque performers on the London stage: Ada Harland, with whom she had worked at the Strand; Lisa Weber, from the Covent Garden; Pauline Markham, from the Queen's; and Harry Beckett, the only male member of the company, a comic actor who had worked with Thompson and for her husband at Liverpool's Prince of Wales Theater.[3]

By the time Thompson and her company docked in New York on

Lydia Thompson as Ixion.
(Prints and Photographs Division, Library of Congress)

August 23, the troupe's publicist, Archie Gordon, had already begun his publicity campaign for Thompson's debut at Wood's Broadway Theater, now scheduled for mid-September. The campaign focused on Thompson's European and British celebrity. Members of the New York press received an eight-page biography, which claimed that Thompson provoked such adulation among her male fans that her European tour had resulted in suicides and duels:

> At Helsingfors [Helsinki] her pathway was strewn with flowers and the streets illuminated with torches carried by her ardent admirers. At Cologne, the students insisted on sending the horses about their business and drawing the carriage that contained the object of their devotions themselves. At Riga and other Russian towns in the Baltic, it became an almost universal custom to exhibit her portrait on one side of the stove to correspond with that of the Czar on the other side. At Lemberg, a Captain Ludoc Baumbarten of the Russian dragoons, took some flowers and a glove belonging to Miss Thompson, placed them on his breast; then shot himself through the heart, leaving on his table a note stating that his love for her brought on the fatal act.[4]

The Season, tongue-in-cheek, warned on August 29: "She has become really quite dangerous. . . . We are [*sic*] an old stager, and have a heart not at all susceptible of female charms, but we are positively becoming quite afraid of Miss Lydia Thompson, and, judging from the newspaper reports of her exploits in Russia and Germany, we should imagine it will become a very grave question with the governments of these respective countries, whether her presence there again can be permitted without endangering the sanity of the whole nation."[5]

The charismatic sexuality suggested by Gordon's publicity campaign material is curiously absent from the visual representations of Thompson and her troupe that accompanied it. The poster for *Ixion*, preserved by the New York Public Library, shows a demure head-and-shoulders engraving of Thompson in street clothes, which, as her biographer puts it, "resembles more a finishing school portrait than a theatrical advertisement." Similar images of Thompson and Markham appeared in newspaper accounts, among them the *New York Clipper*.[6] It is, of course, notoriously difficult to assess the perceived beauty of a person from a vantage point of a century later, and, as we shall see, normative notions about feminine beauty in 1868 were themselves undergoing considerable change – change that was related to the representations of femininity on the burlesque stage. However, there is little in the contemporaneous pictures or renderings of Thompson to suggest that she was a woman perceived to be of such extraordinary beauty by most that the very sight of her was enough to prompt "adoration amounting almost to mania."[7] She was petite, with dark blonde hair, a round face, blue eyes, and a somewhat long and pointed nose. Pauline Markham was the "Blonde" whom some would regard as the most attractive of the troupe. Charles Burnham, writing in 1917, remembered Markham as "the most beautifully formed woman who had ever appeared on the stage." In its generally favorable review of *Ixion*, the *Clipper* critic called Thompson "well proportioned . . . but by no means handsome." A few months later, the *Clipper* complained that the reputation of the "British Blondes" rested on their allure below the waist, not above the neck: "If you would seek for corresponding features of beauty in their faces, the disappointment is great. A more disastrous set of ballet girls, according to their facial index, it has not entered the hearts of men to conceive. In vain do we look for those touches of loveliness which make men fall down and worship the sex; scan them with a lenient eye, the result is the same."[8]

Public discourse, then – both that produced on behalf of Thompson by her publicity apparatus and (perhaps influenced by it) that overlapping discourse that served as a vehicle for and a response to Archie Gordon's efforts in the general and trade press – emphasized the famousness of Thompson, achieved through her ability to elicit the most fanatical devotion from her male following. Even papers that expressed doubts about the accuracy of Gordon's accounts of the mass male hysteria provoked by Thompson, such as the *Spirit of the Times*, a New York sporting and dramatic paper, ran those accounts nevertheless. But the renderings of Thompson accompanying these accounts gave no clue as to the source of this sexual magnetism. The reader – no doubt in keeping with Gordon's plan – would have to see for himself what all the fuss was about.

By the evening of the debut, Monday, September 28, all of the 2,265 seats in Wood's theater were sold. Ticket prices – which the management proudly announced had not been raised for this special attraction – ranged from $1.50 for an orchestra chair to 75¢ in the family circle. To reach the theater, the audience entered on the ground floor of

Pauline Markham, "the most beautifully formed woman who had
ever appeared on the stage."
(Prints and Photographs Division, Library of Congress)

the building, which contained wax figures, statuary, an aquarium, and other displays, and passed by the 800-seat lecture room, where the living attractions were exhibited. Among the latter that day were a dwarf named General Grant, a giantess, and a precocious three-year-old named Sophia Gantz, billed as the "Baby Woman." The theater critic for the *Clipper* penned this telling poem about the attraction with whom Thompson shared billing that evening:

> At Wood's new museum they have
> A living curiosity,
> A baby woman, one they call
> A natural precocity;
> To tell the truth, though, we don't think
> She's very much to talk about,
> Since we can hundreds see each day
> As on the street they walk about;
> For slender, stout, or short or tall,
> Most women babies are – that's all.

A refreshment saloon (nonalcoholic) and shooting gallery were in the basement.[9]

The entertainment in the theater on the second floor began at eight p.m. with Harry Beckett in a farcical curtain raiser entitled *To Oblige Benson*. Then came *Ixion*. The play was a general lampoon of classical culture and mythological allusion composed in punning rhymed pentameter. Because no script of the version of the play presented on the New York stage survives, it is impossible to know how much of F. C. Burnand's 1863 text survives. In Burnand's bastardization of the Greek myth of Ixion, the king of Thessaly (Lydia Thompson) has lost all of his money betting on the horses and cannot pay the dowry for his new wife. He kills his father-in-law, which prompts his wife to lead a revolt against him. Fearing that she will succeed, Ixion calls upon Jupiter for help. The curtains open revealing Ixion crouching before the altar of Jupiter's temple, praying for his help in escaping the wrath of his wife:

Ixion: Come Jupiter [*Music – rumbling noise*]
     What have I done?
     Pale fear!
     My cheek begins to blanch.

Ada Harland, playing Jupiter, suddenly appears on the altar in a puff of smoke:

> Jupiter: Who summons us by journey atmospherical?
>   Whose bawling has made Juno quite hysterical?
>   Is this the worm? [*Examines Ixion through a telescope*]
>   What means this stupid dolt?
>   I've half a mind to hurl a thunderbolt!
> Ixion: Don't be excited, Jupiter, and pray
>   Apologize for me to Mrs. J;
>   I feel, before your royal carriage, humble.
> Jupiter: Carriage? I came here in a volcanic rumble.
>   Whose is the cry raised by gross mortal fears
>   That reaches from our Temples to our ears?

At first, Jupiter does not remember Ixion very well:

> Jupiter: As I am Jove, of course, I ought to know
>   What's going on upon the earth below;
>   But yet your wedding I don't recollect;
>   I hope that Hymen –
> Ixion: Oh, 'twas quite correct.

Jupiter suggests that Ixion come to live among the gods. Mercury (Lisa Weber) accompanies him to Mount Olympus, where he meets and flirts with Venus (Pauline Markham). Cupid does not like the idea of a mortal dallying with his mother and redirects Ixion's amorous attentions toward Jupiter's wife, Juno (Alice Logan). Jupiter discovers them and sentences Ixion to be bound eternally to a giant celestial wheel. But an appeal is made to a greater power than Jupiter – the audience:

> Ganymede: True, Jove; what's one of your most awful nods
>   To the disapprobation of the gods?
>   [*Looking to the gallery*]

But rather than the fiery sky wheel of Greek myth, Ixion at the end of the play is shown behind a giant ship's wheel:

> Ixion: This is the Wheel, friends, which we hope will steer us
>   Safely through the many dangers that are near us.
>   And may it prove, if shoals and rocks are clear,

> A wheel of fortune to the players here.
> On you depends, you, to whom we appeal,
> Ixion's *welfare*, that's Ixion's *weal*.[10]

Burnand's play probably provided no more than a skeletal structure on which were hung topical allusions, popular songs, familiar airs to which new lyrics had been composed, dances, and even more outrageous puns. Thompson's portrayal of Ixion made allusion to "the wickedest man in the world," a notorious rake and con man who had recently launched a lucrative second career as a lecturer on the evils of his past. The plot of *Ixion* easily lent itself to poking fun at recent divorce cases among the socially elite. There was a send-up of the cancan, which had been recently introduced from Paris, as well as a Parisian fashion import, a dress style called the "Grecian bend."

As was the tradition in burlesque, the music for *Ixion* was borrowed from the repertoire of popular songs of the moment, some of which were given new lyrics or a new twist in performance. "Barbe Bleue" was taken from the Offenbach opéra bouffe of the same name then playing at Niblo's Garden. The popular ditty, "Ringing for Sarah," was sung by the entire cast while ringing bells of every size and description. One of the hit numbers was the popular song, "While Strolling through the Park One Day":

> While strolling thro' the park one day,
> In the merry month of May,
> I was taken by surprise by a pair of roguish eyes,
> In a moment my poor heart was stole away.
>
> A smile was all she gave to me.
> Of course we were as happy as could be
> I immediately rais'd my hat,
> Finally she remark'd;
> I never shall forget that lovely afternoon
> I met her at the fountain in the park.[11]

Dances were just as eclectic and exuberant. In addition to the cancan, the show contained jigs, hornpipes, and parodies of minstrel show numbers.

What we can say about the response of the audience that Monday evening – as reported in the daily and trade press – is that it found something in Thompson and her troupe that it liked and liked very much, indeed. Songs and dances were encored several times. The staid *New York Times* characterized the troupe's success that evening as "unbounded": "The wildest symptoms of delight burst forth as each individual of the new company appeared, and Miss Thompson, Miss Markham, and Miss Weber were nearly lost in several floral avalanches which occurred during the progress of the entertainment." Even the *Spirit of the Times*, the paper most critical of Gordon's puffery, had to admit: "Still, there is no question that Miss Lydia has made a great popular hit. . . . Remarkably free from vulgarity and coarseness of mien or gesture, she has captivated her audiences, men and women, by her delightful deviltry." Within a week of Thompson's debut, Wood's was turning away crowds nightly. The theater took in more than $46,000 in October, nearly twice its gross the previous month and more than any other New York theater for the month, outpacing the second-place theater by nearly $15,000. As with nearly all specific performances of American popular entertainment, we know almost nothing about the individuals who constituted Wood's audience on September 28 or on succeeding days, but it is likely that these first audiences were what could roughly be called middle-class men and women.[12]

About the exact nature of the staging of *Ixion* we can only speculate. Several reviews noted the absence of the sort of scenic effects on which the extravaganza depended, pointing out that the performers themselves had to carry the full weight of the show. As for the costumes, carte-de-visite photographs of Thompson and her troupe give us some idea of their nature and extent. One photo, which, judging from the design of the costume, was probably of Thompson as she appeared as Ixion, shows her in a stylized Greek tunic: tight at the waist, a full skirt reaching to within a few inches of the knees, and a scooped but not particularly revealing neckline. She also wears opaque (probably flesh-colored) tights and ankle-length boots. In general, we can say that the costumes worn by the troupe were different in style but no more revealing than those worn by ballet dancers of the period.

The initial critical response to *Ixion* was favorable and focused on the looks and abilities of the principal female performers. The *New York Clipper* called Thompson, Markham, and Weber "perfect blondes, whose flowing golden hair charms all beholders. This burlesque appears to have been written expressly to bring into play the histrionic

powers and fatal fascinations of these ladies, setting the city in a fer-
ment." The reviewer, as we have seen, was given to couching his criticism in verse. Of Thompson's portrayal of Ixion, he wrote:

> In breeches so well she played the cheat,
> The pretty fellow, and the rake complete,
> Each sex was, with different passions mov'd;
> The men grew envious, and the women lov'd.[13]

Although the city was flooded by carte-de-visite photographs of
Thompson, Markham, and Weber, it was Pauline Markham whose
beauty was most celebrated. In 1871 she recalled that Alexander Henderson lodged the cast at the Spingler Hotel, where he made them
virtual prisoners in an attempt to keep their New York admirers at bay.
When Markham contrived to slip out to dinner with one who seemed a
respectable gentleman, he kidnapped her and ordered his driver to take
them out of the city. There he tried to force her to marry him at the point
of a gun. She was rescued by the driver.[14]

The *New York Times* followed a brief notice on September 29 with a
fuller review on October 1. It read in part:

> Miss THOMPSON is a blonde of the purest type, saucy, blue-eyed,
> golden-haired and of elegant figure. She seems to be a sort of
> Prometheus in ardor and ambition, and breathes the breath of life
> into everything she does, whether it be in making wicked advances
> on the wives of the gods, or singing local songs, or in beating DAN
> BRYANT [a famous minstrel performer and dancer] at his own
> trade. It is hard to judge of her as an actress, in a disguise that robs
> her sex of all its charms, for Miss THOMPSON has to swear,
> swagger, and be otherwise masculine as Ixion, but as to the manner
> in which she plays this part this must be said, that she is lively,
> vivacious, and spirited, and although some exceptions may be
> taken to her costume, and that of her companions, no one can do so
> from artistic reasons; the statuesque is certainly not violated in this
> respect; nature has her own. Miss THOMPSON's voice is quite
> sufficient for the duty required in a burlesque of this character,
> where distinctness is one of the requisites. Miss ADA HARLAND
> is a much better dancer – the cleverest and most graceful of the
> troupe, indeed – and Miss WEBER's vocalism is better. . . . Miss

PAULINE MARKHAM, who personates Venus, comes as near a personal realization of the goddess as one can expect of mortal woman. Like Miss THOMPSON she has golden tresses, but her eyes are dark and piercing.[15]

The *Spirit of the Times* was impressed by the response of the crowd, even if its reviewer did not particularly like the piece ("entirely unworthy of the management"). The reviewer was, to some degree at least, impressed by Thompson: "Miss Lydia Thompson appeared in the title role, and made a genuine success. Not that she is the least bit of an actress, for if she were, the part affords her no scope for the display of histrionic talent; but she is a good dancer, has been gifted with a sweet voice, – not very fresh at present, – dresses superbly, and is happy in the possession of a magnificent figure and a pretty face." This paper was one of the first to comment on the troupe's blondeness and how it might have been achieved. After discussing the blonde hair of Thompson and Markham, the reviewer says of Lisa Weber: "[She] too has yellow hair, and it is probably all her own, for the property man rarely furnishes such things, and the chances are that she paid for it herself. Still, whether there is a substratum of objectionable black or brown under the upper crust of tow, we do not know; but to the eye she was fashionable, as well as fascinating."[16]

Ixion ran at Wood's theater until December 28, when it was replaced by the Thompson troupe in another burlesque, *Ernani; or, The Horn of a Dilemma*. Wood's continued to do the best business of any New York theater: nearly $46,000 in November and $40,000 in the third month of *Ixion*'s run. Two days before *Ixion* closed, it was announced that Niblo's Garden had secured Thompson and company for an engagement to begin on February 1. Many regarded Niblo's as the finest theater in America, and in recent years it had become particularly famous for its presentation of extravaganzas and spectacles, including the enormously successful ballet, *The Black Crook*, whose fifteen-month run at the theater had ended the previous January. The huge stage of the 3,200-seat theater was specially equipped to handle the scenic effects, transformations, and elaborate mechanical illusions that had become an expected part of spectacle theater. The theater's considerable experience in and technical resources for spectacle were put at Thompson's disposal in her production of *The Forty Thieves; or, Striking Oil in*

Family Jars, which opened at Niblo's on February 1. The piece was written by prolific English burlesque author H. J. Byron but, once again, seems to have been considerably amended in performance. As in *Ixion*, women assumed the principal male roles, including all forty of the thieves.[17]

Soon after Thompson's move to Niblo's and thus into the New York theatrical spotlight there was an abrupt shift in the tenor of the critical discourse on burlesque. The same papers that had lauded the performance at Wood's attacked it at Niblo's. Burlesque was "re-viewed" as the "leg business" and the "nude drama," and burlesque performers were recast as "brazen-faced, stained, yellow-haired, padded limbed creatures."[18] Instead of innocuous nonsense, burlesque came to be characterized as a cultural epidemic of indecency, impudence, and suggestive sexual display that, far from rescuing the theater from tameness, poisoned it and all society with it. Crowds still flocked to see Lydia Thompson and her troupe, but they did so in the face of what can only be called a hysterical antiburlesque discourse. By the time Thompson ended her run at Niblo's in May, all the major papers had denounced burlesque. Several attacked Thompson and her manager/husband Alexander Henderson personally. Joining this antiburlesque campaign were ministers, legislators, literary figures, and suffragettes.

The burlesque "disease" had indeed spread throughout the New York theatrical scene in the winter and spring of 1869. Although the Thompson troupe left Wood's at the end of January, burlesque remained there: a company headed by Mr. and Mrs. W. J. Florence produced William Brough's *Field of the Cloth of Gold*, in which Thompson had starred at the Strand Theater in London the previous spring. Although, as was the custom by now, the original English version had been altered for American audiences, both versions ended with references to woman suffrage. In the American version:

> Darnley: Who's to speak the tag?
> Henry: I will.
> Francis: No you won't.
> Constance: I will if someone don't.
> Darnley: No, no, not tonight.
>   You're a woman and have no right.
> DeVeau: I'll do it.

Henry: Shut up, old bloat!
Constance: The time will come when we
                    Will have our right and vote.
Darnley: Well, for precedence no more let's parley.
                    Cut the tag and sing the finale![19]

On February 18 Elise Holt, another English burlesque performer (who, in fact, had appeared with Thompson at the Strand the previous spring), opened the new Waverly Theater (formerly Kelly and Leon's Minstrel Hall) in *Lucretia Borgia, M.D.* In the final scene, Holt, dressed in purple velvet pants, a white satin coat, and a white silk hat, smokes a cigar and sings "Up in a Balloon":

> I am, you know, a Madison belle,
> Who did captivate one a magnificent swell,
> He was envoy, embassador or something rare,
> To king what's-his-name, of I do-not-know-where!
> 'Twas at Saratoga, a year come next June,
> We walk'd and we talk'd by the light of the moon;
> There was squeezing of hands, follow'd up by a kiss,
> And as far's I remember, I felt just like this.
> Ah! Up in a balloon, boys, up in a balloon.

Holt brought in three times more business in the first month of the Waverly's operation than in the last month under the minstrel show policy.[20]

By March, burlesque had become so prominent a cultural phenomenon that it was the subject of a burlesque. The week of March 29, Tony Pastor staged *Romeo and Juliet; or, The Beautiful Blonde Who Dyed (Her Hair) for Love.* Scene I was set in "A Street in the Fourteenth Ward, Verona" and Scene III in "The Capulet's Back Garden, Hoboken."[21]

Meanwhile, each staging of a new burlesque seemed determined to outdo the last and its competitors in terms of scale, lavishness of costumes and production, topicality, and daring. In May, Marie Longmore starred in a production of *Robinson Crusoe* at Wood's, which featured, according to the *New York Clipper*, one of the most elaborate processions ever seen on the American stage: "First come twenty-four girls as Amazon warriors, with shields and armor, followed by six negro minstrels, who sing 'De King Am Coming,' accompanying themselves first on the banjo, then the bones, then do a wooden shoe dance. Six more savages appear as ostriches, followed by six negro guards, six female savages, six with bells and fans, six native warriors, and twenty-four female cymbal dancers, who dance and keep good time with their cymbals. The king brings up the rear in his alligator chariot, attended by six negro guards." The procession took half an hour to unfold.[22]

At Niblo's, the Thompson troupe brought in $54,487 in February – more in one month than any other theater had achieved in the past two years and more than in the best month of *The Black Crook*. Business remained strong into the spring. During the final week of May, *The Forty Thieves* was succeeded by *Sinbad the Sailor; or, The Ungenial Genii and the Cabin Boy*, which ran through July. This final production of Thompson's first New York season – a season that lasted forty-five weeks – was, as might be predicted, not well received by the critics. The scene that came in for the most censure was a parody of the slave market scene in Dion Boucicault's 1859 drama, *The Octaroon*. In "The Matrimonial Market," Thompson appeared as a "girl of the period" in a huge blonde wig and a Grecian bend walking dress. In a stump speech she described the qualities of the "new" woman. "She straddles well a velocipede," declared Thompson, and is very much aware of her "own awarishness."[23]

Sinbad closed at Niblo's in late July, whereupon Thompson rested at Niagra Falls before beginning a seven-month tour of the East and the Midwest. Reprising *Ixion*, *The Forty Thieves*, and *Sinbad*, she and the troupe played Buffalo, Philadelphia, Washington, D.C., Baltimore, Cincinnati, Louisville, Chicago, St. Louis, and New Orleans; then they worked their way back north, returning to Cincinnati in January and Chicago in February. At every stop they played to packed houses and to generally favorable press notices. The *Clipper*, which noted the progress of the tour as it did all major road shows, made little mention of adverse criticism in the cities Thompson played. Indeed, the paper commented that in Philadelphia theatergoers seemed disappointed that the performance was not as salacious as the New York press had led them to believe it would be.[24] Until its return engagement in Chicago in February 1870, the troupe caused more of a stir by its topical humor than by anything else. While at Washington's National Theater in October, one of the performers alluded to former president Andrew Johnson, creating a "disgraceful scene" among his supporters and detractors in the audience.[25]

The troupe's first appearance at Crosby's Opera House in Chicago (November 1869) was marked by "an immense audience," which demanded no less than sixteen encores, and favorable press coverage – one paper even noting that "for the relief of the fair sex who are dying to see it, we may say [the performance is] entirely devoid of any improprieties of speech."[26] When Thompson returned in February, however, she was met by a series of personal attacks by editor Wilbur F. Storey of the *Chicago Times*, who only ten weeks before had said she "possess[ed] all of the qualifications for a pleasing actress in light comedy characters." In a letter to the *Times*, Thompson defended burlesque as "harmless entertainment," which, however intellectually frivolous, was not morally objectionable. She denied that double entendres or "extravagant action" had ever been permitted in her performances and took as her motto, *Honi soit qui mal y pense* (roughly, Evil to he who thinks evil of me). Storey redoubled his attacks, charging that Thompson and her troupe "have made an unnecessary and lewd exhibition of their persons, such as would not be tolerated by the police in any bawdy house; that they have made use of broad, low and degrading language, such as men of any self respect would repudiate, even in the absence of ladies; that their entertainments have been mere vehicles for the exhibition of coarse women and the use of disreputable language unrelieved by any wit or humor."[27]

At about six p.m. on February 24, Lydia Thompson, Pauline Markham, Alexander Henderson, and publicist Archie Gordon were waiting in a carriage outside the Wabash Avenue home of Wilbur Storey.[28] When he and his wife emerged, Gordon grabbed Storey and held him while Thompson and Markham horsewhipped him. His wife urged him to draw his gun, but as he put his hand in his pocket, Henderson produced his own gun, warning Storey: "If you draw your pistol I will shoot you like a dog." Their mission accomplished, Thompson and company departed in their carriage.

The following morning the group appeared in a crowded courtroom to answer charges of assault. The assailants' attorneys did not attempt to defend their clients' actions as legal but rather urged the judge's understanding that, because their peripatetic schedule made a libel suit impractical, their behavior was morally and socially justifiable. The judge fined Thompson, Markham, and Henderson one hundred dollars each and Gordon ten dollars. After paying their fines, they rode away from the courthouse, according to one account, to the cheers of two thousand people who had gathered outside.

That afternoon, the matinee performance at Crosby's was prevented by the rearrest of Thompson and company for fomenting a riot. They were fined and released. The evening performance went on as usual, the theater being completely sold out for *The Forty Thieves*. The episode with Storey was made a part of the show. When one character insulted another, the latter ad-libbed: "Do that again and I'll have you arrested for riot." Thompson's character remarked, "I feel like a leaky ship." Why? "Because I had to be bailed out." At the end of the performance, Thompson addressed the members of the audience. She thanked them for their support and explained that, although she had breached the peace in the eyes of the law, "The persistent and personally vindictive assault in the *Times* upon my reputation left me only one mode of redress. . . . They were women whom he attacked. It was by women he was castigated. . . . We did what the law would not do for us." The next day the company left for Detroit, where it played without incident.

In the ten months of its first season in New York and during its subsequent national tour, the Lydia Thompson Troupe became a theatrical phenomenon in the United States. The troupe had maintained its popularity for forty-five weeks (half of them at New York's most prestigious theater), appearing in four different productions in the leading theatrical city in the country. In all, Thompson generated $372,500 in box office receipts in New York – $54,000 in her first month at Niblo's alone.

Although Thompson's was the most successful burlesque troupe that season, others found large audiences as well. Archie Gordon might have centered his predebut hype around the charisma of Thompson herself, but clearly she was not alone responsible for burlesque's popularity. Nor was she alone responsible for the public controversy burlesque provoked or for the extraordinary vilification its detractors would heap upon it. Something about Thompson's brand of burlesque – as practiced by others as well as herself – had struck a remarkably responsive chord among record numbers of theatergoers and, at the same time, a very sensitive nerve among a wide range of individuals who were in a position to have their opinions publicly circulated. Seldom in the history of American theater has a new dramatic form engendered such extreme responses on such a broad scale.

However, Thompson's success in America *was* responsible for transforming what burlesque was understood to be – by those who performed it, those who attended its performances, and those who wrote about it. Every New York theatrical season between 1869 and 1938 included some variant of burlesque that could be traced back to *Ixion* and *The Forty Thieves*. From *Ixion* on, burlesque in America was inextricably tied to the issue of the spectacular female performer, and from then on burlesque implicitly raised troubling questions about how a woman should be "allowed" to act on stage, about how femininity should and could be represented, and about the relationship of women onstage to women in the outside, "real" world.

○ ○ ○ ○ ○ ○ ○ ○

The Intelligibility of Burlesque

> *And way down in front by the footlights glow,*
>
> *The bald-headed men sat in the front row.*
>
> *They had big glasses to see all the sights*
>
> *Including the blondes who danced in silk tights.*
>
> *– Lydia Thompson*

○ ○ ○ ○ ○ ○ ○ ○ ○ ○ ○ ○ ○ ○ ○ ○

In August 1869, while the New York theater languished in its traditional summer doldrums, Richard Grant White reflected on burlesque's remarkable triumph during the season just ended:

> It means something, this outbreak of burlesque acting all over the world. No mere accident has made so monstrous a kind of entertainment equally acceptable to three publics so different as those of Paris, London, and New York. And by monstrous I do not mean wicked, disgusting, or hateful, but monstrously incongruous and unnatural. The peculiar trait of burlesque is its defiance both of the natural and the conventional. Rather, it forces the conventional and the natural together just at the points where they are most remote, and the result is absurdity, monstrosity. Its system is a defiance of system. It is out of *all* keeping. . . . [B]urlesque casts down all the gods from their pedestals.[1]

In a sense, one of the principal projects of this book is to cast White's observation in the interrogatory: What did burlesque mean and to whom? The answers are several, complex, and only partially discernible, but they seem to center around the key quality White ascribes to burlesque: its monstrosity. William Dean Howells, whose essay on burlesque appeared but only months before White's, was similarly struck by the incongruities that lay at the heart of burlesque and its representation of femininity. Strangely enthralled and repulsed by burlesque performers' impersonations of masculinity, Howells declared: "[T]hough they were not like men, [they] were in most things as unlike women, and seemed creatures of a kind of alien sex, parodying both. It was certainly a shocking thing to look at them with their horrible prettiness, their archness in which was no charm, their grace which put to shame."[2]

To cast these two insightful characterizations of burlesque in somewhat more modern (and theoretically grounded) terms, we might say that burlesque is one of several nineteenth-century entertainment forms that is grounded in the aesthetics of transgression, inversion, and the grotesque. The burlesque performer represents a construction of what Peter Stallybrass and Allon White call the "low other": something that is reviled by and excluded from the dominant social order as debased, dirty, and unworthy, but that is simultaneously the object of desire and/or fascination. As they put it, "the low-other is despised and denied at the level of political organization and social being whilst it is instrumentally constitutive of the shared imaginary repertoires of the dominant culture." Because it is by reference to the low that the rest of the cultural hierarchy is defined, the lower strata of the body, of litera-ture, of place, and of culture are frequently – some would say obses-sively – represented in fundamentally contradictory and ambivalent ways that elicit both repugnance and fascination. The result, in the words of Stallybrass and White, is "a mobile, conflictual fusion of power, fear, and desire in the construction of subjectivity: a psychologi-cal dependence upon precisely those Others which are being rigorously opposed and excluded at the social level. It is for this reason that what is *socially* peripheral is so frequently *symbolically* central."[3] Obviously, those in socially higher positions often control the discourses within which the low other will be figured and thus defined. In the case of burlesque, however, the low other produces another discourse, one that – within the confines of the theatrical space – might invert that hierarchy and, worse yet, threaten to call into question the right of higher discourses to determine the vertical order of culture to begin with.

This book's recovery and reconstitution of the history of American burlesque is intended in the first instance to recall to our attention an important though oddly remembered and nearly forgotten strand of American popular entertainment. Today, the term "burlesque" has no meaning as a contemporary phenomenon to most Americans. The associations the term provokes – if any at all – are likely to be of a slightly naughty (but ultimately innocuous) theatrical diversion occur-ring in a vaguely situated past time: somewhere between the 1890s and World War II. At the center of this memory is the emblematic burlesque performer, the stripper, and all that term connotes of the exotic, dis-played female body.

However tinged with connotations of illicit sexuality the contemporary memory of burlesque might be, it has long since been thoroughly recuperated within the mainstream of American popular culture. The piece of music most associated today with striptease (but not written until the 1960s), "The Stripper," made the top-ten pop music charts and then was used in a television shaving cream commercial in which a woman admonished *male* viewers to "take it all off" with Noxzema. In the late 1970s *Sugar Babies*, a Broadway revue with Mickey Rooney and Ann Miller, paid homage to the baggy-pants comics, slapstick, double entendres, and striptease of burlesque as it was in its last moments as a viable entertainment form – the 1930s. It is burlesque as a museum piece, compiled appropriately enough by an academic theater historian. What is today remembered as burlesque – the stripper, the runway, the candy butcher – are features that did not appear until the 1920s, nearly a half century after burlesque's emergence as a distinct American entertainment form.

It is important to reconsider burlesque for other reasons as well. Burlesque is emblematic of the way that popular entertainment becomes an arena for "acting out" cultural contradictions and even contestations and is exemplary of the complexities and ambiguities of this process. It is of particular historical import because its organizing problematic is gender. It emerges at a time when the question "What does it mean to be a woman?" is constantly being asked in a wide range of forums and answered by many different, conflicting voices. Burlesque becomes one of those forums, and the answers it gives via the image of the burlesque performer are themselves complex and contradictory. Furthermore, the refiguring of woman that occurred on the burlesque stage represents the establishment of a model that will prove to be extremely powerful, influential, and, as regards sexual politics, problematic. Lydia Thompson is the figurative mother of Sophie Tucker and Mae West and the grandmother of Bette Midler. At the same time, burlesque also presents a model for the sexual objectification of women in popular entertainment. Thus, it can also be seen as a progenitor of modern pornography.

Nineteenth-century burlesque presents an opportunity to examine a form of popular entertainment that is by its very nature open to multiple interpretations and meanings. To say that burlesque is "open" is certainly not to say that it lacks structure or organization or to say that each new burlesque performance differed radically and unpredictably from those that preceded it – although burlesque performance style probably allowed for more spontaneity than most other contemporaneous forms of popular theater. However, unlike that other enormously popular mode of theater in the decades following the Civil War, melodrama, burlesque makes no attempt to bring all its parts together into a unified and ideologically monovocal whole. There is no moment in burlesque in which we are told what we are to make of what we have seen on the stage, no character who speaks with the voice of moral and authorial omniscience, not even an author to whom we could ascribe the meaning of the "whole thing" if we wanted to. Open forms of popular entertainment – burlesque, vaudeville, street fairs, masquerades, parades, and some forms of television (soap operas and music videos, among them) – have received much less scholarly attention than more determinant forms: the novel, fictional film, and theatrical drama. And yet they demonstrate in striking ways some of the characteristics of popular cultural phenomena in general. In particular, they show us that the popular text and performance are sites of multiple, sometimes conflicting meanings, and that apprehension of a text involves multiple appropriations of it by different groups of viewers or readers for different purposes.

Important in its own right, Lydia Thompson's first American season also serves as a sort of historical reference point for this study. Although Thompson was not the originator of "modern" burlesque in any narrow sense of assigning historical precedence, her appearance in New York in the fall of 1868 marks a watershed both in the history of American burlesque and in the history of the American theater. Quite simply, Thompson and her "British Blondes," as they soon came to be called, took New York and the country by storm. By the same token, however, the more burlesque found a place with middle-class New York theater audiences, the more troubled critics and other commentators became by this success. Thompsonian burlesque, among some at least, was not merely a variation on an established theatrical genre, but something new and troubling in its power to entrance the spectator with displays of women in revealing costumes who were dangerously impertinent in their mocking male impersonations, streetwise language, and nonsensical humor. That first season of modern burlesque in America was disturbing – and threatening – because it presented a world without limits, a world turned upside down and inside out in which nothing was above being brought down to earth. In that world, things that should be kept separate were united in grotesque hybrids. Meanings refused to stay put. Anything might happen. And the burlesque performer – showing herself, showing off, showing up the hapless male characters she took on in repartee – literally and figuratively embodied this world.

The 1868–69 American burlesque season also provides a convenient historical moment in relation to which we can view the sweeping changes in American theatrical culture that led up to it. Thompsonian burlesque emerged in the wake of the most profound cultural reorientation in the history of American theater. It both expressed and contributed to these currents of radical change. Thus, the first season of Thompsonian burlesque in America begins to take on meaning in terms of its place in that larger history of American theater and culture. Within that history, we will be particularly concerned with changes in the relationship between women and the theater – in terms of both the representation of femininity on stage and the place women occupied in the theater audience. Chapters Three and Four provide this necessary historical context; they set the stage for a reconsideration of Thompson's first season in Chapter Five.

The 1868–69 burlesque season has meaning not only as the product of historical processes but also as the predicate for further change. Although the discursive furor over the popularity of burlesque continued for more than a year and both woman's rights advocates and conservative cultural critics opposed it, burlesque became a part of the rapidly developing institution of American show business. Between 1870 and 1940, burlesque troupes toured every part of the United States and its territories – from New York to Klondike mining camps. By the 1890s, burlesque had become a mature entertainment oligopoly, with two circuits (or "wheels," as they were called) of burlesque theaters controlled from New York. Burlesque's industrial institutionalization, however, came at the price of its social and cultural marginalization. Burlesque as a topic of discourse in the popular press dropped from sight, except in the *National Police Gazette*, as it moved out of the mainstream of American popular entertainment and into the shadow world of male, working-class entertainment. In the main, burlesque was tolerated by local officials as an inevitable part of the tenderloin of big cities except when the show "went too far," or when social reformers included burlesque in their litanies of urban vice, as something – like the poor, their houses, and their habits – to be cleaned up.

With the excorporation of burlesque from bourgeois culture came changes in its formal structure and a reconstitution of its representation of femininity. It assumed the three-part structure of the minstrel show in the 1870s, which it kept until the turn of the century. The takeoffs on venerated objects of high culture and punning rhymed couplets spoken by cross-dressed women were gradually eliminated as burlesque increasingly became centered around feminine sexual display – in the cooch dance in the 1890s; in its jazzed-up successor, the shimmy, in the 1910s; and in the striptease of the late 1920s and 1930s. A full generation before Gypsy Rose Lee took the stage at Minsky's Republic Theater on Broadway in the 1930s, Lydia Thompson had declared burlesque of the 1890s to be unrecognizable as the form she had popularized in the United States in 1869.

O O O   **Burlesque as a Cultural Phenomenon**

The subtitle of this volume promises that burlesque will be considered in relation to American culture. It is thus important to make clear at the outset how this notoriously slippery term (culture) is used here and the derivation of its analysis. The study of culture is the study of how groups of people make sense of, find their place within, express their understandings of, and make pleasurable or displeasurable their relationships with the social worlds they inhabit. Thus, to study culture is not to study objects or events in isolation (as if they "meant" the same thing to all people at all times) but rather to attempt to understand the processes by which historically and socially situated groups of people make objects and events meaningful (or not), relevant (or not), pleasurable (or not).

How one makes sense, relevance, or pleasure is socially constrained and, to some degree, at least, socially determined. That is to say several things. First, what sort of culture one makes depends in part on how one is already positioned within the social structure. The markers of social position and identity are many and carry differential weights at different historical moments and within different societies. Certainly, during the period of American history considered here, race, gender, and class are key markers of social positionality.

Conceiving culture as production (of meaning, relevance, pleasure) rather than merely consumption helps to prevent the unthinking assumption of equivalence between cultural objects and cultural production. Although cultural objects (novels, plays, buildings, and so forth) might be tangible evidence of culture (and in the case of historical inquiry might well constitute our primary sources of knowledge about the culture of a past period), they have no intrinsic, unitary meanings and contain no guaranteed effects – any more than, say, a potato is "meant" to be made into vichyssoise or French fries or is bound to make you fat. This is not to say that cultural objects do not, at some level at least, have discernible structures or that anyone can make out of any cultural object anything one pleases. A potato is recognizable as such (and thus different from an apple), and it is certainly easier to make a potato into home fries than into a pot roast. Furthermore, the use to which a cultural object might be put cannot be assumed to be the same as the use for which it was designed or intended. Farmers might grow potatoes more suitable for baking than for boiling and the potato-marketing board might extol in advertisements the glories of a hot Idaho with sour cream and chives, but this does not mean that we can assume that the consumer will use potatoes in this way.

Cultural production does not occur on even terms among groups within society. Because society is ordered in terms of power relations and structured in terms of registers of dominance and subordination, cultural production expresses these relations and these structures. All groups within society produce culture, but not all groups are in a position to disseminate "their" cultural products widely within a society and export them to others, to legitimate and naturalize their tastes in cultural products via social institutions (education, chief among them), or to regulate competing or alternative forms of cultural production via economic power, government policy, and/or legal sanction. Because the primary concern of this study is "low" culture, it is important to keep in mind that it is "low" in relation to other cultures that not only are "high" but also are produced by those in positions of power from which this vertical hierarchy of cultural worth has been constructed to begin with. Cultural production is not merely the result of choices and combinations but of contestations as well.

Like many analyses, this one has been influenced by what has been called the "cultural studies" paradigm, particularly the work of scholars associated or aligned with the University of Birmingham's Center for Contemporary Cultural Study.[4] One strand of this work deals with the cultural production of subordinate groups within contemporary capitalist societies and has emphasized instances of resistance to the dominant culture. We need to make a few qualifications to the domination/subordination model of cultural struggle and to notions of subordinate cultural practice as resistance. First, to reduce society to a hierarchical dichotomy of dominant and subordinate groups and to correspondingly reduce cultural production to that of the dominant and of the subordinate is to grossly oversimplify both social order and culture under capitalism in the West, at least insofar as the past two centuries are concerned. The political and social history of America reveals the coalescence and dissipation of multiple sets of interests all along the scale of power in shifting and frequently contradictory patterns of alliance and contestation. This is not to say that issues of social power and hierarchy are irrelevant. However, the complex and contradictory nature of power relations must be recognized. Furthermore, we need to acknowledge that power relations are expressed within a number of different social registers, only one of which is class. Class is a much less valuable heuristic category when applied to the history of the United States than to that of Great Britain – as the new generation of labor and social historians confirms with each new study. Social history is also a history of relations of gender, race, and ethnicity – related to class relations but not reducible to them.

It is tempting to see the cultural production of subordinate groups merely in terms of its resistance to the power of more dominant groups. To some degree, the theories of cultural inversion and transgression used here to talk about popular entertainment encourage such an emphasis – the discourse of the low other has the potential to challenge the ordering of officially sanctioned culture by pointing to the arbitrary nature of this ordering and the social interests that ordering conceals. It is further tempting to view resistant forms of cultural production as unproblematically and unambiguously progressive – as if there were a solidarity among the discourses of subordination. Historically, however, this has not been the case. In fact, it is just as likely that the structures of domination and subordination will be reproduced in the culture of the subordinate. Emmanuel Le Roy Ladurie calls this phenomenon "displaced abjection." In the Roman carnival riots of 1580, he found, communal solidarity of the rioters was achieved at the expense of "outsiders" who could serve as substitute victims: in this case, Jews and foreigners.[5]

Susan Davis's study of parades and street festivals in antebellum Philadelphia provides an American example. During the first half of the nineteenth century, Christmas celebrations in Philadelphia evolved into raucous and sometimes riotous street festivals whose principal participants were young, native, working-class white men. Christmas was a time when this largely dispossessed and unpropertied group took control of the streets and, dressed in masks and fantastic costumes, extorted hospitality from tavern owners. But this inversive festival of working-class antiauthoritarianism was also used as an opportunity to construct another "other" in relation to which the revelers defined themselves: blacks and immigrants. By the 1840s, when blacks and newly arrived immigrants were competing with native-born white males for work in Philadelphia, the favorite guises of the Christmas revelers were blackface and the caricatured costumes of German immigrants. Thus disguised, they would frequently attack representatives of the very groups they were made up to resemble. The antiauthoritarian character of the celebrations continued – to the extent that after the Civil War, municipal authorities sought to regulate the objects of their ridicule by outlawing impersonations of the police and public officials – but it was part of and inseparable from a larger discourse of nativism and racism.[6]

In short, just as there is no unified "dominant" culture, but rather sets of cultural practices generally associated with and produced for those relatively higher on the ladder of social and power relations, so there is no necessary alliance of the cultural practices or discourses of more subordinate groups. Indeed, "resistant" practices might well be polyvalent, not only directed against those conceived of as "above," but constructing yet another object of subordination. In this process, there is frequently a slide from one register of social power to another – from class to gender, from class to race, and so forth (the displaced abjection

Ladurie speaks of) – or a collapsing of distinctions (condensation, in psychoanalytic terms) between registers – the dandy in the minstrel show, for example, which critiques the manners and dress of the wealthy white fop by attaching them to the figure of the blackface minstrel.

When discussing the discourses and activities that come under the general heading of commercial leisure, it is frequently more useful to think of power relations in terms of subordination's more precise opposite, ordination, than the term with which it is more commonly paired (domination). In the cultural realm, groups in a position to do so rarely exercise their power with the force and directness suggested by the term "domination." Rather, power is expressed through ordination: that is, by attempting to regulate through the arrangement of things in ranks and orders – what is high, what is low; what is us, what is them. Every instance of discourse is itself an act of ordination, an articulation (both in the sense of uttering and in the sense of linking) of signifiers. Thus, just as there can be explicitly ordinative discourse, there can also be insubordinate discourse: discourse that transgresses or inverts existing orderings, discourse that challenges the notion of fixed orders or the ordinative authority of another discourse.

Both the desire to ordinate through discourse and the desire to be insubordinate appear to be as deeply ingrained in human cultures as the desire to tell and listen to stories. Why is it, for example, that, as Christie Davies suggests, "apart from jokes about sex, ethnic jokes of all kinds are perhaps the most popular and numerous of all jokes in the West"? Each Western culture circulates jokes about the alleged congenital stupidity of a geographically or culturally neighboring group: Minnesotans tell jokes about Swedes; Swedes, about Norwegians; Norwegians, about Finns; Finns, about Lapps. Davies argues that such jokes are an expression of anxiety about one's place in an industrial society that places enormous emphasis on skill and knowledge. "In such a world everyone needs to be reassured that they are not really stupid and that real stupidity is safely restricted to the ranks of the Poles, the Irish, or whoever is the butt of the local ethnic joke."[7] In other words, ethnic jokes "work" by reordinating the world, dividing it between an *us* and a *them* – a *them* that is always close to us – geographically or culturally – but is through the joke made ontologically different and inferior.

Ordination suggests the exercise of power bound by the limits of discourse, whether that discourse is a newspaper editorial, a sermon, or an ethnic joke. Similarly, insubordination is resistance contained by discourse: the temporary and circumscribed upsetting of another group's symbolic ordering – graffiti, rude noises at the back of the classroom, the hiss, the boo. This is not to argue that discursive insubordination is without consequence (as students in China tragically discovered in June 1989) or that the exercise of ordinative power is unrelated to other kinds of power (as the Chinese authorities brutally demonstrated). But it does suggest that the struggles over meaning and pleasure occasioned by the emergence of burlesque are more struggles of ordination and insubordination than they are of domination and resistance.

Much of the recent scholarly interest in the potentially resistive and subversive nature of certain forms of public festivals has been prompted by Mikhail Bakhtin's analysis of the "carnivalesque" in the work of Rabelais. For Bakhtin, the carnivals and festivals of early modern Europe were occasions on which the coercive, prescriptive, monovocal, official language of ordinary power relations was replaced by the "heteroglot," collective voices of a populist utopia. Bakhtin describes the way carnivals, fairs, mummeries, travesties, and other popular festivals "worked" through a systematic construction of a discourse of the grotesque, transgression, and inversion. The carnivalesque world is a vision of the world from below and an implicit critique of the everyday world of "normal" power relations.[8]

Through Bakhtin's analysis of the carnivalesque we come to know not only its language but also its relevance. The cultural critique implicit in the carnivalesque and its disorder means that popular festivals cannot be dismissed as meaningless diversions or an escape from business as usual. Critique might serve as the basis for resistance – either symbolic or physical. Carnivals can become riots. What those in power regard as trivial and only play can, under certain circumstances, become serious and violent. Although there are relatively few instances in European history where popular festivals became populist revolts, the threat of things "getting out of hand" was sufficiently recognized that increasingly from the sixteenth century on, authorities attempted to regulate and control fairs, fetes, carnivals, and other public festivals.

Although Bakhtin's work is indispensable to an understanding of "low" cultural production, several qualifications must be made. First, as we have already seen, the utopian and populist vision of inversive popular culture is undermined by the realization that resistance to authority can be deflected and redirected into a discourse of resubordination. Furthermore, as Terry Eagleton and others have pointed out, carnival is a sanctioned, legalized, and hence defused arena for the expression of opposition to the dominant order. Thus, it can be read not as a rupturing of social control but as an instrument *of* social control: carnival allows subordinate groups to "blow off steam" in a ritual and, therefore, in a politically ineffectual space.[9] Finally, we must keep in mind that commercial theatrical popular entertainments of the mid-nineteenth century were by no means identical to the street fairs and carnivals of sixteenth-century France. The spontaneous and participatory nature of the carnivalesque and its blurring of the distinctions between performer and spectator had been suppressed in the historical process of regulation, institutionalization, and commercialization.

In short, Bakhtin has provided a powerful conceptual apparatus with which we can begin to describe the operation of some forms of "low" cultural production. But, when applied to the topic at hand, such an apparatus must be adapted rather than adopted. Simply identifying burlesque or other forms of popular entertainment structured around transgression and inversion as the vestigial remains of a tradition of the carnivalesque fails to capture their complex and contradictory workings as well as their historical specificity. Although it is difficult to maintain Bakhtin's inherent populist utopianism (carnival might well function in this way within the fictive world of Rabelais, but this is certainly not always the case of "real" carnivals), there is no reason to assume automatically that the carnival is merely an instrument of hegemonic control. The former argument oversimplifies the political character of low culture, while the latter conflates intention with effect. Instead, we need to consider these forms of entertainment as specific, historical instances of cultural practice.

○ ○ ○   **Burlesque as a Theatrical Practice**

This study examines burlesque as a historically situated instance of cultural production, or, more specifically, as an instance of theatrical culture. The recognition of the special cultural space marked

out by the theatrical is central to this analysis. Theatrical space is a
space set apart from the space of "regular" activities. Some have seen a
correspondence between theatrical space and the liminal space of tribal
rituals described by anthropologist Victor Turner. Liminality, for Turner, is an in-between state connected generally with rites of passage.
The transformation of an individual or group from one mode of social
existence to another is celebrated through rituals in which the participants act out their "statelessness" by taking on special roles that are
often parodic or inversive of profane reality: male warriors enact female
roles, for example. Liminality confers a license to be different, a difference that would be unallowable in "everyday" life.[10]

Turner sees the "symbolic genres" of modern, industrial leisure as to
some degree analogous to the rituals of liminality in tribal societies: "In
other words, they play with the factors of culture, assemble them in
random, grotesque, improbable, surprising combinations, just as tribes-
men do when they make masks, disguise as monsters, combine with
disparate ritual symbols, or invert or parody profane reality. But they do
this in a far more complicated way, multiplying genres of artistic and
popular entertainments, and within each allowing authors, dramatists,
. . . and others lavish scope to generate not only weird forms but also
models highly critical of the status quo."[11] Turner is quick to point out,
however, that the term "liminal" should be applied only to true passage
rites in tribal or agrarian cultures. The leisure rituals of industrial
societies, including theater, bear an analogous or metaphorical relationship – certainly not a direct one – to the truly liminal experiences
accompanying the transformative rituals of preliterate societies. Turner
even invents a new term, "liminoid," to mark the difference between
the two types of ritual occasions and experiences. Modern, "liminoid"
phenomena tend to be produced by one group in society for another,
rather than being a commonly shared experience of the same group. For
Turner, a "liminoid" experience provides an occasion to stand apart
from and perhaps critique the norms and roles of everyday life but does
not necessarily signal a moment of metamorphosis for the participant.

Both Turner and Bakhtin point to the cultural importance of those
occasions on which ordinary identities, roles, behaviors, norms, and
other markers of one's place in the social structure are temporarily lifted
and another cultural ordering is allowed to take over: an ordering that
always stands in an ambiguous relationship to that which it, within the

space of the ritual, theater, or carnival, supersedes. As noted above, we should not press the "revolutionary" nature either of the carnivalesque or of liminality too far. On the other hand, only in recent decades has the theater in the West become so detached from everyday experience that its nonthreatening, indeed, culturally conservative status, can be taken for granted. In his analysis of the carnivalesque in Rabelais, Bakhtin does not consider actual theater practice, because he believes that after the seventeenth century, dramatic literature consisted mainly of socially inconsequential forms: the comedy of manners, satires, sentimental naturalism, and so forth.

Although Bakhtin does not address the issue, one strategy for controlling not just dramatic literature but the theater as a place for licensed aberration was to institutionalize and "authorize" it. Ben Jonson argued against the abolition of the theater as a whole by proposing that the anonymous authority of "players" be replaced by the responsibility of the text's author. In exchange for ownership of his plays, the playwright would tacitly agree to assume liability for the social consequences of the ideas they contained. As Michael Bristol, in his study of Elizabethan theater, observes: "This individualization of artistic production is the basis for the legitimation of the theater. The author is defined as the owner of his text and thus as an individual who might be punished or subjected to litigation. The audience is decomposed into private individuals who appreciate a text without interpreting it; the actor is an artificial person whose words originate from and are delegated by a well-defined center of authority. In this allocation of functions, there is not one left who can say forbidden things with impunity, and the dangers of an ambiguously allocated or dispersed authority are safely contained."[12]

Splitting theater into dramatic literature, on the one hand, and its performance, on the other, might well have helped to regulate and tame it. However, the very idea of the theater – its impertinent mimicry, its unapologetic artifice, and its upsetting of normality – continued to make it difficult to assimilate within the bounds of unproblematic cultural practice. As we shall see, it took more than two centuries after the colonization of America for the commercial theater to escape the presumption of immorality.

But, obviously, the theater can be and has been "tamed." It can be the place where cautionary tales are told and morality plays – either civic or religious – enacted. The potentially subversive qualities of the theater have been obscured in modern times by its full incorporation into mainstream, middle-class culture: theater is taught in universities and kept alive as a cultural phenomenon by government grants. Moreover, the usurpation of the dramatic theater as a form of popular entertainment, first by the movies and then by television, has rendered it all but moribund as a social force. Thus, many of the cultural reservations people once had about the theater have shifted to these more recent and more popular forms of theatrical entertainment: pornographic films, children's television programming, music videos, televangelism, and so forth. *Hair* and *Oh! Calcutta* were probably the last plays to spark controversy in America about what should be allowed to happen in a theater. Significantly, both aroused opposition because they drew on theater's tradition of subversiveness: parody, irreverence, inversion, the grotesque, and sexual display.[13] Although controversial live theater pieces such as these are increasingly rare, the theatrical remains a place apart from the ordinary ordering of society and, as such, continues to contain within it the power to challenge the legitimacy of that order.

○ ○ ○   Burlesque as a Historical Phenomenon

Any study that claims to be a history of some aspect of popular culture immediately raises the question of whether such a history is, by its very nature, possible. The problems are both evidentiary and, by extension, epistemological. First, we know of any historical instance of cultural production by the material traces it leaves for the historian to analyze. Great pains are taken to preserve certain cultural objects, document their physical production, and celebrate their reception. These are generally not the products of subordinate groups in a society, however, or objects designed for subordinate groups.

Second, in those cases where we do have material evidence of "low" culture, what is this evidence of? As Michael Bristol frames the argument, "could any evidence of the socially and culturally excluded 'other' ever exist even in principle?" In other words, evidence of low cultural production is likely to be preserved only by those groups with an interest in suppressing that culture. Hence, we know the culture of the insane, the criminal, or the low other only through the discourse of

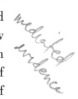

mediated evidence

the asylum, the court, or the censor.[14] By this argument, any attempt to "read" the culture of the subordinate only results in the reproduction of a discourse of domination.

Third, with respect to the nature of culture as an analytical category, objects and texts alone do not constitute culture. Culture is produced as groups of people make sense, relevance, and pleasure out of the symbol systems they encounter in their daily experience. Thus, even if the first two problems associated with a history of popular culture could be overcome, we are faced with a third: How does the analyst study the production of culture as it occurs in the reception of cultural objects? This is obviously a particular problem in the case of theatrical culture, where the object of study is literally the performance of culture – bounded by specific conditions of reception at a particular time, by particular (and, by any criteria of sociological specificity, unknown) groups, in particular places. Add to this the special nature of burlesque – a form given to completely violating the "integrity" of text (script) in performance except as the most general skeletal structure on which to hang a constantly changing variety of topical allusions and bits of business. For example, while the script of *Ixion* still exists, at least as it was written by the "original" author, accounts of its performance by the British Blondes at Wood's Theater indicate that a great deal was added between the writing of the script and its American debut and, further, that changes were made from night to night during its performance. What the critics (either the lovers or haters of burlesque) did not comment on at great length was the play itself. What made burlesque "remarkable" was its performance: the costumes, bearing, gestures, tone, inflections, and attitude of the performers themselves and their rapport with the audience – things no surviving script can begin to capture. Even the most sentimental chronicler of Minsky's burlesque admits that written on paper, the gags, skits, and jokes just make it all the more difficult for a generation who never knew burlesque to understand what was so funny or naughty about it. In a very real sense, "you had to have been there."

All three problems deserve to be taken seriously. The evidence of popular entertainment even in so recent a time as the end of the last century is fugitive and fragmentary at best. Most burlesque scripts have long since vanished without trace. What does survive is a small body of diverse, uneven, irregular, and often vehemently partisan discourse about popular entertainment: materials used in its promotion (posters, photographs, advertisements, carte-de-visite photographs); critical discourse accompanying and responding to it; the recollections of managers, performers, and, in a few cases, members of the audience; fictional stories about it; and the reports of groups for whom popular entertainment was a social problem. In short, we have the least evidence on what made burlesque distinctive and, no doubt, quite different from our contemporary experiences of popular entertainment: the nature of burlesque performances, the immediate circumstances of their reception, and the responses of their audiences.

If my goal were to write the definitive history of burlesque – to explain once and for all what it "really" was and what it "really" meant – then the above problems would be overwhelming. But burlesque was not a thing or an event whose essence or unitary meaning I could capture through historical description – even if I were disposed to write this kind of empiricist history. Burlesque was both a performance structure and, just as important, what groups of people made of and made out of its thousands of performances, accounts of those performances, and representations of performers. To talk of burlesque as if it were a thing is, at the same moment, to acknowledge that as a term it merely stands for the aggregate of all the ways in which an entertainment form by that name was made sense of, relevant (or not), and pleasurable (or not) at innumerable times in a myriad of places by all sorts of different people.

Mark Cousins and Athar Hussain, in discussing the work of Michel Foucault, make a distinction between a history and a case history. A history attempts to reconstitute the past, striving, through the exhaustiveness and adequacy of evidence, to rule out competing explanations. A case history, by which term they describe the studies of Foucault, attempts to make a problem intelligible without requiring that historical comprehensiveness or conclusive proof. Case histories produce knowledge that is always partial, tentative, incomplete, and subject to revision. Their standards of evidentiary adequacy are far from exhaustiveness, and they make no claim to comprehensive historical reconstruction and definitive explanation.[15]

My historical account of burlesque is much closer to the case history than to the exhaustive history. The question I will ask is: How can we make burlesque intelligible as a cultural phenomenon? This qualification of the historical nature of *Horrible Prettiness* does not give me license to treat evidence cavalierly. But, by the same token, it does not result merely from the fact that the evidentiary foundation for any work on burlesque is shallower than any "good" historian would want to construct an exhaustive study. Cultural practices do not lend themselves to exhaustiveness and definitive historical accounts – for conceptual rather than (or in addition to) evidentiary reasons. For if any account of contemporary cultural practice is necessarily circumscribed, tentative, speculative, and partial, so any attempt to understand the cultural practices of a different era is similarly and more severely limited. What follows may well be an account written at the margins of "history," which constantly threatens to lapse into some other category of writing: discourse analysis, criticism, or historical speculation. Nevertheless, that is better than to produce an account that, while more in the histo-riographic mainstream, robs burlesque of the qualities that drew me to it to begin with: its irreducible complexity, its power to elicit fear and fascination, its horrible prettiness.

The Historical Contexts of Burlesque I

The Transformation of American Theater

When I was a boy, I was taught by my parents, who were strict puritans, that all scenic exhibitions were the works of the devil, and should be shunned as a pestilence; and I may say that no person was ever more impressed by this opinion than myself, until very lately, when for the first time in my life I ventured within the walls of a playhouse.

– *"The Perambulator,"* The Rambler's Magazine

The theater is a place where nature is overacted – where false notions are instilled into the mind – where vice is held up to applause, and virtue degraded – where religion is ridiculed – where evil and immodest inuendoes [sic] are thrown out, in order to please the most worthless portion of the community.

– Hopkinsian Magazine

At the theater alone, the higher ranks mix with the middle and the lower classes; there alone do the former consent to listen to the opinion of the latter, or at least to allow them to give an opinion at all. At the theater men of cultivation and of literary attainments have always had more difficulty than elsewhere in making their taste prevail over that of the people and in preventing themselves from being carried away by the latter. The pit has frequently made laws for the boxes.

– Alexis de Tocqueville, Democracy in America

○ ○ ○ ○ ○ ○ ○ ○ ○ ○ ○ ○ ○ ○ ○ ○

When Lydia Thompson arrived in New York in August 1868, she found
a theatrical culture that an American theatergoer from the last decade
of the twentieth century would not have found all that unfamiliar. *time traveler*
Granted, a traveler in time who wandered from the world of *Cats* or *as harder*
Phantom of the Opera into George Wood's Theater on the opening night *of middle class?*
of *Ixion* might have found Wood's collection of stuffed animals and
other museum curiosities a bit odd in the way of lobby decoration, but
little about the theater itself, the audience, the audience's behavior, or
the relationship between performers and spectators would have struck
our time traveler as totally foreign to her notion of what an evening at
the theater is supposed to be. Transported back just one generation
more, however – a few dozen blocks downtown to the Bowery Theater
in 1835, let us say – a contemporary American theatergoer would have
been plunged into a theatrical culture completely alien to her own
experience. She would have found it a noisy, chaotic, probably terrifying
world in which she would have seen very few others like herself (middle-class women), but all sorts of other people she was definitely not
accustomed to confronting in a theater: ink-covered newsboys, aproned
butcher's apprentices, burly stevedores, and, in the theater's third tier,
dozens of prostitutes and their customers.

An enormous historical and cultural gulf separates the theatrical
world of contemporary America from that of the 1830s, and the historical moment of modern burlesque's emergence – the late 1860s –
constitutes the edge of our side of that gulf. The chronicle of modern
burlesque's first season in America means little until we begin to resup-
ply this historical context. As one instance of nineteenth-century American theatrical culture, burlesque must be considered in light of the
fundamentally ambiguous and contradictory place that theater – as
social institution and abstract concept – occupied in American culture
from the colonial period almost to the Civil War. Some of Thompson's

first American fans had witnessed firsthand the radical transformation of theatrical culture that had resulted from struggles over the control of the theater between emerging classes in American society and among differing ideological camps that cut across strict class demarcations. Not all that long ago the theater had been at the center of debates and even riots about the role of leisure and play, about proper modes of representation and mimesis, and about gender relations. Although Thompsonian burlesque appeared at a time when most social groups accepted the theater as a part of mainstream American culture, it reawakened old fears about the power of the theater to undermine the social order. This chapter examines the struggles that were fought over the American theater as a social institution in the decades prior to the emergence of modern burlesque. The next chapter considers more specifically the role of gender representation in those struggles.

O O O   Antitheatricalism in Antebellum America

It was not until the 1820s that the theater secured a permanent institutional toehold in American culture. Its growth was retarded during the colonial and early republican periods by a number of factors, not the least of which was the turmoil produced by two wars. Economic and geographic forces were also responsible for keeping commercial theater at the periphery of American culture. Before the revolutionary war, only a few cities were of sufficient size and wealth to support a permanent theater and a company of actors. As late as 1830, there were only twenty-six cities in the United States with populations of more than eight thousand. Thus, the few colonial acting troupes were by necessity itinerant, traveling days if not weeks between towns and between play dates.

Ironically, two of the wealthiest and most populous American colonies were those least hospitable to traveling players. The settlers of Massachusetts had brought with them from England the Puritan disdain for theatrical entertainments of any kind. When during the winter of 1749–50 two Englishmen offered a performance of *The Orphan* at a coffeehouse on State Street, the General Court responded by legally codifying moral prohibitions against the theater. Thereafter, actors risked a fine of twenty pounds for attempting to mount any public stage play.[1] Nor did the founder of Pennsylvania evince a more tolerant attitude toward the theater. In his 1699 tract, *No Cross, No Crown*, William Penn asked: "How many plays did Jesus Christ and his apostles recreate themselves at? What poems, romances, comedies, and the like did the apostles and saints make or use to pass their time withal?" Penn sought to ensure by law that Pennsylvanians saw no more plays than he assumed Jesus did. The "Great Law" of 1682 set the penalty for infraction at twenty shillings or ten days at hard labor.[2]

By the eve of the Revolution, opposition to the theater had waned in some places, so that in New York, Annapolis, Williamsburg, Charleston, and a few other cities, playbills for a touring company or a local amateur performance did not prompt mob action or the initiation of criminal proceedings. Whatever gains had been accomplished by the first professional actors in the colonies were wiped out during the Revolution, however. At the meeting of the Continental Congress in Philadelphia on October 20, 1774, the delegates passed a resolution to "discountenance and discourage" plays, cockfighting, horse racing, and other "species of extravagance and dissipation" as frivolous diversions from the pursuit of liberty. The first postrevolutionary theater in America was not built until 1781, and it took until the turn of the century for professional theater in the United States to return to the level of activity of 1770.

Colonial antitheatricalism was not, in the main, prompted by a particular instance of an "immoral" performance – indeed, antitheater laws frequently antedated any possibility of their prospective violation – but rather by a deeply held fear of the very notion of theatricality itself and everything that could be associated with it. The philosophical and theological groundings for this fear are to be found in a belief in the ordered, fixed, and immutable nature of the cosmos, and in a further belief in the correspondence between external appearance and essential truth. As Jonas Barish concludes in his history of antitheatrical prejudice, the same qualities that make theater different from the socially sanctioned ordering of things made it an object of criticism from the early sixteenth century to well into the nineteenth. As far as the Puritans were concerned, the theater "[raised] the spectre of an endless feast of fools, a perpetual carnival, or parody of the good society, in which hectic merriment will replace ordered work, a *regnum diaboli* dominated by the anarchy of the sexual instincts."[3]

Singled out for attack by the Puritans and their literal and spiritual descendants in the New World were the twin defining characteristics of theatrical performance: mimicry and spectacle. To disguise oneself and pretend to be someone else – particularly of another rank or gender – was to mock nature and God. Furthermore, the stage identities of players refused to stay put. Actors metamorphosed every day: a king one day became a villainous usurper the next, who became a clown the next, and so on. When male players took on female roles, sexual confusion was added to class confusion. For these deceivers to enact tales of what might have been but was not was to give a false version of the history through which God's work was revealed to man: plays were inherently blasphemous.

Philosophical and religious concerns regarding self-presentation – even on festive occasions – were not limited to actors and the theater. Any subordinate group that presented itself in public in ways that challenged established class distinctions or social hierarchies was subject to the scorn and wrath of groups in a position to determine those distinctions.[4] Even so seemingly innocuous a form of festive identity confusion as the masquerade was viewed as dangerously transgressive by urban officials. In an attempt to boost their sagging box offices in the winter of 1829, several New York theaters suspended theatrical performances and offered masquerade balls. The fashion for masquerades had been imported from Europe and first adopted in the United States as private entertainments in the homes of the wealthy. The Park, the most upscale of New York theaters, was the first to commercialize the masquerade. But within weeks two working-class-oriented theaters, the Chatham and the Bowery, followed suit. As soon as the masquerade craze crossed class lines, prominent citizens – Mayor Philip Hone among them – began to condemn these entertainments for encouraging "licentious privileges assumed by many under the protection of a fictitious modesty." The Common Council of the city persuaded the state legislature to outlaw masquerades in public places and to impose a one-thousand-dollar fine on violators. Such was the popularity of the opportunity to try on a different identity, however, that several theaters found it more profitable to pay the fine than to give their stages back to professional mimics. When in 1857 a Bowery concert saloon attempted to revive commercial masquerades (which were still illegal), the use of the form as a vehicle for popular entertainment was once again viewed as a threat to social order. "The very name [masquerade]," cried the *New York Clipper*, "has an air of crime about it that should cause our citizens to rise at once and crush the hydra-headed monster before it gains a foot-hold in our midst."[5]

Of course, not everyone took the deceit and pretense on which drama is necessarily based quite so literally as the Puritans. After all, the drama might also be a way of teaching those who could not read the word of God for themselves the wonder of his ways. But as Barish points out, fear of the theater's inescapably "pretentious" and deceitful nature has not been limited to religious fundamentalists. "It wells up from deep sources; it is 'anti-predicative,' and seems to precede all attempts to explain or rationalize it. It belongs, however, to a conservative ethical emphasis in which the key terms are those of order, stability, constancy, and integrity, as against a more existentialist emphasis that prizes growth process, exploration, flexibility, variety and versatility of response. In one case we seem to have an ideal of stasis, in the other an ideal of movement, in one case an ideal of rectitude, in the other an ideal of plentitude."[6]

Less troublesome to the Puritans but also a part of both their and others' critiques of the theater was its spectacular nature. The qualities of humility, modesty, and piety were not usually associated with actors. Actors made public spectacles of themselves; they displayed themselves and their talents for money. Whereas the actor's mimetic abilities linked the theater with the sin of blasphemy and the crimes of fraud and bearing false witness, his showing off connected it with the sin of idolatry and the crimes of exhibitionism and prostitution. If mimicry overturned the truth by creating a competing but false history, spectacle called the very nature of truth into question by exaggerating it. The performer made his living by manipulating his body: he shouted, sang, danced, and gestured. His body was his instrument, his tool, yet the work he did with it was not productive of anything but pleasure for those who had paid to watch him show off.

The spectacular qualities of the theater, closely related as they were to the display of the body's abilities and talents, became problematic with the appearance of women on the stage. An immodest and indecorous man was one thing, a woman showing off in public and for money was quite another. A woman who displayed herself onstage was there to be looked at as a woman. Her very presence on the stage was an inescapable reminder of the biological and cultural difference between male and female, a difference that had to be regulated. By going on the stage, an actress not only stepped from the safely contained domestic realm into the topsy-turvy world of theatrical illusion, but she also became part of a commercial exchange by which she sold her "self" for the delectation of male spectators. In the early nineteenth century, a woman on the American stage implicitly asked: "Who, as a woman, am I?" "Where do I belong?"

The first "respectable" actresses on the American stage were valued primarily for their mimetic abilities rather than for their perceived beauty, even if those abilities extended to the convincing portrayal of male characters. It might be argued that the less "herself" an actress was as a woman in the role she played, the less threatening was her presence on the stage. Thus, it is not surprising that well into the nineteenth century (and, in the case of burlesque, well beyond) both actresses and the theater were strongly associated with prostitution: the step from selling one's body onstage to selling it offstage was seen as a short one by many men. Indeed, until the nineteenth century American audiences automatically assumed that any actress was also a prostitute. The libidinous and cultural connection between theatrical spectacle and sexual license helps to explain the fact that during the first half of the nineteenth century, many American theaters reserved the third tier, or upper gallery, for prostitutes and their clients. By 1830, says Claudia Johnson, such an arrangement had become a "national tradition" – so much so that many theater managers considered the operation of the third tier as a place of sexual assignation to be an economic necessity.[7]

Throughout the nineteenth century, some ministers continued to rail against the theater and all that, it seemed to them, the theater stood for. Clearly, this antitheatrical prejudice retarded public acceptance of the theater in some quarters. As late as the 1850s, when Harriet Beecher Stowe was asked to adapt her *Uncle Tom's Cabin* for the stage, she refused, arguing that if the barrier that prevented "young people of religious families" from attending the theater was broken down by "respectable and moral plays," then the same young people would be exposed to all else that *was* immoral about the theater. When Stowe finally did attend a production of a stage version of her work, she arrived

hidden beneath a shawl. One commentator in 1895 estimated that fully
70 percent of the American population in the nineteenth century regarded theatergoing as sinful.[8]

○ ○ ○   **Who Controls the Theater?**

Despite the nagging sense that there was something fundamentally improper if not immoral about the theater, more and more
Americans put aside their religious reservations as the theater finally
began to take hold in American culture in the 1820s and 1830s. Or
perhaps we should say that more and more *male* Americans came to
accept the theater as a social institution and theatergoing as a permissible recreational activity: women onstage and in the audience continued
to be problematic and, at times, controversial throughout the first half of
the century. Therefore, one should keep in mind that in the following
discussion of public acceptance of the theater during this period, public
means *male* public.[9]

In his address at the laying of the cornerstone of the Bowery Theater
in June 1826, Mayor Philip Hone articulated his class's strategy for
legitimizing theatrical entertainment. As the form of amusement "peculiarly calculated to gratify the taste of the inhabitants of large cities,"
the theater might serve as an important instrument to "improve the
taste, correct the morals, and soften the manners of the people." In
other words, he foresaw a theater controlled by enlightened, upper-
class rationalists like himself (or their agents) and used to promulgate
and naturalize the "proper" moral and social values among the masses.
Hone's vision of a democratic theater, accessible to a large portion of
urban American society, was already in the process of being realized,
but the struggle over which group controlled the theater would last
another quarter century.[10]

By the 1830s, the American theater was already becoming a site of
struggle among conflicting social and economic interests. The urban
rich had built, attended, and controlled the first generation of postrevolutionary American theaters. Beginning in the 1820s, however, upper-
class control over theatrical performance and audience behavior was
increasingly challenged by lower-class theatergoers who did not share
the elite's tastes, manners, or notions of commercial leisure. The the-

ater, said the *Spirit of the Times*, had been invaded by "shilling democ-racy."[11] In one sense, the struggle concerned sovereignty over the the-atrical experience itself: what roles should the manager, actors, and audiences play in the theatrical arena? Today, when these roles have all but ossified, it is difficult to imagine a time when the limits of audience behavior and control over the theatrical space were still undetermined and still being tested. A typical evening at New York's Bowery Theater in the 1830s would be perceived as anarchic by contemporary the-atergoers and would almost certainly provoke immediate police inter-vention.

To understand the theater as experienced by a particular audience group in the 1820s or 1830s, we must first examine the physical and social arrangement of space within the theater auditorium. Eighteenth-and early nineteenth-century American theaters were tall, shallow spaces, divided roughly into three areas. Directly in front of the pros-cenium and orchestra was the ground-level pit, where in some theaters well into the 1820s patrons simply stood to watch the performance. Even when rough benches were installed in the pit after the turn of the century, it was difficult to get a good view of the action since the benches were well below the level of the stage itself. The writer of the "Peram-bulator" column in *Rambler's Magazine* suggested in 1809 that "the pit, evidently, should be raised, and so contrived that a person sitting near the stage should see something that passes thereon, without running the risk of being ordered to sit down by the audience behind him, if he should venture to stand up to catch a glimpse of the scenes."[12] Arrayed horseshoe fashion along the walls of the auditorium and elevated above the pit were boxes, in some cases several tiers of them. Above the boxes along the rear of the auditorium were the rows of benches constituting the gallery.

By the 1830s it would have been understood at the Bowery – and, in fact, at nearly every major theater in the land – that the upper gallery, the notorious "third tier," would be occupied by prostitutes and their prospective clients nightly. Brothels-full of prostitutes arrived by sepa-rate entrance an hour or more before the main doors were opened (so as to be off the street when box and pit patrons arrived). In the gallery, prostitutes would sit with their regular customers and be introduced to new ones, drink at conveniently located bars at the back of the gallery, and, on occasion, consummate their business and sexual relations. The

Interior of the Bowery Theater, 1856.
(Prints and Photographs Division, Library of Congress)

link between prostitution and the theater gallery was not seriously challenged until the 1840s, and the connection was not finally severed in all mainstream theaters until well after the Civil War.[13] Because the gallery was the least expensive area of the house, it was also frequented by men who were not necessarily looking for a prostitute. In the South, some galleries were reserved for household slaves who had arrived hours earlier to reserve boxes for their masters. In the North, free blacks were relegated to the gallery.

The middle and upper classes occupied the boxes, where they had a better view of the stage than was provided in the pit, sat in chairs rather than on benches, and were physically separated from the throngs in the pit below and the gallery above. When "respectable" women did attend the theater (always, of course, in the company of a male escort), they sat in the boxes. A better view of the stage did not necessarily mean that patrons sat in the boxes in order to better attend to the drama. For the

single urban dandies, society belles, and middle-class families visiting
the city, the theater was a place to be seen and to see who else of interest
was in the boxes. In the 1820s, before most theaters were fitted with
gaslights, the houselights were left up throughout the evening. In part
this was due to the difficulty in adjusting light levels between the stage
and the auditorium, but it was also done because it was just as important for box patrons to see each other as it was for them to see the stage.
As the *New York Mirror* complained of the Chatham Theater in June
1824, " 'Give us but light,' is still the mental exclamation of every lady
on entering the boxes – for what is the use of spending two hours at the
toilet, if no one can perceive the improvement?" Social intercourse in
the boxes was verbal as well as visual. The "Perambulator" noted in
1809 that he preferred sitting in the pit, where he was less likely to be
bothered by the "fashionables" in the boxes "who think there is nothing
so genteel as to disturb the performance by whispering as loud as most
modest people speak."[14]

Indeed, for many patrons, going to the theater did not mean going to
watch the performance onstage – certainly not with the continuous, rapt
attention we assume to be the normative mode of present-day theatergoers. Dramas were enacted in every part of the house, and undoubtedly these were as easy to see and hear as the action onstage.
Given the general noise level in the auditorium during the performances, a substantial portion of the dialogue in any given play was
probably inaudible. Throughout the three-to-four-hour performance
and several separate dramatic offerings that constituted an evening at
the theater, people shuttled between the auditorium and the lobbies,
bars, and food counters, where it was difficult to get a drink of water but
easy enough to buy spirits of all kinds as well as fruit, pies, custards,
and – in Philadelphia, at least – fried oysters. Writing in 1859, Paul
Preston recalled attending New York's Olympic Theater in the 1840s:
"[T]he dramatic part of the programme was secondary to the social
privilege of interchanging friendly communications. In fact, if . . . a man
about town visited a theater it was mainly with the idea of there encoun-
tering companions of a congenial spirit." Going to the theater for him
meant lounging about in the lobby, drinking, and eating; only if the play
were new did he actually watch the performance.[15]

The pit occupied the physical and social middle of the theatrical
space. Unaccompanied young men with fifty cents to pay for admission,

those who wanted to be closer to the stage, working-class men for whom the theater became an important social ritual, and, occasionally, escorted working-class women all crowded around the footlights in the pit. There they endured uncomfortable seating; the danger of dripping wax from the chandeliers above their heads; barrages of apple cores, peanut shells, and other pieces of refuse dropped or thrown by gallery patrons; and the almost constant hubbub of their fellow pittites. But to be in the pit was to be at the center of the theatrical experience and, in effect, to help to control that experience.

To a degree that would be unimaginable to theatergoers today, early nineteenth-century audiences controlled what went on at the theater. In the 1810s and 1820s that control had been exercised by the wealthy, whose money had built the theaters to begin with and whose patronage of the boxes kept them open. By the 1830s, however, the locus of power had begun to shift to the "shirt-sleeve" crowd, as Mrs. Trollope called them, in the pit and gallery.[16] In one sense, this period represents a struggle between audiences and theater management (with actors frequently caught in the middle) over, to put it in legal terms, what rights and entitlements were attendant upon the purchase of a theater ticket. Once the spectators had been granted admission to the theatrical space, what were the limits on their individual and collective attempts to use that space to express their approval or disapprobation and to structure the performance itself? In the days when the class interests of theater owners, managers, and audiences were more or less aligned, audience control was an issue of little consequence. But by the 1830s, competing sets of interests shared the same theatrical space. Today when we buy a movie or theater ticket, we generally assume that all we have purchased is the right to occupy a particular seat for a given period of time. We further assume that the range of allowable audience behavior (beyond passive sitting) is severely circumscribed – we will be "asked to leave" if we talk above a whisper, shout things at the actors, and so forth. (I even once persuaded the manager to remove a man from a movie theater because his snoring made it impossible for me to hear the dialogue!) In the 1830s and 1840s, however, it was unclear what limits – short of preventing physical damage to the theater – could or should be placed on the actions of audiences.

In part, this struggle over control of the theater was due to what Victor Turner would call its "liminoid" nature. That is to say, the theatrical space is set aside from the world outside it, and – as the epigraph from Tocqueville makes clear – some of the rules and roles that govern conduct and expression in the outside world are suspended as well. Theater managers contributed to the audience's perception that *it* was in control by assuming the role of "your humble servant." As audiences tested the limits of this power, they began exercising it as if it were their right to do so – in exchange for a fifty-cent ticket, they could become part of the group whose "humble servant" was a person who managed a facility and an enterprise worth more than any individual pittite was likely to make in several lifetimes. William Northall recalled an episode at the Olympic Theater in the 1840s when an actor scowled in the direction of the pit in response to a remark by one of its occupants. The next day, the actor received a letter from a representative of the pit "informing him that he must not attempt to frown them down . . . and in future he must behave more respectfully." Paul Preston, who frequently sat in the same pit, remarked some years later: "We were in the habit of doing pretty nearly as we pleased, provided we did not offend public decency, or outrage the proprieties of social life." But even these qualifications did not always apply.[17]

Applause was not reserved for the end of a performance but was likely to occur whenever a line of dialogue or a piece of stage business struck a responsive chord. When audiences found something particularly to their liking, they would insist that it be repeated. Speaking with the voice of the audience in 1846, the *Spirit of the Times* Boston correspondent wrote: "We . . . determine to have the worth of our money when we go to the theater; we made Blangy dance her best dances twice; we made Mrs. Sequin repeat 'Marble Halls,'. . . and tonight we are going to encore Mrs. Kean's 'I don't believe it' in *The Gamester*. We hope she'll prove agreeable and disbelieve it twice for our sakes. Perhaps we'll flatter Mr. Kean by making him take poison twice; the latter depends upon the furor of the moment."[18]

The phrase "calling the tune" originated in audiences' determination to do just that: control what songs the theater orchestra would play. The audience took its job as musical director most seriously on national holidays. A British visitor to New York's Park Theater on Washington's Birthday 1832 reported that the audience demanded at least six encores of "The Star-Spangled Banner," "every patriotic citizen appearing to think himself in duty bound to attempt keeping time, whether or not he had any ear for music, by stamping upon the floor of the box with his feet, so that let the music be what it would, I could not hear a bar."[19]

Theater managers and actors for the most part tolerated the audience's role in structuring the theatrical performance. After all, calls for encores and spontaneous outbursts of applause signaled the audience's enjoyment of that particular part of the entertainment. The other – and much more volatile – side of the audience control issue emerged when audiences expressed their disapprobation. Theater patrons were as quick and demonstrative in expressing their displeasure – for whatever reason – as in expressing their approval. The mildest form of condemnation was hissing, which if general enough could drown out the most stentorian of actors. Shouted insults constituted a further escalation of disfavor, followed by the pelting of offending actors with eggs, nutshells, other foodstuffs, and rocks – the last named brought to the theater in case they were needed for this purpose. One unfortunate actor's portrayal of Richard III in Sacramento in 1856 provoked a fusillade of "cabbages, carrots, pumpkins, potatoes, a sack of flour and one of soot, a dead goose, . . . [and] Chinese firecrackers."[20]

Although not a frequent occurrence, theater riots did take place sporadically in America from the mid-1700s through the 1840s. Given what would strike us today as the chaotic character of a normal night at the theater in the 1830s, it might seem difficult to distinguish between riotous and nonriotous audience behavior. Contemporaneous observers and participants, however, clearly recognized the point at which boisterous expressions of disapprobation became riots. Riots were first of all expressions of groups rather than aggregated individuals. Furthermore, riots were attempts to obtain immediate redress of particular grievances, and the aggrieved group was willing to threaten or use personal injury or property destruction to impose its will.

In his analysis of American riots in the 1830s, David Grimsted distinguishes between riots and revolutionary violence. The latter challenges the existing political and social structure; the former seeks an extralegal remedy of a particular wrong by the limited exercise of violence. In these terms, riots are not anarchic or insurrectionary; however, as Grimsted notes, all riots in Jacksonian America were inextricably linked to the major social and ideological tensions of the era. Such was certainly the case with theater riots. For patrons in the boxes and those who used the theater as an instrument of social and moral control, theater riots served as nagging reminders of the connection between theater and disorder: playful ontological instability onstage was reproduced all too threateningly on a social level this side of the footlights. When class tensions exploded in the Astor Place Theater riot of 1849, with the loss of more than twenty lives, the theater as a place where "the higher ranks mix with the middle and lower classes" became untenable. A fundamental social reordering of the theater was set in motion – a reordering that twenty years later resulted in the establishment of burlesque as a theatrical form.[21]

The specific provocations for theater riots varied considerably, and some seem almost laughably inconsequential: a riot erupted in Providence in 1828 over the British accent of an actor. But in all cases, theater riots were antiauthoritarian in nature. The audience group most involved in theater riots, particularly through the 1830s, was not the proletariat but the artisanal and entrepreneurial working class: the shopkeepers, journeymen, mechanics (skilled workmen), small masters, and apprentices who filled the pits and galleries of many urban theaters and who claimed the Bowery Theater as their own in the 1830s and 1840s. The Bowery Theater audience asserted its collective authority over the theatrical space and experience more vigorously than any other in America and reacted strongly and immediately against any perceived slight or intrusion. Theater riots were demonstrations of class solidarity and theatrical sovereignty.[22]

Tocqueville might well have had the Bowery Theater in mind when he wrote that, in America of the 1830s, "The pit has frequently made laws for the boxes."[23] But the "boxes" were not always willing to tolerate the inversion of power relations within the theater. When a city grew large enough to support more than one theater, the upper classes frequently gravitated toward one of the houses where their taste for opera and English plays and players might better be catered to and where they might exercise greater control over the theatrical experience. In New York, for example, the Park Theater was the "aristocratic" house in the 1830s; the Bowery and the Chatham were for the (literally and metaphorically) unwashed.[24]

Even the physical and institutional separation of classes did not prevent the Astor Place Theater riot of May 1849, the most famous theater riot in American history. The Astor Place Theater represents yet another step in the upper classes' attempt to distance themselves from the democratic theatrical scene. Founded in 1847, the Astor Place was intended as home for Italian opera and for the most fashionable of New York theatergoers. The members of this group, in the words of one observer, "carefully abstained from countenancing even the most refined and elevating dramatic production of their native tongue, and by their example, deterred hundreds of their aping followers, who dreaded the terrible reproach of being out of fashion."[25]

The riot itself grew out of the antipathy of Bowery pittites for English actor William Charles Macready.[26] For several years Macready had been engaged in a rivalry with the Bowery crowd's favorite actor, Edwin Forrest, and at several stops along Macready's 1848–49 American tour the two played opposite each other. The two actors represented antithetical approaches to acting and to the theater. Macready stood for the integrity of the dramatic text, the actor as scholar, and the theater as cultural shrine. Forrest was Jacksonian masculinity personified: bombastic, direct, flamboyant. To the Bowery pit, the rivalry had come to symbolize a contest between the democratic and popular native son and the aristocratic Englishman. Macready's appearance at the Astor Place Theater further underlined the class antagonism implicit in the actors' rift.

When on the evening of May 7 Macready made his first appearance onstage at the Astor Place Theater in the third scene of *Macbeth*, he discovered that parquette and gallery were occupied by a number of Forrest's adherents, who drowned out the hurrahs of the theater's regular patrons with howls and hisses. The Bowery crowd was intent not only on expressing its disapprobation of Macready but also on transferring its notion of republican audience sovereignty to the parquette and upper tiers of the Astor Place Theater. Macready's perseverance in taking the stage at the beginning of the third act further enraged the Bowery crowd, which drove out the orchestra with a volley of chairs thrown from the second tier. Macready himself finally admitted defeat, scurried out the back door of the theater to his hotel, and booked passage on the next ship for England, vowing never to return to such an uncivilized land. The Bowery pittites declared victory over Macready, the Astor Place Theater, and the constellation of antidemocratic ideals for which both stood.

As Peter Buckley notes, up to this point the Astor Place "riot" was in form and consequence little different from the previous theater riots.

The aim – to assert the power of "pit" against perceived antidemocratic and antirepublican forces – was the same. The crowd's tactics – hisses escalating into artillery barrages of increasingly substantial projectiles – followed a familiar pattern. The management allowed the disturbance to run its course without calling for police assistance. What made the Astor Place incident different, however, was the fact that this battle over audience control was fought by the pittites on "foreign" turf, in a theater never intended for them to occupy, and controlled by another audience with radically opposed notions of theater and culture. It was the insistence of some of the Astor Place audience to reassert *their* control over *their* theater that elevated the incident to a much more serious level.

On May 9, forty-seven of the city's most prominent citizens distributed a public letter urging Macready not to be cowed by his reception and assuring him that "good sense and respect for order" would be restored at the Astor Place Theater. A copy was delivered to the mayor, who took the unusual and provocative step of ordering police and militia to protect the theater. An hour and a half before the performance, police began to admit ticket holders to the theater, turning away two hundred whom the management feared might cause trouble. Enough pittites managed to slip through the police screen and take up places in the parquette to alarm Macready with hisses and clenched fists when he made his appearance onstage. The chief of police had them arrested and held in a basement room in the theater. While Macready continued, the crowd outside – which had begun with the two hundred disenfranchised ticket holders – swelled to five thousand and became increasingly agitated. The throng hurled rocks through the theater windows, and the chief of police, fearing that the theater and his men would be overrun, called out the militia. The sight of two hundred soldiers defending the "rights" of Macready and his upper-class supporters further enraged the crowd. The two hundred soldiers panicked and, after firing once into the air, leveled volleys of shot into the thick of the tightly packed mass of people. Eighteen died immediately; four more succumbed later.

As Buckley puts it, "a single riot, even of the order of the one at Astor Place, does not (speaking teleologically) change the 'course' of history." However, as he, David Grimsted, and Lawrence Levine have all argued, the Astor Place riot does mark a watershed in American theater history in several important respects. First, it spelled the end of the era of audience sovereignty and the beginning of a trend toward greater

The Astor Place Theater riot, May 9, 1849.
(Prints and Photographs Division, Library of Congress)

manager control and audience passivity – a trend that would culminate
at the beginning of the next century in silent spectators sitting before
immutable movie screens. Second, after the riot, managers were less
likely to orient their theaters toward a socially heterogeneous audience.
"One theater," says Grimsted, "was no longer large enough to appeal to
all classes." Finally, after 1849, the heterogeneous fare that had characterized an evening at the theater in the 1830s and 1840s – variety acts,
dancers, farce, and tragedy all sharing the same stage – was fragmented
into distinct forms for separate, socially defined audiences.[27]

○ ○ ○   **The Theater Becomes "Sanctified"**
and "Feminized"

Certainly the Astor Place riot provides a convenient historical divide between the theater of the 1830s and 1840s and that of the
1850s and 1860s. But this change did not occur overnight nor as a result
of the riot alone. As noted above, in some cities the "fashionables" had
already begun to withdraw from dramatic theaters and to claim opera as

their exclusive preserve.[28] In addition to this trend, there were two others: the "sanctification" and the "feminization" of the theater.

Two showmen in the late 1840s and early 1850s were particularly responsible for helping to remove the remaining vestiges of religious and moral opposition to the theater and for making theatrical performance acceptable to bourgeois audiences. Moses Kimball opened the Boston Museum and Gallery of Fine Arts at the corner of Tremont and Bromfield streets on June 14, 1841. The Boston Museum, like those opened by Charles Willson Peale in Philadelphia, John Scudder in New York, and Daniel Drake in Cincinnati, began with a collection of paintings, sculpture, and natural history artifacts and presented itself as an educational institution. But, as Kimball and his fellow museum managers quickly learned, the novelty of seeing engravings and stuffed animals soon wore off. Something else was needed to sustain regular patronage. Above the natural history exhibits on the first floor of the museum, Kimball opened a "portrait gallery," which was, in fact, a nine-hundred-seat auditorium. There in his first season he presented musical concerts, dioramas, lectures, and other attractions – indeed, the makings of what would become vaudeville. For twenty-five cents, one gained admission to the gallery with its 161 steel engravings along the walls. As for the show, "the God-fearing folk of Boston could stop to watch or not as they wished."[29]

At the beginning of the 1843–44 season, Kimball assembled a resident dramatic company, assuring his patrons that in "all pieces produced at this establishment all *profane, expletive,* and *indecent allusions* will be totally expunged."[30] But Kimball's most brilliant stroke came later that season when he mounted a production of the archetypal temperance drama, *The Drunkard; or, The Fallen Saved* by W. H. Smith. How could even the most morally scrupulous Bostonian object to watching a dramatized sermon on the evils of drink presented in a museum? *The Drunkard* ran for more than one hundred performances and established theatrical entertainment as an acceptable form of leisure for Boston burghers and upright country folk alike.[31]

In New York, two years before Kimball opened his museum in Boston, Phineas T. Barnum purchased the property of the late John Scudder's American Museum and with it opened Barnum's American Museum on Ann Street in lower Manhattan. Like Kimball, Barnum presented freaks, variety acts, and other attractions in his "lecture

Barnum's American Museum, 1853.
(Prints and Photographs Division, Library of Congress)

room" to augment the appeal of his inanimate exhibits. Associated with
Moses Kimball in the circulation of exhibits, Barnum wrote to Kimball
in 1848 regarding the success of *The Drunkard*. The following season,
Barnum hired a stock company for his museum and turned his lecture
room into a theater proper – still calling it a "lecture room." There he
repeated the success of *The Drunkard* and, in his words, other "highly
moral and instructive domestic dramas, written expressly for this establishment and so constructed as to please and edify, while they possess a
powerful reformatory tendency."[32] Like Kimball, Barnum addressed
the issue of moral reservations about the theater directly, carefully
setting his enterprise apart from the commercial stage: "So careful is
the supervision exercised over the amusements that hundreds of persons who are prevented visiting theaters on account of the vulgarisms
and immorality which are sometimes permitted therein, may visit Mr.
Barnum's establishment without fear of offence."[33]

Note that in this panegyric to himself, Barnum points out the "immorality" that was "permitted" on both sides of the footlights in the

theater as well as the solution to this problem: complete management
control over both the stage agenda and the social agenda in the auditorium. In the museum theaters that followed the example of Kimball
and Barnum, there was no question about who was in control or what
were the limits of audience behavior – any more than there were such
uncertainties in connection with Sunday church services or school
classrooms. Barnum was no more the audience's "humble servant"
than was its Presbyterian minister or school principal.

In terms of ticket price, Barnum's "lecture room" was accessible to
the same audience that attended the Bowery Theater not far away.[34]
Barnum, however, sought an audience that was *socially* different from
those that filled the pit at the Bowery and participated in the Astor Place
riot. The Bowery appealed to the lower ranks of the "older" urban
middle class and the upper echelons of the artisanal working class:
shopkeepers, master craftsmen, and the single journeymen and apprentices who worked alongside their masters in the many small work-
shops that – in the 1830s, at least – still lined New York streets. The
world of their commercial leisure, except for the occasional liaison with
a prostitute, was almost exclusively male and inextricably bound to
alcohol: on the job, in taverns and grog shops, and, of course, at the
theater. Their leisure rituals were those of class and gender solidarity:
asserting their distinctiveness from the capitalists above them and the
unskilled poor beneath, and protecting their ideological turf from intrusion by racial interlopers and meddlesome upper-class reformers alike.

Kimball, Barnum, and the museum theater movement in general
hitched their show business wagons to the ascendant new middle class:
salaried workers, retail clerks, upwardly mobile entrepreneurs and industrial workers, the more prosperous farmers, *and* their families. The
frames of social reference for these workers tended not to be the artisanal workbench and the aggressively masculine rituals of the tavern and
pit, but rather home and family. These families were particularly recep-
tive to the waves of Protestant revivalism that swept through antebellum
America. Within this new middle class, it was women who led their
families to the altar and who coaxed their husbands back to the hearth
at the end of the workday.[35]

At mid-century Barnum and Kimball lured this class to the theater
through the back door of the museum and under the cloak of moral
education. The key to their success was removing the impediments to

middle-class women attending plays. All this required was transforming the theater as a social institution. The markers of gender and class
solidarity were expunged: alcohol, prostitution, boisterous behavior,
and audience control.[36] Barnum's theater was no less a social institution expressive of class interests than was the Bowery Theater, but
Barnum's expressed the inclusiveness and elasticity of middle-class
identity, not the jealously protected distinctiveness of artisanal republi-
canism. Museum theaters also revealed the realignment of genders
within the theater. Women were no longer set apart from the audience –
on the stage and in the third tier – but were included as a valued (and,
indeed, crucial) part of the audience – drawn into the audience by the
respectability of this new theatrical space and leaving it with their
personal reputations untarnished by the experience. Such was the success of the museum theater strategy that within a decade "respectable"
women attended museum theaters in a manner that would have indeli-
bly marked them as prostitutes in the 1840s: without male escort.
In September 1860 the *New York Clipper* somewhat cynically noted:
"*Joseph and His Brethren* are delighting the moral *habitués* of Barnum's
Museum, including the beautiful young ladies who attend so regularly
the afternoon entertainment, and who in such a dramatic temple, do
not find it necessary to have gentlemen to accompany them. Ah! there's
nothing like the moral dodge. Piety fetches 'em."[37]

At the same time that the social stratum from which Barnum drew his
audience was expanding, the economic rug was being pulled out from
under the artisans in the Bowery pit. With the growth of industrial
capitalism between 1825 and 1850, the artisanal work culture and
economy progressively eroded. The rise of factory production, division
of labor, subcontracting, and, in the 1840s, waves of cheap labor from
Ireland and Germany had by 1850 so undermined the artisanal system
that "most of the city's [New York's] leading trades could barely be
called crafts at all, even though some workers still clung to the appella-
tions 'mechanic' and 'journeyman.' "[38] Although there is no accurate
way to gauge the rate or extent of the change, the constitution of the
pit – at least in New York – reflected the deterioration in the status of the
artisanal class. By the time of the Astor Place riot, the pit at both the
Bowery and Olympic theaters had been taken over by teenage apprentices, journeymen, and even newsboys, who had moved down from their
former haunt in the gallery. The "Bowery b'hoys," as they were called,

did not so much constitute a distinctive economic subclass as a subculture based on style (stovepipe hat, pea jacket, red shirt, soap locks, use of street slang, and cocky gait and manner) and social association (affiliation with one of the many volunteer fire companies in the city). The season before the Astor Place riot had seen the stage representation and celebration of these new denizens of the pit in Ben Baker's *Glance at New York in 1848* at the Olympic Theater, specifically through the character of Mose, played by Frank Chanfrau.[39] By the end of the play's four-month run at the Olympic, William Northall complained that "the boxes no longer shone with the elite of the city; the character of the audiences was entirely changed, and Mose, instead of appearing on the stage, was in the pit, the boxes, and the gallery. It was all Mose, and the respectability of the house mosed too."[40]

During the same season he instituted his policy of presenting "pure and domestic" plays at the museum, Barnum took another step toward solidifying the triple articulation among his brand of theater, women, and middle-class respectability. In the fall of 1849, he offered a Swedish singer whom he had never heard perform one thousand dollars per night for up to 150 nights if she would tour the United States under his sponsorship and management. Although largely unknown in America, Jenny Lind had established a considerable European reputation not only for her singing ability, but, more importantly for Barnum's purposes, for her altruism as well. Wherever she sang, Lind gave generously to local charities, and in her hometown of Stockholm, she had endowed a philanthropic foundation. Lind did not know Barnum either, but in light of his offer to deposit the whole of the value of their contract in her London bank before her departure for America, she agreed.[41]

Barnum immediately began to promote Lind as only Barnum could. He took out an ad in a New York newspaper that ran, in part:

> Perhaps I may not make any money by this enterprise; but I assure you that if I knew I should not make a farthing profit, I would ratify the engagement, so anxious am I that the United States should be visited by a lady whose vocal powers have never been approached by any other human being, and whose character is charity, simplicity, and goodness personified. . . . A visit from such a woman, who regards her high artistic powers as a gift from heaven, for the

Mose and Lize in *A Glance at New York in 1848*.
(Prints and Photographs Division, Library of Congress)

An example of Barnum's publicity campaign for Jenny Lind.
(Prints and Photographs Division, Library of Congress)

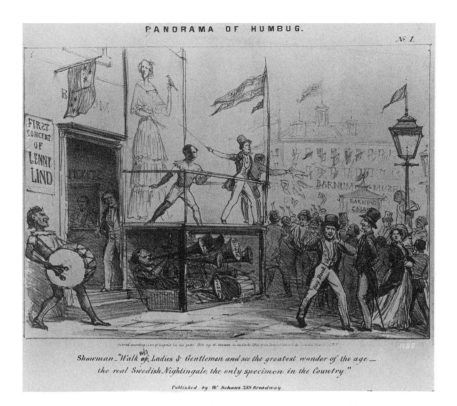

PANORAMA OF HUMBUG.

№ 1.

Showman -"Walk up, Ladies & Gentlemen and see the greatest wonder of the age —
the real Swedish Nightingale, the only specimen in the Country."

Published by W. Schaus 289 Broadway

Barnum's latest attraction: "First Concert of Jenny Lind."
(Prints and Photographs Division, Library of Congress)

melioration of affliction and distress, and whose every thought and deed is philanthropy, I feel persuaded, will prove a blessing to America.[42]

By the time Lind arrived in New York in September 1850, Barnum had helped to engineer a Jenny Lind craze: there were Jenny Lind hats, gloves, furniture, pianos, and, incongruously enough, Jenny Lind–brand chewing tobacco. Her tour was an enormous success, and for once in Barnum's career, one of his attractions very nearly lived up to its billing. Lind donated all of her share of the proceeds from her first New York concert to various local charities and gave at least one benefit concert in nearly every city she played. Naturally, Barnum's publicity machine trumpeted every instance of her beneficence.

It is a mark of P. T. Barnum's show business genius to have found the

perfect feminine theatrical persona to associate with his stage enterprise. Not only was Lind clearly not a woman of dubious moral standing, but also she was one of the most admirable and saintly women in
the world. Who could wonder, wrote the *Albany Weekly Argus* at the
beginning of her tour, that to thousands who had never heard her sing
she was still the most popular woman in the world?[43]

By the 1850s the "feminization" of the American theater audience
was beginning to occur outside the museum theaters as well, and with it
came a further diminution of the masculine power of the pit. As late as
1851, Northall noted that it was unfortunate that women did not usually
sit in the pit, since they would have "a calming effect on men." Increasingly in the 1850s, however, women did move from their traditional place in the boxes into the heretofore masculine domain of the
pit. Or rather, they moved increasingly into what had formerly been
called the pit and was now called the parquette. In new theaters built
around mid-century, the parquette was created through an expansion of
the ground-floor seating capacity of the theater, as theater auditoriums
were lengthened and the amount of space devoted to boxes was reduced. In new and renovated theaters, the bare benches of the pit were
replaced with individual, cushioned seats. The term "parquette" also
symbolically distinguished this space from what it had been before: the
more dignified and restrained behavior of the parquette replaced the
rowdy and demonstrative crowds of the pit.[44]

The social transformation of the theater in the 1850s was uneven.
Some of the more proletarian-oriented New York theaters retained their
rough-and-tumble character long after other theaters had become "respectable."[45] By the end of the decade, however, theatergoing was
generally a very different experience from what it had been twenty years
before. Whether motivated by the example of the Astor Place riot or by a
desire to align themselves with the ascendant middle classes, theater
managers exerted greater control over audience behavior. By the early
1860s, hissing was almost never heard in American theaters; expressions of disapprobation were limited to the withholding of applause.
Managers had begun to sever the connection between liquor and theatergoing, even though the closing of theater bars resulted in a loss of
revenue: so long as liquor was served at theaters, many middle-class
women refused to attend.[46]

Manager control over the theatrical space and, concomitantly, dimi-

nution of the traditional extralegal "rights" of the audience were cod- *legislation*
ified in case law and legislation in the 1850s. Case law concerned two
distinct areas of control: What sort of license was involved in the sale of
a theater ticket? And what limits could be placed on the expression of
audience disapprobation? As to the former, various state courts, citing
an 1845 British decision, affirmed that a theater ticket constituted
merely a temporary license enabling the purchaser to do something
legally that in the absence of a license would be illegal – in this case,
occupying a theater seat, which, if done without purchasing a ticket,
would constitute trespass. As the issuer of a revocable license, the
theater manager had the right to set the terms of that license any way he
chose: he could set whatever price he wanted, restrict entry to particular
categories of persons for any or no reason, and, what is more, decide to
revoke the license at any time he wished and for any or no reason. To
add insult to the audience's injury, on revocation of the license to enter
the theater, the ticket holder immediately became a trespasser and
could be removed "by the use of force necessary for that purpose."[47] In
short, the courts were moving toward the position propounded in an
1882 Missouri appeals court decision: "Theaters are not necessities of
life, and the proprietors of them may manage their business in their
own way. If that way is unfair or unpopular, they will suffer in diminished
receipts."[48]

Again relying on English precedents, American courts ruled that the
audience's right to express its approval or disapproval was qualified and
circumscribed. An audience might hiss a bad performance, but its *rights shift away from audience*
members could not conspire in advance to prevent an actor from taking
the stage by their shouts and hisses. Their responses had to be an
expression of "feelings of the moment," and while their disapprobation
might be "noisy," it could not be "riotous." An 1854 Massachusetts case
reveals how the presumption of rights had shifted from those of the
audience to express itself to those of the manager and performer to
express themselves. The Massachusetts Supreme Court reviewed an
1849 statute prohibiting the disruption of schools, public meetings, or
"other assembly[blies] of people, met for a lawful purpose." The specific
case involved three men whose coughs, laughs, and loud talk disturbed
a temperance meeting. The court not only upheld the lower court's
verdict against the men but also argued that the provisions of the statute
should be extended to *all* lawful gatherings, including amusements:

"Shall not proprietors, authors, composers, artists, visitors, and all other persons interested, be protected in their rights, against wilful disturbance, by the operation of that law, which gives them their rights? And yet those rights can only be preserved by maintaining such meetings from wilful interruption and disturbance, so that the performances may be witnessed, heard and enjoyed." A theater ticket constituted only a license to enter the building; it did not confer the right to "abuse" that license "by tin horns, cracked kettles, and other loud and discordant sounds, [which] might destroy the effect of the most pathetic tragedy, or sublimest oratorio." Obviously, the justices' notion of the theater was derived more from the Boston Museum than from the Bowery.[49]

The state also exercised its "right" to impose controls over theatrical business. Municipal and state statutes gave those governments broad authority to license theaters (and revoke those licenses), limit the hours and days of operation, prosecute obscene performances, and determine who could perform and who could attend performances. A New York appeals court noted in 1875 that the authority of local, state, or federal governments to regulate and license theaters was unquestioned.[50] By the late 1850s, the last vestiges of boisterous and demonstrative audience behavior were to be found in the pits of the Bowery and a few other working-class theaters, now occupied largely by teenage newsboys. In 1859 the New York State legislature passed a law requiring that minors attending the theater be in the company of a parent or guardian. Allowing working-class boys to enjoy the pit's brand of temporary but exhilarating empowerment was bound to lead to criminal behavior outside the theater. "You will be surprised to learn," read a letter to the *Clipper* from Albany, "that they [the legislature] have traced all the larcenies, burglaries, garotting, and thimble-rigging, which distinguish your city, to the theater. . . . There is not a sneak thief, or a confidence man among you who did not receive the rudiments of his calling at the theater."[51]

By the turn of the century, when the first book on American theater law was compiled, it was assumed that proper audience behavior consisted of sitting silently and anonymously. Theatergoers acting in this manner were the "audience" whose rights had to be protected from those who behaved otherwise: "The manager has full right to insist that his patrons behave in an orderly manner and not in such a way as to interfere with the comfort and enjoyment of others. This rule requires propriety of deportment and silence when the play is in progress, as no one may so conduct himself as to deprive others of the full pleasure of what they have paid to see and hear."[52] Theatergoers had become consumers of a theatrical product, no longer actors in the theatrical experience.

○ ○ ○   **The "Other" Theater: The Concert Saloon**

The move to create a respectable, bourgeois theater in America had by 1860 largely succeeded in separating the mainstream theatrical experience from its connections with the more boisterous elements of the working class, alcohol, sexuality, assertive masculinity, and, in general, with what was now perceived as the "vulgarism and immorality" – as Barnum put it – that had been part of the theatrical experience of the 1830s and 1840s. Bourgeois theater in America was constructed in terms of what it excluded as noisy, dirty, disgusting, and vulgar. Thus, the construction by exclusion of a bourgeois theater in America was part of a larger historical process by which the bourgeoisie more generally defined itself in terms of what it had rejected, excluded, outlawed, or repressed. That the theater should be an important site for the construction of bourgeois identity in both Britain and America is not surprising. As Stallybrass and White note regarding the process by which the bourgeois self is constructed, "What starts as a simple repulsion or rejection of symbolic matter foreign to the self inaugurates a process of introjection and negation which is always complex in its effects."[53]

In the case of American theater at mid-century, all of the features of the theatrical experience that had been excluded in the creation of a "respectable" theater were reconstituted in a separate theatrical domain, the concert saloon, which was nothing less than the mainstream theater's negative image, its low-other "identity in difference."[54] Appealing primarily to working-class men, concert saloons sprang up along the Bowery. They featured alcoholic beverages – served by "waiter girls" in, what were for the period, short dresses – and variety acts, all for an admission charge ranging from ten to twenty-five cents. The performance of variety acts in saloons had been common in New York for decades. What distinguished the concert saloons of the 1860s was their incorporation of feminine sexuality as part of the entertainment.

The theatrical press first mentions the concert saloon phenomenon in the spring of 1859. In December, the *Clipper* listed five concert saloons, and by the end of 1861, the paper declared New York to be in the grip of a concert saloon "mania." Concert saloons seem to have differed somewhat in their degree of "illegitimacy," but certainly one can say that their appeal lay in providing what the "legitimate" theater did not: a place where men could go to drink, laugh, talk out loud, be waited on by pretty young women, and take in a show. What constituted the "show" also varied from place to place, but basically concert saloons provided a venue for variety acts, which had once been a standard part of theatrical entertainment but which had been increasingly excluded from mainstream theaters in the 1850s. In one sense, concert saloons were clearly a response to the formality and stodginess of the bourgeois theater experience. The *Clipper* even suggested that they were attracting some male patrons away from legitimate houses.[55]

From the beginning, the fact that the concert saloon was structured around the very elements the bourgeois theater had struggled so hard to expunge made it vulnerable to attack as not just disreputable but as the kind of place that "pander[s] to the vicious tastes of the most depraved characters that infest our city." The focus of bourgeois objections to concert saloons was the waiter girl and her actual or possible connection to prostitution. In January 1862 the *New York Evening Post* declared that concert saloons had become a "truly diabolic form of shameless and avowed Bacchus and Phallus worship."[56]

It is unclear from the lengthy article exactly what form this worship took, but the reporter does offer a fairly detailed description of a concert saloon. A converted theater, the Canterbury Music Hall (on Broadway between Houston and Prince), was among the most elaborate concert saloons in the city. A spacious parquette stretched from the stage at one end of the auditorium back to a bar, which filled the entire rear wall. In front of the bar was an open "promenade" raised some four feet above the parquette, which allowed patrons to stroll about and still see the show onstage. Waiter girls scurried between the bar and their customers (mirrors hung along the walls reflecting their images) and were allowed to drink with the customers. They were "as much stared at and more familiarly known to the audience than the performers on the stage." A

Canterbury Music Hall: "A portico to the brothel."
(Prints and Photographs Division, Library of Congress)

gallery above the parquette had been fitted with individual compartments, where waiter girls could be found serving and drinking as well. "But for the waiter girl feature," the *Post* reporter noted, "the Canterbury might claim to rank as a respectable place of public amusement, the performance on the stage being of average merit, the singing endurable, the negro business no drearier than usual, the dancing pretty good, and in character not much exceeding the usual license accorded to the ballet." Because of the waiter girls, however, the Canterbury was nothing less than "a portico to the brothel."[57]

The *Clipper* also railed against the immorality of some concert saloons (although it found nothing objectionable about the Canterbury), but it argued that most concert saloons were like barbershops: the fact that "respectable" women do not frequent them does not necessarily imply that anything untoward goes on in them. Furthermore, the function of the waiter girls was no different from that of ballet dancers at legitimate theaters: both were hired to show off their figures. Indeed, the paper reasoned, if one wanted to mount a case of immorality, it was easier to do so against the legitimate theater, where "these 'immoral exhibitions' of female legs and bosoms upon the stage of the regular theater are *given before ladies and children*, and often call a blush to their cheeks; whereas, the same style of exhibitions on the concert saloon stage are given in the presence of the male sex only, who don't know how to blush."[58]

In April 1862 the New York State legislature passed an "anti-concert saloon" bill, which had the effect of closing most concert saloons in New York City and driving others underground. After 1862, the concert saloon in New York City operated in the twilight of unprosecuted illegality. Concert saloons sprang up in other cities across the country in the 1860s, their nature and longevity dependent on the accommodations proprietors could make with local authorities. In Minneapolis, for example, antitemperance sentiment prompted concert saloon managers not to call public attention to their enterprises. They operated for several years before they began advertising in the local newspapers in 1868.[59]

It is, of course, impossible to determine the degree of the connection between the concert saloons and prostitution; moreover, that connection is largely irrelevant to the present discussion. What *is* important is that the phenomenon of independent, working-class women engaging in commerce in a working-class theatrical space was perceived by those in a position to make laws as tantamount to criminal sexuality. As Christine Stansell and Ruth Rosen have argued, in the 1850s "prostitution" meant not so much literal sexual commerce as a whole symbolic constellation of qualities attendant upon the working-class woman's economic and social independence from her family and resistance to or distance from patriarchal control. In the increasingly difficult struggle to distinguish the respectable "lady" from the woman who was not, bourgeois culture saw all manner of divergence from the rigid norms of "true womanhood" as whorishness. And because sites of working-class commercial leisure – such as the concert saloon, dance hall, and lake steamer – represented the intersection of feminine economic independence and social autonomy, they were singled out for particularly vehement attack as dens of prostitution. As Stansell puts it, "Insofar as sex retained its associations to exchange and money, women's presence in a commercial culture of leisure, based on the purchase of pleasures, could in itself imply sexual willingness."[60]

○ ○ ○   **The Return of the Repressed**

In September 1868, when Lydia Thompson and her troupe appeared at Wood's – one of the many museum/theaters that followed in the wake of Barnum's success – she faced an audience of clerks and shopkeepers, men and women, for whom theatergoing was, for the most part, socially and morally unproblematic. Theaters had been made safe and respectable, the theatrical experience predictable, and the audience quiescent. In the interval between Harry Beckett's curtain raiser and *Ixion*, the audience might have looked around at the museum exhibits, but they did not rush to the bar for a drink; there was no bar in the theater. Ironically, it was the presence of respectable, middle-class women and men in the audience that made burlesque so problematic, and it was only in relation to what the bourgeois theater had become since the Astor Place riot that burlesque seemed so transgressive. Mainstream American theater had by 1869 reached an accommodation with the middle and upper strata of American society. The theater would continue to be a liminoid space, where things were not what they seemed and where pleasure might be taken in the construction of unreal worlds. At times controversy over the nature and propriety of those pleasures and those unreal worlds strained that accommodation. But onstage and in the audience, the theater's inherent power to transgress and invert existing power relations was much more circumscribed than it had been a generation before. The manager of a new theater in Worcester, Massachusetts, could face his audience on opening night in 1857 and promise that "while I control this house nothing will ever occur on these boards that will cause a blush to mantle the cheek of the most fastidious." In 1865 New York theaters began scheduling matinees on Saturdays primarily for women. The world of the mainstream theater and the world of the social establishment in America had by 1869 become more congruent than it had ever been.[61]

When Lydia Thompson moved to Niblo's Garden in the winter of 1868–69 and into the heart of the middle-class theatrical world, she upset this accommodation. At the historical moment when women had finally become socially invisible as a part of the theater audience, Thompson and her troupe made women visible in a way that could not be ignored. Just when the voices of class division within the audience had been silenced, Thompson and her sisters spoke in the undignified slang of the marketplace and street. Just when sexuality in the audience had been stifled, the third tier evacuated, and the concert saloon closed, the "leg business" put the issue of female sexuality on center stage. All that had been repressed in the righteous, moral, conservative middle class's conquest of the theater returned in burlesque. Theater once again became unpredictable; the relationship between performer and audience became unstably and uncomfortably direct. The fear that even playful ontological duplicity onstage might upset the natural order of things resurfaced. "While I control this house," the Worcester theater manager could proclaim, secure that his claim to control would not be questioned. Control over the theater had been hard won. Burlesque challenged the very notion of hierarchy on which control was based. Who could control these women with their "idiotic parodies" of masculinity, their "horrible prettiness?"

But it would be an overstatement to say that Thompsonian burlesque's threat to theatrical and cultural order came without warning in the fall of 1868. The rapid emergence of the concert saloon and its even more sudden demise (at least in New York City) reveal how easily the bourgeois theater's low other could take economic form and how far bourgeois culture was willing to go to legally suppress it. The concert saloon episode also reveals that for bourgeois culture the "problem" of the theater continued to be the ideological nexus formed by gender and class. The suppression of the concert saloons was an attempt once again to remove "disreputable" working-class women from the theater audience, but this by no means solved the "problem" of women in the theater. Rather, between 1860 and 1868 the site of the problem merely shifted from one side of the footlights to the other. The nature of the problem is suggested by the *Clipper*'s 1861 admonition to legitimate theaters: if they do not want their patrons to be bored by "seeing the same play over and over again, . . . they will be compelled to keep up their attractions – they must give their patrons novelty."[62] Increasingly in the 1860s, the form that novelty took was the female form. The problem presented by the presence of women on the American stage nagged at bourgeois culture continually from the 1830s onward. It came to the fore anew in the 1860s and to a head with burlesque.

4

○   ○   ○   ○   ○   ○   ○   ○

The Historical Contexts of Burlesque II

Women on the Stage

The first dance which I saw upon the stage shocked me. . . . The dresses and the beauty of the performers were enchanting; but, no sooner did the dance commence, then I felt my delicacy wounded, and I was ashamed to be seen to look at them.
– *Abigail Adams*

Depend upon it, the way in which stage dancing is now conducted is but a tribute to an impure and perverted taste, and no woman, in my opinion, can look upon it with pleasure without parting with a portion of woman's pure and most holy feelings.
– *Timothy S. Arthur,* The Maiden

At Barnum's is the place to see

The dancing of the bears

When Driesbach and his family

In winter time appears;

But oh, how better far to me

Is Wheatley's Demons' rare dance,

For in the famed "Black Crook" we see

That most bewitching bare dance.

– Spirit of the Times

○ ○ ○ ○ ○ ○ ○ ○ ○ ○ ○ ○ ○ ○ ○ ○

Although the opposition provoked by Lydia Thompson and her troupe
was extraordinary in its fervor, its tone and substance had a familiar
ring. Paralleling the struggle over the constitution and behavior of the
theater audience in nineteenth-century America was a struggle over the
roles – in both senses of the word – that women would play on the stage. *Women's roles*
From the late 1820s forward, the debate was not so much over whether
women should appear onstage, but how, quite literally, they should
appear onstage. So long as women portrayed dramatic characters, what
a "woman onstage" signified could be more or less controlled through
the words written for her by the playwright. But when women appeared
in spectacle pieces – whether ballet or equestrian drama – their bodies,
not someone else's words, bore the burden of signification.

Spectacle can have the effect of freezing the dramatic narrative's
movement toward closure and the (attempted) imposition of final
meaning. It can open up the stage to pleasures other than those generated by words, ideas, and narrative logic. It reminds us that what is
staged is staged for us to see. And when what was seen onstage, displayed for the audience *to* see, was a woman's body, that body was
transformed into a more fascinating and terrifying specter than any the
nineteenth-century stage manager could conjure with trapdoors and
painted flats: the specter of female sexuality. The struggle over the
appearance of women onstage, then, was a struggle between spectacle
and mimesis, display and drama, desire and repression. Ultimately, it
was a struggle *over* women's sexuality, played out through public debates over the length of ballet dancers' costumes.

○ ○ ○   **American Melodrama: Rituals of
Democracy and Patriarchy**

Prior to the 1830s, the drama performed in American theaters was seldom "American." Managers relied on English plays of the

eighteenth century, the Bard, and translations of French dramas – and for solid economic reasons. Thanks to the absence of an international copyright agreement protecting dramatic works, they could produce these plays without paying a penny in royalties.[1] Furthermore, the first professional actors in America were themselves British, steeped and trained in that country's dramatic literature. Both factors militated against the early development of a cadre of American playwrights: Why should managers buy American works when they could poach them from abroad for free? Why should Americans with literary pretensions write for the stage when their only real protection against filching was to jealously guard every copy?

The cry for a native drama began to be heard loudly toward the end of the 1820s by critics and audiences alike, as "shirt-sleeve republicans" invaded the pit and demanded a drama better suited to their Jacksonian ideology. The 1830s and 1840s saw a groundswell of American play-writing to accompany the growth of the theater. But whether domestic or foreign, the drama presented on the antebellum stage derived from the same ideological source, what David Grimsted has called the "melodramatic vision." Such was the power of this vision that no viable dramatic alternative to it emerged during this period.[2]

At the melodrama's core was its hero. Whether he was highborn or lowborn, the hero's qualification for that role always stemmed from his innate virtue. He had an intuitive moral compass that invariably pointed the way to what was right, good, and wise. But this inner sense did not lead the melodramatic hero into Byronic opposition to the social order: in this world, the dictates of the pure heart were always consonant with those of society.

Wherever the play was set and regardless of the social stratum from which the hero sprang, the plot of the melodrama frequently revolved around romantic love. By the rules of the form, the hero and the heroine had to overcome all obstacles to the fulfillment of their preordained union. Their feelings for one another grew from love rather than from passion. The former was ennobling, chaste, restrained, and led to so-cially sanctioned domestic bliss; the latter was evidence of an ignoble nature and always led to ruin (for women) or vanquishment (for vil-lains).

Establishment of the socially accepted notion of the domestic scene was all-important to the melodramatic vision. And since that scene

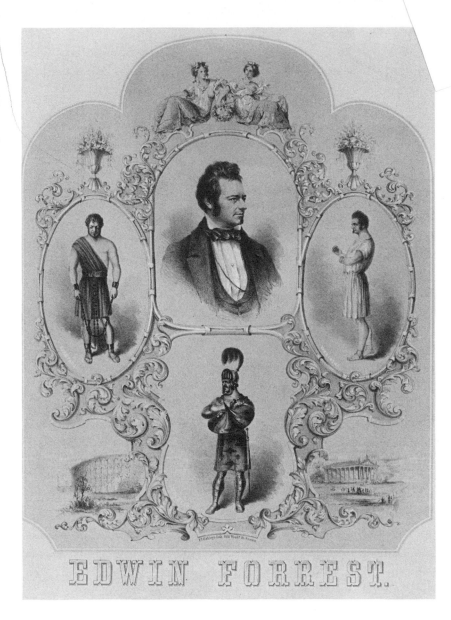

Edwin Forrest, the archetypal hero of the melodrama.
(Prints and Photographs Division, Library of Congress)

depended on the virtue of the heroine, feminine purity was the foundation on which the melodramatic social world rested. Although no major melodramatic character embodied alloyed moral qualities, the heroine in particular had to be without blemish. As Grimsted puts it, "Virtue and the heroine stood almost indistinguishable at the center of the melodrama, the one a personification of the other."[3]

The melodramatic heroine was, to a large extent, the stage embodiment of the "true" woman, whose spirit pervaded sentimental novels and sermons alike, and whose image was reproduced in paintings, prints, and magazines. She stood somewhere between man [*sic*] and the angels. To her fell the responsibility for providing social and moral stability in a rapidly changing world and for ensuring the perpetuation of that righteous moral and social order through the bearing and nurturance of children. Her tools were spiritual rather than physical; her greatest power resided in the example — of goodness, perfectibility, sincerity, purity — she represented. In the melodrama, the heroine's exalted position as heaven's agent was combined with her excruciating vulnerability. Any hint that the heroine was not all she appeared to be immediately and forever disqualified her from *being* the heroine.[4]

The cult of the true woman imbued every aspect of the representation of women, perhaps most strikingly in women's fashions during the period when melodrama was at its height (1836–56). The "sentimental style," as Karen Halttunen calls it, addressed a potential contradiction in the true woman's presentation of self. Cardinal among the true woman's virtues was sincerity, which on a physical level meant transparency and consistency. The face and body were important outward signs of the true woman's inner being: one had to be able to see the latter shining through the former. How, then, could the sentimental style clothe the true woman without severing the intimate connection between outward appearance and inner nature? How could it devise a fashion that was, in effect, morally transparent — revealing not the corporeal body beneath but the spiritual being inside it?[5]

The answer was to make the clothed body stand metonymically for the ideal of the true woman's inner self. The sentimental style produced "sincerity" by refiguring the body so that the soul could be seen directly on the outside. Dress forms became elongated, narrow, and slim-waisted, with yards of material billowing down over padded hips until it trailed along the floor, giving the impression that the upper body rested

Sentimental fashion, 1848.
(Prints and Photographs Division, Library of Congress)

GODEY'S "AMERICANISED" PARIS FASHIONS.

"Americanized" versions of Parisian couture.
(Prints and Photographs Division, Library of Congress)

on a bell-shaped pedestal. Colors became muted. A self-effacing style of dress mirrored a modest nature. Through this maneuver, the sexuality of the body itself could be obscured; carnality was not allowed to compromise spirituality.

This transparency of self-presentation extended to a woman's face, hair, demeanor, and deportment. The face was to be kept free of make-up, since the use of any artificial means of enhancing its beauty constituted cosmetic deception. Women were to rely on "moral cosmetics": cleanliness and diet. Hairstyles were also kept simple: pulled back from the face and parted in the middle, in a style called *à la Madonna*. In illustrations, the true woman is invariably depicted as dark-haired, blonde hair being, in Lois Banner's words, "a clear indication to nineteenth-century culture of an underlying sensuality." Currier and Ives prints and *Godey's Lady's Book* illustrations show the true woman as fragile, doll-like, small-featured, and petite. She is never animated and is seldom engaged in any physical activity. She stands or sits, hands folded in front, gazing demurely into the middle distance or at the floor.[6]

Although they could be physically and intellectually resourceful, the heroines of melodrama for the most part enacted the role dictated by the ideology of the true woman. The inherent duplicity of the drama, which constantly threatened to undermine the entire project of representing the true woman onstage, was elided in that actresses portrayed not so much other people as epiphanies of an ideal. By visually and dramatically stressing the spirituality rather than the materiality of women, the melodramatic heroine deflected attention away from her sexuality. She was still beautiful and desirable, to be sure, but as the dramas relentlessly demonstrated, only villains allowed themselves to be sexually aroused by the sight of her. In short, through the melodramatic vision, the "problem" of women onstage was contained.

○ ○ ○   **Ballet: Spectacular Femininity**

Through the 1840s, an evening at the theater did not mean seeing merely a dramatic work enacted. The stage performance, which stretched over three hours or more, combined dramatic fare – comedies, melodramas, or tragedies – with a variety of other entertainments.

Othello might be preceded or followed by a farce; between the acts of *The Provoked Husband*, the audience might enjoy a magician, an acrobat, orchestral music, songs, or other attractions. The rationale behind the hodgepodge that constituted theatrical performance in the first half of the nineteenth century was simple enough: in appealing to a heterogeneous audience, the manager felt obliged to include something for everybody.[7]

Dance was a part of this theatrical mélange. Where they could be made to fit into the plot, dances were sometimes interpolated in dramatic works themselves, and hornpipes and rope dances were performed between acts. In their endless search for novelties, managers looked to Europe and Britain for the latest theatrical fashion that might be transplanted in America. It was as a result of one such talent search that ballet was brought to the American stage. In February 1827, desperate to keep the Bowery Theater economically viable in its first years, manager Charles Gilfert brought over the celebrated French ballet dancer, Madame Francisque Hutin, to perform between *Much Ado about Nothing* and the concluding farce. Stage chronicler Joseph Ireland described the audience's response: "The house was crowded, and an anxious look of curiosity and expectation dwelt on every face; but when the graceful danseuse came bounding like a startled fawn upon the stage, her light and scanty drapery floating in air, and her symmetrical proportions liberally displayed by the force of a bewildering pirouette, the cheeks of the greater portion of the audience crimsoned with shame, and every lady in the lower tier of boxes immediately left the house."[8]

Many in the European-oriented upper classes championed Hutin (among them Mayor Philip Hone of New York), but other, more conservative elements railed against ballet in terms that anticipated the anti-burlesque rhetoric of forty years later. Samuel F. B. Morse called ballet "the public exposure of a naked female," while reformer and abolitionist Arthur Tappan urged women to boycott the theater entirely: "Let an institution that has dared to insult you be forever proscribed." As would also be the case forty years later, what constituted nakedness must be understood in cultural context. Hutin wore loose trousers gathered at the ankle and covered by a long silk skirt. She was hardly naked (not an inch of flesh beneath her waist showed), nor was her costume even translucent. A woman in the audience on the evening of Hutin's American debut wrote to a friend that the dancer's display was "no worse than others on the stage," adding that she "dances beautifully." What so disturbed Morse was the fact that every time Hutin pirouetted, her skirt flew up and the trousers beneath gave shape to the lower part of the female body.[9]

Upon its arrival on the American scene, ballet obviously presented a problem for the Victorian theater and for sentimental ideology more generally – although ballet was considered a problem more by some (Morse and Tappan, for example) than by others. The problem was how to contain the ballet as spectacle. Although ballet could be narrativized and ballerinas cast as characters in a dance drama, narrative and mimesis were superimposed on ballet as spectacle. Ballet appealed directly to the senses, and its effect was not mediated or channeled by words. The ballet dancer's talent did not lie in her ability to impersonate but in the grace and agility of her body. Ballet feminized dance and called attention to the female performer in a way and to a degree unthinkable in melodrama. The ballet dancer's presentation of self conflicted sharply with that ascribed to the true woman. Her art was predicated on the display of the physical self, not its effacement. She was constantly in motion, not standing passively by. Her costume foregrounded the materiality of the body, flaunted the physicality of women, revealed the outline of that secret half of the female body that sentimental fashion kept hidden. The very lengths that fashion went to conceal the lower body invested in its veiled and partial revelation enormous sexual energy. This accounted for the vitriolic diatribes, the conflation of a glimpse of trouser-clad thigh with total nudity, *and*, thus, the fascination with ballet that paralleled the condemnation it provoked.

The dominance of the romantic style of ballet permitted its partial social and moral recuperation in the 1830s. When the celebrated French dancer, Madame Celeste, toured America in 1834, she brought with her the form and conventions of romantic ballet, which had emerged in Europe over the preceding four years: the trappings of a supernatural world inhabited by imps and witches and by beautiful maidens who are transformed into swans or butterflies or celestial bodies. The romantic ballerina also helped to dematerialize the revealed female stage body. In keeping with her ethereal roles as fairy and nymph, the romantic ballerina frequently was herself small and extremely slight. As late as the 1850s, one commentator described the dancers in a touring French troupe as "open umbrellas with two pink handles."[10] An 1846 Currier and Ives lithograph of Fanny Cerito in *La Sylphide* shows her literally floating, *en pointe*, a foot above a stage lake. The sylphlike figure of the romantic ballerina, when combined with the otherworldliness of the roles she assumed, helped to mitigate the transgressiveness of ballet. By tying the world of ballet to nature and to the platonic adoration of women, romanticism kept it separated from the world of flesh-and-blood human beings and their passions. A change in costume, initiated by Marie Taglioni (the first to dance *La Sylphide* in Paris in 1832), allowed a better view of her ankles, but it more effectively concealed the area above. Taglioni was the first to use a stiffened muslin or tartalan skirt, which fell well below the knees, with pink or flesh-colored tights beneath.[11]

Some indication of the degree to which romanticism had helped to edge ballet toward the American social and moral mainstream is provided by the success of Madame Celeste's 1834 tour. During that tour, which lasted two years, the twenty-five-year-old dancer earned more than $100,000. President Andrew Jackson introduced her to his cabinet, and the governor of New York saw her in *The Maid of Cashmere*, one of the ten most successful New York stage productions to that time. This success came in the face of considerable anti-French feeling in America caused by the French government's refusal to compensate the United States for damage to American ships inflicted as a result of Anglo-French military actions.[12]

Despite Celeste's acclaim, the social status of dancers generally in America in the late 1830s was still lower than even that of dramatic actresses. The dancer who did more than any other to elevate the social status of ballet dancers in America arrived in May 1840. The principal rival to Taglioni in Paris, Fanny Elssler was brought to New York to play the prestigious Park Theater. Anticipating the more conservative climate in America, she lengthened the skirt of her costume by a full foot. The enormous success of her debut on May 14 marked the acceptance by upper-class audiences of ballet and resulted in her being welcomed in the highest social circles. Mayor Philip Hone called on her at her New York hotel, former president John Quincy Adams went to the Park to see her, and President Martin Van Buren received her. The *Spirit of the Times* proclaimed her engagement at the Park the beginning of "a new era in the dramatic annals of this city." One dance historian re-

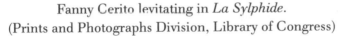

Fanny Cerito levitating in *La Sylphide*.
(Prints and Photographs Division, Library of Congress)

garded her two-year tour of America as "the most important cultural event of the 1840s."[13]

Elssler's talent as well as her sensitivity to Americans' moral reservations about ballet helped to pave the way for a steady stream of European ballerinas to America in the 1840s and to spur the development of a few homegrown dance stars. All of them followed the romantic pattern closely, portraying evanescent sprites and bewitched shepherdesses — unattainable and in some cases nonhuman ideals of beauty and grace. Ballet became morally and socially acceptable (although, at first, only marginally so) by containing the ballerina within a silent, removed world; within plots that alluded to the settings of high-art literature and painting; and within a body that promoted rather than detracted from the illusion that the audience was watching a creature with the same materiality as a fairy.

The connection of ballet with high art is extremely important here. Positioning ballet discursively as "art" helped to reduce the inherent transgressive potential of the partially revealed female form and to play down the role of the baser passions that might be aroused by its display. It also helped upper-class audiences to rationalize whatever pleasures they might take from viewing ballet – base or otherwise. In this case, as in many others from that day to this, the social and moral transgressiveness of some instance of cultural practice is closely linked to its relationship to class. What would be condemned as depraved if it emerged from the lower social strata is celebrated as art (or, at least, condoned) if its provenance is upper-class.[14]

○ ○ ○   **Living Pictures**

A striking example of what happens when a potentially transgressive cultural practice moves from an upper-class site to a working-class one is provided by tableaux vivants or living pictures, as they were called – a form frequently cited as an antecedent to burlesque.[15] Throughout the 1830s New York theaters and museums offered "personifications" of famous paintings and statues "performed" by individuals or companies as entr'acte entertainments or as a part of dramatic vehicles. Living pictures fed the nineteenth-century fascination with verisimilitude by presenting human figures arranged to imitate paintings or statues surrounded by appropriate scenery and props. In a typical living picture exhibition, the stage curtain would part to reveal models frozen in position to the accompaniment of music or spoken commentary. After a few minutes, the curtain would close, allowing the stage and models to be rearranged for the next picture. By the late 1840s, some enterprising showmen had realized that interest in their exhibitions might be increased through the representation of paintings and statues of nude or partially revealed subjects. Among the poses presented by Dr. Collyer's Model Personification at New York's Apollo Rooms in September 1847 was Hiram Power's statue, *The Greek Slave*, with which New Yorkers were familiar from its exhibition in the city earlier in the year. Despite the fact that this male nude statue was represented "with the strictest accuracy" – as the advertisements proclaimed (the model wore flesh-colored tights) – the New York papers praised Collyer's exhibitions for celebrating the fine arts. The *Herald's* critic saw "nothing that could offend the most fastidious."[16]

The success of Collyer's three-month New York run prompted the

mounting of competing displays and the spread of living picture exhibitions into more working-class venues. Most of the exhibitions were in
halls rented especially for the purpose (rather than mounted as a part of
regular theatrical programs), and they proved so popular that one paper
complained they were draining legitimate theaters of customers.[17] This
proliferation of humanized art also brought with it an increasing
reliance on female subjects and models. *Venus Rising from the Sea*,
Suzanna in the Bath, and *The Three Graces* were frequently chosen for
impersonation, along with other paintings that afforded opportunities
for revelation of the female form.

   With the "proletarianization" and concomitant feminization of living
pictures in early 1848, press discourse on the form shifted suddenly
from praise to condemnation. The *New York Herald*, for months a champion of living pictures, was suddenly struck by "the progress of exhibiting the almost naked figures of men and women, under the designation
of model artists. . . . They are rapidly degenerating from the taste and
propriety which characterized them in Palmo's or Pinteux's, and has
[*sic*], at last got so low, in some of the bystreets at three, four, or five cents,
thereby inviting newsboys, loafers, and the veriest ragamuffins about
town to see them." The editorial went on to compare living pictures to
another dangerously transgressive cultural practice: masquerade. "We
remember the rise, progress, and fall of masquerading, as an amusement. The exhibition of semi-naked figures as models of art, seems to be
running the same course; and we should not be surprised to see the necessity of the legislature passing a law regarding such exhibitions. In
some of the out-of-the-way streets and lanes, these exhibitions are really
too bad, and their further tolerance in our city would be a disgrace."[18]

   City officials moved to suppress living picture exhibitions in the
spring of 1848. They survived, however, by blending into the milieu
seldom frequented and usually unnoticed by middle-class New Yorkers:
that of the lowest stratum of working-class commercial entertainment –
the storefront shows and cheap museums that lined the lower part of the
Bowery and adjacent streets. In the early 1860s living pictures were
featured at New York concert saloons. Advertisements for living picture
exhibitions were just titillating enough to draw in the curious and the
country naive, while the shows themselves delivered much less in the
way of flesh than had been promised, which usually succeeded in
keeping the police and moral censors at bay.

By the 1860s, the living picture as an entertainment form had been split into two class-bound genres: sensational living pictures that promised working-class men a glimpse of the partially revealed female body (still hidden, of course, beneath tights) and tableaux vivants of sentimental or patriotic subjects produced for middle-class audiences (men and woman), which did not emphasize women as objects of sexual display. The latter were increasingly absorbed into dramatic works, where they were used to freeze dramatic action at a particularly emotional or poignant moment. The final scene of the dramatization of *Uncle Tom's Cabin* called for a tableau depicting the apotheosis of little Eva: "Gorgeous clouds, tinted with sunlight. Eva, robed in white, is discovered on the back of a milk-white dove, with expanded wings as if just soaring upward. Her hands are extended in benediction over St. Clare and Uncle Tom, who are kneeling and gazing up to her. Impressive music. – Slow curtain."[19] By integrating tableaux into melodramas or patriotic plays, their spectacular qualities could be channeled and controlled and made to serve the semiotic interests of the drama by visually reinforcing a particular sentiment. By breaking the transgressive alliance between the lower classes and feminine sexual spectacle, a de-eroticized form of living pictures was recuperated within the boundaries of bourgeois acceptability.

O O O   The Rise of Feminized Spectacle

The suppression of the concert saloons and the removal of "salacious" living pictures to the netherworld of Bowery storefronts did not result in the banishment of the specter of female sexuality from the legitimate theater. Nor did enveloping the ballet in sylvan mists succeed in completely containing its transgressive potential for long. The fact of the matter was that, despite the periodic protestations of critics, editorial writers, and ministers, the combination of women and spectacle drew audiences to the theater more surely than any other strategy in the 1860s. During the turbulent war years, theater managers discovered that audiences would put aside news of war's horror for an evening if offered something novel and sensational to witness onstage. In the summer pause between the 1863–64 and 1864–65 seasons, the *New York Clipper* noted that "the manager who secures the prettiest ballet, the best formed actresses, and all that, can rake down the 'loot,' as the rebels call their plunder."[20] The years immediately preceding the advent of Thompsonian burlesque on the American stage saw an increasing reliance on feminine spectacle in the legitimate theater and a corresponding discursive drama, enacted in the daily and trade press, pitting desire against denial.

Even in the pages of the same paper one can observe the battle between the felt need to uphold the inviolability of pure womanhood and the libidinous pleasurability of watching women onstage whose costumes and demeanor were sure signs of their impurity. In May 1859 the *Clipper* ran a poem on its front page, entitled "The Dancer" by "One of the Nameless" – one of several in this vein published that year. Written in the voice of a ballet dancer, it admonishes male theatergoers to consider the forces that might have driven a young woman to reveal her legs onstage:

> This is the leg that you criticise
> With an air so unique, sagacious and wise;
> 'The calf is a little too large for the thighs;
> Or the ankle is not in proportion.'
> Do you ever think of the sacrifice?
> Or the self-abnegation of Modesty's sighs
> When the knot of her virginal zone she unties;
> And up rolls the curtain, that gluttonous eyes
> May feast on her proper person?
>
> .   .   .   .
>
> Oh, God! to think of the terrible knell
> That rang out the spotless virtue that fell
> And rang in the cankering weeds that dwell
> In the place of the rose-virginity!
> To think of the pallid lips that pled
> For life and health and warmth and bread
> Till frenzy had pluck'd from an innocent bed
> The flower of femininity![21]

This lament to the loss of respectability that invariably accompanied a woman's appearance in the leg business onstage and its implicit critique of the pleasures to be derived thereby might just as well have appeared in an antitheater religious tract.

Twenty months later, however, the *Clipper*'s critic drools over the prospect of reveling among these same "cankering weeds." In his review of Laura Keene's extravaganza, *Seven Sisters* (which played to crowded houses for eight months), he describes it as

> a show piece, in the full acceptation of the term. It shows us a number of beautiful young girls, and their equally seducing and fascinating legs. Excuse me, ladies, for being so bold. It reveals the 'hidden mysteries of alabaster bosoms,' – for some of the girls wear shockingly low-necked dresses – and exposes [*sic*] to view the physical development and finely molded limbs of the aforesaid 'damsels possessed of great beauty.' . . . Just to think of a bevy of beauties, dressed in good, tight-fitting clothes, with understandings of fascinating symmetry, and all hands going into all sorts of positions before you![22]

The rise of what might be called "feminized spectacle" in the early and middle 1860s occurred along three lines: equestrian drama, especially as practiced by Adah Isaacs Menken; burlesque, of the pre-Thompsonian, American variety; and the ballet spectacle, made popular by *The Black Crook* in 1866. Each represented a different type of spectacle that was built partially or wholly around feminine sexual display, and each contained its own strategies for both producing male scopic pleasure and containing the moral and social transgressiveness that pleasure necessarily entailed. Together, they made up the immediate background against which the representation of women in Thompsonian burlesque would be considered at the end of the decade.

○ ○ ○ **"The Menken"**

Nearly every history of burlesque includes in its survey of antecedents the appearance of Adah Isaacs Menken in the title role of *Mazeppa* at New York's Broadway Theater on June 13, 1861 – or rather each cites one scene from this potboiler as one of burlesque's progenitors.[23] The play itself was by 1861 a rather worn-out melodramatic workhorse on the American stage. Adapted in 1830 from a Byron poem, *Mazeppa* was about a nobleman, Ivan Mazeppa, who falls in love with a beautiful woman already betrothed to an evil and cowardly count.

Mazeppa challenges him to a duel, which he wins, and offers to spare the count his life in exchange for safe passage from the count's castle. In best melodramatic tradition, the count reneges, orders his henchmen to strip Mazeppa and bind him faceup to the back of a wild stallion, and releases the wild beast to charge into the mountainous wilderness, where, he knows, exposure and starvation will do the job he was unable to accomplish with his sword. Of course, the melodramatic credo dictated that Mazeppa extricate himself (offstage) from this seemingly fatal situation and return to vanquish his would-be murderer and rescue his beloved.[24]

The only feature that distinguished *Mazeppa* from legions of other such melodramatic concoctions was the use of a real horse in the scene of the count's ultimate treachery and Mazeppa's apparent demise. For the scene, a ramp was constructed as part of the set, running from downstage right diagonally and at a sharp upward angle to upstage left, where it disappeared into the wings. A docile mare or pony was trained to play the role of the unbroken steed – that is, trained to walk along the narrow ramp. For the ride itself, a dummy was frequently substituted for the stripped and bound Mazeppa, but, of course, the play worked best with audiences on those occasions when the actor playing the role (or his stuntman double) submitted himself to the very real danger of having his thinly clad body lashed sunny-side up to the nag for the brief but perilous canter up the ramp.

Playing Mazeppa as a britches role had been tried unsuccessfully by several actresses prior to Menken's debut in it, first in Albany and a week later in New York City. That Menken succeeded where others had failed was due in part to her willingness to make the famous ride, but the members of the opening-night audience at the Broadway Theater did not turn out for an exhibition of horsewomanship. They had been drawn in large measure because of the publicity surrounding Menken and her appearance in this role – publicity that had been carefully constructed to prompt but a single question in every spectator's mind: Would she really ride naked across the stage?

Menken was the first female American theatrical star not to run away from the charges of moral and social transgressiveness that were almost sure to attach themselves to a popular actress. Rather than attempt to make her offstage life invisible by hiding it behind a cloak of hyper-respectability, as many previous actresses had felt the need to do, Men-

"The Menken."
(Prints and Photographs Division, Library of Congress)

ken took the Bohemian tack of declaring herself exempt from most of the strictures usually applied to women because – like the male literary mavericks to whom she attached herself in New York and San Francisco – she was an artist. Indeed, she was the first to cultivate a persona built around the flouting of bourgeois moral and social norms, and, what is more, to build a career on the interplay between extratheatrical discourse (much of which she purposefully generated or stimulated) and the roles she played onstage.

Menken defined and presented herself in terms of the very qualities that marked her difference from the norms of pure womanhood. Although probably not Jewish by birth but only by virtue of conversion on her marriage to actor Alexander Menken, she nevertheless claimed Jewish heritage for the rest of her life, contributing Zionist poetry and essays to the Cincinnati *Israelite*. She kept her black hair in a shockingly short bob, a style that did not become fashionable in America until the 1920s. Married four times in her thirty-three years and divorced thrice, Menken received the attentions of many men and, in her later years while living in Europe, carried on an affair with Alexandre Dumas, which she publicized by distributing to friends jointly autographed carte-de-visite photographs of her sitting on his ample lap.[25]

As for her stage appearances, Menken did not mount the wild beast nude – even though posters for the play depicting a clearly female Mazeppa certainly promised as much. But she did make her ride sensationally attired in a pink body stocking and light tunic. Unlike previous stagings of the famous scene, Menken insisted that the audience's first sight of the bound and splayed Mazeppa be with the horse already in full stride. As she performed in it, the scene was a blur of equine movement played against a moving landscape drop and lighted by bursts of stage lightning. The clatter of the horse's hoofs on the narrow ramp was all but smothered by the orchestra's deafening accompaniment and sound effects suggesting a violent rainstorm. Given the context and its expectations, the spectators might well have read the scene before them as involving a nude woman on horseback. Menken's carefully laid plan to become New York's next theatrical phenomenon succeeded. *Mazeppa* ran at the Broadway for the next eight months. Her 1863 tour of California and Nevada earned her over $100,000.

Menken was the first American actress to use Barnumesque tactics to promote herself. She gave out so many different versions of her parentage, ethnic identity, and early life that even the most basic biographical facts remained obscure during her lifetime: she was the daughter of a British aristocrat, an American army doctor, a Spanish Jewish noble-man; her mother was French, or Spanish, or Creole. Like P. T. Barnum, she knew the value of manufactured controversy, and she relied on this promotional strategy even though as a woman the stakes were much higher for her than for the paunchy, self-righteous museum proprie-tor.[26]

Menken's success in *Mazeppa* inspired other actresses to take to horseback or to don close-fitting trunks and hose in other britches roles. Nearly five years after Menken's first New York gallop, the *Clipper* predicted that during the next season "many a fresh and fiery Mazeppa, many a luscious and sculpturesque French Spy [another of Menken's cross-dressed roles] will make their debut on the dramatic course, attired in those undress costumes which never fail to make such charac-ters attractive to 'venerable roues' and aged young men."[27] But the limited success of the Menken imitators suggests that her tremendous appeal was based on something more than pink tights and daring-do. It certainly exceeded the inherent popularity of any of the vehicles in which she played, which were at their best merely serviceable. Au-diences paid to see "The Menken," as she later dubbed herself: the poetess who held her own in literary debates with Walt Whitman on one coast and Artemus Ward on the other; the stunning beauty whom, so one of her husbands claimed, every man who saw her onstage instantly desired; the iconoclast who defied convention; the star whose private life contributed as much to her persona as her stage performances.

Menken might well have exercised an even greater influence on theatrical representations of femininity in America had her career on that continent not been so truncated. After her initial success in New York City in 1861, Menken spent most of the next two years touring outside the city – nine months of that on her enormously profitable western tour. When she returned to New York in the spring of 1864, she discovered that the adulation of tens of thousands of San Franciscans and Nevada silver miners did not impress New Yorkers a great deal, so she left for London in April. Except for a brief reprise of *Mazeppa* at the Broadway in the spring of 1866, Menken did not play in the city again, returning to live in London and Paris until her death in August 1868.

Certainly, however, her link to Thompsonian burlesque was more than merely brevity of costume – as the standard histories of burlesque suggest. Here was a new model of theatrical femininity: independent, ostentatious, outspoken, free-spirited. Menken knew all of Barnum's tricks, but her public image was as far from Jenny Lind's as it was possible to get and still be tolerated by bourgeois society. As we have seen and will see again with *The Black Crook*, ballet dancers might scandalize with their bold presentation of feminine physicality, but they did so silently in a removed romantic realm. Living pictures probably offered a better opportunity to gaze at the revealed female form than Menken ever did aboard Black Bess, but its practitioners were not only mute but also frozen in place. Like Lydia Thompson, Menken combined spectacle, feminine sexuality, and speech – a combination that was for nineteenth-century bourgeois males particularly fascinating and potentially disconcerting. In doing so and in succeeding – however briefly – within the context of mainstream American theater, Menken moved feminine spectacle to a new level. Nevertheless, despite the sensation of her physical appearance onstage – when she made the famous ride or used a male role as an excuse to wear a revealing costume – neither Menken nor her imitators provoked the sort of moral outrage that burlesque elicited a few years later. Menken's primary dramatic vehicles, particularly *Mazeppa*, blunted the force of her potential transgressiveness by their familiar and comforting melodramatic ideology.[28]

○ ○ ○ **Pre-Thompsonian American Burlesque**

"Through the 40's and 50's," wrote Constance Rourke, "the spirit of burlesque was abroad in the land like a powerful genie let out of a windbag, finding a wealth of yielding subjects. The legitimate theater came to a standstill; and many reasons were found for this condition.... The truth was that a vigorous burlesque had usurped the stage, turning the serious drama upside down." At mid-century, the term "burlesque" – as used in the American context – covered a number of forms of comic entertainment. The travesty aimed at a specific work of high culture, removing its characters from their lofty positions as princes and peers and resituating them in considerably more prosaic settings. Romeo and Juliet were transplanted from Verona to Hoboken, for example. If the targeted intertext was very familiar to the audience, its travesty might well mock it scene for scene, speech for speech. Whereas the travesty might or might not involve music, the extravaganza and the pantomime always did. Both these forms drew on myths, fairy tales, and children's stories as frames for contemporary comic allusions, visual humor, dances, spectacles, and popular songs. The pantomime, whose primary American practitioners were the Ravel family and George L. Fox, was distinguished largely by its continued reliance on some vestige of the commedia-del-l'arte traditions of the form: stock characters and situations; a heavy dose of broad, sometimes violent slapstick; and the obligatory transformation scene. Clinton Baddeley calls extravaganza "burlesque without an object." Extravaganza might include parodies of popular songs and retain the rhymed-couplet form of more traditional burlesque, but its humor was diffuse, undirected toward any particular object. As the various forms of burlesque became increasingly loose and intermixed in the 1860s, the extravaganza came to stand for any inversive, comic, musical spectacle.[29]

The burlesque proper (although the term was never used with great precision) usually aimed at a larger target than did the travesty, taking as its object a type of theatrical entertainment, style of acting, or dramatic fashion.[30] Some English burlesques were performed on the American stage prior to 1840, but the American fashion for burlesque began with William Mitchell's assumption of the management of New York's Olympic Theater in December 1839. Mitchell, an English comedian, staged more than 230 burlesques, extravaganzas, and farces during his eleven-year reign at the Olympic, many of which were written by him and his two assistants, William Hardcastle and William Northall. Few theatrical trends, performers, or works were safe from lampoon. One of his best-remembered burlesques took on New York's craze for romantic ballet, occasioned by the appearance of Fanny Elssler at the Park Theater in May 1840. While Elssler was dancing *La Tarantula* at the Park, Mitchell himself was dancing the lead in *La Mosquito* at the Olympic. The pudgy, red-faced Mitchell, arrayed in the obligatory tutu, performed, he assured the audience in the program, in "the genuine Bolerocachucacacavonienne style."[31]

Mitchell delighted his mostly working-class audience with send-ups of whatever their "betters" found fashionable in literature or the theater, frequently within a matter of days of the object's initial New York appearance. The opera *Zampa; or, The Red Corsair* at the Olympia became *Sam Parr with the Red Coarse Hair*. Charles Dickens is said to have enjoyed *Boz; or, The Man Over Bored*, Mitchell's burlesque of the effusiveness with which New Yorkers welcomed the novelist's 1842 visit. To mark the opening of the superfashionable Astor Place Opera House in 1847, Mitchell presented a burlesque entitled *Upper Row House in Disaster Place*.[32]

William Burton and John Brougham took up where Mitchell left off when the Olympic closed in 1850. From 1848 to 1856 Burton managed the Chambers Street Theater (formerly Palmo's Opera House), where, as one contemporary manager claimed, he "did everything Mitchell did, and did it in a better way, with better players and better plays."[33] Not even the angelic Jenny Lind was exempt from burlesque's barb. In September 1850 Burton lampooned Barnum's extravagant promotion of the Swedish singer in *She's Come, Jenny's Come*, which represented Lind as one of Barnum's museum freaks alongside the Fat Boys, Tom Thumb, and an anaconda.

"If America has ever had an Aristophanes," wrote Laurence Hutton in 1891, "John Brougham was his name."[34] An Irish actor who apprenticed in burlesque writing in London for twelve years, Brougham arrived in New York in the early 1840s; there he acted in and wrote burlesques before briefly managing his own theater, the Lyceum on Broome Street (1850–52). Over the next twenty years he wrote, acted in, and occasionally produced his most successful burlesques. Like his fellow burlesque authors, Brougham frequently mocked the fads and pretensions of his own industry. The noble American Indian became the subject of innumerable melodramas in the 1830s and 1840s in the wake of the popularity of Edwin Forrest in *Metamora*. In 1855 Brougham produced his *Original, Aboriginal, Erratic, Operatic, Semi-civilized, and Demi-savage Extravaganza of "Pocahontas."* Two years later he took direct aim at Forrest's histrionics in *Met-a-mora; or, The Last of the Pollywogs*. Brougham played the Forrest role of Metamora, which he mimicked so perfectly that even his entrance was greeted with "shouts of laughter."[35] He also parodied the stilted style and creaking dramatic mechanics of the original text, written by John Augustus Stone in 1829:

> *Exit all but Metamora*
> It's very probably that you'd like to know
> The reason why the Pollywog don't go

> With his red brethren. Pray, take notice, each,
> He stops behind to have an exit speech.
> And here it is: . . .[36]

More so than his fellow burlesque writers, Brougham's targets extended beyond the world of the mid-century theater. Even his send-ups of Indian plays struck at the larger issue of their hypocritically romantic representation of Native Americans.[37] In his most pointed work, Brougham's burlesque veered toward outright social satire. In *Much Ado about a Merchant of Venice* (March 1869), Brougham used the familiar vehicle of the Shakespearean travesty to attack the rampant corruption of New York City politics, justice, and business – this at a time when the lease on his theater was held by none other than the legendary swindler, Jim Fisk. Despite published disavowals by Brougham, the personal targets of his attacks were only thinly disguised (if at all) in the play. Fisk, recognizing if not himself at least his shady practices excoriated in the work, closed down the theater after only ten weeks of Brougham's management.[38]

To be sure, the play had its share of the punning nonsense audiences had long come to expect from burlesque:

> Bassanio: It's strange that your *adored* one doesn't show.
> She must be as deaf as a *door* nail.
> Lorenzo: That's so!
> In yonder room it isn't high,
> The precious *jewel* of my life doth lie.
> Bassanio: The *jew ill*, say you, is her father sick and in your *attick*
> room lies rheumatic?
> Lorenzo: Now, *see Bassanio* –
> Bassanio: No, *sea bass* am I,
> In Fulton Street to be hung out to dry?[39]

But over the travesty of the play was laid a heavy layer of social satire. Portia's "quality of mercy" speech became:

> The quality of mercy is so strained
> In this, our day, and all our prisons drained
> By legislative pardons, that our city
> Will need, I fear, a Vigilance Committee

To stem the current of outrageous crime
that leave blood marks upon the banks of time.[40]

During the Civil War Brougham deserted New York for the calmer environment of London. When he returned, he found that a new element had come to the fore in burlesque: feminine spectacle. Burlesque had always provided opportunities for women to play men's roles and vice versa. Beginning in the mid-1850s New York producers and playwrights began to capitalize on this feature of the form and to combine the comic, inversive qualities of traditional burlesque with the spectacular qualities of the extravaganza. The 1850s had seen a raft of fairy spectacles, which helped to set the pattern for *The Black Crook* by relying on elaborate scenic effects and dance for their appeal.[41]

One of the few prominent actress/managers of the period, Laura Keene, played a key role both in opening up the burlesque form and in making feminine spectacle an expected part of it. Keene's Varieties Theater, the second she had managed, opened in 1856. The theater was aptly named, as Keene drew her productions from every form of light entertainment available and did not hesitate to throw them all together in a single piece. Her first big success at the Varieties, called simply *Novelty*, was built around the all-too-real dilemma of a theater manager (Keene) trying to come up with an idea for a new production. With the help of a little stage magic, she is shown burlesqued snippets of the current fare at other New York theaters. The result was a theatrical stew of comic business, amazonian processions, and transformation scenes. She followed *Novelty* with *Variety*, which employed the same plot device and whose playbill described it as "a highly original miscellaneous, ancient, modern, highstorical, upper-atrical, musical, semi-burlesque and wholly scenic extravaganza, in one act." *Variety* was even more popular, running for nearly five months.[42]

The piece that more than any other helped to effect the merger of burlesque with spectacle was Keene's *Seven Sisters*, which opened in the late autumn of 1860. Like its predecessors, it was short on plot but long on spectacle. The *Clipper* called it an "extravagant extravaganza." Its one major innovation was having nearly all parts – male and female – played by women, arrayed in "shockingly low-necked dresses." The *Clipper* critic's enthusiasm for "a bevy of beauties, dressed in good, tight-fitting clothes" already has been noted. He also applauded the final scene of the piece, which, from his description, sounds like an 1860s' stage version of a Busby Berkeley musical number: "a beautiful lake formed of $500 worth of mirrors, revolving pillars, descending goddesses on aerial cars and all that sort of thing. It is immense."[43] Other members of the audience must have shared his enthusiasm, as *Seven Sisters* set the record for the longest uninterrupted run in the history of the American stage to that point: 253 performances stretching over eight and one-half months.

One reason for the play's long run was that its slight and extremely flexible plot allowed for new features to be added at any time. In February 1861, after *Seven Sisters* had played for more than sixty-five nights to an estimated 85,000 people, Keene added a patriotic tableau, "The Dream of the Secessionist." The thirty-four states of the Union were represented by thirty-four "virgin damsels" who quarrel among themselves until "four of the quiet ones step in as peacemakers." In March, the *Clipper* joked: "We shouldn't wonder if the Seven Sisters should be transformed into the tragedy of Macbeth before Miss Keene is done with it." Keene kept her "Grand Burlesque Spectacles," as she advertised them, running continuously at her theater for three and one-half years. *Seven Sisters* was followed by *Seven Sons* and it by *Blondette*, which broke the first run's record by more than forty performances.[44]

Laura Keene was by no means the only New York manager to cash in on the popularity of this motley combination of stage effects, platoons of amazon marchers, music, and burlesque comedy. Just up Broadway from Keene's theater at the Winter Garden, Charles Gayler staged a burlesque of *The Tempest* in the summer of 1862. It featured two novelties. The first was Emily Thorne, an English burlesque actress from London's Adelphi Theater, brought over to play the role of Miranda – apparently the first instance of an English burlesque actress being featured in an American burlesque production. The *Clipper*'s critic, never shy about these matters, called her a "beautiful English blonde [who] has a splendid pair of legs – we say it boldly, legs." The second novelty was a runway thrust out from the stage into the parquette and running directly underneath the side boxes, "thereby affording the occupants of the parquet seats a splendid chance for a closer scrutiny."[45] Gayler thus anticipated the modern burlesque runway (which the Minsky family claims to have innovated in 1917) by more than half a century.

By the end of the Civil War, then, burlesque in the United States had split into two distinguishable subgenres based on their reliance on spectacle. John Brougham continued to write and produce burlesques in the older, more thematically focused style, occasionally pushing its punning verbal humor in the direction of social criticism and eschewing both elaborate stage effects and feminine spectacle. What in the 1860s came to be called "burlesque spectacle" retained the inversive and parodic qualities of burlesque humor but based its appeal more on a feminized variant of the visual spectacle of the extravaganza and the pantomime. In its spectacular mode, burlesque was a pastiche in both form and substance. Its narrative motion was halting at best, coming to dead stops while amazonian processions, dances, or set-piece scenic effects took over the stage. It struck at no particular target and lacked any semblance of thematic coherence. Yet the very looseness of the burlesque spectacle's dramatic construction allowed it to scatter its wit across a wide field of contemporary fashions and foibles. It also allowed individual productions to adjust and update their humor continuously without undermining narrative logic – there was little enough of that to begin with. As San Francisco theater historian Ettore Rella puts it, in the 1860s "burlesque ceased to develop in the direction of puncturing the excessive or false dignity of a legitimate play; or re-scaling the megalomania of personality stars; or making public farce of back-handed political machinations. Shapely legs and ballet routine became the *sine qua non* of what was still called burlesque. . . . Two people in conflict on a raised platform against a dark drape, the art of the speaking voice and the emotional gesture, were looked upon as primitive absurdities."[46]

The feminization of burlesque in the 1860s undoubtedly contributed to its popularity and to its reorientation toward visual spectacle. However, the presence of fetchingly costumed women in principal parts and the appearance of armies of them in mock-military production numbers raised moral and social concerns about burlesque for the first time. As Leland Croghan concludes, the burlesques of William Mitchell, William Burton, and John Brougham might prick the fulsome expressions of Victorian moral sensibility in their lampoons of melodrama, but they were also careful to stay within the boundaries of bourgeois moral propriety. Neither of the two most sanctimonious theatrical vehicles of the age, *The Drunkard* and *Uncle Tom's Cabin*, was the object of a major burlesque – the moral vision they espoused was felt to be above such treatment. Brougham's burlesques, wrote Hutton, "ridicule nothing which is not a fit subject for ridicule, they outrage no serious sentiment, they hurt no feelings, they offend no portion of the community, they shock no modesty, they never blaspheme."[47]

The feminization of burlesque, raising as it inevitably if implicitly did the thorny issue of female representation onstage and, more generally, the role of women in American society, represents the passing of burlesque's moral and social innocence. From that point on burlesque and the leg business were conceptually joined, the former almost always implying the latter. In the 1860s burlesque became something for bourgeois culture to watch – both in the literal sense of deriving pleasure from its spectacle of feminine physical display and in the sense of exercising moral oversight. It was only a matter of time before the combination of burlesque's inherent impertinence and the form's domination by female performers would be seen as a serious breach of social and moral propriety.

○ ○ ○   **The Black Crook**

One of the most popular and successful stage spectacles of the nineteenth century and the piece most frequently cited in survey histories as the direct predecessor of Thompsonian burlesque came about, we are told, by accident. During the 1865–66 season, theatrical entrepreneur Henry Jarrett, backed by his partner, wealthy Wall Street speculator Harry D. Palmer, planned to produce an elaborate ballet spectacle, *La Biche au Bois*, at the Academy of Music on Fourteenth Street. They had already purchased scenery and engaged a ballet troupe in London when, on May 21, the academy burned to the ground. Left with the scenery and dancers but no theater in which to present them, Jarrett and Palmer approached William Wheatley, manager of Niblo's Garden, about producing the spectacle at Niblo's, which for several years had been home to extravaganzas. Wheatley apparently had the idea to integrate the scenery and ballet into a production of a play he had already purchased, *The Black Crook* by Charles Barras. In late June, Jarrett was dispatched to London to bring back David Costa's ballet troupe while Wheatley supervised extensive renovations at Niblo's to accommodate the elaborate scenic effects planned for the spectacle. Wheatley also began to promote *The Black Crook* on the basis of the scope of its production and the costs incurred in mounting it. The *New York Times* enumerated (what Wheatley claimed to be) the costs for each aspect of the project, from $500 for transporting 110 tons of scenery and costumes from London to $5,000 for digging out the cellar beneath the stage to accommodate machinery and traps, for a total outlay of over $25,000.[48]

Barras's script, which he had written in 1862, is part melodrama, part extravaganza, part spectacle, but not at all burlesque. In a plot built entirely to romantic specifications, two lovers in a mythical middle-European and vaguely seventeenth-century village, Rudolph and Anima, are separated when the evil Count Wolfenstein claims Anima as his new bride and turns Rudolph over to his equally evil alchemist, Herzog, the "Black Crook." Herzog has made a pact with the devil to provide him with one young soul each year in exchange for another year of life. He sends Rudolph on what he believes will be an impossible and fatal mission to recover a hidden treasure to finance his assault upon Wolfenstein's castle. As melodramatic luck would have it, along the way Rudolph saves a dove from being eaten by a serpent. The dove turns out to be the queen of the fairies, Stalacta, who takes Rudolph to her undersea grotto. The rest of the story – with a few twists and turns to provide opportunities for the ballet troupe to perform and to stretch the piece out to more than five hours – is entirely predictable. Rudolph secures Stalacta's help and magical powers in defeating Herzog and Wolfenstein, the Black Crook is taken away to hell, and Rudolph and Anima are reunited. The final scene "transforms" from forest glen to Stalacta's golden grotto.

Contrary to some accounts, which describe *The Black Crook* as a standard (some say substandard) melodrama into which ballet and scenic effects had to be awkwardly inserted, Barras's manuscript clearly indicates that the play was written as a melodrama in spectacle form, with opportunities for song and dance built in.[49] Joseph Whitton, Wheatley's box office manager in 1866, recalled some years later that Wheatley had originally purchased the rights to *The Black Crook* because he saw in it a "clothes-line on which to hang the expressive costumes, dances, scenic displays, etc." The plot, wrote Whitton, was hardly original, being "a medley made up of *The Naiad Queen, Undine, Lurline*, and two or three other spectacle dramas of like nature."[50]

The Black Crook opened at Niblo's on September 12, 1866, to an overflowing house. Initial reviews were, save one notable exception, extremely laudatory. Not surprisingly, they emphasized the spectacular aspects of the production – especially the scenery, stage mechanics, and costumes – and the ballet. The *New York Tribune*'s critic, although calling Barras's drama "rubbish," wrote: "Scenic Art has never, within our knowledge, been so amply and splendidly exemplified. In respect to the Ballet, it is the most complete troupe of the kind that has been seen in this country." The *Times* called it "well worth seeing, as it is decidedly the event of this spectacular age." The *Clipper* dubbed it the "greatest dramatic sensation of the day." The production ran for the next sixteen months (474 performances), making it the nineteenth century's second longest continuous run.[51]

As with Keene's *Seven Sisters*, part of the reason for *The Black Crook*'s longevity was the constant addition of new attractions to its production. In May 1867, after it had played for nearly nine months, Wheatley added new sets and more dancers. In October, he introduced a mechanical donkey and a baby ballet: "a march of intricate military evolutions performed by over a hundred youngsters, varying in height from 35 to 45 inches." Even after thirteen months and "millions" of auditors, the *Tribune* critic wrote: "Children cry for it. Countrymen coming to town clamor for it, and will not be comforted unless they see it. The rural visitor, in fact, divides his time between Niblo's Garden and Trinity Church, and he certainly sees a good deal at both places."[52]

The "stars" of *The Black Crook* were undoubtedly the principal dancers: Marie Bonfanti, Rita Sangalli, and Betty Rigl – especially Bonfanti. There were no cross-dressed roles in the production, and neither the male nor the female actors received any press attention. Of the human elements of the production, it was the dancers whom everyone noticed. Within a week of her debut, the *Clipper* penned an ode to Bonfanti:

> O, who could be better,
> Than Marie Bonfanti?

Tho' her clothing is scanty,
She's the card to a letter
For any establishment.
Ah, who could withstand her
Light foot and white hand, her
Every soft blandishment?

. . . .

If we were to marry,
No longer we'd tarry,
We'd take such a fairy
As you, charming Marie;
For, being perfection,
You must have affection,
And your salary is sufficient to run a fashionable
  restaurant every week.[53]

Bonfanti's style was still that of the romantic ballet, popularized by Marie Taglioni more than thirty years earlier. Choreographer David Costa, Sangalli, and she had all studied under Carlo Blasis, director of the La Scala ballet school, in Milan, Italy, which stressed harmony, balance, and effortlessness of execution. The movements of the small and slender Bonfanti were controlled and restrained. Thirty years later, her name evoked in a writer of the *New York Dramatic Mirror* a memory of "the light of a bird in the air, the flutter of the bough in breeze, the very spirit of dance itself. When she ceased the beholder drew in his breath again, like one awakened from a dream and screamed for more."[54]

The reviews of *The Black Crook* usually included some reference to the "large number of female legs," as the *Tribune* put it, to be seen in the production. The *Clipper* noted: "Everybody is talking of it and the many beauties it reveals to our bewildered gaze. It is an undress piece of a model, artistic character." The following week, the paper joked: "It used to be that Menken's undress uniform 'took the rag off,' but these demons at Niblo's have scarcely a rag left upon them to take off." The "demons" appeared in the most celebrated and controversial dance in the production, the "Pas de Demons," which closed the second act. What made the dance controversial were the costumes worn by the principal dancers: close-fitting pantaloons, which stopped at mid-thigh, and a sleeveless bodice, both done in polka dots. The *Times* reviewer, who saw the demons as wearing "no clothes to speak of," nevertheless acknowledged that the demon dance was "the ballet success of the night. . . . No similar exhibition has been made on an American stage that we remember, certainly none where such a combination of youth, grace, beauty, and *elan* was found. The curtain was rung up three times at the close of this act, in compliance with peremptory demands of the house." So popular was the demon dance that Wheatley published a timetable of the production, so that men "may drop in, take a peek at his favorite scene, or dancer, or leg or something and enjoying the sight, return to the bosom of his family."[55]

As would be true of Thompson's appearance at Niblo's a little more than two years later, as the full extent of the popularity of *The Black Crook* with its more than fifty "undressed" dancers became apparent, some commentators reconsidered the moral and social implications of this kind of production at so "respectable" a theater. The *Clipper*, evincing once again its schizophrenic stance toward the leg business, asked in October (only two weeks after the "bare dance" poem was published) if *The Black Crook* put Niblo's on the slippery slope toward the moral abyss into which tableaux vivants had already plunged. It also transformed the "charming Marie" and her fellow dancers into dangerously foreign others:

Mr. Palmer, who brought a number of foreign dancing girls to this country, has not enhanced his reputation thereby, and we question whether this introduction of such undressed performers at a first-class theater like Niblo's will not injure the heretofore excellent character of that house. Manager Wheatley may find the model artiste dancers a profitable source of revenue just now, but will such prosperity compensate him for the probable injury done to his theater by the exhibition of Palmer's scantily attired women? Will not such nudities drive away the ladies and other respectable patrons of the house? It is true that they draw, and so did Colyer's model artists until their exhibition was suppressed. . . . If Mr. Palmer's aspirations lie in that direction, why not take his imported nudities and exhibit them in some place more suited to such exhibitions than Niblo's Garden?[56]

The most consistently negative criticism of *The Black Crook* in the daily press came from William Bennett's *New York Herald*. An editorial again made the connection between the production and salacious living pictures:

> Nothing in any Christian country, or in modern times, has approached the indecent and demoralizing exhibition at Wheatley's Theater in this city. . . . The Model Artists are more respectable and less disgusting, because they are surrounded by a sort of mystery – something like a veil of secrecy which women do not look behind and which men slip in stealthily to see. But the almost nude females at Wheatley's are brought out boldly before the public's gaze. . . . Our respectable citizens should cry it down, and the police should arrest all engaged in such a violation of public decency and morality. . . . If any of the Herald's readers, in spite of its warnings and advice, are determined to gaze on the indecent and dazzling brilliancy of *The Black Crook*, they should provide themselves with a piece of smoked glass.[57]

It is possible, however, that the picture of indecent sexual pleasure painted in the editorial was designed to entice the *Herald*'s readers to stock up on smoked glass rather than lobby their aldermen to close down the show. In his "inside history" of *The Black Crook*, written thirty years after its debut, Joseph Whitton claimed that Bennett's criticism was calculated to promote the play.[58] If this was the case, it surely must be the first instance in American theater history of a newspaper purposely emphasizing the moral and social transgressiveness of a theatrical production as a covert advertising ploy on behalf of the theater management. It would also be further indication of the inherently contradictory feelings of desire and denial that the feminine spectacle provoked in the minds of bourgeois males.

This contradiction is apparent even in the discourse of *The Black Crook*'s chief nonjournalistic antagonist, one almost certainly not in league with Wheatley. Charles Smyth, a Protestant minister in New York, was so incensed by what he had seen at a performance of *The Black Crook* that on Sunday afternoon, November 18, 1866, he rented the Cooper Institute for a three-hour sermon, heard, reportedly, by three thousand people. The sermon, excerpts of which were printed during the following weeks in the *Clipper*, *Herald*, and other papers, makes clear that Smyth had observed this lewd exhibition closely:

> The first thing that strikes the eye is the immodest dress of the girls; their short skirts and undergarments of thin, gauze-like material, allowing the form of the figure to be discernible through it in some instances; the flesh colored tights, imitating nature so well that the illusion is complete; with the exceedingly short drawers, almost tight fitting, extending very little below the hip, also of this material, arms and back apparently bare, and bodice so cut and fitted as to show off every inch and outline of body above the waist. . . . The attitudes were exceedingly indelicate – ladies dancing so as to make their undergarments spring up, exposing the figure beneath from the waist to the toe, except for such covering as we have described; stretching out a foot so as to place the limb in a horizontal line drawn from the hip, and turning the foot thus held out towards the audience.[59]

Smyth's denunciation of *The Black Crook* does not seem either to have stirred public sentiment or to have slowed the flood of patrons to Niblo's. The play continued to run to full houses for months and months. During the one full calendar year of its run (1867), *The Black Crook*'s receipts were more than twice those at any other New York theater and greater than the combined box office of the Broadway, New York, Fifth Avenue, and French theaters. Indeed, it has been suggested that, like Bennett's "gold-edged abuse," Smyth's attack provided Wheatley with invaluable publicity.[60] One must wonder, however, whether such attacks changed the composition of the audience. Henry Jarrett claimed to have counted 1,345 women among the "fashionable" audience of 2,397 on opening night. Kristina Gintautiene maintains that women continued to attend despite the trumpeted indecency of the spectacle, but that some did so anonymously by wearing veils over their hats. The *Clipper*, which frequently commented on such things, does not note a desertion of female patrons, despite its prediction that the play's "nudities" would "drive away the ladies."[61]

What was there for commentators to object to in *The Black Crook*? What occasioned the comparisons with the living picture exhibitions that had been driven off the New York stage and into Bowery storefronts? What bounds did the production exceed that had not already been breached by previous examples of feminine spectacle? Obviously, William Bennett's regular warning to his readers that *The Black Crook* was indecent enough to warrant legal suppression helped to raise the issue of the production's moral propriety, regardless of what one felt about the validity of or motive behind his charges. Critics also were struck by the sheer scope of the spectacle, by the combination of elaborate scenic effects with female physical display on an unprecedented scale. As everyone acknowledged, the drama itself was singularly unremarkable and, given the production's constant revision during its run, singularly unimportant. *The Black Crook* was not a dramatic narrative punctuated by spectacle, but rather a series of spectacular features loosely tied together by a narrative. The production's appeals bypassed the logical and intellectual faculties and went straight for the senses, enveloping the audience in an intoxicating, magical, glittering world inhabited by a seemingly endless array of fairy queens, sprites, demons, naiads, and coryphées. Within a week of opening night, the *Tribune* said, *The Black Crook* had become "a symbol among us. . . . The spectacle remains in the popular consciousness as the first attempt to put on the stage the wild delirious joy of a sensualist's fancy." The final transformation scene, wrote the critic, "will dazzle and impress . . . by its lavish richness and barbaric splendor. All that gold, silver, and gems and lights and women's beauty can contribute to fascinate the eye and charm the senses is gathered up in this gorgeous spectacle. Its luster grows as we gaze, and deepens and widens, till the effect is almost painful."[62] It was the "barbaric splendor" of the production, its five-hour assault upon the senses and libido, that seems to have fascinated and disturbed those who wrote about *The Black Crook*.

As for the costumes, about which Rev. Charles Smyth complained in such amazing detail, contemporaneous photographs and descriptions indicate that most of the dancers in most numbers wore some variation of the standard, knee-length ballet tutu, worn over tights, which had been seen on the New York stage for decades. The one major exception was the pantaloon costume for the "Pas de Demons," which provoked charges of nudity. One theater historian has contended that dancers in *The Black Crook* omitted tights altogether, making the play "the first show of its kind on the American stage to make a feature of the diaphanously draped or semi-nude feminine form."[63] Photographs of the original cast, including those in the demon costume, do not bear this out, however. Furthermore, given Smyth's admirable powers of observation and description, one would think such a scandalous omission would have prompted at least a mention by him, if not another three-hour sermon. Indeed, he singled out "flesh colored tights" for objection.

Even with tights, the demon costumes were, to some eyes at least, transgressive enough. Their "exceedingly short drawers" revealed the shape of the female anatomy from waist to knee, an area that fashion had so carefully concealed beneath crinolines, petticoats, and, in the 1850s, huge metal hoops. The fact that the costumes were cut as pants also greatly increased their transgressive power. As Lois Banner has noted, in 1851 Elizabeth Cady Stanton and Amelia Bloomer attempted to reform women's fashions by introducing what derisively came to be called "bloomers": baggy trousers worn under calf-length dresses. Response to the costume was so negative, however, that even Stanton herself gave it up after only two years. In a time when culture consigned men and women to two very separate spheres and when trousers constituted the surest sartorial marker of masculine identity, many viewed the wearing of pants by women as a dangerous symbolic usurpation of male power. Then as (unfortunately still) now, a woman who asserted herself within the family was accused of "trying to wear the pants" – the presumably single pair allotted to each household being the exclusive property of the male member. Indeed, such was the association of trousers with masculinity that women had not begun to wear divided undergarments (the precursors of "pant-ies") until the beginning of the century. When Madame Hutin first appeared in New York in the late 1820s, her ankle-length pantaloons (worn, of course, beneath a ballet skirt and over tights) were cause for comment. But neither they nor bloomers were designed to be worn without a covering skirt. Banner cites one dress reformer of the period who observed that "the major problem with the bloomer was that it brought into plain view a garment women had only recently begun to wear as underclothing." The same could be said about the demon costume but taken further. It was not baggy but form-fitting, not ankle-length but thigh-length.[64]

Like all transgressive forms that remain within the boundaries of bourgeois culture, *The Black Crook* represented a dialectic of transgression and containment, excess and recuperation. The lavish, "almost painful" spectacle of sight, sound, motion, color, and displayed feminine physicality was yoked to a romantic, melodramatic plot. The single

most transgressive element of the production, the ballet costume, retained its associations with that art form, which, by this time, was much
more culturally acceptable than it had been three decades earlier. The
choreography was kept solidly within the mainstream of romantic ballet. But perhaps the most important reason *The Black Crook* remained
within the pale was that it was not a burlesque. There was no impertinent, inversive burlesque humor in the piece; it was played straight, not
for laughs. In the original production, at least (*The Black Crook* was
revived eight times in New York), there were no cross-dressed roles.
This is not to say that there was no comedy in the production, but it was
not burlesque comedy. The controversial demons spoke not a word.

Ixion Revisited

It means something, this outbreak of burlesque acting

all over the world.

– Richard Grant White

○ ○ ○ ○ ○ ○ ○ ○ ○ ○ ○ ○ ○ ○ ○ ○

With the historical backdrop in mind, we now return to the performances of that first season of modern burlesque in America, begun by Lydia Thompson when she took the stage at Wood's in the fall of 1868. This chapter asks more directly, How can those performances – their immense popularity as well as the controversy they provoked – be made historically and culturally intelligible?

In the first place, it seems clear that – given its amazonian marches and processions, its mock-masculine and mock-military costumes (including short pantaloons à la *The Black Crook*'s demons), its predebut publicity emphasizing Thompson's fatal physical charms, and its status as an imported European novelty – Thompsonian burlesque was viewed, in part at least, as another "leg show," a continuation of feminine display in the tradition of *The Black Crook* and other ballet spectacles. Particularly after Thompson's move to Niblo's, comparisons with *The Black Crook* were almost inevitable – barely seven months had passed since the play ended its sixteen-month run there. No doubt many wondered if Thompson's troupe would "out-crook" *The Black Crook*.

Nor did the ballet spectacle die with the end of *The Black Crook*'s run. In little more than a week after the demons put away their polka-dot costumes, William Wheatley had mounted a new spectacle, *The White Fawn*, although it was not nearly as successful as its predecessor. Even before *The Black Crook* closed, it spawned imitators, and with each one audiences and critics alike compared its scenic wonders and revealing costumes to those they had seen at Niblo's. As the *New York Herald*'s critic wrote of *Cendrillion*, a burlesque spectacle that opened at the New York Theater in December 1866, "When the ladies of the ballet made their appearance in the glare of calcium lights which fizzed away in every part of the stage, the most lively discussion took place among the audience as to whether their dresses were up or down to the recognized standard at the rival establishment." In its review of *The Forty Thieves* at Niblo's in February 1869, the *New York Clipper* assessed the scale of the Thompson troupe's feminine spectacle in relation to the two previous ones at Niblo's: "And while we are talking about legs, we would state that such a display of legs has never before been seen in this city; even *The Black Crook* and *White Fawn* could not equal the present production, for this outstrips them all. It is in this respect, and in the magnificent costumes that *The Forty Thieves* excels all previous productions."[1]

O O O   **Olive Logan and "The Nude Woman"**

Although many critics viewed Thompsonian burlesque against the background of *The Black Crook* and other ballet spectacles, some commentators saw in burlesque something much more troubling and threatening. Lydia Thompson and her fellow burlesquers were not mute, otherworldly imps and sprites whose romantic choreography constituted an adjunct to an otherwise unobjectionable melodramatic plot. Burlesque dances were the antithesis of romantic ballet, with its controlled, effortless harmony of movement and balance.

The most sustained and vociferous attacks against the transgressiveness of burlesque came from Olive Logan, a thirty-year-old actress and woman's rights activist. She launched her campaign against burlesque on May 12, 1869, as a speaker at the convention of the American Equal Rights Association, held at New York's Steinway Hall. Logan spoke for eighteen minutes to an audience that included Lucretia Mott, Frederick Douglass, Henry Ward Beecher, and Susan B. Anthony. She called for women to enter the arena of politics to set right a system "which is now all wrong." Midway through her remarks, she ruled out the stage as a possible avenue of advancement for women: "I can advise no honorable, self-respecting woman to turn to the stage for support, with its demoralizing influences, which seem to be growing stronger and stronger day by day; where the greatest rewards are won by a set of brazen-faced, clog-dancing creatures with dyed yellow-hair and padded limbs who have come here in droves from across the ocean."[2]

Perhaps because it came from an actress who was also a campaigner for woman's rights, Logan's admonition regarding the theater and her characterization of burlesque were widely reported and reprinted in newspapers across the country. Three days later, in a letter to the *New York Times*, she pointed out that her antipathy was not directed toward "decent young women" who sought careers on the stage but rather female stage celebrities and theater managers, whose requirements for a position were:

1. Is your hair dyed yellow?
2. Are your legs, arms, and bosom symmetrically formed, and are you willing to expose them?
3. Can you sing brassy songs and dance the can-can, and wink at men, and give utterance to disgusting half-words, which mean whole actions?
4. Are you acquainted with any rich men who will throw you flowers, and send you presents, and keep afloat dubious rumors concerning your chastity?
5. Are you willing to appear tonight, and every night amid the glare of gas-lights, and before the gaze of thousands of men, in this pair of satin breeches, ten inches long, without a vestige of drapery on your person?[3]

This was not Logan's first public denunciation of feminine spectacle. Two years earlier she had railed against *The Black Crook*'s "leg business." The "nude women" of its corps de ballet, she claimed, were "met with a gasp of astonishment at the effrontery which dared so much. Men actually grew pale at the boldness of the thing; a death-like silence fell over the house, broken only by the clapping of a band of *claqueurs* around the outer aisles." But to Logan the threat to the theater and to public decency represented by burlesque performers was far worse than that posed by the dancers in *The Black Crook*. The latter were, at least, French ballet dancers who "represented in their nudity imps and demons. In silence they whirled about the stage; in silence trooped off. Some faint odor of ideality and poetry rested over them." The burlesque performer, on the other hand, compounded her nudity with raucous impertinences and self-conscious winks and leers. Worst of all, she did not hide her salacious impudence behind a portrayal of another character or creature: "The nude woman of to-day represents nothing but herself. She runs upon the stage giggling; trots down to the foot-lights, winks at the audience, rattles off from her tongue some stupid attempts at wit, . . . and is always peculiarly and emphatically herself, — the woman, that is, whose name is on the bills in large letters, and who considers herself an object of admiration to the spectators."[4]

A few weeks after her letter appeared in the *Times*, Logan was commissioned to write a piece on the "nude drama" for the July issue of *Packard's Monthly*. Immediately she began promoting its appearance in yet more letters to newspapers. In the *Packard's Monthly* article, entitled, "The Nude Woman Question," Logan divided the theater into two dichotomous categories. There was the legitimate drama, whose modest practitioners studied long and worked hard to perfect their mimetic talents, whose appeals were intellectual and aesthetic, and whose effects were morally elevating. However, this drama had been overrun by its illegitimate opposite: the leg business. Its practitioners had no acting talent but commanded huge salaries for displaying themselves "stripped as naked as [they] dare" on the stage. The burlesque performer subverted the legitimate drama by perverting its essential features. Songs were rendered vulgar and senseless. Even the innocent verses of a child's nursery rhyme were made prurient when performed with "the wink, the wriggle, the grimace, which are not peculiar to virtuous women." The "poetry of motion" that was ballet in burlesque became the artless jig. The burlesque performer was made to play the banjo and the bugle, musical instruments that "look queer in a woman's hands." These instruments were inappropriate for women to play on the stage not only because they were "masculine," but also because they were associated with Negro minstrelsy, in whose hands "these accomplishments amuse us without disgusting us." The morally uplifting language of the drama in burlesque became the double entendre and the "ribaldrous innuendo."[5]

According to Logan, the nude women of burlesque were not actresses; their professional calling was not the theater. Rather, they belonged to the branch of show business called variety or the concert saloon. At these resorts "of only the lowest and vilest," where respectable women did not appear, the nude woman for some time had been one of a variety of attractions: "a tid-bit, hugely relished by the low and vile who went to see her; but only permitted to exhibit herself economically, for fear of cloying the public appetite." But now the practices of the haunts of the degenerate working-classes had taken over the same stages where Shakespeare's creations once walked. Instead of being a tidbit on a variety program, the nude woman was now "exhibited ceaselessly for three hours, in every variety which an indecent imagination can devise."[6]

Clearly, for Logan the issue was much more than the brevity of costumes — although the revelation of the "lower part" of women's bodies was inherently indecent "for good and sufficient reasons, which no man, who has a wife or mother, should stop to question." Logan constructed burlesque as the complete antithesis of theater. It was an "other" kind of enterprise (business rather than theater), and the burlesque performer was an "other" who desecrated the stage properly reserved for authentic actresses and ballet dancers. The burlesque performer was a sexual other, who reveled in the display of the female body as a sexed and sensuous object. She was a transgressive other, whose "business" was predicated on subverting and perverting the very essence of the legitimate theater. She was a low other, dragged up from the netherworld of the working-class saloon, armed with the instruments of that other low other, the Negro minstrel, and thrust onto stages she had no right to occupy. She was no actor; she merely showed herself. And she succeeded to the degree that she revealed herself to be what she was: a woman. It was the undeniable libidinal and monetary success of this strategy of sexual objectification and display that most alarmed Logan: "When it becomes a question between suffering, struggling virtue, and vice which rolls in luxury, and gathers unto itself wealth by the sheer practice of its wickedness, no woman who loves honor in her sex can hesitate as to the course to be taken." Logan saw burlesque as a revolutionary, anarchic, demonic force that threatened to overrun the theater. The only recourse was to drive it from the stage and stone its managers through the streets. Thus, Logan used a military metaphor to end her piece: "Firm in the belief that this indecent army *can* be routed, I call on all honorable souls, both in and out of the profession, to stand by my side and strike hard blows. We shall get hard blows in return, no doubt; but poor indeed must be the panoply of that warrior who can not hold his own against the cohorts of the nude woman."[7]

Just as Logan constructed the drama and burlesque as the legitimate theater and its pernicious inverse, so she implicitly constructed two antithetical strategies for the advancement of women in American society. The strategy that she propounded called for women to learn a trade and to pursue it with determination so that they would not have to rely on men to support them: "Now, girls, be men! Learn your business

thoroughly. Let no employer have it in his power to say your work is
slovenly, and that you're only working along until you can catch *a man*;
and that one man can work faster and better than three women."[8]

Literature and drama, Logan said, were the two realms of work
where a woman was on an equal footing with a man and where women
had already demonstrated their ability to achieve the same success and
financial rewards as men. This strategy of dogged determination, self-
reliance, zealous acquisition of vocational skills, and hard work demanded that a woman suppress her own sexuality, because female
sexuality merely ensnared women in the web of marital dependence.
Thus, for Logan, burlesque was not only a threat to public decency but
also, and more important, an insidious inversion of her strategy for
female economic emancipation. The "nude woman" succeeded mon-
etarily but not because of her hard work and training. She merely
advertised her sexuality and was paid for doing so. Her singing required
no training, her dancing no skill. She did not even have to act; she only
needed to be herself. According to Logan, the burlesque performer
succeeded to the degree that she was willing to display what made her
dependent on men. Her subjection to the regime of the male sexual
gaze reenacted onstage woman's subordination within the institution of
marriage. Implicitly, Logan feared that, given the obstacles women
faced in trying to compete with men in the workplace, the expressive
and lucrative sexuality of the burlesque stage would represent for young
women an easier route to economic independence.[9]

Logan's antipathy for burlesque reflects larger concerns regarding
female sexuality and (male and female) passion that were shared by
many in the feminist movement. As William Leach notes, by the 1870s
most American feminists agreed that in order for sexual equality to be
achieved, sexual passion had to be brought under the control of women
and carefully regulated, rationalized, and channeled exclusively into
procreation. Lucinda Chandler, for example, admonished mothers to
teach their daughters the latest scientific facts about physiology and
reproduction; she also urged women to "discard all prominent devices
to distinguish sex" in their dress and appearance so as not to arouse
male sexual interest. Feminists considered male sexual passion to be
inherently irrational and dominating and therefore dangerous in the
extreme. Thus, in the context of mid-nineteenth-century feminism, it is
not difficult to understand why Olive Logan and her sisters regarded

burlesque – a popular entertainment form predicated on sexual difference, irrationality, and the flaunting of feminine sexuality – as antithetical to their vision of a new sexual and social order.[10]

O O O   **Burlesque as Disease and Criminal Sexuality**

Logan's attacks on burlesque were but the most sustained
among a barrage of vilification hurled in the popular and trade press in
the spring of 1869. The first sign of serious opposition to burlesque
came in November 1868, when the *New York Times*'s editorial stance
toward Thompson and burlesque in general began to diverge sharply
from that of its dramatic reviewer. An editorial of November 8 commented favorably on a resolution voted by the Ministerial Union at its
recent meeting in Chicago. The resolution began by charging that
"spectacles now become common in theaters and opera houses have
reached a pitch of degradation both in their visible indecencies and
theoretic immoralities unprecedented in our own country and hardly
equalled in any other, and are now making fearful inroads upon female
delicacy, youthful purity, and public morality." The resolution went on
to urge state legislatures to pass laws against "immorality" in theaters.
According to one minister quoted in the editorial, more men and
women had been ruined by the theater than by saloons or brothels. It
was not so much spectacle and gaiety itself that the ministers objected to
but its popularity and ubiquity, which threatened to swamp taste and
virtue:

> Look at the glaring and flaunting spectacular shows! Look at the
> everlasting ballet! Look at the Opera Bouffe! Look at the sensual
> exhibitions of the feminine form! Listen to the salacious music! See
> the appeals to the sensational and the pandering to the base and
> vulgar elements of human nature! Hear the gross innuendo and
> notice the foul suggestion! Who will deny that these things are
> immensely damaging to the public taste and terribly ruinous to the
> public morals?[11]

Thompson's move to Niblo's Garden merely fanned the flames of the
Times's outrage by adding elements of spectacle to the "base and vulgar" qualities inherent in burlesque. In his review of *The Forty Thieves*,

the paper's theater critic reprised in seriocomic form the objections raised against burlesque with an all-too-straight face in the editorial pages. The "mania for burlesque" had become an epidemic, infecting every part of New York, whose spread the board of health was powerless to stop. The "patients" had a tendency "to dispossess themselves of their clothing, and it requires the greatest exertion to keep anything on them; then follow a series of piercing screams called comic singing, distorted and incoherent ravings called puns, and finally, strong convulsions, denominated break-downs and walk-arounds. Exhaustion supervenes after a fit of two or three hours each night." The "infection" had been brought to New York from England – each arriving steamer carrying a cargo "of the golden-hair, which once landed on our shores develop[s] into the true raving, roaring, stamping-mad burlesque." Although "some dismal folk" had predicted the destruction of the community as a result of this "disease," the theater critic was more concerned about its deleterious effect on the drama. Burlesque was "dangerous" because "it defies criticism. It is folly to weigh the merits of a pun, the strength of rival feminine heels and toes, and those areas of the human form which ought to be concealed from promiscuous gaze." "No burlesque," he continued, "ever succeeded on its literary merits. Its wit is tolerated only from a bewitching mouth. . . . Its object is to upset decorum, to upset gravity, to disarm judgment, and to intoxicate the senses."[12]

Although the reviewer mocked the alarm with which his own paper's editorial writer regarded the social consequences of the popularity of burlesque, it is worth noting the manner by which he (albeit only half seriously) characterized that entertainment form. Burlesque had become a disease, a contagious infection; the burlesque performer had become both the diseased body and the carrier of the disease within the civic body. Burlesque produced a female body out of control and unable to control itself. It was an exposed public body that insisted on calling attention to itself: a raving, convulsive, incoherently screaming, hysterical, mad body. It was dangerous because it represented the antithesis of the rational, governed and governable "corpus" of the drama. Its appeal, based on sensory intoxication and moral and cultural anarchy, short-circuited rationality. Its effects were immediate, affective rather than cognitive, and visceral, and they required no explanation – indeed, critical judgment had nothing to say about the workings of the burlesque body; its effects were seen and felt and could not be calculated or parsed. It was a body displayed for all to see.

Furthermore, instead of whirling about in a removed realm oblivious of the audience's presence – as did the dancers in *The Black Crook* – the burlesque performer addressed the audience directly, aware, as one of Thompson's characters put it, of her own "awarishness." This directness of address and complicity in her own sexual objectification struck commentators forcefully and further separated burlesque from the innocence of the ballet spectacle. Regardless of the role she might play, the burlesque performer, to use Logan's words, was "always peculiarly and emphatically herself, – the woman, that is, whose name is on the bills in large letters, and who considers herself an object of admiration to the spectators." Intimacy with the audience was an expected part of the burlesques and acting styles of William Mitchell, John Brougham, and their male colleagues. Of one of Brougham's performances in 1857, the *Herald* wrote: "Now he interpolates a joke bearing a reference to some political topic of the day, now he talks confidently to the leader of the band and to an extent which, sublimely violating all the principles of illusion, produces a most amiable fraternity between stage and audience."[13] What made this informal, self-referential style transgressive in Thompsonian burlesque clearly was its appropriation by female performers.

Specific criticism of *Sinbad*, the show that followed *The Forty Thieves*, was almost totally obscured in the popular press by more general condemnations of burlesque and by reports of physical attacks and libel suits involving Thompson's husband and manager, Alexander Henderson, and the *Spirit of the Times*. The latter were provoked at a dinner party held at a Manhattan hotel in mid-May and attended by theatrical managers, members of the press, and, according to one account at least, some members of the Thompson troupe. What Henderson said in after-dinner remarks on this occasion became the subject of considerable debate. The *Clipper*'s account – one of the more dispassionate – had Henderson criticizing the state of American theater in general and gloating over the success of his own venture here. He also berated the dramatic press for its attacks on burlesque, calling the ill and absent E. H. House of the *Spirit of the Times* a liar. Henderson upbraided a former member of the Thompson troupe (unnamed, but presumably Ada Harland) for breaking her contract with him in order to form her own company, intimating that he had had a romantic liaison with her. Henderson's remarks – impolitic at best – embroiled him in a bitter, personal battle with the *Spirit of the Times*.[14]

The specifics of this dispute and the motives of the parties involved (one paper claimed that Henderson and George Butler of the *Spirit* were both romantically interested in the same burlesque performer) are of only incidental interest here. What is of considerable import is the figuring of burlesque in the discourse of the affray. Here, for the first time, burlesque is represented explicitly as criminal sexuality.

George Butler, present at the dinner and now filling in for House as dramatic critic of the *Spirit*, responded to Henderson's remarks at the dinner party in a May 22 article, entitled "Light Reading about a Light Manager – The Shovel-Nosed Shark of the Sea of Vice." Just as the shovel-nosed shark lives by eating the scraps thrown overboard by ships, so Henderson "with cold-blooded instinct, foreseeing the effect which nude female forms and floating yellow hair glowing under the bright blaze of calcium lights would have upon the sensual portion of the public . . . thrust himself into the midst of a school of dancing girls and mermaids of the ballet, and thus surrounded by these entrancing sirens, this voluptuous rover of the sea swam gaily after the gilded galley of burlesque with its silken sails, silver oars, and perfumed atmosphere, in keen quest of the rich pickings which fell from its sides."[15]

Once he dropped the ichthyological metaphor, Butler made clear how he viewed the relationship between Henderson and the performers: that between pimp and prostitute. The members of the troupe were "bound to him by ties unnecessary to mention." To Butler, the connection between the "nude drama" and prostitution was literal and causal, not metaphoric: "There are sad proofs enough how these gilded larvae breed to a vocation, and many a girl who months ago was modestly content with plain attire and an honest name, now basks her nude limbs in the hot gaze of an abandoned crowd, or streams like a yellow meteor along the pave, luring weak followers to her new ambition. Worse than this, under this seeming popularity of vice, sanctioned by the profession of the stage, the very public women of the city have taken new courage in their calling."[16]

On May 27 George Wilkes, the *Spirit*'s owner and editor, received a note from Henderson's attorney demanding to know who had written this article. For the May 29 issue of the paper, Wilkes himself wrote the editorial rejoinder to the note, declaring that he was responsible for anything printed in its columns and commending the author of the May 22 piece for his restraint in only calling Henderson a shovel-nosed shark. Wilkes stated that Henderson and all other "merchants in nudity . . . who live by exhibiting half-naked girls upon the stage" should not only be driven out of the dramatic profession but also should be driven out of town. New York had enough of its own "muck" without "this flaxen scrofula, this worse than yellow fever, from the slums of London" imported by Henderson. The *Spirit*, he promised his readers, would do everything it could to rid the city of this "epidemic." The following week, Butler accosted Henderson at Niblo's after a performance of *Sinbad*, called him an "English son of a bitch," and struck him several times with a whip.[17]

In the wake of the Henderson/Butler affair, the *New York Times* jumped aboard the anti-Henderson bandwagon and continued its anti-burlesque campaign in the process. Noting that Henderson had "spread his tentacles" throughout the New York theater district (a reference to his leasing of James Wallack's Broadway Theater for the summer), the *Times*'s theater critic called for a swift end to the 1868–69 season and to its "blight of burlesque." The English style of burlesque was "destructive to popular taste" and "the worst combination of stupidity and incompetence." Burlesque offered only "cheap rhymes, pre-Adamite puns, impudent distortions of grave political and social subjects . . . [and] uncouth and immodest imitations of negro dances by young women." Its only appeal was the chance to see "brawny nakedness."[18]

The day before this article appeared, the *Times* noted with approval remarks made in London at the annual Theatrical Fund Dinner to the effect that burlesque had turned away from acceptable topics and had now exceeded the bounds of decency by ridiculing national heroes and patriots. Even worse, it had "laid rude hands on women, whose mission envelops them in sanctity." The reason the speaker gave for burlesque's "progressive demoralization" of the theater was that theater audiences were now composed largely of "a transitory mob of uncultivated, uncritical people."[19]

Although this reference to "uncultivated" audiences was made with respect to the English scene, it contributed to a more general effort to fix the class and gender orientation of the American audience for burlesque as something other than that for "legitimate" theater – either directly or by implication. In its review of *Robinson Crusoe* at Wood's in May, the *Clipper* commented on "a very rough crowd of boys" in the gallery. The following April, when Lydia Thompson returned to Niblo's, the paper again mentioned the absence of "respectable" people in the audience. Although the house was full, women were few and not "of the class we were accustomed to see at the leading establishments." The reviewer saw no need to discuss the plot or staging of the piece being performed. "The crowd who bow down and worship at the shrine of the blondes . . . don't trouble themselves about the quality of the performance as regards the acting; they go there to see legs and busts, and to listen to double entendres and all that kind of thing."[20]

As we shall see, the audience for burlesque in the United States did indeed become largely male and working-class after 1870. Looking back on her first season on the New York stage a number of years later, however, Thompson recalled that at Niblo's "ladies and children were my greatest patrons. The matinees would look like perfect flower gardens."[21] Of course, it is difficult to determine who actually saw Thompson and the other burlesque troupes perform in New York that spring or whether the character of that audience had already begun to change. Two things should be noted in the absence of more definite demographic information. First, primarily by implication but sometimes directly, the discourse on burlesque also constructed, discursively, an audience for it. If burlesque was an epidemic of "flaxen scrofula," then its patrons were, by extension, its infected victims. If burlesque impudently ridiculed what should have been above ridicule, then its patrons abetted this anarchic transgression. If burlesque was tantamount to prostitution, its patrons were consorts. Furthermore, it is possible that the discursive construction of burlesque and its audience helped to change the social constitution of burlesque's "real" audience, making it more difficult for "respectable" (read: middle-class) women to attend without stigma.

○ ○ ○   William Dean Howells and the "Horrible Prettiness"

Because it was the center of the theatrical trade, the site of Lydia Thompson's American debut, and the point of origin of most national theatrical trends, New York was the focus of the greatest portion of discourse on burlesque during the 1868–69 season. But burlesque was not merely a local, New York phenomenon, even before the first national tour of Thompson's troupe in the fall of 1869. In the May 1869 issue of the *Atlantic Monthly*, William Dean Howells looked back on the theatrical season in Boston as it drew toward its summer hiatus.[22] The most notable feature of the season to Howells was the remarkable success of English burlesque. This "child of opéra bouffe and the spectacle muse," as Howells called it, had been staged in five of the city's seven theaters over the winter, making its first appearance even before the season began the previous summer.

Whereas Olive Logan responded with alarm to what she saw as burlesque's satanic subversiveness, Howells was both fascinated and horrified by its grotesqueness. What struck him most forcibly about burlesque was its blurring of categorical distinctions and its creation of unnatural hybrids. Logan dealt with burlesque performers by consigning them to an ontological category all their own: they were antiactresses who produced antitheater. For Howells, they presented a different critical and epistemological problem: they refused normal categorization, they exceeded his attempts to capture them in language. If to Logan burlesque performers were a nude army, to Howells they were a monstrous apparition. If Logan responded by taking up arms against them, Howells responded by covering his eyes and running to the safety of the normal world outside the theater.

When he saw his first burlesque the previous summer, Howells was shocked by the brief costumes of the female performers. He was even more stunned by the fact that their faces were not those of exotic theatrical creatures but rather of young women whom one might see working at the Jordan Marsh department store. The strange unseemliness of their costumes and actions was made all the more shocking by the conventional familiarity of their visage. It was this incongruous juxtaposition that made them "a horror to look upon" and made it difficult for Howells not to cry out to one of them "that she need not do it; that nobody really expected it of her."[23]

But clearly, Howells said, there were those in the audience who did expect it of her and who saved their loudest expressions of appreciation for the show's star. Whereas the shop girls in their pink tights were "dyspeptic and consumptive in the range of their charms," the star "triumphed and wantoned through the scenes with a fierce excess of

animal vigor." Dressed as a prince, "she had a raucous voice, an inso-
lent twist of the mouth, and a terrible trick of defying her enemies by
standing erect, chin up. hand on hip, and right foot advanced, patting
the floor." She dominated not only those with her on the stage but those
who, like Howells, stared slack-jawed at her from the audience as well:
"It was impossible, even in the orchestra seats, to look at her in this
attitude and not shrink before her."[24]

The English burlesque troupe that played Boston in the winter featured women who were "very pretty, very blonde, and very unscrupu-
lously clever." The show they put on was full of dance, but the dance
had "nothing of the innocent intent" that had characterized *The Black
Crook* or the other ballet spectacles. The piece ended with a "walk
around" borrowed from the minstrel show, in which each performer
in turn attempted to outdance the one who had preceded her. Each
"plung[ed] into the mysteries of her dance with a kind of infuriate grace
and a fierce delight very curious to look upon. Each dance inspired the
succeeding dancer to "wantoner excesses, to wilder insolences of hose,
to fiercer bravadoes of corsage" until "the spectator found now himself
and now the scene incredible. . . . A melancholy sense of the absurdity,
of the incongruity, of the whole absorbed at last even a sense of the
indecency."[25]

Howells was also struck and confounded by the delight the female
performers seemed to take in their assumption of male personae. One,
who had appeared ill at ease as the soubrette in the curtain raiser,
"seemed quite another being when she came on later as a radiant young
gentleman in pink silk hose and nothing of feminine modesty in her
dress excepting the very low corsage." The transformation effected by
her masculine impersonation was beyond Howells's ability to compre-
hend: "A strange and compassionable satisfaction beamed from her
face; it was evident that this sad business was the poor thing's *forte*."
Another performer's assumption of masculine airs and attitudes was
such that she "must have been at something of a loss to identify herself
when personating a woman off the stage."[26]

But in their guise of masculinity, there was no intention to deceive the
spectator or to suppress their femininity. They produced a monstrous
hybrid gender that both aroused and repulsed Howells: "[T]hough they
were not like men, [they] were in most things as unlike women, and
seemed creatures of a kind of alien sex, parodying both. It was certainly

a shocking thing to look at them with their horrible prettiness, their archness in which was no charm, their grace which put to shame."[27]

Although burlesque produced in Howells a sort of personal, guiltily pleasurable unease, it did not prompt him to call for civic action to eliminate it from the stage. The audiences Howells saw around him at burlesque performances – "honest-looking, handsomely dressed men and women" – lacked "that tradition of error, of transgression" required for burlesque to flourish for long. The taste for burlesque was an imported and foreign one to Boston audiences, and Howells predicted that by the next season burlesque would pass from fashionable to old-fashioned. His prediction, he said, was not based so much on a belief in the stage's inherent ability to reform itself as on the conviction that burlesque had already reached a point of transgressiveness beyond which it could not go: "[N]o novelty now remains which is not forbidden by statute."[28]

The personal (as opposed to social) and sexual (as opposed to political) parameters of Howells's response to burlesque were, no doubt, bound up with his own psychosexual instability. Despite growing up in what, for its time and locale, must have been a sexually progressive household, Howells as an adolescent suffered a neurotic fear of sex, with which he spent most of his life coming to terms. When he was twenty years old and editor of the *Cincinnati Gazette*, he found the sight of boisterous shop girls in a restaurant so disturbing that he collapsed and left his job. He became a proponent of the cult of pure womanhood, which worshipped the sexless ideal of woman as embodiment and guarantor of moral goodness. For a while, he eschewed the theater altogether as a demoralizing influence. But for Howells, no matter how good or pure, women were inherently infected by the disease of sexual passion, which if expressed, led to chaos. As his essay on burlesque makes clear, burlesque was disturbing precisely because it was a medium through which female sexual passion – whether in the frenzied convulsions of the minstrel show breakdown or the hermaphroditic release of masculine impersonation – could be powerfully expressed. And it horrified him.

However, we need not discount Howells's construction of burlesque as the idiosyncratic panic of a psychosexual invalid. Howells shared his fear of feminine sexuality as a chaos-inducing disease with an entire social caste, which desperately clung to a Victorian code of gentility and

sex roles even as it was progressively undermined by the swirling currents of social change in the years following the Civil War. His puritan-
ism was but an extreme instance of a much more widely shared set of
norms. "At almost no other time in western history," points out one of
his biographers, "was the fear of passion so extreme. For reasons hard
to determine, sex became a metaphor for chaos."[29]

Howells's bewilderment at the oxymoronic incongruity of burlesque
was echoed by two other commentaries, which appeared during the
summer of 1869. In its July 3 issue, *Appleton's Journal of Popular
Literature, Science, and Art* complained that of the seven theaters still
open in New York, fully six were presenting burlesque or pantomime.
Pantomimes, with their visual humor and surprising transformations,
were amusing without being shocking. Burlesque, however, was a different matter:

> It sets out with respecting nothing – neither taste, propriety, virtue,
> nor manners. Its design is to be uproariously funny and glaringly
> indecent. It seeks to unite the coarsest fun with the most intoxicat-
> ing forms of beauty. It presents women garbed, or semi-garbed, in
> the most luxurious and seductive dresses possible, and makes them
> play the fool to the topmost bent of the spectator. One is dazzled
> with light and color, with gay songs, with beautiful faces and
> graceful limbs, and startled at the coarse songs, the vile jargon, the
> low wit, and the abandoned manners of the characters. The mis-
> sion of the burlesque is to throw ridicule on gods and men – to
> satirize everybody and everything; to surround with laughter and
> contempt all that has been reverenced and respected.[30]

Richard Grant White began his sardonically subtle attack on burlesque in the August 1869 issue of *Galaxy* by saying:

> It means something, this outbreak of burlesque acting all over the
> world. No mere accident has made so monstrous a kind of enter-
> tainment equally acceptable to three publics so different as those of
> Paris, London, and New York. And by monstrous I do not mean
> wicked, disgusting, or hateful, but monstrously incongruous and
> unnatural. The peculiar trait of burlesque is its defiance both of the
> natural and the conventional. Rather, it forces the conventional
> and the natural together just at the points where they are most

remote, and the result is absurdity, monstrosity. Its system is a defiance of system. It is out of *all* keeping. . . . [B]urlesque casts down all the gods from their pedestals.[31]

In short, Thompsonian burlesque was so fascinating and so transgressive to bourgeois audiences in 1868–69 because it combined visual elements of feminine spectacle with the impertinence and inversiveness of the burlesque form – a merger effected onstage almost entirely by women and expressed through their bodies, language, movements, and gestures. It was this combination and not merely skimpy costumes that so outraged Olive Logan, moved the *New York Times* to declare burlesque "immensely damaging to the public taste and terribly ruinous to the public morals," provoked ministerial associations to see in it unprecedented immorality, caused William Dean Howells to shrink before its transgressive power, and prompted Richard Grant White to call it – quite accurately – a monstrosity "out of all keeping."

○ ○ ○   **Burlesque's Problematic Femininity**

What were the qualities of this monstrous union, and how were they articulated in such a way as to cause the whole to be infinitely more alluring and threatening than any of its individual attributes? Clearly, the power of Thompsonian burlesque to delight and to horrify is inextricably bound to its status as the most thoroughly feminized form of theatrical entertainment in the history of the American stage to that time. Indeed, no form of American commercial theatrical entertainment before or since has given the stage over to women to a greater degree. John Brougham's burlesques might have involved crossdressed roles, Adah Isaacs Menken might have played Mazeppa to a female heroine, the corps de ballet in *The Black Crook* might greatly have outnumbered the men in the cast, but in *Ixion* every part except one was played by a woman. Even that solitary male member of the troupe, Harry Beckett, played a woman. Thus, in 1868 no other form of theater had ever put before its audience the issue of the representation of women and femininity as boldly or as inescapably as did Thompsonian burlesque. That it did so not as a "serious" dramatic treatment of the place of women in American society but rather in a form that united "the coarsest fun with the most intoxicating forms of beauty" merely heightened its impact.

What audiences saw on this stage full of male-impersonating, revealingly attired, slang-spouting, minstrel-dancing women was a physical and ideological inversion of the Victorian ideal of femininity. Lydia Thompson, although not nearly so large as the burlesque stars of a decade later, was certainly statuesque, as were the other principals in the troupe. There was nothing of the frail, ethereal, steel-engraving lady about her. Her corseted costume emphasized her bust, hips, and legs, calling attention to the markers of sexual difference the sentimental costume kept hidden. Whereas the sentimental feminine ideal had been consistently depicted as dark-haired, much was made of the blondeness of the British Blondes and the means by which this tint might have been achieved.

As Lois Banner argues, the "look" of Thompson and her troupe was that of the voluptuous woman, a challenge to the sentimental ideal of feminine beauty that emerged in the early 1860s. The British Blondes themselves might have helped to influence a radical shift in notions of female beauty between the 1850s and the 1870s, from the slender, asexual steel-engraving lady to the large-breasted, big-hipped ideal of the feminine physique. The origins of the voluptuous model of femininity are obscure, but two sources might have been working-class and immigrant communities, where girth was associated with economic well-being, and urban street subcultures – "Bowery girls" and prostitutes. The female counterparts of the Bowery b'hoys in the 1840s and 1850s, Bowery girls flaunted their limited economic and domestic independence by adopting a mode of dress and public behavior that inverted bourgeois norms. In an age when fashion called for muted colors in dress and scrupulous modesty in demeanor, the Bowery girls wore gaudy, short-skirted dresses that showed off hips and busts. Groups of them strolled the streets with what Christine Stansell calls "self-conscious boisterousness."[32]

In the 1850s and 1860s the most threatening challenge to type was without question that represented by the urban prostitute. The decades around mid-century saw an outpouring of commentary on the "problem" of prostitution, which was, as Michel Foucault has argued, a displaced discourse on sexuality and women in general. It was also a discourse on the "problem" of class, occasioned by the same process of bourgeois class consolidation and rejection that had created the mainstream American theater at precisely the same historical moment. If the elimination of the rowdy pit and all that it stood for was in part, at least, an action directed against "lower-class" males, then the commentary on prostitution was, as Stansell puts it, "one response to the growing social and sexual distance that working-class women – especially working-class daughters – were travelling from patriarchal regulation."[33]

To most bourgeois males, the prostitute and the lady were two ontological categories, the former representing the antithesis of the latter. The prostitute, then, was not defined in any narrow legalistic sense (indeed, there was no law against prostitution in New York City in 1850), but rather and more loosely included any working-class woman whose dress, demeanor, or actions transgressed bourgeois notions of feminine propriety and respectability.[34] A woman might be branded a prostitute if she returned the gaze of a man on the street. It had not been long since all actresses, unless otherwise specified, were assumed to be prostitutes. The *New York Evening Post*'s condemnation of the Canterbury Music Hall as "a portico to the brothel" implicitly consigned every woman who worked in a concert saloon to the category of prostitute. And the *New York Clipper*'s 1859 poetic moral location of the "dancing girl" among "the cankering weeds that dwell / In the place of the rose-virginity" leaves little doubt that similar assumptions were being made in the 1860s about women who dared to participate in feminine spectacles.[35]

It is difficult to overestimate the alarm provoked within bourgeois society by the specter of prostitution. It was more than merely an issue of lapsed morality or hygiene, as it would become in the twentieth century. The prostitute constituted, in Lydia Nead's words, "an agent of chaos bringing with her disruption and social decay." Part of the urgency of discourse on prostitution after 1850 stemmed from the fact that the practice was by this time much more publicly visible than it had been in the earlier decades of the century. Women who were identified as prostitutes (for whatever reason) could be seen strolling along Broadway, occupying the same sidewalks as respectable women. Having recently driven prostitutes from the third tier, the bourgeoisie now encountered them parading openly along the boulevard. The fear this sight aroused was that it breached the very categorical distinctions – of class and gender relations – on which the respectable bourgeoisie had constituted itself.[36]

By 1868, it was becoming more difficult to distinguish a respectable woman from her opposite on the basis of appearance alone. Although their move was still controversial, some middle-class women had shed their drab colors and simply cut dresses for a more assertive, colorful style in a play, claims Banner, to wrest some degree of fashion-determining power from the upper classes. This "statement of rebellion against the elites" may have involved adapting the style of those women from the working classes – the Bowery girls and prostitutes – who had assumed it to begin with as a marker of difference.

In that year Elizabeth Linton, writing in the *London Saturday Review*, gave the British instance of assertive bourgeois fashionability a name: the "girl of the period." Henry James, reviewing a collection of essays on "modern women" that Linton had edited, contended that American womanhood had not yet fallen victim to this epidemic of vulgarity, but his description of its effects suggests that he had seen the American version of the "girl" strolling down Fifth Avenue: "a painted, powdered, 'enamelled' creature, stained with belladonna and antimony, crowned with a shock of false hair, wearing her walking dress indecently high and her evening dress abominably low. . . . She frankly sells herself; she marries for money, without a semblance of sentiment or romance." According to Linton, the British "girl" had adopted her style of dress, makeup, and deportment from that of "the celebrities . . . [and] obscurities of the *demi-monde*" of Paris. James found that her American sister was marked not only by dress but by attitude as well: "Accustomed to walk alone in the streets of a great city, and to be looked at by all sorts of people, she has acquired an unshrinking directness of gaze. She is the least bit *hard*."[37] What was so remarkable about young middle-class women looking back when looked at on the street was that until recently this "directness of gaze" had been a trait associated with prostitutes.

Others noticed a change in bearing among some middle-class young women. In 1865 a *Clipper* writer commented on the boldness of a woman he encountered on the street, but he put it down to a wartime shortage of men:

> Why, it is an undeniable fact that the girls actually make love to the men in these rebellious days. One of 'em made advances to us in Broadway the other day, before all the people; we asked her if her

intentions were honorable, and she burst out laughing right in our face. We had an awful time before we shook her. One can scarcely move a step without being tackled by some nymph in human shape and gaiter boots. It's getting to be a nuisance.[38]

Here, the writer seems to have been referring to a prostitute, but the fact that it is unclear what kind of "girl" he meant suggests something of the confusion provoked by the appropriation into bourgeois fashion of elements of working-class and subcultural style and manner.

The most extreme sartorial expression of this style of self-presentation – the Grecian bend – came precisely at the moment Lydia Thompson arrived in New York, and, in fact, was burlesqued in both *Ixion* and *Sinbad*. Introduced from France in the summer of 1867 and popularized the following season, the Grecian bend style combined a tightly laced corset, which forced the body into an exaggerated s-shaped configuration (bust thrust outward in front, buttocks behind), and high-heel shoes, which projected forward the upper part of the body even more. To further emphasize the hips, the uppermost part of a double skirt was pulled up at the sides and gathered at the back. This vogue, which Banner calls "the most erotic style of the century,"[39] so distorted normal posture that some women found it impossible to sit upright in a carriage. Songwriters, quick to exploit any fad, poked fun at women who so discomforted themselves for the sake of fashion in comic songs that filled music stores in 1868. In one, a gallant young man mistakes fashion for infirmity:

> One morning as I was walking out to promenade,
> I met a girl who look'd just like she was going to fall,
> I politely told her so, the offer I then made
> Of my left wing, when she began to squall.
> She call'd me a brute and said I was not polite
> And that my ways I'd better amend,
> The hump-tilt and toeing she assur'd me was right,
> Like any other Grecian Bend.
> Oh, my eyes, to what you see attend,
> Watch them close, those girls on a Grecian Bend.[40]

The Grecian bend was clearly related to the look of the voluptuous woman. In both cases, bust and hips were prominent.

As James's description of the girl of the period suggests, blonde hair dye and the heavy use of cosmetics became briefly fashionable among more adventuresome middle-class women in the late 1860s for the first time in the nineteenth century. Both previously had been employed only by working-class women and prostitutes. Banner suggests that the popularity of Thompson's troupe was largely responsible for the sudden fashionability of dyed blonde hair. If so, this shift must have been sudden indeed. In November 1868, barely two months after Thompson's debut at Woods, a *New York Times* story on the popularity of blonde hair observed that only a few years before, the idea of a woman (read: middle-class woman) dyeing her hair blonde would have seemed "barbaric." Now, one saw women with dark eyes and eyebrows but blonde hair everywhere. The following spring, a *Times* article charged that the "rage" for blonde hair led to the greater use of cosmetics. Women who dyed their hair a light color had to exaggerate their make-up so that their faces would not look "as yellow and jaundiced as jealousy or an Asiatic." The same article accused fashionable women of adopting styles without taking into account their provenance. The "vulgar looking" chignon had been borrowed from the "blackamoors of Africa." As for the false beauty spot, which was worn again for the first time in the century, "The ladies do not know from what class of fashionables or age of the world this fashion is descended to them, nor what greater blemish resulting from dissipation this blemish of the patch was originally intended to conceal, or else they would abandon its use at once." In another article, the same writer implicitly compared the new fashion with the morally transparent costumes of earlier decades: "Women have no chance to allow their garments to become a truthful part of themselves, the expression or embodiment of mind or sentiment. It is nothing but change, change distinguished only by its rapidity and ingenuity."[41]

G. J. Baker-Benfield has linked the rise of gynecology in the years after the Civil War with the bourgeois class and gender identity crisis, of which the troubling stylishness and assertiveness of middle-class women was one aspect. A stable and ordered society was seen as dependent on the maintenance of patriarchal power in the home – power that kept women in their proper place as submissive wives and mothers. Any steps women took beyond their established roles threatened the entire system by inverting power relations. Unable to conceive of male/female

"The Grecian Bend Song" sheet music cover.
(Prints and Photographs Division, Library of Congress)

relationships except in terms of domination and subordination, many bourgeois males regarded any movement toward female independence as an attempt to usurp the male role in society. Women, in other words, were trying to become men. A former president of the American Medical Association wrote in 1870 that the unnatural practices of "rebellious women" (including masturbation, contraception, and abortion) represented a threat to American civilization on a par with the barbarian threat to the Roman Empire.[42]

This fear of the unruly woman was a concomitant fear of unbridled female sexuality. The medical literature on women at mid-century regarded them as inherently unstable biopsychological systems, whose maintenance required professional control and periodic intervention. Whereas man's nature was seen as governed by his higher organ, the brain, woman's nature was determined by the sexual and reproductive organs of the lower body. When the constraints of morality and self-control were for whatever reason relaxed, women reverted to a state of biological and sexual anarchy.[43] Throughout the latter half of the nineteenth century, doctors, reformers, and the legal system devised ways to control women who "transgressed" bourgeois sexual norms – from female castration and clitoridectomy (the latter first performed in the United States in the late 1860s) if she were middle-class, to declaring a woman feebleminded or a criminal if she were working-class.[44]

Given this context, it does not require a great leap of historical imagination to see that Thompsonian burlesque enacted in a comic and only slightly removed fashion onstage a serious social drama then unfolding on city streets, in hospitals, in magistrates' courts, and around the middle-class family hearth. At stake in the drama outside the theater was, to many, nothing less than the preservation of the bourgeois, patriarchal social order. Burlesque had become another arena where this drama of bourgeois crisis was acted out – an arena and an enactment that, to some middle-class men in the audience, were dangerously out of control.

It was on the body of the female burlesque performer that burlesque's power to upset rationality and unseat bourgeois male authority was most clearly inscribed, and it is no coincidence that this body "figured" so prominently in the discourse on burlesque. The issue of the female body was most frequently couched in terms of immodesty: the burlesque performer revealed what should have been publicly concealed.

"She Stoops to Conquer" sheet music cover.
(Prints and Photographs Division, Library of Congress)

legs → nudity
✳

low

other and mixing

What the burlesque costume revealed, of course, was not just legs, but legs as the synecdotal sign of the lower body and of female sexuality in general – hence, the symbolic transformation of mid-thigh pantaloons and opaque tights into complete nudity.[45]

After decades of referencing the norms of femininity, primarily in terms of the "high" – angels, spirituality, ideality, fairies – bourgeois males saw that burlesque constructed femininity with reference almost exclusively to the "low" – the lower body, the profane, the working classes, prostitutes. The figuring of burlesque is an excellent example of the process described by Peter Stallybrass and Allon White by which the bourgeois subject defines itself "through the exclusion of that which has been marked out as 'low' – as dirty, repulsive, noisy, contaminating." The low other represents "a mobile, conflictual fusion of power, fear, and desire in the construction of subjectivity: a psychological dependence upon precisely those Others which are being rigorously opposed and excluded at the social level." Yet, as they go on to say, this exclusion is part of a larger and more complex process of both negation and introjection. In the construction of the excluded low other, two types of the grotesque are produced; the grotesque in terms of which the "otherness" of the excluded is defined, and the grotesque "as a boundary phenomenon of hybridization or inmixing, in which self and other become enmeshed in an inclusive, heterogeneous, dangerously unstable zone."[46]

The creation of the bourgeois self was predicated on the exclusion of the popular as that which was not respectable, tasteful, or clean. "[W]hen the bourgeoisie consolidated itself as a respectable and conventional body by withdrawing itself from the popular, it constructed the popular as grotesque otherness; but by this act of withdrawal and consolidation it produced another grotesque, an identity-in-difference which was nothing other than its fantasy relation, its negative symbiosis, with that which it had rejected in its social practices." Burlesque, then, was both denied and desired as part of the popular, and a particularly problematic domain of the popular at that – one that was structured as a comic inversion of the bourgeois world.[47]

In the critical discourse, burlesque coalesced into a force that threatened to rupture the norms of bourgeois culture through its celebration of an upside-down version of that world. Above all, what burlesque denied was the legitimacy of rationality and its power to impose order and meaning. The emblematic trope of burlesque was the pun, which short-circuited language's sense-making power through a purposive confusion of sensory affinity with logical association. To be sure, puns had been a part of burlesque on both sides of the Atlantic for decades. But in Thompsonian burlesque, women set off these linguistic fire-crackers and stink bombs.

Burlesque resisted the critics' attempts even to describe it as a form of theater. It was seen as having no form or of promiscuously taking on too many. Burlesque would not hold still long enough to be pinned down. Its plots were punctured by half-hour processions, suspended for gratuitous outbreaks of dancing, or abandoned all together for minstrel show breakdowns. Indeed, to discuss the "meaning" of burlesque was in a sense to miss its central point: it worked by turning meaning inside out. With the pun it exploded the possibility of stable meanings, or in the case of a female performer impersonating a male character dancing a minstrel show jig, it piled too many meanings on top of each other. Burlesque delighted in incongruity and miscegenation: Minerva was played by a man who constantly drank from a hip-pocket flask.

Having anesthetized rationality, burlesque gave its stage over to unauthorized impertinence. Burlesque was inherently antiauthoritarian. For if rationality was achieved through the suppression of the irrational, then the celebration of irrationality was a ritual act of insubordination. When the targets of humor were the venerated, the authorized, the sacrosanct, then laughter became an affirmation of the right of a nobody to question the stature of a somebody. Burlesque flaunted the language of the street, of the uncultured, and of the urban working classes: slang. In doing so, it flouted the right of bourgeois culture to determine the propriety of public discourse. Burlesque reveled in its illegitimacy.

The celebration of the body and of the irrational in burlesque was visual as well as linguistic. The "nudity" of the burlesque performer challenged the authority of bourgeois culture to define her as sexually invisible (she made a spectacle of herself). At the same time, she aroused instinctual, irrational urges in her male spectators by encouraging them to "see" her for what she was, thus producing a double social transgression. Again, the physical spectacle, which was clearly also a sexual spectacle, of burlesque completely short-circuited the intellectual and the rational. Its effects were both sensuous and sensual.

The burlesque performer's transgressive sexuality was not even clothed in the modesty of imitation. She was, as Logan put it, "peculiarly and emphatically herself, – the woman . . . who considers herself an object of admiration to the spectators." The appeals of burlesque were not only sensuously direct, they were rhetorically direct as well. Burlesque acknowledged its audience, addressed it directly, and showed off for it; the burlesque performer made no pretense that her relationship with the audience was distanced by her absorption within another persona. She was aware of her own "awarishness."

But the burlesque performer, at this point in burlesque's history at least, was not merely a mute object of sexual display. In fact, it was her "acting out" that bothered some critics much more than her "showing off" her body. In the upside-down world of burlesque, masculinity was but a caricature of itself, a female impersonation. Taking on the markers of masculinity, the burlesque performer was licensed to act in a very unladylike fashion: she swaggered about the stage wearing short pants, played the banjo, danced the jig, commanded battalions of her fellows in close-order drill, and exuded in her speech and stance the knowing, cocky worldliness of the man-about-town. It is not difficult to imagine Howells's embarrassed fascination at the sight of a burlesque performer's imitation of manliness – embarrassment provoked by the denaturalizing of the postures of masculinity. After seeing her, how could he stand with his hands on his hips without thinking that pose a self-parody? Burlesque produced not the unproblematic sensual display of the ballet dancer but a monstrosity, a "horrible prettiness," that provoked desire and at the same time disturbed the ground of that desire by confusing the distinctions on which desire depended.

○ ○ ○   **At the Intersection of Fashion, Gender, and Class**

In March 1868, just after the Thompson troupe had moved to Niblo's, the *Clipper* reprinted in its entirety an article from the *Northern Monthly* under the headline "Busts and Legs." The article explicitly links the transgressive quality of female fashion with that of "nude woman" onstage. It also leaves little doubt that both these forms of indecency are indicia of the larger threats to bourgeois patriarchy represented by the lower classes and by unruly women. Because it exposes the logic that tied the symbolism of feminine spectacle to the social crisis outside the theater, this article warrants detailed examination.[48]

The first problem with the revealing fashions now being worn by middle-class women, the article says, is that they make available promiscuously a sight that properly belongs only to a husband. "What husband will fail to claim that the woman whom he takes to his arms and heart contracts to keep the glories of her womanhood sacred to his only eye? And what father or brother will fail to visit with the severest reprobation the first advance toward undue revelation of form of either daughter or sister; simply because he, in common with the husband, recognizes such exposures, if continuing, as incompatible with purity of soul, and threateningly dangerous to purity of body?" The article makes explicit the connection between scopic and sexual possession through an anecdote. A "certain husband," watching his wife dance at a ball in a revealing dress, was asked by a stranger who the object of their mutual gaze was. He replied: "That? Oh! that is my wife; but, by the Prophet! I am inclined to think, by the way she dresses tonight, that she is the wife of every gentleman in the room!"

Then, in a remarkable eruption of patriarchal paranoia, the article speculates as to the motives behind a woman's desire to so display herself: "[W]hat does the married woman – a lady in position and really spotless as to action or intention – hope to gain by exhibiting in ballroom or opera box what her husband was silly enough, at some time or other in their acquaintance, to believe would be held sacred from all eyes but his own? Is it to make him proud and happy by showing what a prize he has drawn in the physical lottery? Is it with a far seeing eye to some coming day, when there may be another marital partner wanted and a complementary belief that more 'pipe' must be 'laid' against the future by the exhibition of more bust than brains?" If neither of these is the case, then there are but two other possible motives, one of them infuriating, the other so terrifying that it cannot be spoken of directly: "[T]he wife, unsatisfied with the devotion of one, and feverishly craving that dangerous need, general admiration, is willing to win it at a price which brings it to her blended with sneers and coarse speculations; or that there is a worse devil tempting, whose name is by no means pleasant to mention in such a connection." Obsessed with trying to

figure out which of these disturbing forces drives his own wife's transgressive fashionability, the bourgeois male sits beside her in their opera
box, notes the opera glasses directed at her, and says to himself: "There
is only one comment upon this spectacle – it is simply sickening!"

By making herself this spectacular object, the middle-class wife,
wittingly or not, has aligned herself with nude women on the stage and,
through this alliance, with a working-class conspiracy to undermine the
social order. The ballet dancer – and, by extension, all women involved
in the leg business – merely finishes "what her prouder sister has left
incomplete" by revealing the lower part of her body as well as the upper
half. As if illustrating Stallybrass and White's argument that "the human body, psychic forms, geographical space and the social formation
are all constructed within interrelating and dependent hierarchies of
high and low,"[49] the article connects the lower limbs of the ballet dancer
with "lower humanity":

> It has been well and wisely said that if kings and nobles disdain
> lower humanity, and reduce its members to poverty and suffering
> by refusing to take order for their welfare, that lower humanity has
> yet the terrible power of asserting its brotherhood by commu-
> nicating the diseases contracted through that want and suffering;
> and the thought will obtrude itself here, do the "wealthy, curled
> darlings" of our ball rooms and opera houses, rioting in the mag-
> nificent indecency already reprobated, quite remember to what
> they prove themselves akin in the act? Who it is that aids them in
> the great work of corrupting themselves and others? Would they be
> quite content, if they once paused to think seriously on the subject,
> with the reflection that there are two sculptors, and only two, for the
> waxen statue of Immodesty, so laboriously toiled at, and so widely
> worshipped: bust by Mrs. A. or Miss B. of Fifth Avenue or Murray
> Hill; legs by M'lle Kitty Wriggle, or the Theater Unmentionable,
> and a social standing not far removed from that of the back slums?

To make sure the reader will not miss the full political – indeed,
metaphysical – implications of the alliance among the diseased working
class, its Medusan stage accomplices, and their middle-class, female
fellow travelers, the article ends by asking how long it will be before the
current form of theatrical spectacle "is re-presented in another shape,
which France saw at one of the principal churches of Paris in the wildest

hour of the Reign of Terror – modesty, purity, decency, all dethroned, and a naked courtesan set up and worshipped as the true cynosure for human eyes, and the proper substitute for an outlived and exploded God?"

This article helps further to account for Thompsonian burlesque's simultaneous threat to patriarchy and extraordinary appeal among bourgeois males. By offering her displayed body to the gaze of theatrical spectators, the burlesque performer carried to its logical conclusion the process of bodily and hence sexual disclosure at work in women's fashions. The evening dress made public the "glories of womanhood," the pleasurable sight of which properly belonged exclusively to the husband within the private space of the bedroom. Feminine spectacle in the ballroom loosened the tight Victorian bond between male scopic pleasure and domestic patriarchy. Marriage gave men the right to sexually possess a woman, which included the right to the sight of her sexuality. By displaying herself in a way that invited men to look upon her as a sexual being, that woman "gave away" a portion of her husband's proprietary rights. She cracked open the door to *his* secret treasure vault and exposed its contents to anyone who cared to peek. As the ballroom anecdote suggests, fashion allowed women to trade scopic monogamy for, if not promiscuity, at least polygamy.

But the same fashion that robbed a bourgeois husband of his sole claim to the sight of his wife's body also enabled him to stake a claim to the "sight rights" to dozens of other men's wives and unattached women. The internal conflict between cuckolded husband and predatory visual interloper provoked by the ballroom scene could in the liminoid space of the theater be palliated by making the exchange of feminine display for male scopic pleasure a commercial transaction, a transaction that opened up an important social distance between burlesque performer and male spectator. As a woman who displayed herself for money, the burlesque performer immediately gave up any claim to consideration as a "respectable" bourgeois woman. She became the low other whom the bourgeois male could safely gaze upon without immediately seeing his wife or sister in her place. The construction of the burlesque performer as low other, as a working (and working-class) woman trading in sexuality – in other words, as a prostitute – was a necessary strategy in the negotiation of male scopic pleasure.

Yet this strategy was, and would continue to be, problematic. In the first place, as the *Northern Monthly* article and Howells's essay make clear, the two ontological categories that bourgeois males constructed to distinguish their wives and sisters from the nude women of the stage were not watertight. Thompson and her troupe did not perform in Bowery basement dives but in middle-class theaters attended by bourgeois men *and women*. Furthermore, as fashion drew more and more on the look and style of stage women, the two categories were drawn closer together. In the case of burlesque, the power relationships at work between performer and spectator were much more complex than the terms "display" and "scopic pleasure" suggest. Desire always entails a partial relinquishing of power to that which is desired. The spectator might feel that his position as customer establishes him as the party for whose benefit the performance is staged, but it is the performer who controls what is offered. Thompsonian burlesque offered much more than merely display. It was display bound up with irreverence, impertinence, masculine impersonation, and verbal insubordination. Sometimes men like Howells found it impossible to maintain the necessary barrier that in their minds separated the alien creatures of the stage from ordinary women.

Burlesque is figured in the antiburlesque diatribes as the reemergence of the theatrical suppressed. The bourgeois theater, which had struggled to rid itself of all marks of its former working-class connections, was invaded by troupes of women whose language, dress, and actions – indeed, whose very transgressiveness – marked them as part of "lower humanity." Furthermore, these holdovers from the recent era of the concert saloon were not performing in resorts haunted by the "low and the vile," but rather in the "first theatre in America," Niblo's Garden. The combination of female sexual transgressiveness and working-class origins (which were already so closely aligned as to be almost synonymous) pointed almost invariably in the direction of criminal sexuality: prostitution. More than Menken, the living picture exhibitions, or ballet spectacles, Thompsonian burlesque seems to have rekindled the fear that once again the middle-class theater was being contaminated by displays of feminine sexuality tantamount to soliciting onstage and by women whose very connection with such displays placed them in the same category as the prostitutes whom one might pass along Broadway. Howells may have been describing a young woman's initiation into the life of a brothel when he wrote of a burlesque performer who "coldly yielding to the manager's ideas of the public taste, stretched herself on a green baize bank with her feet toward us or did a similar grossness. . . . [I]t was hard to keep from crying aloud in protest, that she need not do it; that nobody really expected or wanted it of her. Nobody? Alas! there were people there – poor souls who had the appearance of coming every night – who plainly did expect it, and who were loud in their applauses of the chief actress." Even though the *Spirit of the Times*'s dispute was with Alexander Henderson and not, apparently, with Lydia Thompson herself, George Butler could not resist casting Henderson's relationship with the troupe as that of pimp to a stable of prostitutes. They were, he said, bound to Henderson "by ties unnecessary to mention." When Wilbur Storey wanted his readers to grasp the extent of Thompson's transgressiveness in Chicago, all he had to do was to link it with prostitution. The troupe had made "an unnecessary and lewd exhibition of their persons, such as would not be tolerated by the police in any bawdy house."[50]

As Mary Douglas points out, at times of particular social tension, the discourse of ordinating groups frequently falls back on the imagery of the body in an attempt to protect or redefine moral and social boundaries. The existing social order is mapped on a civic body so that threats to it can be articulated as infectious agents and transgressive elements in society reproduced as diseased or deformed bodies. In antiburlesque discourse, the image of the displayed theatrical woman condenses bodily filth, disease, foreign contamination, and the collective excrescence of the urban poor. One of the first signs of the discursive shift that accompanies Thompson's debut at Niblo's in February 1869 is the *Times*'s tongue-in-cheek description of burlesque as an "epidemic," imported by foreign women, whose victims suffered convulsive dancing, incoherent ravings, and obsessive exhibitionism. In June the *Tribune* called burlesque performers "a sort of fungus on the stage, and the fungus has now become excessive and intolerable." Commenting on *The White Fawn*, the *Northern Monthly* article warned the roué that he knows not of the dancers' "variety of flaccid lymph or bony thinness, their clammy, inodorous flesh." And the *Spirit of the Times*'s attack on Alexander Henderson concluded by saying that New York had enough of "its own home muck before Henderson imported this flaxen scrofula, this worse than yellow fever, from the slums of London; and we intend to do our best to cure our city of the epidemic."[51]

*artificial/
unnatural*

Even less vitriolic responses to burlesque still regarded the performer's body as unnatural, one whose sexual features had been ar-
tificially enhanced. Olive Logan was particularly incensed by the practice, presumably followed by burlesque performers, of padding hips and
legs. "The art of padding," she wrote, "has reached such perfection that
nature has almost been distanced, and stands, blushing at her own
incompleteness, in the background." Elsewhere she referred several
times to burlesque performers as "brazen-faced, stained, yellow-haired,
padded limbed creatures."[52] A few weeks before Logan's diatribe
against burlesque at Steinway Hall, the *Clipper* linked the artificiality of
burlesque performers with their foreign origin:

> They do say that nearly all of our native American actresses are
> about to leave for England in order to go through the necessary
> training to fit them for an appearance before an American public.
> They have a manufactory over there where novices are taken in and
> put through a regular course of sprouts for the New York market.
> Legs are repaired and made to conform to the American standard;
> bosoms are filled out and developed more in accordance with
> existing notions; the blackest hair is transformed into the purest
> blonde; while modesty, delicacy and innocence are at once made to
> give place to impudence, profligacy and immorality, as better
> suited to the American market.[53]

transformation

Marilyn Moses contends that the artificiality of the burlesque performer – her tightly corseted costume emphasizing hips and bust,
painted face, dyed blonde hair, and tights filled out with padding – were
controversial because they inverted the sentimental ideal of feminine
purity and naturalness.[54] Certainly, the look of the voluptuous burlesque performer was diametrically opposed to that of the steel-engraving lady. Yet the romantic ideal of ethereal, natural femininity was
already being challenged outside of the theater by bourgeois fashion.
Indeed, this challenge was most strongly felt in the fall of 1868 with the
introduction of the Grecian bend. The inversion of Victorian feminine
physicality was "there to be read" in the self-presentation of the burlesque performer – a reading Logan, for one, was quick to make.

More important, however, the carefully constructed sexuality of the
burlesque performer linked her with her stylish middle-class sister – the
obvious transgressiveness of the former commenting on the barely

sublimated eroticism of the latter. Implicitly, the burlesque performer asked, "What's the difference?" Thompson herself made the comparison explicit in *Sinbad* when, in the "Matrimonial Market" scene, she delivered a stump speech dressed as a girl of the period: huge blonde wig, short Grecian bend walking dress, and high heels.[55]

For William Dean Howells and Richard Grant White, both burlesque and the burlesque body were grotesque and monstrous, unnatural combinations of separate and exclusive categories. To Howells, burlesque performers were monsters composed of masculine and feminine natures: "though they were not like men, [they] were in most things as unlike women, and seemed creatures of a kind of alien sex, parodying both." Whenever one of these "creatures" attempted to reassert her "feminine" nature, the result gave Howells "a curiously and scarcely explicable shock," as "in the case of that dancer whose impudent song required the action of fondling a child, and who rendered the passage with an instinctive tenderness and grace, all the more pathetic for the profaning boldness of her super-masculine dress or undress." White wrote: "I saw once a very large and elaborately-carved set of chess-men which a mischievous boy had taken apart and screwed together with the black pieces on the white standards, and the white on the black, the bodies and heads of the pieces being misplaced in a like manner. This was a sort of burlesque." White saw the monstrousness of burlesque reaching its apotheosis in *The Forty Thieves*, in which "the forty robbers were represented by forty young women, who, as a part of their daily drill, at the command of their captain, pulled out forty matches and lit forty cigarettes; in which a donkey danced a break-down, and Morgiana, pouring the poison into the jars in which the forty were concealed, exclaimed, 'They do die beautiful.' "[56]

Thus for the bourgeois male, the pleasures to be derived from Thompsonian burlesque were almost certainly guilty and troubling pleasures. To the degree that he saw in the performer the likeness of his wife or his sister, he was prompted to connect the topsy-turvy world of sexual relations in the theater with the threat outside of it represented by women's new assertiveness. To the degree that he submitted himself to the allure of her low-other sexuality, he risked contamination and corruption through her implicit connection with the working class and with prostitution. In different ways, Logan, Howells, White, and the others who commented on burlesque in Thompson's first season in

America all pointed to burlesque's transgressive potential: its power to resurrect the spirit of a suppressed, prebourgeois theatrical culture; its inversion of the male-ruled world outside the theater; its overwhelming sensuality; its unapologetic celebration of the absurd and the nonsensical; its confusion of roles, stations, and categories. Only by imagining the monstrosity of Thompsonian burlesque can we begin to understand the discursive vacillation between celebratory delight at burlesque and shrill recrimination. Only when we come to see burlesque as a monstrosity "out of all keeping," as White called it, can we begin to sense the imperative to tame burlesque or at least to keep it out of sight.

○ ○ ○ ○ ○ ○ ○ ○

The Institutionalization of Burlesque

Upon my grave please lay a wreath:

I almost played a week for Keith.

– William Jerome

○ ○ ○ ○ ○ ○ ○ ○ ○ ○ ○ ○ ○ ○ ○ ○

On July 2, 1869, a *New York Times* editorial announced the death of "British burlesque," at least as far as New York City was concerned. The editorial viewed Lydia Thompson's scheduled departure from Niblo's Garden to launch a national tour as evidence that "our unwelcome guests having at last exhausted public patience have received formal notice to quit. Their share in the theatrical revels of New York is nearly at an end." For the *Times*, the final ignominy suffered by the New York stage at the hands of burlesque had been Alexander Henderson's leasing of the city's most prestigious dramatic venue, James Wallack's Broadway Theater, for a summer season of burlesque and pantomime. Wallack's decision to "submit to the unwholesome fascinations of the foreign manager" had "shattered the faith of his old clientelle." However, Henderson's relinquishing of the lease to accompany his wife on tour meant that "at the end of this month we shall have the satisfaction of recording [burlesque's] dismissal from this last stronghold. After that, we shall hear of it no more." Burlesque had been, the *Times* reasoned, but a momentary fascination, an "abnormal theatrical stimulant" creating an "artificial and delusive prosperity." But as with all such "unnatural" arousals of the theatrical and social body, "the deathly reaction is inevitable." The week before, the *New York Clipper* also had noted a falling off of business at Niblo's and suggested that burlesque might be merely a passing fancy.[1]

In addition to continuing the discursive construction of burlesque as an unnatural, foreign, contaminating other, the *Times* editorial signaled the beginning of burlesque's descent from the sunshine of bourgeois theater into the shadows of male, working-class entertainment. Despite the *Times*'s premature death knell, Thompson and her troupe would continue to "stimulate" New York audiences at Niblo's, Wood's, and Wallack's season after season between 1870 and 1877. But as dozens of burlesque troupes sprang up in the wake of Thompson's extraordinarily successful first New York season and subsequent national tour, the form itself underwent an aesthetic and social mutation, to the point that by the 1890s Thompson could declare that her brand of burlesque had been "retired" from the stage. Lydia Thompson did not set out to inaugurate what American burlesque had become by the 1890s, Bernard Sobel observes; indeed, she would have considered such "credit a discredit."[2]

This chapter moves the story of burlesque beyond its initial season and considers the process of its integration into the American show business system as an autonomous form of popular entertainment in the 1870s. That process entailed its marginalization and social reorientation toward a working-class male audience. It also involved the curious formal merger of Thompsonian burlesque with another popular entertainment form structured around the figure of the low other: the minstrel show. The rise of burlesque and its social transformation historically parallels the rise of variety and its development into vaudeville. Although burlesque and vaudeville are today frequently conflated, their early histories reveal sharply contrasting strategies for dealing with sexuality, cultural transgression, and their ties to "lower-class" culture.

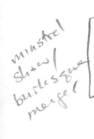

minstrel show/ burlesque merge/

❍ ❍ ❍ The Diffusion of Burlesque

The details of the process by which burlesque's audience moved down the social hierarchy from middle to working class and, concurrently, lost its following among middle-class women are extremely difficult to recover. As early as April 1870, when Thompson returned to Niblo's in *Pippin; or, The King of the Gold Mine*, the *Clipper* commented on the small number of respectable women in the audience and referred to the rest of the spectators as "the crowd who bow down and worship at the shrine of the blondes" and who "go there to see legs and busts." Yet the following week the *Clipper* declared that its reporter had seen some of the most prominent men in the city at Niblo's.[3]

Much easier to document is the formal and institutional transformation of burlesque in the early 1870s. The success of *Ixion* at Wood's prompted an immediate proliferation of competing burlesque troupes in New York, the first drawn from the Thompson troupe's own ranks when Ada Harland and Lisa Weber left to form their own companies in

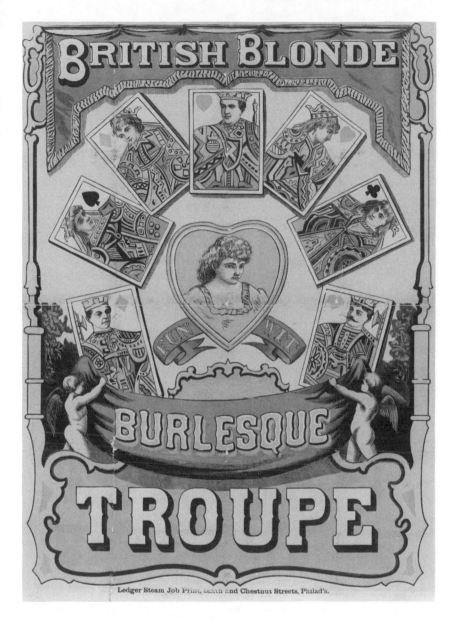

The first of many rivals to Thompson's troupe in America:
The British Blonde Burlesque Troupe.
(Prints and Photographs Division, Library of Congress)

February 1869.[4] Even before the beginning of Thompson's extensive U.S. tour in the summer of 1869, Harland's troupe had already hit the road: while Thompson was concluding her engagement at Niblo's, Harland was appearing in *The Forty Thieves* at the Academy of Music in Providence, Rhode Island. By the time Thompson reached San Francisco in June 1870, she had been preceded there by Elise Holt's company in *Lucretia Borgia* by fully a year. Taking their cue from Olive Logan's recently published essay in *Packard's Monthly*, the San Francisco newspapers greeted Holt's appearance with the same antiburlesque diatribes that confronted Thompson in New York.[5]

When Thompson finally arrived to play San Francisco's California Theater the following summer, she found her former colleagues — Eliza Weathersby, Ada Harland, and Harry Beckett — already in residence at the California's chief rival, McGuire's Opera House, calling themselves the British Blondes. Nevertheless, Thompson attracted what one paper claimed was a record audience for the theater. At one point, the gallery was so enthusiastic that the manager had to take the stage to appeal for order. The two companies battled each other, song for song and novelty for novelty, for several weeks before each headed out on separate tours of California.[6]

Such extensive tours were only possible and profitable because of the new network of rail lines that now stretched from coast to coast. Traveling theatrical companies, or "combinations" as they were called, could be routed from city to city week after week for months on end. As noted earlier, the success of touring *Black Crook* companies had helped to confirm the economic viability of the rail-based combination system. Thompson followed *The Black Crook*'s model of a long New York run followed by an extensive national tour, the former serving as a key marketing point for the latter. The dozens of burlesque troupes that popped up from Syracuse to Cincinnati in the wake of Thompson's New York success pushed the combination model one step further. With the few notable exceptions of companies that were established around former members of Thompson's troupe, these new burlesque combinations were assembled *as* touring companies. The members of the Occidental Burlesque Troupe, Blanche and Ella Chapman and Company, Jenny Wilmore's London Burlesque Combination, and the Wallace Sisters Burlesque Troupe (merely a few of the early touring companies) had never performed together in New York City except in a rehearsal hall, and they might well have played together for an entire tour without getting any closer to Manhattan than Providence. The effect might have been, as one San Francisco correspondent to the *New York Clipper* put it in 1870, to "flood . . . the land with mediocre performers."[7] Certainly, railroad networks broadened the scope of theatrical entertainment across the country and worked to centralize its control, as local theater managers became increasingly dependent on imported combinations and less so on resident stock companies. As an emerging theatrical novelty that usually did not depend on a particular star (as did some earlier combinations), nor on elaborate scenic effects (as did *The Black Crook*), burlesque in 1869 was perfectly positioned to take advantage of both the railroad and the combination system.

○ ○ ○   **Burlesque and Minstrelsy**

The person usually cited as the key pioneer of the touring burlesque company and credited with developing post-Thompsonian burlesque's new formal structure is Michael Leavitt. As Irving Zeidman, relying on Leavitt's own account, tells the story, Leavitt was by 1870 an established show business entrepreneur with a flair for the sensational who had built his success on the importation of European acts. "On one of his trips he became intrigued with a European tent show, called Rentz's Circus. The first successful minstrel show which he feminized went under the name of Mme. Rentz's Female Minstrels. . . . Eventually, Leavitt conceived the idea of merging the lady minstrel show, vaudeville, and musicalized travesty into one production which he called burlesque, and thus was evolved the first Rentz-Santley show, [which became] the model for most of the reputable burlesque shows of the 1880s and 1890s."[8]

However, the circumstances surrounding the emergence of this new form of burlesque are a bit less clear-cut.[9] Simultaneously (summer and fall of 1870), a number of managers attempted to meld the gendered nature of burlesque entertainment with the tripartite structure of the blackface minstrel show, producing a hybrid female minstrel form.[10] The *Clipper* listed their engagements under its regular minstrelsy column, along with news of standard blackface troupes. The paper's Pittsburgh stringer gives us the first indication of the nature of this brand of

One of the first female minstrel troupes: The Rentz-Santley Company.
(Prints and Photographs Division, Library of Congress)

performance in his account of Ada Tesman's Female Minstrels at the
Masonic Hall in November:

> Ten people appeared in the first part; seven ladies and three gentle-
> men. The ends were occupied by James Roone, tamborine, and
> Mike Foley, bones. Gaynor Roone was interlocutor. The ladies
> were costumed in white dresses and had blue bows on the bosoms.
> All were endowed with more or less beauty – the more predomi-
> nating – and so far as appearance went the first part was a success.
> Ada Tesman and the Stevens Sisters sang quite cleverly, but the end
> men were not up to the standard. . . . The party gave a very
> creditable olio, and closed the entertainment with a farce of
> "Wanted: 1,000 Milliners."[11]

Since the 1840s, the minstrel show had consisted of three parts. In the
first part, the ensemble sat in a semicircle, with a whiteface interlocutor

*Structure of
minstrel
show*

in the middle and two eccentrically dressed and made-up blackface comedians (end men) at either end, their customary names, Tambo and Bones, referring to the instruments they played. This arrangement allowed the interlocutor to pose questions and riddles for the end men and other members of the company to perform in songs and dances, supported on occasion by the full company in chorus. The second part of the show, called the "olio," involved a succession of variety acts performed by individual members of the company. The performance concluded with an afterpiece or burlesque: a piece of sketch comedy – sometimes a travesty of a popular piece of literature or drama, some-times set on the old plantation – that always relied on familiar blackface dialect humor.[12] At first female minstrel troupes used male performers as interlocutors and end men, the latter appearing in blackface. As far as can be determined, "female" minstrels always appeared as white characters, sometimes adorned with blonde wigs.[13] Before long, the male interlocutor and end men were dropped from the female min-strel's format and the first part was performed only by the women of the company, with a few men appearing in the olio and concluding farce. Over the next twenty years, the arrangement of the cast in a semicircle was replaced by an opening production number performed by the entire female company, punctuated by individual numbers and bits of busi-ness. But burlesque retained the overall tripartite structure of the min-strel show, including its olio and concluding farce, into the twentieth century.[14]

How are we to account for what seems on the surface to be a curious hybridization of two such disparate forms of popular entertainment? The minstrel show was an all-male form; burlesque, obviously, was dominated by female performers. The minstrel show worked by playing with and playing up racial differences between white audience mem-bers and the caricatured blacks impersonated by white performers onstage; burlesque had little of this ethnic or racial basis to its humor. The economics of popular entertainment played a major part in producing female minstrelsy. Since its establishment as an autonomous form of popular entertainment in the mid-1840s, minstrelsy had ap-pealed to a broad aggregate of principally working- and lower-middle class audiences. Although its origins were urban and New York City was its birthplace and important hub, minstrel shows had appeal through-out the country – in both cities and villages. It was, one historian claims, the most popular form of entertainment in America at mid-century.[15] Even in New York, where in the 1850s ten minstrel companies competed, minstrelsy attracted Bowery b'hoys and girls as well as the "respectable" working class newly added to the theatergoing audience by P. T. Barnum and Moses Kimball. It drew audiences from the neighborhoods of lower Manhattan and from among rural visitors to the city, who in the late 1840s were as likely to spend an evening listening to E. P. Christy's Minstrels sing Stephen Foster as they were to gawk at Barnum's oddities.[16]

In the years after the Civil War, as Robert Toll argues, minstrelsy had to adjust to new and unfavorable economic conditions. It had to face competition from variety, which gradually severed its connection with the concert saloon and its "pretty waiter girls" and oriented its low-cost, modular entertainment toward the family minstrel audience.[17] Toll further contends that minstrelsy was challenged by the explosive growth of feminine spectacle that occurred in the wake of *The Black Crook*. However, the timing of the formation of the first female minstrel troupes – dozens of them appeared within the space of months at the beginning of the 1870–71 theatrical season – suggests two additional factors. Feminine spectacle began to compete seriously for the minstrel show audience in the wake of the success of Thompsonian burlesque, *and*, as a result of a shift in the audience for burlesque from the middle to the working classes in the wake of the antiburlesque hysteria of 1868–69. For all the above reasons, minstrelsy desperately needed a transfusion of public interest. In February 1871 the *Clipper*, noting that the minstrel business had been declining for two years, asked: "Has the taste for negro minstrelsy diminished, or is the apparent public apathy in that style of amusement to be attributed to a lack of novelty and freshness in the entertainments presented?"[18]

In the scramble to retain their audience "share," minstrel companies tried to broaden their appeal and their markets. Troupes traveled more widely and more deeply into the hinterlands than ever before, advertised their shows with huge pictorial billboards and massive parades, added more performers and specialty acts to the olio, and, in general, moved away from the representation of a white fantasy of blackness that had been their stock-in-trade for a quarter century. Replacing white male minstrels in blackface with white female burlesque performers was, Toll suggests, but one survival strategy minstrel entrepreneurs

Minstrel company sheet music cover. Note the prominence of the
"wench" character.
(Prints and Photographs Division, Library of Congress)

devised at a time of increased competition and diminishing interest in their traditional offerings of eccentric dances, banjo solos, dialect humor, and blackface grotesquerie. What resulted, of course, was not an augmentation of the minstrel show audience, but rather the creation of a new entertainment form, which drew away from minstrelsy a portion of its male audience. Burlesque's predication on female spectacle and sexuality was incommensurable with minstrelsy's family orientation.

Traditional minstrelsy did become "feminized" in the 1870s, but on its own terms, with the increasing use of female impersonators to play blackface prima donna roles. Males playing low-comedy "wench" roles had been common in minstrelsy since the mid-1840s. The 1870s saw the popularity of a very different representation of blackface femininity: the serious impersonation of demure, well-dressed, handsome young women, who, represented as mulattoes, sang teasingly of the first blushes of romantic love in falsetto voices.[19]

[margin note: new femininity in minstrelsy]

With female minstrels cleaved away in the early 1870s and despite the novelties managers innovated in their attempt to build patronage, minstrelsy did not veer sharply away from its traditional audience or format in the 1870s and 1880s. Rather, it reasoned that if audiences had responded enthusiastically to a dozen minstrels in the 1850s, a doubling or quadrupling of the cast would revive that enthusiasm twenty years later. The fashion for elephantine minstrel companies reached its height in 1879 with J. H. Haverly's Mastadon Minstrels, a troupe of forty performers complete with brass band, elaborate scenic effects, transformation scenes, and tableaux.[20]

[margin note: enlargement of minstrel companies]

As with so many cultural changes, economic forces provide a necessary but insufficient basis for explanation. Notwithstanding their surface dissimilarities, there were some formal parallels between minstrelsy and burlesque. In both, narrative and dramatic continuity played only a minor role. In the case of Thompsonian burlesque, the drive toward narrative resolution was constantly suspended for songs, dances, and bits of visual business – interruptions hardly generated by the narrative logic of the piece. In effect, the olio portion of the minstrel show was in burlesque interspersed within a larger dramatic vehicle rather than separated out into its own segment.

It is clear that the style of singing and dancing in Thompsonian burlesque was influenced by minstrelsy even before the former's American introduction. Minstrel shows were popular in Great Britain as early

as 1836 – a popularity that fed easily into the burlesque and extravaganza traditions. By the 1860s, as Michael Booth puts it, "The lively,
eccentric, and sometimes grotesque dances of the minstrels were imported wholesale onto the extravaganza and burlesque stage, and a
deluge of hit minstrel tunes had appropriate new lyrics written for
them." In America, Olive Logan complained that burlesque performers
playing the banjo and the bugle "looked queer" not only because these
were "masculine" instruments, but also because they were associated
with minstrelsy. Whenever American burlesque producers saw an opportunity to do so, they worked in more specific references to minstrel
show conventions. Recall, for example, the amazonian march in *Robinson Crusoe* in which the twenty-four female warriors were accompanied
by "six negro minstrels, who sing 'De King Am Coming,' accompanying
themselves first on the banjo, then the bones, then do a wooden shoe
dance." By the same token, the spirit of burlesque pervaded minstrelsy.
The concluding afterpiece or farce of the minstrel show was frequently
a burlesque of a form of high culture or a travesty of a particular work.
From the earliest days of minstrelsy, Italian opera was a favorite target
of minstrel show burlesque. In 1833 *Fra Diavolo* became, at the hands
of pioneer minstrel T. G. Rice, *Bone Squash Diavolo; or, Il Nigeretta*.
Shakespeare was a frequent subject of travesty from the 1820s until the
eventual demise of commercial minstrelsy in the 1880s.[21]

The two forms shared an extraordinary structural flexibility and, in
their separate ways, could respond to particularities of place, time, and
audience. The "script" for a Thompsonian burlesque was constantly
altered to work in local and topical allusions, which could be altered or
dropped according to audience response.[22] In the minstrel show, the
interlocutor had even more immediate control over the show's largely
improvised first part. He could fine-tune the performance through his
choice of musical selections and his set-piece exchanges with the end
men.[23]

But the link between burlesque and minstrelsy is considerably
stronger than that suggested by these formal similarities. Both forms
worked upon principles of transgression and inversion. Both were constructed around ironic, low-other characters, whose speech, costume,
behavior, and demeanor helped to structure different but homologous
ideological problematics: gender and race, respectively. As low-other
constructions, both the burlesque performer and the blackface minstrel

were subject to simultaneous contrary interpretations by their audiences.

The sexual objectification of the burlesque performer confirmed the
authority of the male spectator to visually possess her, while, at the same
time, her inversive and transgressive performance pointed to the social
and sexual system within which both spectator and performer were
situated. Similarly, the black man represented by the blackface minstrel
was obviously an object of ridicule, a construction of thoroughgoing
otherness that allowed white audiences to see themselves as both ontologically different and constitutionally superior. Furthermore, in the
years leading up to national dissolution, the construction of blackness
in terms of its depiction in minstrel shows implicitly (and sometimes
explicitly) sanctioned the ideological precepts underlying slavery and
racial oppression. However, it would be simplistic to regard the minstrel
show simply as a spectacle of racial hatred rendered palatable to the
audience through comedy. The very low otherness of the blackface
minstrel allowed him to serve as the vehicle for a displaced, bottom-up
critique of the social order, an order in which the white audience itself
had been figured as low other.

As Jules Zanger argues, a great deal of attention has been directed –
and rightly so – toward the unrelievedly racist nature of blackface
minstrel characters. Much less attention has been focused on the construction of the only white figure in the minstrel show's first part, the
interlocutor, and his relationship to the blackface end men. The interlocutor was not merely a generic white man but was himself a caricature
of upper-class white American society. Specifically, Zanger observes,
"he caricatured the humanitarian reformer, the liberal preacher, the
academic savant, that is, anyone, who from the vantage point of superior class, education, or morality, presumed to lecture the mob."[24] This
caricature is apparent in the interlocutor's exaggeratedly formal costume, in his patrician and patronizing demeanor, and perhaps most in
his prolix speech and love of arcane, multisyllabic words. His exchanges
with the end men set up a contrast between his excessively high-flown
verbiage and their "low" language. The end men persistently misin-
terpreted the interlocutor's questions and misunderstood his words.
Humor resided in the gap between the registers of their low, naive mode
of apprehension and articulation and his cerebrality and pomposity. As
in burlesque, the pun was a favorite weapon for undermining the inter-

locutor's linguistic authority and puncturing his inflated image. In the process, says Zanger, "The resultant laughter of the white audience is directed primarily at the discomfiture of the Interlocutor and only secondarily at the foolishness of the End Men who, in this regard, are acting as instruments of the white audience's will."[25]

The end man's apparent stupidity frequently was a cover for low cunning and guile – qualities the oppressed have always used to manipulate hierarchy to their advantage, and qualities the white working-class audience could appreciate when they were directed at upper-class snobs. This sly insubordination comes through in minstrel songs and first-part banter, as well as in the afterpieces. One such afterpiece, the "Virginny Mummy," published in 1864, demonstrates that the audience's allegiances were not with the upper-class characters in the sketch, and, while also distanced from Ginger Blue, the stock plantation black character, the audience's perspective was clearly more closely aligned with him than his employer, Colonel Rifle.

The play opens with Colonel Rifle checking into a hotel after having been away for two years. He sends for a porter to check his mail at the post office:

Ginger Blue: Did you call me, massa?

Rifle: I called the waiter. Are you he?

Ginger: I ar one ob dem.

Rifle: I ar one ob dem! and how many does it take to make one of dem?

Ginger: Dar's whar you hab me. I guess it takes a right smart chap, anyhow.

Rifle: Well, you are an original.

Ginger: No, I'm a Virginian.

Rifle: Ha! ha! ha! Come here; can you run an errand for me?

Ginger: If you isn't sent nobody else.

Rifle: What do you ask me that for?

Ginger: 'Cause if dar's two, we'll be sure to quarrel 'bout the pay when we come back.

Rifle: But suppose I don't choose to pay you; what then will be the consequence?

Ginger: It will be rather hard to hear you when the bell rings.

In order to impress her scientist father and win the hand of his daughter, Rifle contrives to deliver to him an Egyptian mummy, who is, of course, Ginger Blue. His face painted white and his body wrapped in cloth, he is ordered to stand stock still in an upright sarcophagus. One of the daughter's other suitors, Charles, also a scientist, attempts a sketch of the mummy while Ginger delivers sotto voce asides to the audience:

Charles: Now for a sketch. . . .
Ginger: What de debbil is he gwan to do?
Charles: I'm afraid I won't be able to hit the dark shades of the
         face.
Ginger: As long as he don't hit me on de shin, I don't care.
Charles: But as close as my genius will admit of, I will come to it.
                                                    [*Crosses to L.*]
Ginger: Dat sabe me de trouble ob comin' to you.
Charles: But I can scarcely believe that it lived 3000 years ago.
Ginger: Eh! eh! honey. You is right – only half ob it.
Charles: No doubt it was some great personage, and stood very
         high in his native country.
Ginger: When I was up in de tree arter de 'possum.
Charles: Probably a king.
Ginger: Yes, wid a *dom* come to it.
Charles: That had led triumphant armies across the plains of Egypt
         after the retreating enemy.
Ginger: Or rader a pack ob dogs fro' de cane brake arter de bear

    .   .   .   .

Charles: He might have been an artist, and handled the brush.
Ginger: Yes, indeedy – de white wash brush.
Charles: Or an astronomer, and read the stars.
Ginger: I guess the book was upside down.
Charles: Or had an ear for music.
Ginger: Jist gib me de banjo, dat's all.
Charles: Oh, what a field imagination may trace to find out what it
         is.
Ginger: You put me in de cornfield. I show you what it is.
Charles: I wonder if his race were all that color.
Ginger: I guess you find me a pretty fair sample.
Charles: And such a prodigious height, almost a giant.

Ginger: Yes, almost; but not quite.

Charles: I wonder what his name is.

Ginger: Ginger Blue, all de world ober.[26]

Ginger Blue would have been recognizable to minstrel show audiences as one of two principal stereotypes of black masculinity: the
"southern darkie" or "plantation darkie." He dressed in tatters, spoke
in the stage dialect white minstrel performers devised to represent black
southern speech, and betrayed his rural origins and naiveté when confronted with any aspect of urban culture. But he was also good-
humored, earthy, and, as we have seen, frequently possessed of a disin-
genuous native cunning.[27]

The other principal type was the northern urban dandy, who went by
Zip Coon, Dandy Jim, or one of a dozen other names. Dressed in a
long-tailed coat, tight pants, ruffled shirt, and gloves, and carrying an
eyepiece on a long cord, Dandy Jim condensed two caricatures into a
single figure. Strutting pretentiously around the stage, and spouting
malapropisms he took for "l'arned" speech, he represented the free
black male who aped the dress and manner of the white dandies he
passed on the street. As such, he served to reinforce the notion that any
attempt to "civilize" black males outside of their "native" plantation
culture would result in a grotesque travesty of white culture. Laid over
this caricature, however, was another: that of the white social type
Dandy Jim took as his model – the overweening, self-centered, wealthy
man-about-town, who lived off his family's prosperity, contributed
nothing to his community, and whose life revolved around fashion and
the pursuit of women.[28]

Zanger concludes that the structure of minstrel shows reveals "a
systematic irreverence and antagonism toward the most prominent
aspects of American Victorian high culture, toward its pomposity, its
artificiality, its sanctimoniousness, as well as toward its learning, its
humanitarianism, and its cultivation." Similarly, Alexander Saxton sees
minstrel shows as expressing "class identification and hostility," the
blackface convention rendering "permissible topics which would have
been taboo on the legitimate stage or in the press."[29] Considered in this
way, the minstrel show can be regarded as an instance of displaced
abjection. That is to say, the minstrel show licensed an inversive, insubordinate critique by the "low" of high culture and society, and yet

that inversion was only accomplished through reordination: the construction of another low-other figure representing a social group threatening the audience from below.

In both burlesque and minstrelsy, the form's transgressive and inversive qualities were borne by the bodies of its performers. Burlesque constructed a body that was a horribly pretty parody of masculinity, inversive in its flaunting of the female performer's lower parts (hips and legs) and transgressive in its size, display, and connection with feminine working-class sexuality. The blackface minstrel body was unequivocally grotesque. Mikhail Bakhtin distinguishes between the classical body and the grotesque body. The classical body is closed, finished, smooth, symmetrically proportioned, separated from other bodies and from connections with the outside world, and separated from its connections with procreation, birth, and death. The grotesque body, on the other hand, is "a body in the act of becoming." It seems to outgrow its own limits. It is all protuberances and orifices, shoots and branches. The grotesque body emphasizes those parts and their functions that connect the body with other bodies and with the world outside itself: nose, mouth, anus, belly, phallus; sneezing, eating, defecating, urinating; birth and procreation. "Of all the features of the human face," says Bakhtin, "the nose and mouth play the most important part in the grotesque image of the body." And most important of all is the mouth: "It dominates all else. The grotesque face is actually reduced to the gaping mouth; the other features are only a frame encasing this wide-open bodily abyss."[30]

Especially in the case of the end men, their makeup was not designed to present a convincing imitation of what anyone could possibly perceive as "characteristic" black physiognomy. Their mouths were gaping holes surrounded by a huge circle of red, and their eyes were outlined in white as if frozen in a state of permanent surprise. In images of minstrels in the many posters and sheet music covers that advertised minstrel troupes, black facial features were depicted in even more grotesque fashion: wild, bulging eyes; gigantic, flaring nostrils; equine teeth set within flapping lips; absurdly large feet with distended heels. Usually, Bakhtin notes, eyes play no role in the construction of the grotesque, because they tend to express self-sufficient individuality – a quality "not essential" to the grotesque. The grotesque "is interested only in protruding eyes."[31] The eyes of blackface minstrels appeared ready to

The first of many rivals to Thompson's troupe in America:
The British Blonde Burlesque Troupe.
(Prints and Photographs Division, Library of Congress)

One of the first female minstrel troupes: The Rentz-Santley Company.
(Prints and Photographs Division, Library of Congress)

The High Rollers Extravaganza Company: "Bend Her."
(Prints and Photographs Division, Library of Congress)

The High Rollers Extravaganza Company: "Mamie Lamb."
(Prints and Photographs Division, Library of Congress)

The Bon-Ton Burlesquers: "A Warm Reception."
(Prints and Photographs Division, Library of Congress)

The High Rollers Extravaganza Company: "Initiating a High Roller."
(Prints and Photographs Division, Library of Congress)

Phil Sheridan's New City Sports Company.
(Prints and Photographs Division, Library of Congress)

The Rose Hill English Folly Company:
"Hot Time in the Old Town Tonight."
(Prints and Photographs Division, Library of Congress)

launch from their sockets. In jokes, songs, and sketch humor, minstrel characters were represented as fixated on animalistic bodily functions, particularly eating, drinking, and – albeit disguised under cover of primitive courtship – sex. In the "Virginny Mummy" sketch, while Ginger Blue is supposed to be standing motionless in an upright coffin, he is constantly waiting for a chance to snatch food or drink. He drinks a medical potion in the doctor's laboratory because it smells like whiskey, gulps down the doctor's breakfast while no one is looking, and consumes the contents of the sugar bowl.[32] The minstrel show even elaborated an alternative aesthetic of physical beauty to correspond with its grotesque construction of the body. Such an aesthetic fetishizes all the parts of the female anatomy that protrude. Tambo and Bones envisioned their ideal woman with gargantuan feet and lips so large that they could not be covered in a single kiss.[33]

Onstage, the end men's bodies refused to accept the delineation between self and outside space and rejected any semblance of balance or order. They squirmed restlessly between and during interrogations by the interlocutor as if unable to control a manic desire to dance. As Toll puts it, "Even while sitting, they contorted their bodies, cocked their heads, rolled their eyes, and twisted their outstretched legs. When the music began, they exploded in a frenzy of grotesque and eccentric movements."[34]

As Bakhtin points out, the two canons of the body – the grotesque and the classical – were never immutable or without interaction, cross-fertilization, or fusion.[35] In the 1870s the minstrel stage contained both the grotesque figure of the end man and the classical figure of the prima donna. Furthermore, in attempting to relate Bakhtin's work to latter-day commercial entertainment forms, we must always keep in mind the indisputable social and ideological differences between them and the tradition of medieval carnival on which he predicates his theory of the carnivalesque and its significance. The minstrel show was not a spontaneous popular outpouring but a carefully calculated piece of show *business*. This said, it is still useful to think of the blackface minstrel in terms of Bakhtin's notion of the grotesque, vestiges of which he sees surviving from medieval times in Western folk art and lore. All the minstrel body lacked to conform exactly to Bakhtin's schema was an explicit emphasis on the genitals, which was elided in the minstrel show in deference to the mixed nature of its audience, but which reemerged in only slightly sublimated and displaced form. Thus, it was not just because the minstrel character was a caricature of the excluded and despised social other (the black man) that he served as a vehicle for social critique, but because he was at the same time constructed as a grotesque clown, who, functioning in a similar fashion to fools and clowns of medieval times, brought even the loftiest down to earth and made the most abstract flesh.

In the body of the Thompsonian burlesque performer, there was a tension between classical and grotesque modes. Compared with the steel-engraving lady of a few decades before, the burlesque performer's body placed much more emphasis on the materiality of the body, espe-cially its lower regions – hips and legs. The grotesque in Thompsonian burlesque was also created through its yoking together of conceptual categories that "should not" be joined, particularly in its construction of an alien, hermaphroditic sexuality. Still, nothing in the carte-de-visite photographs of Lydia Thompson and Pauline Markham resembled the thoroughgoing grotesquerie of the blackface minstrel. Rather, with their ample hips and busts protruding out of tightly corseted costumes, they represented a tension between the expansive materiality of the grotesque and the enclosed and contained classical body.

Ironically, in the 1870s when the minstrel show's figuring of the female body was moving closer to the classical mode, the burlesque body was moving in the opposite direction as star burlesque performers became more voluptuous. May Howard, one of the first women from Leavitt's Rentz-Santley Company to form her own troupe, boasted in the 1890s that she would hire no woman who did not weigh at least one hundred and fifty pounds. In 1899 W. B. (Billy) Watson built his entire troupe, Billy Watson's Beef Trust, around the size of his female per-formers, some of whom weighed as much as two hundred pounds.[36] The 1880s and 1890s were the heyday of the voluptuous body type in American fashion. Nevertheless, May Howard and her colleagues far exceeded bourgeois norms of ideal feminine size. Something of the transgressiveness of the burlesque performer's bulk can be seen in this passage from David Graham Phillips's 1917 novel, *Susan Lenox: Her Rise and Fall* – published at a time when notions of the ideal female body were again in transition. The young heroine signs on as a singer on a riverboat, where she is assigned a dressing room with two veteran burlesque performers:

When the two women stripped and got into their tights, Susan with polite modesty turned away. However, catching sight of Miss Anstruther in the mirror that had been hung under one of the side lamps, she was so fascinated that she gazed furtively at her by that indirect way.

Violet happened to see, and laughed. "Look at the baby's shocked face, Mabel," she cried.

But she was mistaken. It was sheer horror that held Susan's gaze upon Violet's incredible hips and thighs, violently obtruded by the close-reefed corset. . . . Susan had never before seen a woman in tights without any sort of skirt.

"You would show up well in those things," Violet said to her, "that is, for a thin woman. The men don't care much for thinness."

"Not the clodhoppers and roustabouts that come to see us," retorted Mabel. "The more a woman looks like a cow or a sow, the better they like it. They don't believe it's female unless it looks like what they're used to in the barnyard and the cattle pen."[37]

In summary, then, the marriage of burlesque and the minstrel show in the early 1870s was facilitated both by economics and by an underlying structural logic emanating from the homology between the blackface minstrel and the burlesque performer. An important consequence of this union was to direct the course of burlesque's development as an autonomous popular entertainment form downward toward the minstrel show's working-class audience and away from mainstream bourgeois theaters and audiences.

By the spring of 1872, the *Clipper* had stopped listing the activities of female minstrel troupes under its minstrelsy column, signaling the paper's recognition of this hybrid form's institutional and economic autonomy. Although Lydia Thompson continued to play New York's mainstream theaters in the early 1870s in revivals of her old hits and variations on them, the term "burlesque" increasingly came to be associated with Michael Leavitt's brand of entertainment and less and less with Thompson's. After finally gaining control over Madame Rentz's Female Minstrels in 1871, Leavitt reconstituted his troupe around Mabel Santley, one of the first stars of the new burlesque form. Leavitt's Rentz-Santley Company may have been the first to organize songs, dances, skits, olios, and afterpieces into an annual "edition," which was rewritten each season – a practice that was taken up in the twentieth century by Flo Ziegfeld in his revues.[38]

Dozens if not hundreds of troupes were launched in the 1870s. Within the overall tripartite structure adopted from the minstrel show, there was considerable variation in performance emphasis and detail. Some troupes continued the trappings of the minstrel show's first part; some abandoned it for the opening number. Some troupes advertised elaborate afterpieces; others touted the size and talent of their olio. Many troupes added living pictures, a practice that eventually became standard in burlesque. Each troupe – regardless of what else it featured or how it structured its performance – contained variety acts, both in the olio and, as songs and dances, in the first part.

O O O   **Burlesque and Variety**

At the same time that burlesque was being consolidated as an autonomous entertainment form in America in the 1870s and 1880s, variety was also emerging as a separate popular entertainment institution. Both burlesque of the 1870s and variety reflect the fragmentation of the antebellum theatrical performance tradition and audience that occurred in the wake of "bourgeoisification" of the American theater in the 1850s and 1860s. Variety, the performance of brief entertainment acts, had been a part of American theater from the beginning. In antebellum theater, dancers, magicians, acrobats, monologuists, and other variety artists had appeared either as a part of dramatic vehicles or as ancillary parts of an evening's entertainment. In the 1850s, variety became marginalized as theater managers reduced the diversity of performance fare in conjunction with their strategy to attract a less heterogeneous audience. As we have seen, variety was reconstituted as a part of concert saloon entertainment in the late 1850s and early 1860s, its appeals aimed primarily at working-class men.

In the 1870s the same railway network that made touring burlesque companies possible and profitable also made it possible to assemble troupes of variety artists and send them on the road. Indeed, burlesque companies and variety combinations frequently followed each other into theaters along the same routes. However, while the entrepreneurs controlling burlesque were consolidating their positions as purveyors of sexual titillation for the common man, a few variety managers, chief among them Benjamin Franklin Keith, saw an opportunity to transform variety into a form with middle-class appeal by severing its connections with working-class culture and with working-class sexuality. Variety became incorporated into bourgeois theater as vaudeville at the same time and as a part of the same process that resulted in the excorporation of burlesque. The terminological shift from variety to vaudeville signifies not so much a change in performance structure as changes in the form's institutional structure, social orientation, and audience.

Even though it may seem on the surface to have little direct relationship to the history of burlesque, this shift is worth examining in some detail. Vaudeville and burlesque were negative reflections of each other. Each defined itself in terms of what the other was not. Thus, by looking at the manner by which vaudeville was constructed as a form of popular leisure, we can better understand what burlesque represented both to its devotees and to those who attended vaudeville in part, at least, because it was *not* burlesque.

Even before the 1862 crackdown, some New York concert saloon managers had attempted to attract a mixed audience by featuring "ladies matinees" during which all drinking and smoking were forbidden. It is unknown whether such matinees succeeded in overcoming women's reluctance to frequent places where, in the evenings, their less "respectable" sisters were the primary attractions.[39] It was not until the early 1880s that a clown turned concert saloon manager, Tony Pastor, demonstrated that by relying on high-quality talent, variety could be made profitable in the absence of liquor, and, further, that by severing the concert saloon's connection with liquor and sexuality, its audience could be expanded to include women as well as men. Having managed a "respectable" concert saloon in the Bowery for a number of years, Pastor finally moved out of the saloon business and into the variety business in 1881, when he took over the theater in the Tammany Society building on Fourteenth Street, just a block east of Union Square. By this time Union Square had become the center of the New York theater district, and its proximity to the retail shopping area stretching up Broadway between Fourteenth and Twenty-third streets (the "ladies mile," as it was called) helped to position Pastor to attract a more upscale, "family" audience.[40] Pastor made his the most famous variety theater of the 1880s and 1890s by offering his audiences a steady flow of the best talent available, which, as a performer himself, he helped to nurture and develop. Pastor banned drinking and smoking in his theater and removed blue material from the acts he booked.

O O O   **B. F. Keith and the Rise of Vaudeville**

Pastor certainly played a major role in establishing a new audience for variety and, in New York at least, in loosening variety's ties to prostitution and rowdy, working-class leisure. But as a performer/ manager whose ambitions did not exceed the walls of his one theater, Pastor was by 1890 a throwback to an earlier era in theater history. Others also saw the potential of using variety to cater to the entertainment tastes of what Albert McLean calls the "new folk": the class of urban white-collar workers and their families that expanded enormously between 1870 and 1910 and that "was to form the basis of the mass consumer market."[41] The key figure in the transformation of variety as a performance medium into vaudeville – the appropriation of variety as the basis for a large-scale system of purpose-built theaters, peripatetic performers, and booking agents – was Benjamin Franklin Keith. Keith came to many of the same conclusions regarding the future of variety as did Pastor. But unlike the popular rotund clown, Keith was an ambitious entrepreneur with no performance heritage. Furthermore, Keith's brand of vaudeville emerged from the context of the Boston dime museum rather than the concert saloons of the Bowery.

Having toured with circuses for several years as a seller of gimcracks, Keith joined the staff of Bunnell's Museum in New York in the late 1870s.[42] Like Wood's, where Lydia Thompson had played a decade earlier, Bunnell's was a dime museum, one of the first to charge so small a fee for admission to its stage show and collection of curiosities. Bunnell's exhibition of wax figures, two-headed chickens, and bearded ladies – standard fare at American dime museums by the late 1870s – was a far cry from what the founders of the American museum movement had envisioned in the 1790s. These public-spirited citizens, such as Charles Willson Peale of Philadelphia, had seen the need to make available to the public places for the demonstration of the latest scientific advances as well as exhibitions of the flora and fauna of the yet unexplored American continent – a sort of architectural National Geographic.[43] By the 1840s, most American museums had come under the control of men who used the institution's scientific legacy as a means of circumventing religious and moral prohibitions against theatrical amusements. As we have seen, P. T. Barnum was instrumental in the transition of the American museum from temple of science to palace of freaks. Barnum acquired Peale's New York Museum in 1843 and, largely through his advertising genius, made it by 1851 the most popular and famous museum in the country.

The exhibition room with attached lecture hall of the early nineteenth-century museum had by mid-century evolved into an area for the display of curiosities and a theater; in more modest museums, a portion of the room was set off for theatrical performances. On the stage would "perform" certain of the human curiosities – the rubber-skin man, the bearded lady, the alligator boy – as well as variety performers. The combination of variety acts with human and inanimate curiosities helped to solve a nagging structural problem with the dime museum. Even Barnum found that a Feejee Mermaid or a General Tom Thumb could not be located (or manufactured) on a frequent, regular basis. Inanimate curiosities – stuffed animals, wax figures, religious relics – usually remained attractions for only a brief time. The use of itinerant and local performers gave museum managers a base on which to build a regular clientele. The half man/half dog might be transparently bogus, the collection of African death masks dusty and familiar, but there was sure to be something to entertain museum patrons on the variety bill.

By the late 1870s, when Keith encountered them professionally for the first time, museums had become associated with the working and lower-middle classes. Barnum's, Bunnell's, and Moses Kimball's Boston Museum were at the pinnacle of American museums in the 1870s and drew from the most diverse audience. Most others were much less pretentious affairs. In New York, they lined the Bowery, some occupying quickly renovated storefronts.[44]

After a year at Bunnell's and another traveling with Barnum's circus, Keith moved his family to Boston, where in early January 1883 he converted a hat store at 565 Washington Street into "reception rooms" for a single attraction, "Little Alice, the Baby Queen," a tiny, prematurely born infant. At what Keith first called his New York Dime Museum, Little Alice was soon joined by other attractions, including Dora "the beautiful tattooed lady" and Miss Mary Cole "with the extraordinary and luxuriant growth of hair." By May, Keith and his partner had opened a second-floor "Theater Room" for the performance of variety acts, which were repeated hourly.[45]

For the next several years Keith and a succession of partners struggled to make the museum profitable. Being unable to match competing museums' emphasis on museum attractions, Keith featured variety and dramatic performances. In the summer of 1885, he instituted a "continuous performance" policy for his stage shows: the variety bill was repeated throughout the day without lowering the curtain, so that there was always a show for the patron to see between ten in the morning and the museum's closing at ten that evening. Keith claimed that 19,000 patrons visited what he now called the Gaiety Theater and Museum in the first week of continuous performance.[46]

With the success of continuous performance, Keith set his cap for a more upscale audience than the one that came to the Gaiety for its museum attractions. His theater was well situated to attract a more middle-class family audience. The four-hundred-room Adams House Hotel was next door, and directly across the street was the R. H. White department store, one of the largest in New England. Within a few blocks in either direction on Washington Street were six of Boston's nine theaters. Keith's problem in attracting a "respectable" audience to his variety shows was quite different from that of Tony Pastor's. In Boston, variety did not have nearly so strong a connection to rowdy, drunken, morally questionable entertainment as it did in New York. In the 1860s liquor licensing laws prohibited theatrical performances of any kind in taverns. Moreover, the number of saloons in the city was strictly regulated, thus removing the temptation to skirt the law in order to gain a competitive advantage. Thanks to Moses Kimball, middle-class theatergoers in Boston associated variety with wholesome, family amusement, not immorality, salaciousness, and drink. Even before Kimball's success with *The Drunkard* in the early 1840s, he had offered a variety show that became "the accepted diversion of the most decorous Bostonians." In short, Keith's problem was not removing the taint of immorality from variety so much as it was severing its connections with working-class leisure in the minds of his prospective middle-class patrons.[47]

Now convinced that his future and fortune lay with appealing to more bourgeois tastes, Keith in 1886 acquired the lease on the recently renovated nine-hundred-seat Bijou Theater, giving him one of the most distinctive theaters in the city. Within eight months of the opening of the Bijou as a variety and comic opera venue, the *Clipper* announced that Keith had found a new way to "coin cash."[48] Legitimate theater patrons were attracted by the chance to see lyric theater at a fraction of the price charged at other houses. Keith also made sure that anything that might offend even the most proper Bostonian was expunged from variety acts. Special efforts were made to attract female shoppers and their children to afternoon performances. The move to the Bijou put some conceptual distance between variety and its origins as a dime museum, with its freaks and gawking farmhands. However, Keith shrewdly maintained a vestige of the museum in the lobby's "art gallery," which provided a sense of continuity for Gaiety regulars. For this group, which most likely rarely attended regular theaters, the Bijou was a palace of wonders, with its horseshoe-shaped, electrically lighted proscenium and domed Moorish ceiling. For the newer middle-class patrons, the theatrical environment of the Bijou was a bit more eccentric but no less impressive than what they found in legitimate theaters. Both groups and those in between were made to feel at home at the Bijou, and the modular format of the variety portion of the bill ensured that no segment of the audience would go away completely disappointed.[49]

What Keith accomplished was nothing short of a reintegration of the American theatergoing audience, which had been fragmented in the 1850s. But his idea of the reintegrated audience was hardly that of the antebellum theater, with its noisily contentious class factions and struggles between management and audience over who "called the tune." Keith's notion of an entertainment that would "appeal to all classes of people equally" assumed the centrality of bourgeois values and norms of appropriate discourse, bearing, subject matter, and behavior both onstage and in the audience. As he recalled in 1911, his aim was to "give the public a nice, refined, pleasing theatrical entertainment." Performers put it another way, calling the circuit of vaudeville theaters that would eventually bear his name the "Sunday School Circuit," meaning that nothing could be uttered onstage that could not be said in church.[50]

Patrons were similarly expected to behave with proper bourgeois decorum. Armies of uniformed ushers policed all parts of the theater, handing out fliers asking ladies to remove their hats and gentlemen not to stamp their feet, smoke, or talk during the acts. A bit of polite applause was all that was tolerated as audience response. In the early days, some of Keith's working-class patrons had to be taught how to behave, and Keith was not above playing the role of schoolmaster. At one performance he took the stage to remonstrate the gallery, whose occupants had dared to raise their voices in approval of an act. "I know that you mean no harm by it," Keith said, "and only do it from the goodness of your hearts, but others in the audience don't like it, and it does not tend to improve the character of the entertainment, and I know you will agree with me that it is better to omit it hereafter." At the Bowery Theater in the 1830s such an admonition might have led to a riot; it certainly would have occasioned a hail of peanuts, apple cores, and assorted other missiles upon the head of the manager injudicious enough to infringe on the audience's rights. Fifty years later, however, and in the context of Keith's reintegrated popular theater, the response (as Keith remembers it, at least) was quite different: "As I walked off, I received a round of applause from the whole house including the gallery. And that was the last of the noise from the gallery gods."[51]

The Keith brand of vaudeville included not just squeaky-clean acts and well-behaved audiences but theater environments that were shrines to bourgeois notions of taste, luxury, and cleanliness. Edward F. Albee was placed in charge of the construction and decoration of the expanding chain of Keith vaudeville theaters, and it was his sense of what bourgeois patrons would regard as "refined" along with his obsession with detail that expunged from the Keith vaudeville environment any hint of its proletarian origins.

Albee's influence on the direction of vaudeville can perhaps best be seen in his supervision of the construction and decoration of Keith's new Boston house, which was called simply B. F. Keith's New Theater. Opened in 1894, it was the first of a new generation of vaudeville palaces and as such the first, as one chronicler of the Boston stage puts it, "to appropriate the splendors of the legitimate theater and even of the opera house for lowly, despised variety entertainment."[52] Albee drew inspiration not only from the scale and amenities of the legitimate theater but also from what the American bourgeoisie assumed European palaces, villas, and public buildings must look and feel like – which meant what they would look and feel like if they had utilized the latest American building and decorating techniques. The Washington Street facade of the New Theater incorporated marble pillars, pilasters,

gargoyles, *and* ornamental ironwork, as well as stained glass and elec-
tric lights. In the lobby there was a "Bureau of Information," with
telephones, messengers, and writing desks. The lobby and hallways
were floored in white marble and lined with leather sofas, original
paintings, and huge plate-glass mirrors. Restrooms became a "smoking
and reading room" for gentlemen and "suites of rooms . . . furnished
with dressing cases and every toilet requisite" for the ladies. Albee's
mania for cleanliness extended even to the state-of-the-art boiler room,
where patrons who were given the grand tour found a red velvet carpet
leading to the furnace, "oiling cans . . . standing on gilt onyx-topped
tables, just as if they were handsome toilet bottles," and stokers wearing
spotless white uniforms.[53] No doubt Keith's obsession with the whole-
someness of the acts appearing on his stage and with rigidly defined
norms for audience behavior and Albee's equally compulsive standards
of cleanliness were indications of a deeply felt need to separate their
enterprise and themselves from all associations with "the low."[54]

○ ○ ○   **Vaudeville and Burlesque:
Consolidation and Excorporation**

Although Keith and Albee were by no means the only entrepreneurs responsible for effecting the shift from variety to vaudeville,
their strategies set the tone for this nascent show business industry.[55]
They were key figures in what Frederick Snyder has called the "respectability mania," by which middle-class audiences were attracted to variety by a combination of morally unexceptionable acts, tightly policed
audience behavior, and theater environments that realized bourgeois
dreams of European upper-class splendor.[56] The rise of vaudeville is
but another chapter in the history of the consolidation of the American
bourgeoisie – consolidation accomplished through simultaneous cultural incorporation and excorporation. In terms of performance, vaudeville was simply the aggregate of all the forms of entertainment from
which it took attractions. Vaudeville existed only as a distinctive presentational, environmental, and institutional form; in terms of content,
vaudeville was nothing and everything. Although certain types of acts
became standards on the vaudeville program, virtually every show business attraction that could fit on a stage appeared in vaudeville – with, of

course, the important qualification that it had to be morally unobjectionable and satisfy middle-class notions of propriety and taste. Vaudeville absorbed a number of forms of popular entertainment that previously had been relatively independent of any particular presentational venue: shadowgraphy, magic lantern shows, puppetry, and magical illusion, among them. In the mid-1890s, vaudeville even gave a home to a carefully sanitized and refined version of living pictures. At Koster and Bial's Music Hall (which, despite its name, was by 1895 a vaudeville theater on the order of Keith's or Proctor's), nine tableaux from Gounod's *Faust* were presented in the spring of 1895, accompanied by excerpts from the opera score. At the same theater the following spring, projected motion pictures made their American debut. Vaudeville would provide the infant motion picture industry with its most important outlet for exhibition during its first decade. Before vaudeville theaters installed their own projectors and booths in the early 1900s, films, projectors, and operators traveled the vaudeville circuits just like jugglers or animal acts.[57]

The transition from variety to vaudeville also marked the incorporation of a diverse audience. The admission price at a Keith theater – as low as fifteen cents for a balcony seat during the day to as much as seventy-five cents for a box seat in the evening – placed vaudeville within the reach of a much larger segment of the population than did the legitimate theater. By the same token, Keith had so completely removed vaudeville from its working-class context that Mrs. Jack Gardner, the "grand dame" of Boston society in the 1890s, bought a box at Keith's New Theater for the 1894–95 season.[58] Because Keith's brand of continuous performance vaudeville bent over backward not to offend the most delicate moral sensibilities, and because its theaters were open from late morning on, vaudeville was the first form of commercial theatrical entertainment to draw a large portion of its audience from unescorted, middle-class women. By the 1890s, vaudeville theaters were frequently located in or near busy retail districts, where women could drop by after shopping excursions.

These women also brought their children. By 1900 vaudeville was in fact "family" entertainment: it was estimated that at some theaters fully one-half of afternoon audiences and one-fourth of evening audiences were made up of children. As the treasurer of Keith's Providence theater put it in 1900, "The general character of the performance with its infinite variety and nothing to tire, its large amount of music and its generous proportion of laughter provoking features, appeals with special force to the children, to whom the ordinary drama is but a bore and anything but interesting or attractive." Middle-class mothers even felt secure leaving their children at Keith's theaters while they shopped.[59]

One of Keith's strategies for incorporation was the suppression of difference both in the audience and onstage. Both advertisements and ticket prices projected an image of vaudeville as an egalitarian institution. Whether a person paid fifteen cents or five times that amount for admission, once he or she passed through the door of a Keith theater that person became simply a "patron," entitled to use all of the house's facilities and to be treated with equal solicitousness by an army of ushers and attendants. Keith's publicity machine touted vaudeville as the realization in popular entertainment of American democratic ideals. Promotional brochures describing the Keith theaters reveled in the seeming contradiction that theaters aping the architectural excesses of European autocratic cultures were constructed for the American people. A 1913 booklet distributed at the Keith Palace in Cleveland describes it as

vaudeville as democratic

a millionaire's playhouse, a gigantic poor man's clubhouse, one of the most interesting experiments in democracy imaginable! In ancient Egypt, E. F. Albee would have erected a five-million dollar tomb for himself and he would have employed skilled artists to paint or carve the principal events of his life on the vases. . . . In Italy, Germany, France, or Denmark, he would have built vast halls to dazzle the eyes of the few who were commanded to be his guests. . . . In America? Being an American and being president of the B. F. Keith circuit of theaters, he erected his palace for the people. . . . And with tremendous capital at hand, he was as particular to make it a beautiful palace as was a Chinese, Italian or German monarch. It was erected, decorated, and furnished with the same good taste and elegance that a monarch would expend on his residential palace. There is no precedent as in foreign palaces. All are equals when once inside and beyond the bronze gates. First come, first admitted. It's all decidedly a Yankee idea! . . . Who ever heard of such a thing before E. F. Albee had his wonderful dream that came true?[60]

equality
on
bourg.
terms

But in exchange for becoming the socially undifferentiated "patron," the audience member implicitly agreed to abide by Keith and Albee's rigid code of bourgeois manners, demeanor, behavior, and restraint. Everyone was "equal" so long as everyone played the role of a member of the bourgeoisie. Ushers and, in some of their earlier theaters, bouncers ensured that those bold enough to deviate from this code were either brought into line or deprived of their citizenship in this new egalitarian society.

What Keith's patrons saw and heard onstage was touted as an infinite variety of attractions, but it was an infinity within a tightly circumscribed universe of attractions whose values could not be construed as significantly different from those Keith ascribed to the ladies and gentlemen in his audience. One of the first excisions Keith required of all acts playing his theaters was anything resembling "blue" material, including double entendres – that is, words or phrases in which one could discover two possible meanings: one innocuous, the other sexually suggestive. Douglas Gilbert claims that every Keith theater had a notice tacked to its backstage bulletin board. It read in part: "If you have not the ability to entertain Mr. Keith's audiences without risk of offending them, do the best you can. Lack of talent will be less open to censure than would be an insult to a patron. If you are in doubt as to the character of your act consult the local manager before you go on the stage, for if you are guilty of uttering anything sacrilegious or even suggestive you will be immediately closed and will never again be allowed in a theater where Mr. Keith is in authority."[61]

The extent of Keith's determination to eradicate difference as the basis of pleasure in his theaters can be seen in a letter he wrote to his Boston booking manager in 1912. Keith, then already retired from the day-to-day operation of his vaudeville empire, reflected on his early career as a sidewalk peddler of a device called the "endless match." He had become so adept at demonstrating the device that he challenged "the ability of the famous 'Irishman who can always light his pipe in a gale of wind.'" Having made this innocuous ethnic reference, Keith immediately apologizes, which leads him to comment on the removal of ethnic and other types of humor of difference from his theaters:

Many of us remember the time when free reference was made to and enjoyed by all classes in our public entertainments. But by degrees this has all gone by, and it is well it has, for in many cases the picture was so over-drawn as to be not wholly untrue but derogatory to the character represented, so that we are all glad that it has been eliminated. At one time our public officials were equally scored in a humorous or attempted humorous way which was often as badly portrayed as the different nationalities had been, so that they came to object so sternly as to prohibit entirely the attempted humor. Next came the "Mother-in-law," who was freely referred to, always humorously, without a thought of harm or injuring the feelings of those to whom the title might apply. One day a gentleman wrote me a letter about it, and I at once saw the justice of his polite protest and immediately ordered the expression out of all my theaters, and it has not since been used to my knowledge.[62]

Although some variety acts played both burlesque and vaudeville in the 1890s and despite the fact that the two forms are today often confused, their underlying principles were as different as night and day. In a world predicated on the suppression of difference there is no place for transgression, since transgression is nothing less than the presentation of a potentially troubling difference from established norms and codes. Whether the impertinent impersonations of masculinity in Thompsonian burlesque, or the overlaying of gender difference on racial otherness in the female minstrels, or the later running battles with municipal authorities over its sexual transgressiveness, burlesque was all the things vaudeville wanted no part of. Burlesque was structured around the body of the burlesque performer, its size and display foregrounding sexual difference and marking it as the body of the low other. Without the performer's body, there was no burlesque. Vaudeville had no body. The eight to twelve acts that constituted the standard vaudeville bill were less a fragmented vaudeville body than they were interchangeable parts in vaudeville's performance machine. Indeed, vaudeville managers were among the first show business entrepreneurs to apply the principles of industrial standardization and mass production to popular entertainment: each act had to conform to vaudeville's performance requirements (no less than seven and no more than twenty minutes) and each had to fulfill a particular function in a performance system that had been carefully constructed to manipulate the expectations and desires of the audience.[63]

O O O   **The Industrialization of Vaudeville
and Burlesque**

Although vaudeville and burlesque were imbued with very
different performance spirits, after 1890 both forms emerged as popular
entertainment industries that aspired to monopoly. Burlesque took its
cue from patterns of industrial concentration that were already apparent in vaudeville and the legitimate theater.[64] By the beginning of the
new century, vaudeville had become the dominant force in American
show business. Vaudeville expanded first into other large urban centers,
which had experienced a fivefold population increase since the Civil
War. In 1900, when there were no fewer than twelve vaudeville theaters
in New York City, Keith's four theaters alone were selling more than a
million tickets each year, his Boston house attracting 40,000 patrons
each week (a figure representing 14 percent of the city's total population) and grossing more than $20,000.[65]

As early as 1895, some vaudeville entrepreneurs began to realize the
competitive advantage to be gained by linking their own theaters or
small circuits with others so as to monopolize the time of particular acts
for an entire season and in doing so to bargain for lower weekly salaries
by eliminating gaps in their schedules.[66] By 1901, Keith was obliged to
protect his own position. In January he called a meeting of the country's
major vaudeville interests, east and west, persuading them to form a
classic oligopoly to reduce the salaries of performers, respond to the
formation of a labor union by vaudeville performers, and limit competition among members by carving up the country into protected territories
for each circuit. By the end of the meeting, sixty-two of the sixty-seven
most important vaudeville theaters in the country had been united
under the banner of the Vaudeville Managers' Association (VMA).[67]

Keith and other founders of the VMA realized that the keystone of
their plans to insulate themselves from potential competition and
higher business costs lay in the mechanism by which acts were booked.
Consequently, they formed under the VMA umbrella a booking office
through which every act had to secure its time on any of the members'
circuits. The booking operation covered its costs and made a handsome
profit for its parent organization by charging a 5 percent commission on
the weekly salary of every act booked. Vaudeville performers, who

already paid 5 percent to their agents, now saw salary levels cut (as competition among theaters and circuits evaporated) at the same time that they were charged an additional 5 percent booking fee.[68]

While Keith and Albee were contemplating the need for a vaudeville trust, burlesque theater owners and producers were coming to the same conclusion. As burlesque became consolidated in the 1880s and 1890s as a set of theaters devoted largely if not exclusively to it and as a group of producers who organized touring shows, it followed much the same pattern as legitimate theater and variety during the same period. Individual theaters negotiated separately with producers to fill out each week in a given season. In the 1890s, as burlesque expanded into more cities and more theaters in the largest cities, competition for troupes increased. In response, new companies were formed, challenging the position of established troupes. Rivalry among theaters and fear among existing troupes that newer ones might usurp their positions prompted both producers and theater owners to meet in 1900 to organize their respective ends of the business as the Travelling Vaudeville and Burlesque Managers' Association of America. The thirty-three principal burlesque theaters included in the trust made it possible for a troupe to play a full forty-week season (with seven "repeat" weeks).

The burlesque trust was not nearly so successful an oligopoly as the Vaudeville Managers' Association, however. Unlike the Keith organization, no single force in burlesque theater ownership was dominant enough to hold its competing factions in line. Furthermore, in vaudeville, power was inherently invested in theaters and in booking agencies, against which any individual act was virtually powerless. Burlesque was comprised of two much more equally matched forces: theater owners and producers. When in 1903 theater owners protested the custom by which the weekly box office gross was split with the burlesque company, producers promptly announced that they would supply only six weeks of the following season's forty-week schedule. Theater owners dropped their protest. By 1905 the theater owners had split into two bitterly opposed circuits or "wheels" of theaters: the Western Wheel or Empire Circuit and the Eastern Wheel or Columbia Circuit. Each had its own producers and its own personality. The Empire Circuit became known for "hot" shows that tested the limits of civic tolerance. The Columbia Circuit vacillated between eschewing sensationalism, self-righteously advertising itself as "refined" and "clean" burlesque, and, when this strategy failed to draw business (which was most of the time), competing with the Empire at its own game.[69]

As a branch of show business, burlesque's high-water mark occurred at the same time as vaudeville's: around 1910. However, burlesque in its heyday remained in the shadow of its respectable bourgeois opposite. In 1912 approximately seventy touring burlesque companies played at one hundred theaters across the country and employed five thousand persons. A burlesque company fully booked on one of the wheels could expect to gross $100,000 in a season. By comparison, in 1906 *Billboard* listed over four hundred theaters that were devoted totally or in part to vaudeville (thirty-three of them operated by Keith alone), and the total audience for vaudeville by the turn of the century already exceeded one million. With the exception of San Francisco, burlesque was largely an East Coast and Midwest phenomenon. Strong religious and moral objections prevented it from taking hold in the South. Burlesque was also primarily a big-city phenomenon by 1910, as distinct from vaudeville, which played in any number of medium-sized American cities. By 1912, a few burlesque theaters rivaled first-class vaudeville houses in scale and appointments (Chicago's Star and Garter and Columbia; Brooklyn's New Empire; and, grandest of all, the Columbia Circuit's flagship Columbia Theater at Forty-seventh and Broadway), but most burlesque theater owners and managers rightly assumed that their patrons were not principally interested in marble floors and onyx oil-can stands.[70]

Within two decades of Lydia Thompson's American debut, burlesque had become a show business industry whose success was based on catering to the audience that first the legitimate theater and then vaudeville had excorporated: white working- and lower-middle-class males who continued to seek commercial entertainment apart from women and their families. This core audience was augmented by more middle-class single and family men on a night out with "the boys," farmers taking in the sights of the big city, and even a few intellectuals who preferred its earthiness and gaiety to more "respectable" forms of entertainment. Burlesque offered them an aesthetic form and a place of their own. Industrialization regularized the burlesque form. Each week saw another burlesque company come to town, but patrons knew that regardless of the name of the troupe on the poster, they could depend on the structure and content of the week's show being yet another slight variation of a tried-and-true formula: ethnic comics, variety acts, sketches, and, of course, a chorus of "divine creatures" in revealing costumes. Industrialization also located burlesque in particular theatrical spaces, which gradually became devoted to it exclusively. Whereas Lydia Thompson and the female minstrel troupes that succeeded her in the 1870s played theaters that might have featured a melodrama the week before and a variety ensemble the week following, by 1890 it was much more common for burlesque troupes to play only in burlesque theaters. The isolation of the burlesque form in its own autonomous wheels of big-city theaters made great economic sense for both theater owners and burlesque producers. But it also had the effect of further separating the burlesque experience from the bourgeois mainstream of American theater and culture and creating a self-contained burlesque world.

O O O O O O O O

Burlesque at Century's End

I long to do something to startle society

As I sit in my opera box,

Where our talk the divine music shields,

My mind wanders off several blocks

From dear Wagner to Weber and Fields.

And at Del's when the opera's done

As I sup on things dainty and dear,

I'd pass it all by just for one

Swiss cheese sandwich accompanied with beer.

– Fiddle-dee-dee

○ ○ ○ ○ ○ ○ ○ ○ ○ ○ ○ ○ ○ ○ ○ ○

As burlesque became marginalized in the 1870s as a working-class form – its performance structure and content separated from that of vaudeville and its venues removed from the realm of bourgeois theater and into urban houses catering almost exclusively to its male audiences – it also largely disappeared from view in the mainstream press. Now that the threat to bourgeois values had been safely contained within working-class culture, commentators ceased railing about burlesque in the pages of middle-class magazines. Now that burlesque was on the road and not in New York's leading theaters, the opening of a new burlesque show went unnoticed and unreviewed by the daily press. Between the early 1870s and its slow death after 1930, burlesque surfaced sporadically in mainstream media only as a problem associated with the lower strata of urban culture, as something that needed to be policed, restrained, cleaned up.

In the latter decades of the nineteenth century, discourse on burlesque was relocated in relation to its new "lower" class male audience. To be sure, theatrical trade papers covered burlesque as an aspect of show business, but irregularly and usually on the back pages. Burlesque figured most prominently during this period in forms directed toward its likely audience: in the tens if not hundreds of thousands of carte-devisite photographs of burlesque performers sold for a few cents each in the 1870s and 1880s, in the color posters that were plastered across the front of local theaters in advance of an arriving troupe, and in the pages of "men's" papers, which could be found in barrooms, barbershops, and pool halls (and, no doubt, carefully hidden in "respectable" households as well) in cities and towns across the country.

The first half of this chapter considers the traces of burlesque culture of the 1880s and 1890s that survive in these sources, particularly the *National Police Gazette* and burlesque posters. Unfortunately, aside from them and sporadic coverage in theatrical trade papers, there is

evidence problem

little evidence on which to construct a picture of the world of burlesque in its first three decades as a male, working-class entertainment form. Most of the burlesque scripts from this period have long since vanished; its early stars or entrepreneurs (with the exception of Michael Leavitt) did not leave memoirs, and its primary audience of plumbers, drummers, and factory workers did not keep diaries that anyone bothered to save. Nevertheless, the *Police Gazette*'s fundamentally ambivalent treatment of burlesque and the inversive universe of the burlesque poster together provide us fascinating, if limited, insight into the possible meanings of burlesque for its audiences.

The second half of this chapter takes up burlesque's further structural transformation in the 1890s as the form focused even more on female sexual spectacle, causing the burlesque performer to lose her "voice" and much of her transgressive power. Also as a result of this transformation burlesque became linked to yet another popular entertainment form structured around a low-other figure: the freak show. As with the minstrel show, there would seem to be little similarity between burlesque and the display for profit of physical oddity and deformity. Yet, like the relationship between burlesque and minstrelsy, burlesque and the freak show were joined at a deeper level of structural homology.

O O O   **Burlesque in the Barbershop:
The *Police Gazette***

Begun as a chronicle of what it saw as the alarming rise of criminal activity in the country and of instances of police corruption, the *National Police Gazette* (known to most simply as the *Police Gazette*) struggled through a number of proprietors before being sold in 1878 to Richard Kyle Fox, who would own and edit the paper until his death in 1922. Fox, a seller of newspaper advertising who had only recently arrived in New York from Belfast, acquired the paper in settlement for debts owed him by an engraving firm that had itself become the paper's owner in the same manner. Even before Fox took over the paper's operation, the *Police Gazette* had found ample opportunities to link women on the stage with its regular accounts of criminal malefaction. In weekly columns bearing such titles as "Epidemic Evil" and "Vice's Varieties," the paper ran lurid stories on sensational crimes culled from newspapers and sent in by stringers from all over the country. Waiting their turn for a haircut and shave, readers might learn about "Negroes Outraging a White Man in Nansemond Co., Virginia" or "A Drunken Woman Ravished, Stripped Naked and Murdered." They might also read about Frank Rivers, proprietor of several concert saloons in New York and Philadelphia, whose "green and yellow villainy, elaborate, deliberate, persevering fraud, . . . shocking brutality, loathsome sensuality, barbarous outrage and impudent duplicity and imposture" were unmatched by any other criminal past or present. An orphan ("young, pretty, and of pure reputation") answered an ad in a Philadelphia newspaper for "ballet girls" at one of Rivers's concert saloons. Promising her a position and ballet lessons, Rivers "persuaded that orphan girl to consent to her own destruction and permanent dishonor" and, after he had had his way with her, threw her out. Rivers had, of course, sealed the unfortunate woman's fate: "Through four years immediately following that melancholy night, this outraged and friendless girl travelled along the desolate ways that wind through the 'chambers of death,' sinking, as in all such cases, into lower and yet lower gradations of dishonor and abandonment, till at the expiration of the aforesaid time, she finally breathed her last breath and heaved her last sigh in one of the vilest dens of sin and iniquity in . . . Philadelphia."[1]

Under Fox's editorship, the *Police Gazette* settled on crime, sports, and theatrical sexuality as the objects of its journalistic discourse – a formula that would make the paper the most famous and successful tabloid of its type in the United States. After a few years the latter two subjects came to predominate. Representations of women in the *Police Gazette* were sharply bifurcated. Fox continued the paper's long-standing tradition of running stories of the ruin of young women in the city. These women were almost always bourgeois, often from small cities or towns, and, as with Frank Rivers's orphaned victim, frequently drawn into the maelstrom of moral and physical degeneration through their contact with working-class show business. A November 1878 cover story (complete with full-page woodcut) related the demise of Georgina Livingstone, "an accomplished and well bred but fallen girl" from a "noted and aristocratic" Ohio family who, "frenzied with remorse," attempted suicide in an Indiana brothel. The following week there appeared a first-person account of a young woman raised in "a quiet, peaceful village in West Virginia, far from the city's feverish pulsations, sin and dissipation," who was seduced, taken to New Orleans, and abandoned. Unable to find work, "I took the awful leap in the dark, which thousands of unfortunates similarly situated have done before me. I became a woman of the town, and a terrible life I have found it."[2]

In these stories the downward path is always irreversible, and moral deterioration always leads to physical and mental collapse. The "impulsive" daughter of one of the wealthiest men in Cincinnati left her husband for another man, who abandoned her in Chicago. There she wound up in a "maison de joie," where "she plunged into the turbid tide of dissipation with a zeal that astonished those around her. . . . Such a course of excessive dissipation brought its natural results, and her mind began to give way under the fearful strain imposed upon it." She was finally committed to an asylum, where "today the rich casket, despoiled of its jewels and converted into a living tomb, is all that remains of Blanche Bennett."

Under Fox, however, what had been an almost totally unrelieved morality drama lamenting the fall of good bourgeois women under the influence of sensuality, alcohol, and the lure of the city was juxtaposed with the paper's celebration of burlesque's feminine sexuality. Beginning in late 1878, the *Police Gazette* began featuring woodcuts of burlesque performers under the heading, "Favorites of the Footlights." No stories of moral degradation accompanied the likenesses, merely brief captions describing the image as that, for example, of "Miss Jenny Hughes, the accomplished and popular vocalist and burlesque artist" or "Miss Farrington, a comely and graceful coryphee." "Footlight favorites" appeared in every issue of the *Police Gazette* for more than twenty years.

In stories specifically about burlesque performers, they were represented as women freed from the moral restraints of bourgeois culture, both onstage and elsewhere. In an 1880 article entitled "In the Off Act," the author is invited by the scene painter at a burlesque theater to visit him backstage during a performance. During the olio, four "jolly girls" in the troupe pass the time with the two men drinking beer and playing poker: "There was a blonde prince in blue and silver, a brunette cavalier in scarlet and gold, and two awfully magnificent indescribable somethings in the costumes anyone . . . will be able to imagine for themselves."[3]

The image of four "magnificent" women in revealing burlesque costumes playing poker with two sports is an interesting and telling one. The author is invited backstage for a privileged look. What he discovers is that offstage burlesque performers retain their glamour and allure, but they also enjoy the same diversions as working-class men: drinking beer and playing poker. They become in this story a sort of positive obverse of William Dean Howells's alien sex: they are clearly described as embodying both masculine and feminine qualities (one is dressed as a prince, another as a cavalier), and yet here the combination attracts rather than repels.

However, the combination of expressive sexuality and freedom from bourgeois restraint could also produce a much more threatening figuring of the burlesque performer: the predatory female who used her allure to ensnare and manipulate her male victims. It was in these waning decades of the nineteenth century that the gold digger first appeared in American popular culture. She might be represented specifically as a burlesque performer or more generally as a "chorus girl" or "soubrette." She was the opposite of the middle-class woman as victim, for whom the theater was but an early stop on her way down into a moral, physical, and social abyss. The gold digger was a working-class woman, who, by virtue of that class status, was represented as having little if any "reputation" to lose. For her the stage was an arena where she could use her physical charms and her position as an onstage object of desire to achieve the material trappings of bourgeois culture by manipulating the affections of her male admirers.

In some representations, the gold digger's power over men is treated lightly, with a wink and a nod, almost in celebration of her ability to extract what she wants from bourgeois culture by transgressing its code of feminine propriety. In a *Police Gazette* short story from 1899 about "Dolly of the Casino," a naive young woman is initiated into the ways of the gold digger. On her first night she overhears one of her fellow chorus girls report: "The fellow with the blond mustache in the box last night blew me off to six bottles. . . . I'm getting a friend to find out what business he's in, and if he's got any coin. I'm an expensive piece of furniture, I am." When Dolly expresses her puzzlement as to how the woman can afford an apartment costing two hundred dollars a month on her salary of fifteen dollars a week, "The girl looked at her a minute and then burst out laughing." Dolly then determines to take advantage of her own situation. One night she receives a twenty-dollar bunch of flowers from a man who, she is told, "has more money than he knows what to do with." She goes out with him to dinner, and over a third bottle of champagne he offers to set her up in an apartment. Several months elapse in the story's narration. We learn that Dolly has dyed her hair blonde, and, despite the fact that he gave her diamonds and a brougham, she has thrown over her first sugar daddy because he wanted to leave his wife to marry her. "I wouldn't marry the best man living," she explains. "You marry a man and there your finished. He grows tired of you. Keep on the stage and they'll all run their legs off trying to get you to smile at them."[4]

Appearing alongside tales of cunning Dolly and jolly, poker-playing burlesquers were representations of the gold digger's other side: the ruthless, greedy home breaker and femme fatale. As early as 1871, the *New York Clipper* – another source of contradictory representations of feminine sexuality – explained why the predatory female was so dangerous. Contrary to popular belief, the editorial began, women by nature are not morally superior to men. They are just as prone to vice as men, but their vices are of a different nature because of the different constitution of the feminine psyche:

> By nature women are plastic, more governed by impulse and passion than reason, generally of an emotional, nervous temperament, with strong affinities and repulsions, but capable, when guile or vice have destroyed the natural disposition, of degenerating into cold, calculating, cunning beings, making all things subservient to one pet object or ambition. Their softness and pliancy make them loveable to the ruder and coarser being, but, as eastern civilization has taught us, softness, pliancy, gracious words, and graceful actions are not always accompanied by the good feelings which they seem to indicate. What could exceed in suavity the manners of a Hindoostani court, and what, when the mask is removed could exceed its grossness and cruelty? . . . Few will dispute the fact that a bad woman is worse than a bad man. . . . There is a certain circle marked by society, and, so long as women keep within it, they are very careful of their characters; but once let them step outside of it and they become more thoroughly reckless than men ever become.[5]

In other words, once a woman steps out of the circle of bourgeois respectability, she reverts to a primal predatory state in the face of which some men are powerless.

An 1880 story in the *Police Gazette*, entitled "Bewitched by an Actress," illustrates the fact that "a woman of shameless manner and impure life will have over a man an influence that cannot be shaken – an influence which some angel of purity could never possess." A middle-class man, married to a pretty woman of "thoroughly domestic" tastes, takes up with a "variety actress of the higher class" (a burlesque performer) whose profession is, by her own admission, "the means to another end." She is blonde (of course) and of a complexion "that paint and powder could never give." The man's wife discovers his infidelity and confronts the actress. "I don't want him," she responds. "When I have bled him, completely, and got all out of him I can get, you are welcome to him." To complete this cautionary tale, the narrator reports that he saw the husband sometime later: "His face showed that a pulmonary complaint from which he suffered was making rapid inroads upon his health, and I saw the impress of the hand of death." The implicit warning of this tale was, of course, directed primarily at bourgeois men and those who aspired to that stratum, since the gold digger would hardly waste her time "bleeding" a man who had nothing to give.[6]

Representations of the predatory woman and her effects on bourgeois men were by no means limited to the pages of the *Police Gazette*. In his study of misogyny in Western painting of this period, Bram Dijkstra points out that "diabolical women with the light of hell in their eyes were stalking men everywhere in the art of the turn of the century." Images of innocent, maternal femininity of only a few decades before had given way to cruel Dianas, fatally attractive Salomes, voracious vampires, and personifications of animal brutality and implacable natural forces. Even when women were depicted as flowers – by the late nineteenth century already a hackneyed symbol of decorative femininity – they became "a nightmare vision of woman as a palpitating mass of petals reaching for the male in order to encompass him." Both the woman as vampire and the image of the young working-class woman represented "the personification of everything negative that linked sex, ownership, and money." The alternative to harnessing women's sexuality through marriage and procreation was seen as the wasting of male vitality in the satisfaction of women's sexual and material greed. But perhaps because these paintings were produced for the class whose men had the most to lose from this "nightmare confrontation with the flower of evil," the consequences of their yielding to feminine power were devastating. As Dijkstra puts it, "For the men of the second half of the nineteenth century . . . it seemed that the pleasures of the body were to be paid for with death." Gustave Moreau (1876), Edouard Toudouze (1886), and other painters returned to the Salome story, in which a man quite literally loses his head over a dancing girl.[7]

The threatening power of feminine sexuality embodied by the burlesquer and her more generic sister, the chorus girl, was kept in check in the working-class discourse on burlesque by displacing that power into the register of class relations. The predatory chorus girls in cartoons, stories, and other media were either explicitly or implicitly from the working class – the very fact that they were in burlesque or some other form of "illegitimate" show business removed them from the *Clipper*'s "certain circle" of middle-class respectability. Their victims, however, were frequently from the upper class and always at least from the middle class.

O O O   **The World of the Burlesque Poster**

Nowhere is this mapping of gender power relations over those of class more apparent than in the color posters produced to advertise traveling burlesque troupes from the 1870s on. Along with a number of other "firsts" he claims in his memoirs, Michael B. Leavitt takes credit for introducing lithographic theater posters to the United States when he brought back a supply of one-color lithographs from a trip to Europe in 1872. By the latter part of that decade, when lithographs began to take the place of block printing in theatrical advertisements, Leavitt claims that his six to eight touring burlesque companies each used $8,000 to $20,000 worth of posters every season.[8] Vaudeville relied on unillustrated playbills ("quarter sheets") for advertising, its weekly change of all eight to twelve acts making the preparation of elaborate lithographs by any given theater uneconomical. Burlesque troupes, on the other hand, traveled as full ensembles, performing the same "show" over the course of an entire forty-week season. Posters were its principal advertising medium. By 1890, full-color lithographic burlesque posters adorned theater fronts everywhere burlesque played in America. Highly pictorial, the posters' illustrations sometimes referred to the theme for a given troupe's show that season. More often than not, however, the posters advertised the troupe itself, illustrating not so much what a prospective patron would see onstage but rather the nature of burlesque's imaginary world.

A sampling of burlesque posters from the 1890s and early 1900s, preserved as copyright deposits at the Library of Congress, offers a glimpse into that world. It is first of all an inverted, reordinated world dominated in every respect by women. Wearing the various costumes of the burlesque stage, women crowd the mise-en-scène of these posters, forming platoons, parades, and chorus lines massed in the foreground of the image or extending through the background into infinity. In some cases, it is an exclusively female world; in others, greatly outnumbered males serve as onlookers, functionaries, or victims.

What is most striking about these posters is their celebration of charismatic female sexual power. Several posters represent this power through inversion, by placing burlesque-costumed women in traditionally masculine roles. In the High Rollers Extravaganza Company's poster for its burlesque of *Ben Hur*, "Bend Her," two gigantic, statuesque women (one of them wielding a horsewhip) drive careening chariots. An Imperial Burlesquers' poster, "Imperials Always to the Front," depicts a military drill team of well-endowed women, creating a pun on the poster's verbal legend. The posters leave no doubt that this sexual power is deployed in the domination of men. In the Bon-Ton Burlesquers' "On the String," five lilliputian men bound up in ribbons dance about the feet of a Gulliver-sized burlesquer while she pulls their "strings." In another High Rollers poster, "A Ten Strike," men have become human-headed duckpins sent flying by an athletic burlesquer bowler using balls marked "youth," "song," "dance," "wit," and "beauty." Her sisters stand, hands on hips, imperiously looking on or sit haughtily sipping wine. The prize for the most bizarre iconography among the posters must go to "The Beautiful Indian Maidens," in which a tribe of amazonian Indian warriors gather at a riverbank. In the background a stag flees for his life from his spear-hurling female pursuers, while in the foreground one of the huntresses holds her catch by

The High Rollers Extravaganza Company: "Bend Her."
(Prints and Photographs Division, Library of Congress)

the neck, displaying it for the viewer: a tiny, duck-headed, tuxedo-clad
man. Nearby, a flower-garlanded maiden emerges from the water
clutching a lobster-bodied, man-headed creature by the tail, while he/it
looks helplessly up at his captor.

Although it does not take an art critic to decipher the symbolism of
women launching bowling balls at male duckpins or amazonian warriors preying on duck-headed dandies, the burlesque posters' celebration of female sexual power and its goals is even more direct in other
examples. Several posters explicitly depict the economic manipulation
of men by gold-digging burlesquers. In "Dining a High Roller Girl after
the Show," a burlesquer triumphantly lights a cigarette while her un-
conscious, bald-headed victim slumps in his chair, his bulging wallet
open on the floor. In another from the same company, entitled "How the
High Roller Girls Do It," a chorus girl clips the tail from her poodle to
send one of her many admirers a lock of "her" hair.

If we assume that the "model viewer" of these posters was male (as it
almost certainly was, given the largely male audience for burlesque),
then burlesque's upside-down world of enormous, powerful women
and powerless, victimized men is explicable only when one takes into

The Imperial Burlesquers: "Imperials Always to the Front."
(Prints and Photographs Division, Library of Congress)

The Bon-Ton Burlesquers: "On the String."
(Prints and Photographs Division, Library of Congress)

The High Rollers Extravaganza Company: "A Ten Strike."
(Prints and Photographs Division, Library of Congress)

The Beautiful Indian Maidens.
(Prints and Photographs Division, Library of Congress)

The High Rollers Extravaganza Company:
"Dining a High Roller Girl."
(Prints and Photographs Division, Library of Congress)

The High Rollers Extravaganza Company:
"How the High Roller Girls Do It."
(Prints and Photographs Division, Library of Congress)

The Bon-Ton Burlesquers: "365 Days Ahead of Them All."
(Prints and Photographs Division, Library of Congress)

account the class difference between the men within that world and the intended viewer, inscribed in the posters largely by his absence from their sadistic narratives. The threatening qualities of that world, where women dominate and men are willingly if helplessly submissive, are defused and made pleasurable to the viewer by the construction of those dominated men as upper-class others. All of the male victims of the posters' wily chorus girls and gargantuan amazons are represented as unmistakably upper-class: they wear tuxedos, starched shirts, and even pince-nez. Furthermore, they are frequently depicted as "baldheads": the corps of wealthy, sexually frustrated but effete old men who, from the days of *The Black Crook* onward, are said to have occupied the front rows of feminine spectacles armed with opera glasses. The baldheads epitomize the male victims of gold diggers in these posters. Their pathetic fascination with feminine sexual display makes them easy marks, while their wealth makes them favorite targets. Moreover, there is little danger that the chorus girl will have to pay the sexual price the baldhead presumably desires in exchange for his slavish devotion and lavish gifts. As "Dining a High Roller Girl" makes clear, when the moment of truth comes, he turns out to be ineffectual, if not impotent.

The Rose Hill English Folly Company: "Our Boquet of Beauties."
(Prints and Photographs Division, Library of Congress)

Iconographically, the upper-class "mashers" are frequently represented in terms of a metonym for the luxurious life-style they offer – the lobster. In a High Rollers poster featuring Mamie Lamb, Lamb rides a red-hot stove turned carriage pulled by two giant lobsters. In a Bon-Ton Burlesquers poster, "A Warm Reception," a lobster dances with a burlesquer atop a dining table while three seated male admirers raise their champagne glasses in salute. In the 1890s new and spectacular restaurants opened along Broadway to accommodate the theater crowd and other "men about town." Rector's, Shanley's, Maxim's, Bustanoby's, and Churchill's all featured gilded interiors and specialized in expensive late-night suppers – so-called bird-and-bottle dinners. If a "sport" or a baldhead wanted to show off his "bird," these lobster palaces, as they were called, could oblige. If he desired more privacy, private dining rooms were available. Lobsters came to signify culinary extravagance, the elaborate setting in which such expensive fare was served, and the man who attempted to impress his dining companion by ordering it. The image of the wealthy sugar daddy entertaining a chorus girl at one of these lobster palaces was a familiar one by the turn of the century, particularly after the Harry Thaw murder trial in 1906 when, it was revealed, architect Stanford White had met and entertained Floradora Girl Evelyn Nesbit at Rector's.[9]

The world of the burlesque poster establishes for the working-class male burlesque audience a network of fantasy power relations that extend out from the figure of the sexually expressive, physically captivating burlesque performer. Her sexual appeal is guaranteed by its economic value. It can be used to obtain the trappings of the high life through an inversion of "normal" sexual power relations: the woman is clearly in control of the situation; the wealthy admirer is clearly taken advantage of. But in the exercise of that power, the burlesque performer becomes for the poster's viewer one of the working-class "us" whose domination is over the upper-class "them." The joke is on the baldheaded, tuxedo-clad men in the posters, not on the working-class men who are largely absent from them but present in the burlesque theater.

In the one poster in this collection in which recognizably "lower-class" men are prominently featured, the sexual power relations are quite different. A High Rollers poster, entitled "Initiating a High Roller," shows a gap-toothed, red-nosed, union-suited hobo holding a rope by which a burlesque performer, her hands tied behind her back, is

The High Rollers Extravaganza Company: "Mamie Lamb."
(Prints and Photographs Division, Library of Congress)

The Bon-Ton Burlesquers: "A Warm Reception."
(Prints and Photographs Division, Library of Congress)

suspended by her ankles over a barrel of beer. Five leering, lumpen-proletariat colleagues celebrate the baptism. Here the iconography of the burlesque world is itself inverted. The lobster-bodied swell held by the tail in the "Beautiful Indian Maidens" poster has been replaced by the upside-down figure of the chorus girl. The imagery of being "on the string" is repeated here but with the woman consigned to the other end. What results from this overturning of the already inverted world of the burlesque poster obviously is not, however, the reestablishment of bourgeois ordination, but rather another example of displaced abjection. The male figures in "Initiating a High Roller" do not stand in any direct way for the male, working-class burlesque audience. They are constructed as creatures of another low-other order – an ironic order marked in every way as low*est* in the burlesque poster-world hierarchy. Their "lowestness" is established by both their distance from bourgeois norms and by their inverted appropriation of the markers of upper-class style. If the qualities that mark the public image of the bourgeois male at this time are sobriety, moderation, industriousness, and gallantry, then the men who officiate at the initiation of the High Roller Girl are his opposite. They are irredeemably dissolute, drunken, and lecherous. Furthermore, except for their derby- and union-suit-wearing leader, they are dressed in the castoffs of upper-class male fashion: crumpled top hats and patched and ragged swallow-tailed cutaway coats.

The full irony of this image of lumpen-proletariat men in control of the world into which the burlesque performer must be initiated can only be seen in relation to the posters where the burlesquer dominates her rich admirers. The lowest of the low are shown to be in control of the process by which women are sexually empowered and endowed with the ability to make fools of those who in the "real" world of social relations sit atop its power hierarchy. The image of the burlesquer as initiate into an antibourgeois counterculture appears in another poster, in which the oppositional values of that culture are made clear. In the poster for Phil Sheridan's New City Sports Company, fourteen burlesquers wearing bat-ribbed capes and holding aloft torches form a semicircle in the middle of which stands the devil. He points toward a huge open book resting on the back of a grotesque demon, where a new member of the company has just signed or is about to sign her name. An innocent stands behind her (she is the only woman not dressed in burlesque costume), a look of horror on her face. Has she just witnessed

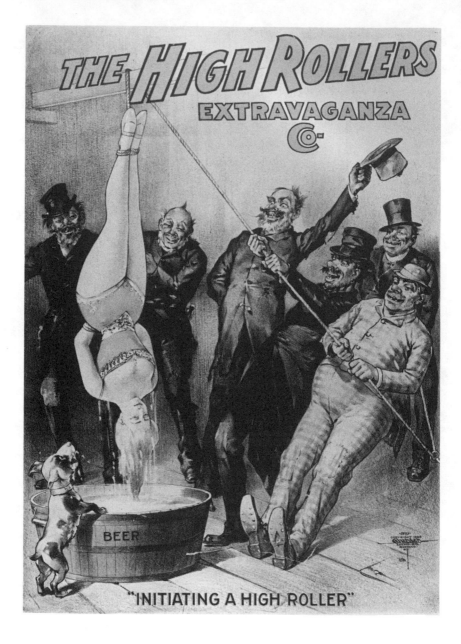

The High Rollers Extravaganza Company: "Initiating a High Roller."
(Prints and Photographs Division, Library of Congress)

the transformation of the novitiate from demure maiden to demonically empowered charmer? Is she next? A crowned skeleton looks down on the scene from his throne. The burlesque performer, then, does not so much learn the tricks of manipulating the "real world" social hierarchy as she is converted from adherence to its norms and values to a hedonistic credo based on sexual pleasure and material exploitation of the system.

Where does the intended viewer of the poster fit into its system of transgression and inversion? What, according to the logic of the posters, are the pleasures to be found inside the burlesque theater by the male, working-class spectator? The posters promise first of all that admission to the burlesque theater will buy the theatrical and hence spectatorial services of beautiful women — women so charming and desirable that they are able to ensnare the wealthiest of men. The High Roller Girl will perform for whoever has the price of a ticket. Part of her allure is her power to turn the tables on those men who would attempt to possess her, to dominate them and reduce them to midgets, comatose old men, ducks, and lobsters. But the burlesque patron is exempted from this threat of domination. He is in on the joke and rejoices at his working-class sister's ability to fleece and humiliate rich old men with much more money than good sense. She (the burlesque performer) is certainly a predator, but he (the spectator) is not the victim. Whatever extraclass sexual threat the burlesque performer might represent to the spectator is further defused by her construction as an exotic other. She is both the most desirable of women and so different from other women that she seems to belong to a separate species or to inhabit a separate world. The burlesque performer is the amazon warrior, the Roman charioteer, the devil's handmaiden. In the fantasy realms of stage and poster world, she is so distanced from ordinary women and real-life sexual relations that he can take pleasure in her display of charismatic sexuality without feeling threatened by it. He can even indulge masochistic fantasies of being dominated by her, knowing that sitting in the audience he is safely distanced and insulated from her power. She is to him an unobtainable object of desire, and that very unobtainability is his shield against her power. It is significant that when bourgeois discourse imagined women cut free from restraints on sexual expression, it usually consigned them to the category of criminal working-class sexuality — prostitution. They were either pitiful, doomed victims or vira-

Phil Sheridan's New City Sports Company.
(Prints and Photographs Division, Library of Congress)

ginous home wreckers. In the discursive universe of burlesque posters, on the other hand, sexually expressive women were constructed as exotic other without implication of criminal sexuality.

○ ○ ○   **Taking the High Road: The "Respectable" Burlesque of Weber and Fields**

As the burlesque performance became increasingly routinized and with the industry's oligopolistic structure militating against radical formal innovation, burlesque wheels, companies, and theaters differentiated themselves from each other principally according to the degree of their reliance on feminine sexual display. From the 1890s onward, burlesque was torn between two contrary strategies: whether to produce "hot" shows, which emphasized the displayed female body and blue humor, or to produce "clean" shows, which downplayed sexuality. The adoption of the first strategy usually elicited the best response from burlesque's core, working-class audience. However, it almost guaranteed that the audience would be limited to working-class males, and it ran the risk of calling burlesque to the unwanted attention of the police, reform groups, and politicians. The latter strategy was used in an attempt to broaden the audience for burlesque to include more women and more middle-class men. It was also the mode hot houses reverted to in the wake of a crackdown by civic authorities. The problem with the clean burlesque tack was that, in the absence of sexual display, there was little to attract patrons to burlesque that they could not get (and in better quality) from vaudeville.

The most successful examples of the clean burlesque strategy at the turn of the century were the productions of Weber and Fields.[10] The two men were so successful, in fact, that they left burlesque entirely. Joe Weber and Lew Fields began their career in comedy playing Bowery dime museums in the late 1870s. Not yet sixteen, they made their first appearance on the burlesque stage in 1884, when they performed their Dutch knockabout act at Miner's Bowery Theater. "Dutch" was an Americanization of *deutsch*, and a Dutch act relied on heavy German dialect and stereotyped "national characteristics" for its humor. As Mike and Myer, their act began:

Mike: I am delighfulness to meet you.

Myer: Der disgust is all mine.

Mike: I receivedidid a letter from mein goil, but I don't know how
        to writteninin her back.

Myer: Writteninin her back! Such an edumuncation you got it?
        Writteninin her back! You mean rotteninin her back. How
        can you answer her ven you don't know how to write?

Mike: Dot makes no nefer mind. She don't know how to read.[11]

For the next five years they toured with several variety companies. In
1890 they formed the Weber and Fields Own Company, which show-
cased the pair's enormously popular Dutch act. In 1896 they took over
the Imperial Music Hall at Broadway and Twenty-ninth Street.

Weber and Fields were a throwback to the days of the actor/manager
(they had toured with Tony Pastor's variety company in the 1880s), and
in many respects their Weber and Fields Music Hall was sui generis.
Unlike other burlesque theater managers, who used touring companies, Weber and Fields relied on their own stock company, a number
of whose members were stars in their own right: De Wolf Hopper, Sam
Bernard, David Warfield, and Fay Templeton, among them. In the wake
of the disastrous legitimate theatrical seasons during and immediately
following the depression of 1893–94, Weber and Fields were able to
attract to their theater first-order stars from comic opera, comedy, and
drama. They effected their greatest coup in 1899, when they lured
comic opera star Lillian Russell, at the time the highest-paid actress on
the American stage, to replace the departed Fay Templeton as their
principal comedienne. She demanded a salary of $1,250 per week,
guaranteed for a thirty-five week season. The only way their tiny 665-
seat theater could break even under such terms was to auction off seats
for Russell's season. One box fetched $1,000, and an orchestra seat sold
for as much as $100. Among those buying seats were Stanford White,
Louis Sherry, and Randolph Hearst.[12]

"It is unfortunate," wrote Weber and Fields's biographer, "that there
is no other word than 'burlesque' for these shows."[13] Indeed, by the
time of Lillian Russell's season at the Weber and Fields Music Hall,
their brand of entertainment was so far removed from what was being
performed as burlesque elsewhere that it was hardly included in that
category by audiences or critics. In a sense, Weber and Fields brought

back some of the spirit of Thompsonian burlesque. Their productions were, roughly speaking, travesties, each relying on their New York audience's familiarity with a popular play as a framework for new songs, production numbers, and bits of comic business. As with *Ixion* and *Sinbad*, Weber and Fields's shows worked in topical allusions.

The second production to be mounted at their theater in 1896, *The Geezer*, is representative of the Weber and Fields brand of comic entertainment. Written by Joseph Herbert with a score by John Stromberg, *The Geezer* was a takeoff on *The Geisha*, a popular musical comedy imported from London, which happened to be playing at Daly's Theater just up the street. The plot centered around the efforts of the Chinese foreign minister to find a wealthy American bride for his emperor: her dowry is needed to pay off war reparations to the Japanese. John T. Kelly played the role of the Chinese minister with an Irish accent, while Sam Bernard played another Chinese character with a Dutch brogue. The principal female role was that of Nellie Fly, an obvious reference to journalist Nellie Bly. Nellie Fly is so eager to interview the Chinese emperor that she masquerades as an American heiress and offers to become his betrothed. She describes herself to his agent as

> primarily a journalist, eternally an American. I am not a new woman, as I am said to be over seven. I travel so fast that greased lightning is distanced. My cheek is peachy and plenty. Your emperor is qualified to rule a nation. I am qualified to rule an emperor.[14]

Three other women appear as Lady Faith, Lady Hope, and Lady Charity, chorus girls who have married British peers. New Yorkers would have recognized them as send-ups of May Yohe, the American actress who had married a lord. They sing:

> We are three marvels of ultra propriety,
> Though we have had to the verge of satiety
> Poverty, wretchedness, more than a moiety.
> When we were classed in a class lower middle,
> Our feelings we'd vent with a low tarra-ra-diddle.
> Now we move in a superior set.
> We walk and we talk a la grand minuet.

Married and settled, we are highly respectable.
Conduct is perfect and morals dissectable.
Still we must add with sincerest regret:
It's irksome to be a society pet.

There were other shots at contemporary personages and foibles: The-odore Roosevelt, civic reformers, Newport society, and yacht racing, among them.[15]

Even before Russell placed her imprimatur upon their venture, We-ber and Fields attracted a very different audience from the one that frequented Miner's burlesque house downtown, where they had begun in burlesque. So popular was *The Geezer* that they were able to raise ticket prices nearly to the level of legitimate theaters without losing patronage. They drew their audience from across a broad social and economic spectrum, attracting both men and women with their own famous comedy routines, the considerable talents of their stock com-pany, and the songs of John Stromberg, some of which became popular tunes of the day. Like the Imperial Music Hall, whose premises Weber and Fields now occupied, their music hall continued to sell alcohol at its bar. However, drinks were sold only before the show and during inter-missions. Although their shows did feature – as the *New York Times* critic said of their 1901 production – "a whole army of pretty girls in astonishing garments and active dances," neither sexual display nor blue humor was a major part of their appeal. Thus, women and some men who would have been embarrassed to be seen entering a burlesque house had no such compunction about going to Weber and Fields's. As the *Times* put it in 1897, "Everybody goes there and laughs immoder-ately while there. The nonsense of the performers employed there just suits the fancy of the hour."[16]

The Weber and Fields partnership was dissolved in 1904, shortly after new fire regulations forced the closing of their music hall. Their farewell performance as a team occurred at the New Amsterdam The-ater on May 30, 1904, where, according to the *New York Herald*, a capacity crowd "composed of representatives of society, clubdom, the world of first-night, the theater and every walk of life, called for the curtain to rise again." Long before they left the stage, however, Weber and Fields had left burlesque behind – at least as burlesque was then being practiced. Zeidman views their defection from the burlesque ranks as a serious blow to the form. When they deserted burlesque for travesty, he says, "Burlesque was left with its girls and dirty after-pieces."[17]

○ ○ ○   "Cooch" and the Rise of Twentieth-Century Burlesque

Few burlesque producers or theater managers followed the example of Weber and Fields. Many more took the opposite path, building their shows around undisguised feminine sexual spectacle, which had no narrative or dramatic relationship to the rest of the show. Reliance on sexual display in burlesque greatly increased after the Chicago World's Columbian Exposition of 1893. It was here that the "cooch" dance was introduced to American audiences. Within months, practically every burlesque troupe in American had added a Fatima, Little Egypt, or Zora to do her version of the famous *danse du ventre*.

It is both ironic and appropriate that the cooch dance, the immediate forerunner of the striptease, should enter burlesque by way of an attempt to popularize the new science of anthropology. Planned as a commemoration of the quadricentennial of Columbus's discovery of the New World and as a showcase for American technological and cultural progress, the Columbian Exposition featured 65,000 exhibits housed in $18 million worth of buildings constructed on 686 acres of reclaimed swampland along the shore of Lake Michigan some five miles south of the city's center. In the six months of the fair's operation, more than twenty million visitors passed through its gates, nearly three times the attendance at Philadelphia's Centennial Exposition in 1876. In all, it is estimated that between 5 and 10 percent of the U.S. population made a pilgrimage to Chicago for the fair.[18]

The Columbian Exposition was planned as two separate but related sites. The monumental White City was the fair's formal side, containing exhibits devoted to G. Browne Goode's twelve "departments" of knowledge — everything from fine arts to fish products. The Midway Plaisance, a mile-long avenue stretching from White City to Washington Park, kept commercial and "popular" attractions safely removed from the exposition's high-toned, educational side while allowing fair officials to realize considerable income from concessionaires. Officially, the

Midway was operated under the auspices of the exposition's Department of Ethnology, and it was planned as part of an ambitious project to introduce the science of anthropology to the American public and to bring together anthropological artifacts and data that might form the core of a great museum collection.[19] In White City, visitors could be examined and measured by Franz Boas or Joseph Jastrow, gauging their forms against statues of the ideal racial type (whose models were Harvard and Radcliffe undergraduates). Along the Midway they could compare their culture with that of others from around the world in dozens of village exhibits. There were "villages" from Persia, India, Japan, Egypt, Algeria, Sweden, Ireland, Lapland, Java, Turkey, and Germany. Amid the villages were other opportunities to mix education and entertainment, among them Hagenbeck's menagerie of performing exotic animals and George Ferris's new piece of amusement technology: the dual Ferris wheel, whose huge cars could lift 2,100 riders two hundred feet above the fair.

Together, the two sites of the exposition constituted, in the words of the Smithsonian's Bureau of American Ethnology, "one vast anthropological revelation." But, as Robert Rydell has argued, the Midway's cultural microcosm was not an exercise in cultural relativism. Rather, it "provided visitors with ethnological, scientific sanction for the American view of the nonwhite world as barbaric and childlike and gave a scientific basis to the racial blueprint for building a utopia."[20] The ethnological exhibits were neatly ordered along what was presumed to be an evolutionary hierarchy of racial progress. At the west end of the Midway, the farthest from White City, were the exhibits of the most "primitive" peoples: the Dahomey (Africa) and American Indian villages. Nearer the center were the villages of the Middle Eastern and Asian worlds. Closest to White City and thus to the pinnacle of evolutionary development were the Teutonic and Celtic races – two German and two Irish villages. The logic of this spatial articulation was not lost on visitors and reporters. A correspondent for *Frank Leslie's Popular Monthly* noted that the Dahomey village was peopled by sixty-nine blacks "in all their barbaric ugliness," who were "blacker than buried midnight and as degraded as the animals which prowl the jungles of their dark land." After viewing them, the reporter could see that American blacks were but one step removed from these "wild people." The

Japanese were clearly more advanced. They were "closest to the American heart of all the semi-civilized races."[21]

At this "semi-civilized" midpoint along the Midway's evolutionary avenue, visitors to the "Streets of Cairo" and Algerian village exhibits witnessed the belly dance being performed publicly for the first time in the United States. The dancers, wearing baggy trousers and midriff-length tops, gyrated to the accompaniment of male musicians sitting cross-legged on the stage behind them. In his autobiography, the Midway's director, Sol Bloom, recalled that when the fair-going public translated the exhibits' advertised *danse du ventre*, "they delightedly concluded that it must be salacious and immoral. The crowds poured in. I had a gold mine." As long lines formed daily in front of the Egyptian, Persian, and Algerian exhibits, a predictable outcry was raised (principally by those who had not seen the dances themselves) against the performances. Even the secretary of the National Association of Dancing Masters wrote fair officials to complain about "objectionable" dances. He was told that the performances were part of ethnological exhibits, and under the terms of the fair's contracts with their proprietors, action could be taken only if the dress of the participants were inappropriate.[22]

The "cooch," or "cootch," or "hootchy-kootchy" phenomenon – as belly dancing quickly came to be called – points out the contradictory nature of the fair's construction of femininity. Inside the White City, women's accomplishments were granted a more prominent place than at any previous international exposition. Yet the exhibits and activities organized to showcase the contributions of women to world culture juxtaposed representations of women as innovators in art, the sciences, and the professions with those of women as child bearers and helpmates. Insofar as representations of the female body and women's sexuality were concerned, however, there was no such confusion: both were carefully obscured. The hundreds of classically styled bas-relief and statues of women to be found everywhere in the White City hid the body behind "wind-blown drapery, floating vegetable matter, and opportune posture." The fair's official attitude toward the naked female body, noted Thomas Beer, seemed to be that it was "most obscene."[23] At the same time, on the other, "popular" side of the fair, all that had been suppressed in the White City's representation of the female body as frozen, solemn, and chaste reemerged in the undulations of the cooch dancer. Just as the African and American Indian exhibits encouraged visitors to compare the more "primitive" branches of the human evolutionary tree with the most advanced, cooch dancers served as a reminder of the atavistic nature of women in a "semi-civilized" state.

Bram Dijkstra has related the representation of women in bourgeois painting of the period to current theory regarding their place in the evolutionary hierarchy. Noting the smaller cranial cavity and body size of women as compared with men, Herbert Spencer had argued in 1873 that women represented an arrested state of evolutionary development. The view that, at her current stage of evolution, woman was somewhere between the primitive savage and the civilized white male was common in scientific circles on both sides of the Atlantic by the 1890s. Charles Darwin himself maintained that some of the physical features of women were "characteristic of the lower races, and therefore, of a past and lower state of civilization."[24] In bourgeois painting, Dijkstra argues, this view of woman as a partially civilized savage was expressed in images of woman as a

> creature of animal impulse [who] sought to separate the male from godlike capacity for spiritual transcendence and drag him back into her regressive realm of mere physical existence. The only part of male being that woman truly understood was his sexuality, and it was therefore through this least effectively evolved element of his being that she tried to reach him and drag him back down to her own low level on the evolutionary scale. Thus woman became a nightmare emanation from man's distant, pre-evolutionary past, ready at any moment to use the animal attraction of her physical beauty to waylay the late nineteenth-century male in his quest for spiritual perfection.[25]

But clearly, the cooch dancer, while she might be uncivilized, was no threatening virago. The threat her sexuality might represent was defused through her construction as exotic, ethnological other. Like the amazonian Indian warrior in burlesque posters, the belly dancer was another kind of woman, whose expressive sexuality tantalized but whose power was contained and distanced by her exotic otherness. She was a woman, to be sure, but as far removed from the modern, American bourgeois woman of the White City as was the Dahomey tribesman from the white middle-class male who was entranced by her dance. The cooch dancer's dance also confirmed that this exotic other was ruled by sexuality, but through the dance this sexual possession was rendered fascinating and not threatening. By the 1890s, Dijkstra notes, what some saw as women's peculiar love of dance was explained as an outlet for pent-up sexual energy. In *Man and Woman* (1894), Havelock Ellis wrote: "One reason why women love dancing is because it enables them to give harmonious and legitimate emotional expression to this neuro-muscular irritability which might otherwise escape in more explosive forms."26 Dance, then, whether represented in the innumerable paintings of frolicking maidens or in performance, could be seen as the authorized expression of feminine sexuality. "Indeed," Dijkstra tells us, "turn-of-the-century men adored the stage spectacle of a woman who lapsed into self-induced fits of orgiastic transport – and all in the name of art [or ethnology]. What could be more intriguing than to watch a woman, safely isolated from the audience, revert publicly to the 'savage' source of her being?"27

Within weeks of the fair's closing on October 29, 1893, cooch dancing arrived in New York City as a part of a sampling of fair exhibits erected at the Grand Central Palace at Lexington and Forty-third Street. At the Streets of Cairo exhibit, four dancers did a show each hour, and before long a line fifty or more deep formed at the ticket counter. Inside the hall, several hundred spectators at a time watched Stella, Zora, Ferida, and Fatima perform their *danse du ventre*. At the first performances on Saturday, December 3, "a number of ladies, most of whom were thirty years and upward and evidently from very respectable families, were there." Some of them hurried from their seats when the star performer, Ferida, began her dance. The police arrived to close down the exhibit, which occasioned, in the words of the *New York Times* reporter, "an entertaining and beautiful" incident. As the police entered from the rear, men in the front row, who had been engrossed in the display before them, turned to see who was interrupting their pleasure. When they recognized a police inspector, they mustered "as much enthusiasm as their disappointment would allow" and cried, "That's right, old man! Hooray for Inspector Williams!"28

When the proprietor reopened on Monday, the police were there to arrest three of the dancers (one had refused to perform again): Zelika Zimmerman, Zora Zimman, and Tatma Mesgish. The next day they appeared in court for arraignment, and their attorney asked if one of them would demonstrate her dance in order for the judge to rule on whether performances could continue until their case was heard later in the week. Zelika, dressed in "red silk Turkish trousers, a blue Eton jacket, trimmed with gold, and a white gauze waist drawn in tight," "wriggled and twisted, turned, cavorted, and kicked through an exhibition in which there was not the slightest sign of graceful movement." Nevertheless, the judge ruled that the show could go on until the trial. "Oh, it won't harm anybody for a few days," he said. "Out in Chicago I saw it myself." When the case did come to trial, the dancers were convicted of immoral conduct and fined fifty dollars each. The performances continued despite this legal setback but with such restraint that the police captain on hand attested "not even a church member could take offense at that."[29]

Chicago burlesque theater owner and producer Sam T. Jacks took credit for introducing "Little Egypt" to burlesque at his theater at Madison and State streets. Whether or not he earned that distinction is less important than the fact that by the turn of the century, the cooch dancer had become a standard feature in burlesque companies. Her absorption into burlesque is signaled in burlesque posters, where her black hair and exotic costume become part of the iconography of that world. In the Rose Hill English Folly Company's "Hot Time in the Old Town Tonight" (1899), for example, she leads a parade of innumerable burlesque performers under a banner reading "We Are the Leaders of Fun."

At the St. Louis fair of 1896 a new twist was added to the cooch dance, which eventually found its way into burlesque.[30] Such was the competition among the tents along the Midway Plaisance that barkers hectored passersby in an attempt to entice them inside to see the "real stuff," each promising a more revealing show. The winner, apparently, was Omeena, a "World's Fair" celebrity, who "does what is called a 'take off' of the genuine article. She takes off almost all of her clothing, and is sufficiently suggestive to satisfy the most blase old roue. She executes the couchee-couchee or houche-couchie, or tootsie-wootsie . . . in the presence of men only." This immediate precursor of the striptease represents the further sexualization of the cooch dance, although striptease did not become an integral part of burlesque until the mid-1920s, the period of burlesque's final decline.[31]

The Rose Hill English Folly Company:
"Hot Time in the Old Town Tonight."
(Prints and Photographs Division, Library of Congress)

The inclusion of the cooch dance as a standard feature of burlesque after the 1890s centered the form once and for all around undisguised sexual exhibitionism. The cooch dance linked the sexual display of the female performer and the scopic desire of the male patron in a more direct and intimate fashion than any previous feature of burlesque. Here, all pretense that the performance was about anything other than sexual pleasure was dispensed with. The spectator's desire was not diffused among a company of performers or mediated by drama but focused exclusively on the body of a single woman. She, in turn, played only to him; her movements served no function other than to arouse and please him. Her dance was a pas de deux involving her body and his gaze. She was an exhibition of direct, wordless, female eroticism and exoticism.

The innovation of the runway around 1917 linked performer and spectator in an even tighter scopic embrace. Morton Minsky, whose family operated New York City's most famous burlesque theaters in the 1920s, recounts in his autobiography the origins of the runway. The Minsky brothers' first burlesque theater, the National Winter Garden, had been designed as a movie theater without stage lighting. In an effort to bolster sagging ticket sales, brother Abe suggested imitating the *Folies Bergère* and extending the stage into the audience by means of a runway. The troupe of six dancers "was able to get so close to the audience that they could actually smell their perfume and hear their heavy breathing. It was sensational! Never before had an audience been able to get so close to the performers." From then on, the most expensive seats in the house were those closest to the runway. "To tell the truth," admitted Minsky, "burlesque was on its way to becoming nothing more than a legal way of selling the illusion of sex to the public."[32]

By 1922, when the Mutual burlesque wheel was formed, cooch, which was now performed to the rhythms of jazz, had been renamed the "shimmy." Zeidman describes the Mutual shows, which were built around the shimmy and the runway: "The chorus girls on the runway, yelling, shimmying directly at and over the men, the music blatant, jangling and dissonant, the audience alternately hooting or derisively encouraging – it was a demonic, orgiastic spectacle. Hands upraised to a merciful heaven, the girls would sprawl out on the runway, twist, writhe, squirm and shake, each to her own inventive obscene devices."[33]

○ ○ ○   **Cooch and Carnival**

Working-class men in America's small towns and villages, far from the nearest burlesque theater, also became part of the audience for Fatima, Omeena, Little Egypt, and hundreds of their sisters as cooch dancing rapidly joined carnival sideshows and appeared along the midways of agricultural fairs in the early years of the new century. Ever since, exhibitions of feminine sexuality have been touted in sideshows featuring Siamese twins, hermaphrodites, pinheads, and pickled fetuses. A generation after Lydia Thompson shared the bill at Wood's Museum and Theater with Sophia the giantess, feminine sexual spectacle once again became associated with the freak show. And it still was a century later. When asked to name the principal attractions of the carnival in the late 1960s, the editor of the carnival trade paper, *Amusement World*, put "girl shows" at the top of his list:

That's what the boys *really* come to see. Don't let anyone tell you otherwise. There are damned few carnivals, particularly little ones, which don't carry at least one girl show. "Revues" they call them, but they're actually kootch. . . . Carnivals that hit the rural South or the Pennsylvania Dutch country . . . have to carry as many as three girl shows to handle customers who spend the whole night going from one to the other and returning to the first and starting it all over again.[34]

This historical symmetry is not coincidental. Nor is it coincidental that dime museums reached their apex of popularity in the same decade that burlesque became an autonomous branch of American show business, or that in the 1870s burlesque stars and freaks constituted the two most popular genres of carte-de-visite photographs.

The heyday of the dime museum was the 1870s, when at least fifty museums operated in New York City alone, most of them concentrated along the Bowery and lower Broadway. Nearly every major American city sported at least one museum: Bradenburgh's in Philadelphia; Drew's in Providence; and Kohl and Middleton's in eight cities, including Chicago, Louisville, St. Paul, and Cleveland. In the 1890s the rise of vaudeville drew patrons away from the museums, which declined rapidly after the turn of the century. The "human curiosities" that had always constituted the core of the dime museums' appeal left the museums for circus sideshows, becoming part of the latter during its "golden age" (1870–1920). By the 1890s, a major circus sideshow had over fifteen exhibitions plus a troupe of cooch dancers and a band, frequently made up of black musicians. As the circus declined in the 1920s in the face of competition from the movies, amusement parks, and radio, freaks shifted venues for the last time, becoming part of traveling carnivals. By 1937 three hundred carnival units toured the United States, and in each the freak show (called a "kid show" or "ten-in-one") was an important if not central attraction. According to *Amusement World*, at least one thousand shows still toured the country in the late 1960s, attracting an audience of seventy-five million people.[35]

Here, the term "freak" stands for these human attractions not to derogate them but to signify their status as show business performers. The difference between a person with a medically defined physical abnormality and a freak is, of course, the discourse through which each is constructed. Robert Bogdan tells the story of Jack Earle, an unusually tall University of Texas undergraduate, who was spotted by the side-show manager when he visited the Ringling Brothers Circus. "How would you like to be a giant?" the manager asked Earle.[36] The phys-ically exceptional person becomes a freak when his or her abnormality is made the basis for the commercial construction of radical otherness. That otherness is structured as a grotesque essence, which confuses and thereby challenges the boundaries between key self-definitional cate-gories: self and other, male and female, human and animal, large and small.[37]

It is the shock of resemblance and similarity in this radical other, and not the freak's total alienness, that is at the heart of the freak's power to enthrall and disgust. Siamese twins fascinate because they transgress the boundaries of physical autonomy, creating a doubled self that is neither a single body nor two separate ones. Hermaphrodites were frequently exhibited so as to construct an incredible but tantalizing androgyny: costume and makeup arranged so that in one profile he appeared to be a bearded male, while in the other she was a smooth-faced and sexually differentiated female. All manner of physical abnor-malities were made the basis of half man/half animal freaks: hyperhir-sute men became Jo-Jo the Dog-faced Boy and Lionel the Lion-faced Man; phocomelics (individuals with vestigial arms and legs growing directly from their torsos) were transformed into seal children; and skeletal deformities, skin disorders, and other types of disfiguring con-ditions were made the basis for human/animal hybrids: frog boys, snake boys, pony boys, alligator boys, bird girls, mule women, and, of course, the Elephant Man.

In his study of the freak show, Leslie Fiedler explicitly links the experience of watching an exhibition of human biologic abnormality and that of witnessing sexual spectacle. Both share "the sense of watch-ing, unwilling but enthralled, the exposed obscenity of the self or the other. And only 'freaks,' therefore seems a dirty enough word to render the child's sense before the morphodite or Dog-faced Boy of seeing the final forbidden mystery: an experience repeated in adolescence when the cooch dancer removes her G-string and he glimpses for the first time what (as the talkers say) 'you'll never see at home.'" However, the parallel Fiedler draws between the experience of watching a freak show and that of glimpsing the hidden mysteries of the cooch dancer needs to be taken a step farther. The cooch dancer is not like a freak, she is one. Her exhibition is structured around the tension between her similarity to "ordinary" women the male audience member sees and knows outside the tent and her fascinating otherness produced by her expressive and displayed sexuality. As Fiedler notes, there is an erotic element to all confrontations between the "mark" (the carny term for the audience member) and the freak. The mark pays to see what has been concealed: the body of the freak, the sight of which guarantees the authenticity of his or her otherness. Before he was "rescued" by Dr. Frederick Treves, John Merrick, the Elephant Man, was exhibited as the object of a kind of striptease – his draped body finally uncovered at the end of his manager's lengthy spiel. Even Treves's later "medical" lectures merely served as a different discursive frame for what was still in essence a climactic moment of exhibitionism. "After all," concludes Fiedler, "Merrick's total horror could be seen only in total nudity."[38]

But if there is always an element of the erotic in the display of the freak's body, there is also always an element of the freaky grotesque in the cooch dancer's sexual display. Just as the microcephalic is transformed on the stage of the freak show into a pinhead, the biologically sexed woman makes herself into a different kind of sexual creature when she takes on the role of cooch dancer. Her authenticity is also guaranteed by the revelation of her body and its hidden mysteries. Pagan Jones, a cooch dancer touring with carnivals in the late 1960s, compared performing in big city clubs and in carnival sideshows. At the former, she said,

> All the guys do there is drink and smoke and chatter. . . . They hardly even look at the performers. You don't know what the hell they want and neither do they. . . . But out in front here [at the carnival], you know exactly what the boys want every second and you try to give it to them. . . . The marks out there don't want a chorus line; they don't want show tunes; they don't want choreography or ballet. All they want is sex – bumps and grinds – they want to see something they don't see at home.[39]

Girl shows are distinguished by how "strong" the dancers are allowed to perform – in other words, by the extent of sexual abandon of the dancing routines and the degree of genital display. In the larger and more sedate carnivals (those that play state fair dates, for example), the performance might end with a strip down to the G-string or its removal for a moment just before the dancer leaves the stage. In smaller shows, however, where "stronger" acts are the norm, the performance might end with a gynecological anatomy lesson as the performer caters to what Arthur Lewis calls "insatiable male curiosity about the exact nature and geographic disposition of 'women's parts.' " At one show he witnessed, several regular marks brought flashlights with them. "These they used in businesslike fashion in order to examine, clinically and under laboratory conditions, what they 'couldn't see at home.' "[40] As a part of the cooch dancer's body, biologic equipment possessed by half the world's population – including women left "at home" by some of the marks – is transformed into a site of fascination and mystery. William Dean Howells never would have recovered from the sight.

O O O   **Burlesque Enters the Twentieth Century**

By the turn of the century, burlesque was institutionally an autonomous, modern, oligopolistic branch of American show business, its two wheels encompassing enough theaters for a full season's work for the several thousand performers, stagehands, and ancillary personnel who worked in burlesque. With industrialization and the minimizing of competition brought about by the creation of the burlesque trust, the formal qualities of burlesque also became more standardized. Each company with a "franchise" on one of the two wheels came out with a new show each season, which included a first part (an opening production number and attendant sketches, frequently featuring ethnic comedians, or a one-act sketch interrupted by musical numbers), an olio of individual acts, and a concluding afterpiece.[41]

The links with Thompsonian burlesque had become tenuous. By the 1890s, Lydia Thompson could write that burlesque as she knew it "has been retired for a time," its glories now "merely memories of the stage." The very word "burlesque" had been "cruelly used and abused" by its latter-day practitioners. Today, she lamented, "the startling posters, composed of bald headed men and floating Venuses . . . coupled with the word 'burlesque' are enough to make the better class of theatergoers fly from the very name."[42] The middle-class women who had

"The Black Crook" in name only. An 1893 burlesque troupe
appropriates the name.
(Prints and Photographs Division, Library of Congress)

been much in evidence at Wood's and Niblo's had long since deserted
burlesque (except the productions of Weber and Fields). They and their
children were flocking to Keith's. Depending on local licensing laws,
alcohol was still firmly connected with burlesque – either sold on the
premises or in saloons conveniently situated for a quick nip between
acts.

Gone were the full three-act burlesques of highbrow culture, although some of the spirit of burlesque survived in parodies of popular
stage and literary works done as afterpieces. Gone also was the intricate
punning humor of Thompsonian burlesque articulated by female performers and the gender inversiveness that humor entailed. The sexual
transgressiveness of Thompsonian burlesque survived into the new
century in the cooch dancer and, by the late 1920s, the stripper. But the
burlesque performer's transgressive power was circumscribed by her
construction as exotic other, removed from the world of ordinary
women. Her power to reordinate the world was similarly limited by

largely depriving her of speech. Burlesque was a world controlled by women only in the posters outside the theater. Inside, the appeals of burlesque became increasingly bifurcated: verbal humor provided usually by male comedians and sexual display provided by female performers. To be sure, the woman performer did sometimes figure in burlesque sketch humor, but frequently her revealingly costumed body occasioned humorous remarks by male comedians or her words provided the comic situation that, through riposte and reaction, they could exploit. They were funny; she gave them something to be funny about.

Billy Minsky himself concocted a burlesque skit, "The Gazeeka Box," which illustrates the role of women in much of twentieth-century burlesque humor. The straight man pushes a large curtain-covered box onstage just as the comic passes by. The straight man offers to sell this "Gazeeka Box" to the comic for only one hundred dollars. When the comic refuses, the straight man demonstrates its power. After passing his hand over the box and uttering some magical incantation, a parade of beautiful women, dressed in evening dresses, emerges from the box, each of them kissing the straight man as she walks offstage. After the requisite display of delight and excitement, the comic pulls out his wallet, but the straight man has now raised his price to two hundred dollars. The comic refuses to pay, and the straight man once again causes a procession of women to emerge from the box; this time they wear flimsy kimonos. The comic gets even more excited, but the straight man has raised his price to five hundred dollars, which the comic refuses to pay. A third time, the straight man pronounces the incantation, and the women appear wearing revealing lingerie. The comic, now deliriously aroused, counts out five hundred dollars, and the straight man leaves the stage. Unable to wait another second, the comic repeats the magic words, but this time the box yields a chorus line of ugly old hags who chase the comic from the stage.[43]

Even when their roles in burlesque sketches did not revolve around sexual display, women were frequently there to serve as the objects of sexual humor. Ann Corio recounts a sketch devised by burlesque comic Harry Conley and performed by him for sixty years. Harry plays a Rube who comes on stage with his plain and equally rustic wife. The entire sketch consists of Conley's character hurling verbal abuse at his wife Minnie while she stands impassive and mute:

If you go to cross a street, why don't you cross? First you're on one side of the street, then on the other, then you're in the middle of the street, going back and forth . . . running back and forth doing your damdest *to get me killed*! I know what you're after. You don't fool me. You're trying to get that *hundred-dollar* insurance policy!

You walk down the street; everybody's looking at you, everybody's laughing. Making a damned fool out of yourself and me, too. You and your . . . ingrown knees! You walk like you've got diaper rash! . . .

Then when you come back from the doctor, calling up the doctor, don't know what you're saying over a telephone. Calls up the doctor, she says, "Doctor, would you look around your office and see if you can find my panties!"

Doctor came back to the phone, he says, "I've looked every place and I can't find your panties."

"Then I must have left them at the *dentist*!"

I'll hit you so damned hard on top of your head I'll knock your eyeballs so far down in your stomach you'll have to take off your pants to see where you're going.[44]

In addition to illustrating two variations on the theme of the voiceless woman to be found in twentieth-century burlesque humor, the silent women in these sketches constitute the two poles in terms of which femininity was represented in burlesque. On the one hand, there is the beautiful, exotic, and sexually arousing woman, multiplied in the first sketch with the aid of the Gazeeka Box. Indeed, the Gazeeka Box can be seen as standing metonymically for burlesque itself, with its ability to produce phalanxes of captivating, sexually displayed young women as if by magic from behind its closed curtain. This numerical plentitude of feminine sexuality continues a representational strategy evidenced in burlesque posters of the 1890s, which feature many more women than would actually have appeared in any burlesque company. But as in the world of the burlesque poster, the women who emerge from the Gazeeka Box – although they tease and promise sexual availability – are in the end objects of merely scopophilic pleasure. When the comic attempts to go beyond looking by purchasing the machine, it offers him the opposite of desirable femininity.

The second sketch is structured around another representation of undesirable femininity, the working-class wife. Unlike the crones in the Gazeeka Box sketch, she provokes not disgust but contempt. Her silence is admission that she "deserves" the unrelieved comic calumny heaped on her by her husband, even his threat of physical violence. The sketch, only a small portion of which is quoted above, is a catalog of all the inadequacies and faults a working-class husband might project upon his wife: she is so physically unattractive as to make *him* a laughingstock, yet she is also unfaithful; she is stupid, yet she schemes to have her husband "accidentally" killed in traffic to collect his insurance.

So customary was it for women to be the mute objects of sexual humor in burlesque sketches that á special term had to be invented to designate one who actually spoke: the "talking woman." Jean-Paul Debax, among others, has argued that the mute woman is one of *man*kind's oldest fantasies and that reducing women to silence represents the deployment of the masculine will to castrate. "Women's will to revolt necessarily passes through the use of language, the tongue. Language, the tongue, is woman's weapon."[45] The silencing of the sexually expressive woman in burlesque in the 1890s, then, had double significance. The burlesque performer had become objectified both in the sense of becoming an object of male scopic pleasure and in the sense of being removed from the stage as a speaking, ordinating subject. Even if the punning rhymes, slangy exclamations, and impersonations of masculine discourse did not derive from the pen of Lydia Thompson and her sisters in the 1860s, the power of burlesque language to call attention to society's categories and hierarchies was based on the fact that it came out of the mouths of women. As the burlesque performer's mouth became the only part of her body that did *not* move in the cooch dance, the shimmy, and the striptease, she literally and figuratively lost her voice. To be sure, she still had her body with its power to enthrall, captivate, and, to some extent, dominate her male partner in burlesque's scopic pax de deux. But without a voice it was all the more difficult for that body to reclaim its subjectivity.

Burlesque in the Twentieth Century

*Certain romantic-minded commentators led me to believe
that burlesque was the sole contemporary guardian of the
Rabelaisian spirit, but "Rabelaisian" certainly suggests the
vigorous, the spontaneous, and the unrestrained, while no
adjective could be less appropriate to describe the wearily
mechanical antics of a group of underpaid and overworked
performers.*

– Joseph Wood Krutch

*Stop ten people on the street and ask what's their idea of
burlesque and if only one of them says anything but strip-tease,
I'll forfeit a month's salary.*

– A. J. Goldstein

○   ○   ○   ○   ○   ○   ○   ○   ○   ○   ○   ○   ○   ○   ○   ○

In the discourse on American burlesque produced over the last twenty-five years, John Brougham, Lydia Thompson, the British Blondes, female minstrels, and Little Egypt – if they figure at all – are mentioned merely as quaint and removed precursors of the "real" burlesque of strippers, candy butchers, and naughty sketch humor. This latter-day version of burlesque is nostalgically revived on the stage from time to time *as* burlesque: in Ann Corio's *This Was Burlesque*, which ran in New York from 1967 to 1970; in *Sugar Babies*, which also enjoyed a long New York run a decade ago; and occasionally in Las Vegas and Atlantic City casino revues. It is this era of burlesque – from the cooch dancer of the turn of the century to the stripper-dominated burlesque of the form's last years in the 1930s – that forms the subject of this concluding chapter. At this chapter's center is the figure that remains at the center of the popular memory of burlesque: the stripper and all that term evokes of the spectacular, sexual, displayed female body.

○ ○ ○   **Burlesque and the Striptease**

Ironically, the one feature with which burlesque is most closely associated, the striptease, did not become a standard feature of burlesque until the mid-1920s. Within a few years of the introduction of the cooch dance, some performers added to it the removal of parts of their costumes, making implicit or overt allusion to the "Dance of the Seven Veils." Other disrobing acts in burlesque developed independently of the cooch tradition. In 1896 the *Police Gazette*'s theater column pointed out the act of Lona Barrison as "remarkable for its suggestiveness." Dressed initially in a man's evening suit, she undresses to the point that "she gets down to what a mining man would call 'hard pan,' or what I would call the limit. Then she stands quivering and trembling for a moment before the audience, and in an instant she is out of sight." Miss Barrison, the column noted, had thus acquired "a wide reputation for wickedness." As with most of the *Police Gazette*'s commentary on burlesque, it is impossible to tell here whether this wickedness is being advertised or castigated. Three years later, a "disrobing act" was introduced as a feature in the Rose Hill English Folly Company's touring burlesque show.[1] In nondancing disrobing acts, the "setup" was anything that might serve as a pretext for voyeurism: preparing for a bath, donning a swimsuit in a bathhouse, or, perhaps the most common device of all, getting ready for bed. For the most part, these acts, common by the early 1910s, were performed behind backlighted opaque or translucent screens. The nudity that figured as a logical part of the setup was suggested rather than blatant.

Until the late 1920s, even disrobing dancers, whose acts were not concealed behind a screen, stripped down only to flesh-colored tights. The true strip was burlesque's last-ditch and ultimately unsuccessful strategy to stay alive. It represents not the symbol of burlesque's golden age – although it is remembered as such – but rather its ultimate failure to sustain a performance medium sufficiently distinct in its appeals from other forms to draw an audience. The completely revealed female form was twentieth-century burlesque's only trump card. When it was finally played, authorities in New York City moved to close down the game. Even where strip-oriented burlesque evaded closure, it merely briefly forestalled rather than prevented the form's institutional demise.

By the mid-1920s, burlesque was already experiencing financial difficulties. Motion picture palaces had been erected in cities across the country, where, for less than the price of the cheapest seat at a Keith vaudeville theater, one could see three hours worth of films and live entertainment. The movies certainly did not compete with burlesque in terms of sexual display (especially after the Hollywood scandals of the early 1920s), but the usurpation by the movies of vaudeville's preeminence in American popular entertainment had a negative impact on burlesque as well as on its respectable opposite.

Furthermore, burlesque was not the only form of theatrical entertainment structured around the display of the revealed female body. In July 1907 a theatrical manager, whose previous clients had included strongman The Great Sandow, took a lease on the roof garden of the New York Theater. There he offered a loosely structured mélange of songs,

dances, novelty acts, and commentary on the fashions and foibles of the
year, which featured fifty chorus girls and starred Annabelle Whitford
as the Gibson Bathing Girl. *The Follies of 1907* was the first of Florenz
Ziegfeld's twenty-one revues produced in New York over the next quarter century. Ziegfeld was persuaded by musical comedy star Anna Held,
his French-born common-law wife, that New York was ready for an
upmarket feminine spectacle along the lines of the *Folies Bergère*.

The Ziegfeld *Follies* of the early 1900s represented the acceptable
face of feminine sexual spectacle in America and easily blended into the
ideology of bourgeois consumer culture. By the time Ziegfeld's chorus
"girls" paraded onto the stage of the New York Theater's roof garden,
the country was in the midst of what William Leach has called "a
critical moment in the formation of a new culture of consumption," one
based on spectacle. This desire to "show things off," which Leach traces
in the development of the department store, is found in other cultural
arenas as well. As he puts it, "The concept of show invaded the domain
of culture, whether in the shape of a theatrical show, a baby show, a
show girl, a show place, or a showroom. Perhaps inadvertently, the
desire to show things off helped to loosen the resistance to personal
sexual display and performance in public that had hitherto distinguished American social behavior."[2] Appearing comfortable with her
new-found independence and with her expressive but controlled sexuality, the "Ziegfeld girl" was a living display advertisement for middle-
class consumer culture. Ziegfeld lavished time and money on the
chorus's costumes – as many as ten different ensembles in a single show.
No matter how revealing, they were always elegant, an outward sign of
the social and economic status of the wearer. In the 1910s Ziegfeld was
so impressed by the live mannequins employed by Lady Duff-Gordon
in her Fifty-seventh Street salon that he hired her to design gowns for
his productions and hired a number of her models to serve as "show
girls," whose only function was to beautifully wear beautiful clothes.[3]

Ziegfeld's shows succeeded with bourgeois audiences and escaped
(for the most part) public censure only because he managed to package
feminine stage sexuality in such a way that his audiences connected the
Follies not with the working-class sexuality of burlesque but with the
cosmopolitan worldliness of Paris. Ziegfeld carefully removed from his
brand of feminine sexual spectacle all the markers of its working-class
associations. At a time when burlesque stars were still of imposing girth,

Ziegfeld limited his chorus lines to svelte young women who seemed not fully to have blossomed into womanhood. There was nothing sexually awe-provoking or threatening about the Ziegfeld girl. Hers was the contained, manageable, almost wholesome sexuality of the white middle-class girl next door, not the wild, potentially destructive sexuality of the amazon. To Ziegfeld, as Lewis Erenberg points out, "In order to appeal to a man, the chorus girl was active and forward, but not so active that she represented a threat to fragile male egos or posed a challenge to his mastery." She had to combine "sensuality with niceness."⁴ The Ziegfeld girl's sexuality did not need to be constructed in terms of the exotic, alien other, as did that of the cooch dancer. Although Ziegfeld took as her model the *Folies Bergère* performer, the Ziegfeld girl represented homegrown feminine sexuality.

Ziegfeld's success inspired imitation. The Shubert brothers (Ziegfeld's lifelong nemeses), John Murray Anderson, George White, and Earl Carroll, among others, mounted revues patterned after Ziegfeld's *Follies* in the 1910s and 1920s. All featured a chorus of revealingly costumed women. With each passing year and season of revues, the costumes became more and more abbreviated; by the mid-1920s, the choruses in Ziegfeld's and other revues were appearing in tableaux nude or nearly nude from the waist up. What would have been immediately suppressed by municipal authorities had it been innovated for working-class audiences in burlesque was tolerated when produced for the pleasure of middle-class audiences in cabarets and revues. Ziegfeld and his imitators cloaked their shows' sexuality in the trappings of art and glamour. This, combined with the nonthreatening nature of their feminine spectacle, insulated them against most charges of transgressive sexuality.

○ ○ ○   **"Stock" Burlesque**

The movies lured patrons away from burlesque with lavishly appointed theaters, low prices, and long programs of live and filmed entertainment. Cabarets and revues constructed a new mode of feminine sexuality that was more palatable to bourgeois tastes, while at the same time they "outstripped" burlesque in terms of its degree of bodily revelation. Moreover, vaudeville, the movies, and revues all drew off talent nurtured in slapstick burlesque sketches. For these reasons, burlesque was struggling to maintain the audience of working- and lower-middle-class men it had built up since the turn of the century. Yet the oligopolistic structure of the burlesque industry militated against innovation among the wheel producers and theaters. Producers with a franchise on one of the wheels had little incentive to do anything more than recycle old material in a new guise every season. At the same time, franchise agreements kept new producers out of wheel theaters – almost. A season on one of the burlesque wheels was forty weeks, the twelve off weeks coming in the summer when some theaters closed and all theaters experienced a decreased box office. By the mid-1910s, a few enterprising producers organized what were called "stock" burlesque troupes to play wheel houses during the summer months. Other show business entrepreneurs took over theaters in run-down areas of big cities and installed stock burlesque without affiliating with either wheel.

Stock burlesque "innovated" by cutting costs and, more important, by taking salaciousness to a level wheel houses were generally unwilling or thought it unnecessary to go. In other words, stock burlesque was burlesque stripped down to its roughest and barest essentials. In order to minimize police interference, a buzzer or light switch was installed under the box office counter so that the attendant could warn the stage manager backstage to switch to the clean or "Boston" version of the show whenever a likely censor entered the house.[5] If the authorities closed the show, neither the producer nor the theater owner risked a great financial loss. Because Ziegfeld and his fellow revue producers had preempted innovation via elaborate and expensive productions to attract middle-class patrons and because wheel producers monopolized the best burlesque venues, few options were open to independent producers and theater owners other than taking burlesque even farther down the road toward unabashed sexual display.

The more burlesque emphasized striptease, the more everything else in the performance was used merely to pad out the program. By 1930, the trade paper *Billboard* could describe an entire burlesque show (excluding the strippers and cooch dancers) in the following shorthand manner, knowing that any burlesque insider would have no difficulty extrapolating the entire performance: "Spanish ensemble, income tax, some arm, cutaway, ever in love, fight for your honor, hold up, hold this gun, shoot a hole in coat, no more bullets, whole week, good night sleep walker, follow the bell, detour, Jake's hitting the pipe, women love brutes." In 1933 Abe Minsky admitted that not one new burlesque sketch had been written and performed in the past twenty years.[6]

The brothers Minsky (Billy, Abe, Herbert K., and Morton) became stock burlesque pioneers when their father acquired the National Winter Garden Theater on New York's lower East Side in 1913 and turned it over to his two oldest sons, Abe and Billy, to run. After unsuccessfully trying vaudeville, films, and wheel burlesque at this venue, the brothers turned to stock burlesque. In 1917 they constructed a runway into the auditorium so that patrons could examine cooch dancers more closely. During the same season, at least as Morton Minsky remembers it, they also launched striptease by exploiting a dancer's "accidental" strip. Mae Dix did her dance act in a short black dress with detachable white collar and cuffs. At the end of her song one hot summer night, she removed her collar as she walked offstage, trying to forestall the next laundry bill. Someone in the audience demanded an encore, at the end of which she removed her cuffs as well. "Between the heat and the applause, Mae lost her head, went back for a short chorus, and unbuttoned her bodice as she left the stage again." Thus, we are told, was the striptease born at Minsky's.[7]

The Minskys demonstrated that, with a bit of showmanship and a lot of female flesh, stock burlesque could be profitable even in the ghetto neighborhoods of New York. But the increased popularity of their shows also attracted the attention of reformers and the police. The most famous police raid (but only one of many) occurred on the evening of April 20, 1925, when Billy Minsky and eight others were charged with violation of Section 1140a of the New York Penal Code: presenting a performance likely to corrupt the morals of youth and others. The raid was memorialized in Roland Barber's fictionalized 1967 account, *The Night They Raided Minsky's*. The complaint was brought not by the police or the district attorney, but by John Sumner, secretary of the New York Society for the Suppression of Vice. Sumner was particularly incensed by one Mary Dawson, a young woman from rural Pennsylvania, who, performing as Mademoiselle Fifi, ended her strip act that evening bare chested, her arms raised above her head.

While Minsky's and other stock theaters flourished in the interstices of burlesque with cheap shows and plenty of striptease sex, the wheels were coming apart.[8] The Eastern and Western wheels had been fully consolidated in 1913 as the Columbia Amusement Company (the Columbia Wheel). Samuel Scribner and I. H. Herk, who headed the Columbia Wheel, continued the Eastern Wheel policy of presenting relatively "clean" burlesque. When an independent wheel threatened to fill the niche for somewhat stronger shows left by the demise of the Western circuit, Scribner and Herk organized a subsidiary wheel, the American Burlesque Association (the American Wheel) to drive the upstart chain out of business. They succeeded, and the American Wheel offered bumping and grinding cooch dancers and blue humor from 1915 to 1922, when disagreements between Scribner and Herk led to the American's downfall. A new wheel initially associated with the Columbia, the Mutual, was immediately formed to take the American Wheel's place. The Columbia Wheel, still the dominant force in burlesque with thirty-eight shows and a property value of $20 million in 1923, stuck to its policy of cleaner burlesque until the 1925 season, when falling revenues led Scribner to sanction bare-breast tableaux and the removal of tights.

The Columbia shows adapted too late to stop the flow of customers to other entertainment forms, to the Mutual shows, and to the even rougher stock burlesque theaters. Columbia accepted a merger offer from Mutual in 1927. The *New York Herald Tribune* called the 1929–30 season the worst for burlesque since 1868. For the first time in seven years, the Mutual Wheel experienced a decline in receipts. Even with the Columbia merger, Mutual could sustain only thirty-seven full weeks for its shows. Hoping to differentiate itself from stock burlesque, Mutual made what turned out to be the fatal decision to revive clean burlesque the following season. Nineteen shows folded on the road. In 1931 wheel burlesque in America came to an end when Mutual ceased operation as a circuit and its remaining theaters succumbed to stock.[9] Thereafter, there was only stock.

○ ○ ○   **Burlesque Invades Broadway**

Ironically, the Great Depression provided stock burlesque a few years of prosperity in the 1930s. The history of popular entertainment in the United States suggests that, since the late nineteenth century at least, periods of economic retrenchment benefit entertainment forms that serve the lower social and economic strata at the expense of more upscale forms. Vaudeville became a solidly middle-class form in the theatrical seasons immediately following the depression of 1893. After a less severe but nevertheless serious economic downturn in 1907, movie producers and exhibitors moved quickly to attract middle-class patrons. With less money to spend on entertainment during times of economic hardship, commercial entertainment patrons look again at cheaper forms. Entrepreneurs of those "lower" forms find it possible to attract "high-class" talent at bargain-basement rates, and, when legitimate theaters fail during economic depressions, to move their operations into larger and more elaborate theaters. So it was with burlesque in the early 1930s. In 1932, some 150 strippers were employed in burlesque, most of them in their first season. In 1936 *Variety* reported that burlesque had the lowest unemployment rate in the show business industry, with virtually no first-class burlesque talent out of work.[10]

The economic buoyancy of burlesque during the depression, combined with the devastation suffered by legitimate theater, led several entrepreneurs to open burlesque theaters in the heart of the New York theater district: Times Square. The stock market crash of 1929 explosively deflated a thirty-year theater-building boom in New York City. Legitimate productions folded one after another, closing many theaters and forcing most producers and theater owners into bankruptcy.[11] Billy Minsky saw in the ruins of legitimate theater an opportunity to add to the Minsky chain of New York burlesque houses and to do what no entrepreneur had yet done: put burlesque on Broadway. In 1931 he acquired the Republic Theater on Forty-second Street just south of Times Square and reopened it with the Minskys' brand of stock burlesque: strippers, cooch dancers, and four comics, giving two shows daily with ticket prices ranging from 75¢ to $1.50. One month later, Max Rudnick, a Brooklyn movie theater operator, leased the Eltinge Theater across the street from the Republic and also installed stock burlesque – four shows per day, with tickets as low as 15¢. Within months, two more former legitimate houses, The Central and the Gaiety, were running burlesque, each of them with the backing of one of the Minsky brothers. In 1934 the block of Forty-second Street between Seventh and Eighth streets got yet another burlesque theater when the Apollo, which since 1924 had been home to George White's *Scandals* revues, opened as a "grind" (continuous performance) house.[12]

This eruption of stock burlesque out of the working-class neighbor-hoods of Brooklyn, the Bowery, and the lower East Side and into the middle-class realm of the legitimate theater along Broadway ultimately destroyed burlesque in New York City. So long as burlesque remained out of sight, it might experience the occasional raid (as did the Winter Garden in 1925) but not concerted civic, police, and, hence, politi-cal opposition. In an ironic parallel to Lydia Thompson's move from Wood's to Niblo's in the winter of 1869, burlesque's move uptown in the early 1930s brought it once again into the spotlight of mainstream discourse. As in 1869, burlesque was framed in terms of the "low," whose contaminating penetration into the heart of the city and its entertainment district had to be opposed on social, moral, and eco-nomic grounds.

Opposition to burlesque from antivice groups, particularly John Sumner's New York Society for the Suppression of Vice, had surfaced sporadically during the 1920s. As noted above, it was Sumner's com-plaint against "obscene" humor that had precipitated the fabled raid of Minsky's Winter Garden Theater in April 1925. In the absence of other pressures, however, New York magistrates and judges were reluctant to bring the full force of criminal law down upon entertainment entrepre-neurs and performers. To be in violation of Section 1140a of the New York Penal Code, a performance had to be manifestly indecent and likely to be a corrupting influence on minors and others. Because so much of burlesque's sexual transgressiveness was visual rather than verbal, courtroom accounts of burlesque performances conveyed al-most nothing of their suggestiveness. Indeed, in burlesque humor sala-ciousness was usually found in the slide between levels of possible meaning. In the seven-week trial following the April 1925 raid, Sumner tried to convince a jury that some of the Minsky sketches were indecent. In one, entitled "Desire under the El," two comics, straight man Ray-mond Paine and top banana Scratch Wallace, strike out in their at-tempts to "smooth-talk" talking women Chubby Drisdale and Holly Dean:

Paine:　We gotta change our approach! We gotta play hard to get.
Wallace: But are we going to vamp them?
Paine:　No, first we let 'em *scrutinize* and *then* we *vamp* 'em.
Wallace: "Scrutinize 'em!" *That's* playing hard to get?[13]

What the police stenographer who accompanied Sumner to the offending performance could not capture, of course, was the salacious intonation of "scruuu-tin-ize" or the leer that accompanied it. The judge dropped the charges against all performers except Mary Dawson, *a.k.a.* Mademoiselle Fifi. Sumner in his complaint had charged that Fifi's "pelvic contortions" were indecent and immoral. The judge demanded that as a part of Sumner's testimony he demonstrate the pelvic contortions he had found so offensive. Reluctantly, Sumner gave his own interpretation of "The Shame of La Bohème" to the a cappella accompaniment of Paine, Wallace, Drisdale, and Dean. The result was ridiculous but not remotely prurient. Sumner's final charge – that Fifi's dance was indecent because it ended with the display of her bare breasts – was effectively rebuffed by the Minskys' attorney, who forced Sumner to admit that in this respect Fifi's act was no more revealing than any number of "high-class" production numbers currently being performed in revues on the New York stage or than "classic" works of art displayed in art books or local museums.[14] In short, if the authorities gave the benefit of the doubt to the defendants in such cases, there was little unique to a burlesque performance that by 1930s' standards could be construed as blatantly criminal in terms of its sexual transgressiveness.

In March 1932 another Section 1140a complaint was brought against burlesque – this time against the Eltinge Theater – but not by an antivice organization. The complaint was part of a campaign launched by the Forty-second Street Property Owners' Association to drive burlesque off Broadway, particularly off the block of Forty-second Street that featured three burlesque houses. The initial public stance of the organization was that burlesque theaters should be closed because they were indecent and immoral. Posters of half-nude women in front of the theaters offended respectable passersby and enticed children. "Barkers" or "pullers-in" who solicited customers on the street accosted pedestrians. But it soon became clear that the association's real complaint against burlesque was economic: stores and trades built on servicing middle-class customers drawn to the Times Square area by the legitimate theaters were suffering. Not only did the success of Broadway burlesque not produce the same "spin-off" trade legitimate theaters had in the 1920s, but also it flooded the area with "undesirable" characters whose presence, in turn, further depressed middle-class trade. Property owners saw the value of their investments plummet during the depression, and burlesque was a convenient villain. The association did succeed in securing the prosecution and conviction of a barker for unlicensed street hawking (a small victory: the fine was ten dollars), but it failed twice in as many weeks to have burlesque performances declared indecent. Again, on the basis of sketch dialogue read aloud in court, judges acknowledged that the lines might well have double meanings but were not manifestly indecent.[15]

Led by its counsel, former district attorney Joab Banton, the Property Owners' Association shifted its point of attack from the city's judiciary to a much more politically sensitive and vulnerable area: the municipal commissioner of licenses, from whom all theaters had to secure permission to operate. With the license of every burlesque theater in the city set to expire on April 30, 1932, and with the decision whether to renew in the hands of the mayor's appointee, the association mounted an all-out effort to close down burlesque by executive action. The association organized a parade of witnesses before Commissioner of Licenses James Geraghty at the hearings he called in late April and bolstered its case with affidavits solicited from dozens of religious and civic groups. The hearings lasted two and one-half weeks, and testimony ran to more than 1,400 pages.

Early on, Geraghty revealed that he did not need much persuading that some action should be taken against burlesque theaters on Broadway. He announced that his inspectors were prepared to "prove" that the lobbies of burlesque theaters had become hangouts for "men who trade on the shady side of night life." The deputy commissioner of police appeared at the hearings to oppose renewal of the theaters' licenses, saying that he had received numerous letters complaining about their effects on the neighborhood. The director of the League of New York Theaters accused burlesque of "pandering to the very lowest in human nature." Religious groups joined the chorus. Patrick Cardinal Hayes condemned burlesque at the Republic and Eltinge theaters as "breeders of vice." The Catholic Actors' Guild called the form "low and degrading," and a rabbi who took his wife to see a Broadway burlesque show said he found a "hellhole of filth." The association's members blamed burlesque for injuring real estate prices in the Times Square area, for lowering "the general tone of the district and [giving] rise to conditions that were a degradation to the city." One property owner contended that conditions along Forty-second Street were so bad that he had put his building up for sale, and a banker stated that he would not recommend that his firm loan money on any parcel on that street between Broadway and Eighth Avenue.[16]

The burlesque interests were forced to respond to the association's agenda and to a political apparatus decidedly not inclined to grant them the benefit of the doubt. The best they could do to demonstrate that burlesque was not a "hellhole of filth" was to present as evidence "Mother" Annie Elms, the ninety-three-year-old former wardrobe mistress at the Winter Garden Theater, whose career in variety and burlesque stretched back to Tony Pastor's Music Hall. Mother Elms testified that she had not been corrupted by burlesque and that most of the women she had worked with had been of high moral character. The operator of a lunch stand next door to the Eltinge said that he regarded burlesque as an art form and that his business had increased by half since the theater's conversion to burlesque. A stage decorator and painter was called to testify that the audience for burlesque was not made up of shady characters but of plumbers, carpenters, and other working men who could not afford musical comedy. Burlesque was, he argued, "poor man's theater." Joseph Winestock, director and part owner of the Republic, used his time in the witness stand to try to convince the public (if not Commissioner Geraghty) that pressure to close burlesque theaters was the result of a plot hatched by legitimate theater interests, whose customers were deserting their houses for burlesque. "We've been accused of everything except kidnapping the Lindbergh baby," he complained.[17]

Geraghty mulled over the issue for four months before deciding on September 19 not to renew the licenses of the Republic and Eltinge theaters. Geraghty was merely carrying out the policy of Acting Mayor Joseph McKee, who had taken over from Jimmy Walker when he was forced by scandal to step down. The *New York Times* editorially supported McKee's drive against "pornographic exhibitions," declaring that burlesque performances "have sunk to a level of lewdness never before tolerated in this city." However, another licensing decision made at the same time reveals that sexual transgressiveness may not have been the sole or even the primary basis for closing the Republic and the Eltinge. Also before the commissioner in September was a request for a license to operate a carnival on a vacant lot at the corner of Forty-first Street and Eighth Avenue. Dyer Post 37 of the Veterans of Foreign Wars had planned the carnival as a two-week fund-raising activity. The Forty-second Street Property Owners' Association vigorously opposed the license application on the grounds that such a carnival would constitute a "menace," "cheapen the street," and interfere with "normal" business operations. The license request was denied. Some months later, the *Times* itself acknowledged that the real issues in the burlesque licensing issue were economic and political, not moral. The problem burlesque presented to the surrounding property interests, an editorial pointed out, was that "the alleged obscenity of the burlesque shows is exceeded by their external frowsiness. The neighborhood of such theaters takes on the character of a slum." That the association was determined to drive burlesque off Broadway might well be a sign that property values had bottomed out in the area and were set to rebound. Furthermore, the editorial concluded, reformist zeal is always strongest in the months leading up to a mayoral campaign.[18]

○ ○ ○   **The Death of Burlesque in New York**

Although the Republic and Eltinge were "dark" for only a month, McKee's use of the licensing ordinance as a tool for the suppression of burlesque launched a four-and-one-half-year battle between New York burlesque interests and municipal authorities. During this battle the burlesque performance was effectively dismantled, and when it ended burlesque was killed entirely. The Minskys and other burlesque entrepreneurs realized that their only hope of staying in business was to negotiate terms under which Commissioner Geraghty might allow their theaters to reopen. They agreed first not to call their new productions "burlesques," but rather "revues." A company censor would be assigned to each house to ensure "dignity and restraint" in all things. The Minsky shows, their attorney assured the *Times*, would be burlesque only "in the classical sense of the term." In allowing the theaters to reopen, Geraghty warned that their licenses were revocable "on call," and in a further crackdown in March 1933 he ordered the cessation of all strip acts.[19]

Later that year, Fiorello LaGuardia was elected mayor of New York and appointed Paul Moss to the post of commissioner of licenses. Neither had any use for burlesque. Moss and burlesque interests jousted for several years. A state appeals court had ruled that the commissioner of licenses could only refuse to renew a theatrical license; he or she could not revoke a license prior to its expiration except in the case of a successful criminal prosecution against that theater. Moss simply made the licenses for burlesque theaters effective for ninety days instead of one year. In April 1937 LaGuardia and Moss engineered the successful prosecution of five performers and the stage manager at the Minskys' Gotham Theater on 125th Street for violating Section 1140a: the five women had given an obscene performance by stripping to the accompaniment of "soft music and softer lights." Armed with the requisite criminal conviction, Moss ordered the immediate revocation of the Gotham's license.[20]

The next license expiration date for other burlesque theaters in town fell on April 30. A series of sex crimes in the Times Square area, none of which were linked in any way with burlesque, provided a convenient excuse for denying renewal. In revoking the Gotham's license, Moss announced his belief that salacious burlesque performances had "contributed to the wave of sex crimes in the city." Moss called for new hearings on burlesque licenses, which gave antivice groups, property owners, religious groups, and others a chance to take a hand in striking the coup de grace against burlesque. The Knights of Columbus found burlesque guilty of inciting "not only immorality but bestiality and degeneracy." Kings County District Attorney William Geoghan launched his own police raids against Brooklyn burlesque theaters, calling them "places of filth, rottenness, and iniquity" that were "largely responsible for sex crimes in the city." On May 2, Moss refused to renew the licenses of the fourteen operating burlesque theaters in the city and refused to grant an initial license to three burlesque entrepreneurs. Cardinal Hayes publicly applauded Moss's actions, calling burlesque a "stench in the nostrils of decency," and Mayor LaGuardia proclaimed them one victory in his personal war "against the incorporation of filth."[21]

The burlesque interests were stunned. They had expected the traditional and temporary crackdown that permitted municipal authorities to take credit for cleaning up the city but that still allowed them to present some semblance of burlesque – even if they could not call it that. But this time LaGuardia was determined to end burlesque once and for all. The Minskys appealed to the state supreme court, arguing that Moss had overstepped his authority. The attorney representing the city contended that burlesque theaters were a public menace. Their shows were "the cause of many of our sex crimes, and the theaters which house them [were] the habitats of sex-crazed perverts." The appeal failed, and for the first time since September 30, 1869, there was no burlesque to be found in New York City.[22] Moss announced that thereafter no license would be granted to a theater using the term "burlesque" in any way, effectively eradicating the term from the theatrical lexicon of the city. So closely were the Minskys associated with burlesque that Moss also barred the use of their name in advertisements. They closed their houses and announced that they planned to present a "high-classed variety revue" starring black performers at their Oriental Theater. It was not a success. Once again, sexual spectacle was driven out of "respectable" neighborhoods, out of bourgeois consciousness, and into the tenderloin of the city. As Zeidman puts it, "The only remnants of burlesque that persisted on Broadway were the strip clip-joint nightclubs on 52nd Street which succeeded the burlesque houses. They survived for several years only because they were, in the main, unadvertised, unpublicized, and generally unknown – in exact antithesis of the exploitation that brought about the downfall of the burlesque houses. After a while, they became noticeable. . . . So they were closed down also."[23]

One week after Moss closed down burlesque in New York, Brooks Atkinson, the *New York Times* theater critic, wrote burlesque's obituary. The recent war in which burlesque had been defeated, he wrote, was caused in part by the fear of public bodily display in any form: "The human body always terrifies some people. The crusade is an old one." Atkinson explicitly linked the calumny heaped on burlesque in 1937 with the excoriation of Lydia Thompson in the same city sixty-eight years earlier. But to Atkinson, a burlesque fan, the form had contributed to its own demise. At the last burlesque show he had visited, it was not salaciousness but "the absence of art" that offended him most. "Since the striptease bit of midway hocus-pocus started turning burlesque into a peep show about ten years ago, the dark, dead attitude of the audience and the foulness of the comedy have very nearly destroyed the revelry that at one time was both coarse and wholesome and much prized for an occasional night out of bounds. Burlesque was at one time lively fooling." "This column looks forward," he concluded, "to staying away from burlesque forever."[24] Burlesque did continue in other cities for a while, but New York had always been the form's center and trendsetter. When burlesque stopped there, it left the body of the burlesque industry brain-dead. It was only a matter of a few years before burlesque passed from the scene entirely except as a misleading signifier for nightclub strip shows.

○ ○ ○   **The Legacy of Burlesque**

In the years since the death of burlesque, its primary contribution to American show business has been regarded as providing fertile ground for the development of comedic talent that achieved greater fame elsewhere. Phil Silvers, Bud Abbott and Lou Costello, Jackie Gleason, Red Skelton, and Red Buttons are but some of the comics who started in burlesque and then achieved much wider celebrity in radio, film, and/or television. Ironically, for a form structured around women performers for seventy years, burlesque produced no female stars who enjoyed equivalent success in other branches of show business. Stripper Ann Corio, whose success in burlesque occurred in its waning years, made a few B-grade movies. Gypsy Rose Lee was also lured to Hollywood with the promise of a new career on the screen. However, according to Morton Minsky, the studio brass "were terrified that her frank and charming sexuality would come across, so they changed her name back to her maiden name [Louise Hovick] and made her wear costumes that covered her from her ankles to her neck."[25] None of her pictures was successful. She became best known for the play *Gypsy*, which dealt far more with her relationship with her overweening and seriously dotty mother than it did with her experiences in burlesque. Ruby Keeler and Joan Crawford did brief stints in burlesque choruses in their earliest professional days, but neither could be said to have trained in burlesque in the same way that male comics were nurtured there in their craft. By the latter days of burlesque, women's roles had been limited to the display of their bodies – as cooch dancers, strippers, or talking women. Their skills were not easily transferable to other, more family-oriented media.

Without question, however, burlesque's principal legacy as a cultural form was its establishment of patterns of gender representation that forever changed the role of the woman on the American stage and later influenced her image on the screen. When Lydia Thompson and the other members of her troupe appeared onstage in tights and short skirts or pantaloons, they accelerated a trend of feminine spectacle begun more than thirty-five years earlier with romantic ballet. In 1869, the display of the revealed female body was morally *and* socially transgressive. The very sight of a female body not covered by the accepted costume of bourgeois respectability forcefully if playfully called attention to the entire question of the "place" of woman in American society. But unlike the feminine spectacle of romantic ballet or *The Black Crook*, burlesque's transgressiveness was incalculably intensified by its inversiveness and its blurring of central gender distinctions. It was this combination of sexual display and physical and verbal insubordination that caused William Dean Howells to shrink before the horribly pretty creatures of burlesque, Olive Logan to regard them as a rising tide of subterranean filth, and bourgeois discourse in general to cry them off the mainstream stage and into the shadows of show business. As a part of this process of social and cultural marginalization, these two components of burlesque's transgressive representation of femininity began to come unhinged. The wit and humor of burlesque – which when coming from the mouths of Thompson and company was as startling and disturbing as their appearance onstage – gradually became an aspect of burlesque dominated by men. And with the advent of the cooch dance as an essential feature of burlesque in the 1890s, women on the burlesque stage were even further linguistically disempowered.

◯ ◯ ◯ **Images of Feminine Sexuality in the Wake of Burlesque**

It is not surprising that patterns of feminine sexual display originated or promoted by burlesque should find their way into forms of purely visual representation. One of the most popular forms of visual entertainment in the home in the late nineteenth century was the stereograph: a simple viewing device that allowed two side-by-side photographic images shot by a stereographic camera to be viewed as a single, seemingly three-dimensional image. It was, in other words, the ancestor of the "Vue-Master." More than five million stereographic

photographs were made in the United States in the last half of the
nineteenth century, with more than fifty companies producing at least
ten thousand subjects each.

By 1898, companies were staging narratively organized series of
stereographic photographs called "picture stories." These picture stories, which varied in length from several to several dozen images, drew
on jokes and sketches from all areas of contemporaneous popular culture, including burlesque and vaudeville. In "The Maid and the Furnace Man," a series produced in almost identical fashion by several
companies, a bourgeois woman asks her maid to tell her when the
furnace man has come to repair the boiler. In the punch-line image, the
maid delivers the news of the furnace man's departure with two large
black handprints visible to the viewer on the back of her white blouse.[26]
Dialogue or an explanatory legend was printed across the bottom of
each image. Other series worked display of the partially revealed female
body into the narrative. In "How Biddy Served the Potatoes Undressed,"
a series produced by at least eight companies, a bourgeois couple sits at
their dining table. The woman tells the new maid she would like her to
serve the potatoes undressed. In the next image, the maid returns
bearing the same platter of potatoes but wearing one less item of
clothing. The rather obvious situation escalates to the final image, in
which Biddy, down to her petticoat, declares (usually with an Irish
brogue): "Even if it costs me my job, I'll not serve 'em any more
undressed than I already am!"[27]

Some of the more suggestive stereographic series were built around
unadorned male voyeuristic pleasure. In "Love's Young Dream" (1904),
a young woman is shown in her boudoir reclining on a chaise lounge in
petticoat, stockings, and shoes, a mirror in the background reflecting
her image from behind. "The French Corset" (1906) portrays a woman
modeling her new corset before a mirror. A number of the picture-story
series explicitly link the burlesque performer with opportunities for
voyeuristic pleasure. In "Jolly Mr. Jack" (1904), the viewer observes
"The Girls behind the Scenes," as several burlesque performers don
their costumes and tights before the dressing room mirror. "The Living
Picture Model" (1904) shows a woman posed in the classical manner of
reclining nudes, her body loosely draped with a sheet. She returns the
gaze of the viewer.

"How Biddy Served the Potatoes Undressed."
(Prints and Photographs Division, Library of Congress)

Chorus girls were the subjects of stereographs and series of monocular photographs as well. A 1901 photographic series by William H. Rau, depicting the life of chorus girls "at home," shows two young women in corsets and petticoats in their bedroom enjoying chicken salad and oysters after the matinee, reading a "mash" note, and preparing for bed. In an image entitled "The Platonic Kiss," one of the women kisses her image in the dressing table mirror while her mirror image gazes back at the spectator. The ubiquitous mirror in these photographs is, of course, a feature they share with a much older tradition of the representation of women in Western art. Here, they also augment the viewer's scopic pleasure by providing him with multiple views of the woman's body and, in stereographic subjects, by increasing their three-dimensional effect.

The use of photography to analyze animal motion provided the basis for the invention of motion pictures. In her recent study of cinematic pornography, Linda Williams argues that these early photographic experiments reveal that a pattern of feminine sexual display had already been "implanted" in the cinema before its literal invention. Specifically, she analyzes the motion studies of Eadweard Muybridge, who, by using a battery of still cameras to take sequential photographs, produced a massive, eleven-volume work in 1887 entitled *Animal Locomotion*. In addition to many animal studies (particularly of horses), Muybridge

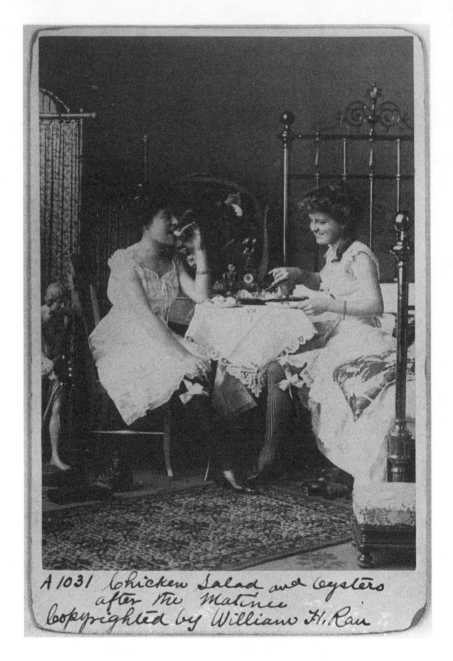

"Chicken Salad and Oysters after the Matinee."
(Prints and Photographs Division, Library of Congress)

photographed naked or partially clothed men, women, and children as they demonstrated all manner of simple motions: from running and jumping to performing carpentry tasks.[28]

Williams remarks on the difference between Muybridge's motion studies of men and those of female subjects. In the male studies, subjects move unselfconsciously within a spare, utilitarian mise-en-scène and are supplied with only the most necessary props. The actions of female subjects, however, are less purposive, as if Muybridge could not quite settle on what types of "female" motions he wanted to study. The women are much more "awarish" than the men; they acknowledge the viewer and even blow kisses to the camera. They wear loose, translucent drapery, which calls attention to their partially hidden forms and emphasizes the difference between being clothed and nude. The mise-en-scène within which they move is more decorative, creating, as Williams calls it, "a more specific imaginary place and time." In some of the male studies, two subjects move in relation to each other – they wrestle, catch balls, or box. But Muybridge could construct no parallel athletic encounters for his female subjects, so he invented imaginary situations in which two women might interact: in one series of images, a women douses another with water; in another, a woman smokes a cigarette while a second woman leans against her chair. Male movement is represented in terms of athleticism or work, female movement in terms of sexual spectacle. Like the burlesque cooch dancer, Muybridge's moving women take on meaning principally in terms of the sexual difference their movements, gestures, glances, and displayed bodies evoke. Despite the fact that Muybridge's work, unlike burlesque, was framed as scientific discourse, his images nevertheless produced a "surplus aestheticism in the fetishization of its women subjects."[29]

Williams argues that while the display of the male body in Muybridge's photographs is effectively naturalized by their activities (sport or work), the display of the female body requires explanation and needs to be situated within some context. Hence, the image sequences of women frequently constitute proto-narratives that attempt to account for their sexual display. Muybridge's narrativizing of feminine sexual spectacle was nothing new. Adah Isaac Menken's portrayal of Mazeppa provided a narrative and dramatic context for her "nude" gallop across the stage, which mitigated the boldness of the ride as spectacle. The assumption by Lydia Thompson and her corps of male roles and quasi-masculine attire served as a rationale for their abbreviated costumes. Even the cooch dancer's appearance in burlesque in the mid-1890s implicitly suggested a story (however threadbare) that "explained" her brand of sexual spectacle: she was a representative of an exotic foreign culture, demonstrating her native customs for the enlightenment of burlesque's ethnographically minded audiences. And stereoptic slide series were little more than proto-narrative inventions that served as frames for shots of partially dressed women.

Twentieth-century burlesque alternated between narrativized feminine sexual display and display as pure spectacle that punctuated the succession of narrative comic bits. Although the former strategy was present in burlesque until the end in the form of sketch humor (as, for example, in Billy Minsky's "Gazeeka Box" sketch), the latter came to dominate burlesque first with the shimmy and then with the striptease. As we have seen, the first strips were given some narrative context: a woman preparing for bed or performing her toilette. The audience played the role of voyeur. By the late 1920s, the narrative context had been eliminated from the striptease; it needed no story to support its spectacle. The striptease is a narrative drama of sorts – a tale of revelation that always begins and ends in the same way – but it makes no reference to any larger narrative that "explains" why the stripper should be removing her clothing. In the place of that larger narrative is the self-evident rationale provided by spectacle: the stripper is what she does, and she does what she does because of who she is. As Williams notes, whether the sight of women's bodies precipitates narrative or, as in the case of some later Hollywood films, acts to retard or suspend narrative through the spectacle of the fetishized female body, it constitutes a textual disturbance.[30] Burlesque is the one form of theatrical text that is structured around this disturbance: the continual eruption of feminine sexual display. Burlesque texts deal with this disturbance either by attempting to contain it within narrative (in which male comics assert through language their control over that eruption while its potentially threatening edge is removed by the woman's corresponding voicelessness) or by attempting to demystify it through the striptease and the spectacle contract between performer and audience: she performs for his pleasure. To be sure, the containment of this eruption may not be complete. As in the case of antebellum ballet, the specter of women's sexuality and all of the mystery and power it represents continues to hover over the spectacle of the woman onstage no matter how much the male viewer is made to feel in control.

○ ○ ○   **The "Smoking Concert" Film:**
Burlesque Meets the Movies

Williams's discussion of cinematic pornography moves quickly from proto-cinematic representations of feminine sexuality to the first stag films of the 1920s. However, within a few years of the movies' emergence as a commercial entertainment form, an important subterranean subindustry developed within the young but increasingly "respectable" motion picture industry – one dedicated to the production of films predicated on feminine sexual display of one sort or another. These films drew heavily on the traditions of sexual display then common in burlesque and photographic media.

The movies became a commercial entertainment form in 1894 when films taken by Thomas Edison's Kinetograph camera were exhibited in peep-show form at Holland Brothers' Arcade on lower Broadway. For a nickel, viewers could watch a thirty-second loop of film run through Edison's Kinetoscope. The subjects of these first motion pictures were performers who had been lured from New York to Edison's tiny studio at his laboratory in West Orange, New Jersey: Sandow the Strongman, vaudeville knockabout comics Walton and May, May Irwin and Fred C. Rice doing a kiss in close-up from their hit Broadway play, and an unnamed woman who performed a rather tame variation on the cooch (a serpentine skirt dance), among others. Edison was slow to move toward projected motion pictures; but when it became apparent that foreign inventors had devised workable projectors, he was persuaded to introduce his own. Actually, Edison had nothing to do with the development of the Vitascope projector marketed under his name; he merely secured exclusive rights to the machine from its inventors, Thomas Armat and Francis Jenkins. Nevertheless, it was marketed as the new screen machine "on which Thomas A. Edison has been working for years" when it was debuted at Koster and Bial's Music Hall on April 23, 1896. For the next ten years, vaudeville provided the infant movie industry its principal venue and its most important audience.[31] That audience, as we have seen, was a diverse one, but at its core were middle- and lower-middle-class families. As ten- to fifteen-minute film programs quickly became standard in American vaudeville over the following season, movie genres were developed to serve the interests of vaudeville's audience and to satisfy the demands of B. F. Keith and other vaudeville magnates that everything on their programs be whole-some, family entertainment: travelogues, news films, brief comic narra-tives, and trick films, among them.[32]

But other audiences in other venues were willing to pay to see films with radically different appeals. One of the Edison Company's chief competitors between 1896 and 1908 (when the two firms joined others in a movie trust) was the American Mutoscope and Biograph Company (AMBCO), founded in 1895 by W. K. L. Dickson and three associates. Dickson had recently left Edison's employ, having done most of the work on "Edison's" first movie camera. Dickson developed a flip-card peep-show device, the Mutoscope, to compete with Edison's Kineto-scope in penny arcades, and a motion picture camera (the Biograph) by the fall of 1895. The Biograph could be modified for use as a projector as well, and the company joined Edison in providing programs for vaudeville theaters in 1896. Although Edison abandoned the Kineto-scope peep-show device when he moved to projected motion pictures, the Mutoscope remained an important part of Biograph's business for the next decade.[33] Between 1896 and 1902, many Mutoscope subjects distributed by Biograph to penny arcades, amusement parks, and sa-loons were the same as those the company screened for patrons at Keith's vaudeville theaters. Others definitely were not. In addition to making films for vaudeville patrons of Admiral George Dewey's trium-phant march through Union Square on his return from the Philippines and of the Atlantic City fire department answering a mock fire alarm, Biograph also produced such Mutoscope titles as "Pajama Girl," "A Hustling Soubrette," and "Poor Girls: It Was a Hot Night and the Mosquitoes Were Thick."

These brief, salacious flip-card subjects – sexually oriented narratives or spectacle displays – constituted the underside of Biograph's business for at least a decade. It was a side the company began to hide as its niche in the "respectable" sphere of the movie business became more secure. By 1908, racy Mutoscope subjects were filmed at its Manhattan studios in the evenings, providing the production staff and actors with extra income. D. W. Griffith, who joined Biograph in that year, might well have obtained his start as a director with "A Scene in a Dressing Room" or "The Merry Widow at a Supper Party." He certainly acted in these "spicy" vignettes – a superb irony given the solidly Victorian representation of women in the many "above-ground" film narratives he directed at Biograph over the next four years. The vast majority of the racy Mutoscope subjects were never copyrighted and have long since disappeared, even though visitors to Coney Island or Ocean City in the 1920s could still see "What the Butler Saw" Mutoscopes in the arcades there. A few were transferred from flip cards to film and copyrighted in 1902.[34] They were "discovered" among the Library of Congress's copyright deposit holdings in the 1960s and restored, along with hundreds of other "lost" films from the movies' earliest years.

A number of the brief Mutoscope subjects hark back to the female motion studies of Eadweard Muybridge – simple movements serving as an excuse for bodily display. For example, three films (called "films" here, although technically they were flip cards), copyrighted in 1903 but probably shot much earlier than that, involve three women wearing men's-style pajamas. In "Pajama Girl," one woman does calisthenics. In "Pajama Statue Girls," she is joined by two other women who throw a handkerchief to each other and freeze in position whenever it is caught. And in "A Dance in Pajamas," two of the three perform a soft-shoe dance while the third looks on and claps. In all three films, the performers play for the camera. In "Girls Swinging," shot in 1897 but not copyrighted until 1903, two young women take turns pushing the third in a swing. As she swings forward, the spectator gets a view of her petticoats.

A series of Mutoscopes shot in June 1901 used the device of the living picture to frame more explicit subjects. All of them employed a stage set concealed by curtains that were held closed by two burlesque-costumed women. In one of these films that survives, a man enters the frame from the side and places a card on an easel that reads "The Pouting Model." He then exits the frame and the two women pull back the curtains to reveal a nude adolescent girl standing with her back to the spectator and posing for a bearded artist seated in the background of the image. After a few seconds (in the tradition of the living picture neither of the framed figures move), the two women close the curtains and the film ends.

One of the most elaborate of the early voyeuristic subjects narra-tivized its sexual display in terms of burlesque. "The Trapeze Disrobing

Act" was made not by Biograph but under the auspices of that paragon of rectitude, Thomas A. Edison. The Edison Company also produced what it called "smoking concert" films around the turn of the century, although the intended venues of these one-minute subjects are less clear than those of the Mutoscopes. In "The Trapeze Disrobing Act," the camera is positioned as if in the front rows of a theater. On the stage, a woman in street dress and hat swings on a trapeze. On the left side of the frame two men occupy box seats, their long beards, hair, and dress marking them as rural bumpkins. While she swings, the woman removes her clothes: hat and blouse, skirt, corset, garters, then stockings. Stripped down to her camisole and petticoat, she turns a flip, removes her petticoat, and winds up sitting on the trapeze bar in trunks and camisole. Throughout her act – and it is clear from the skill with which she accomplishes her strip and trapeze maneuvers that this is a polished "act" – she plays to the rubes, throwing them her corset and garters as she removes them. The more she takes off, the more excited they become. They jump around the box, grab each other, and wildly gesticulate in gleeful appreciation. Interestingly, whereas at this time strip acts in burlesque were usually provided with some narrative context (a woman preparing for bed, for example) to "justify" the strip act itself, in this early film, the context of the burlesque stage provides the rationale for the film's sexual display.

From the surviving films and descriptions of Mutoscope subjects in the Biograph catalog, a pattern of class representation emerges in these "naughty" narrative films that parallels that found in the burlesque posters of roughly the same period. In the depiction of male characters in these films, there is a sharp delineation between bourgeois characters and others. Those portrayed as deriving pleasure from the sexual transgressiveness of women tend to be nonbourgeois. The rubes in "The Trapeze Disrobing Act" are objects of humor in their unrestrained enthusiasm, yet, like the male audience for the film itself, they are allowed to delight in the sexual spectacle before them. In "Foxy Grandpa and Polly in a Little Hilirity [*sic*]" (AMBCO, ca. 1902), another rural character dances with a young woman, who shows off her ankles for him. Bourgeois characters, on the other hand, tend to be punished for sexual desire. In "Professor of the Drama" (AMBCO, 1903), the male "professor" attempts, as the catalog describes it, to "make love" to a young female pupil, but their embrace is interrupted by the woman's

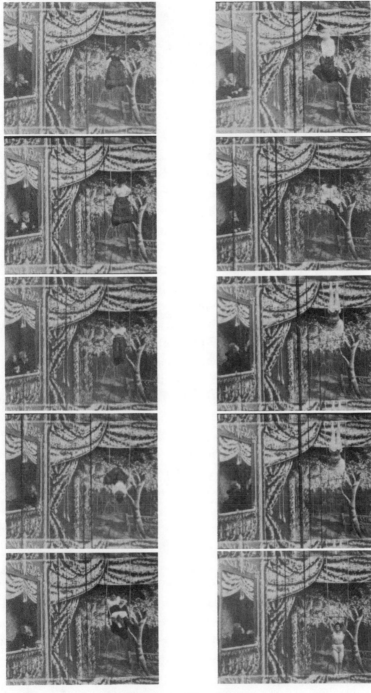

"The Trapeze Disrobing Act."
(Motion Picture, Broadcasting, and Recorded Sound Division,
Library of Congress)

father, who throws the professor out of a window. In "The Doctor's Favorite Patient" (AMBCO, 1903), a doctor is called to the dressing room of an actress. "In treating her headache," the catalog says, "he becomes more affectionate than discrete and when his wife and mother come in, there is trouble."[35]

A three-part Mutoscope series, "The Divorce" (AMBCO, 1903), depicts the consequences of bourgeois infidelity. In the first scene, entitled "Detected," husband, wife, and baby are at home. The husband drops a compromising letter, which is discovered by the wife. In the second, "On the Trail," she seeks the services of a private detective. In the concluding scene, "The Evidence Secured," the detective catches the husband and his mistress flagrante delicto by peeping through the keyhole of their hotel room. He and the wife burst in and confront them.[36]

Linda Williams's discussion of the possible pleasures offered by stag films has relevance to twentieth-century burlesque as well.[37] Unlike the hard-core feature film, whose pleasures are predicated on providing narrative and visual satisfaction, the stag film's pleasurability resides in its ability to arouse but not to satisfy the viewer. That arousal is displaced onto a ritual of homosocial bonding, in which tension-easing jocularity is substituted for sexual consummation. Moreover, the stag film, like burlesque, is characterized by its direct address to the audience, which further contributes to its goal of arousal and further differentiates it from the more "modern" hard-core feature. The latter shares the Hollywood cinema's covert and voyeuristic mode of audience address.

The dynamics of desire, sexual tension, and pleasure were more complex in burlesque than in a stag film screening at a Moose Lodge smoker. With the rise of the striptease, the appeals of burlesque increasingly centered around sexual arousal, and the "address" (whether through glance, gesture, or verbal address) of the stripper was even more direct than that of the female film subject. Mediated representation, whether carte-de-visite photos, stereographs, Mutoscopes, or projected motion pictures, took the already diminished power of the displayed female body in burlesque and contained and controlled that power even more. The carte de visite and stereograph reduced the subject of feminine sexual spectacle to a tiny icon, which could be bought and collected. As a Mutoscope subject, even her movement could be controlled by the spectator, since he controlled the speed at which the cards flipped by. Like the cooch dancer, she might return the gaze of the spectator, but now her gaze was incommensurable with his. In the theater, the body and gaze of dancer and spectator — although they were separated by the footlights and by their respective roles — occupied the same space, the same time, the same materiality. As a photographic or cinematographic image, however, her returning gaze had less power to unsettle since the gulf that separated the displayed woman from the man who looked at her was an unbridgeable, material gulf. He could look; she could only appear to look at him. Silenced, frozen in time, and captured within the film's frame, she evoked only a shadow of a threat.

As in the burlesque posters, the model viewer for sexually oriented motion pictures — the working-class male — was largely absent from their diegeses. He was privileged through this elision: he was given the best position from which to see and enjoy scenes of sexual transgression and spectacle, yet his pleasure was not spied on or punished. Interestingly, although in the burlesque posters bourgeois men were punished by the objects of their desire, in these films punishment came at the hands of a third party: the man's wife or the woman's father or mother. The objectified woman herself had been denied the power of sexual domination — even over bourgeois men.

O O O   **"Unruly Women": The Other Side of Burlesque's Power**

As argued earlier, the burlesque performer's unruliness when combined with sexual display rendered Thompsonian burlesque culturally too hot to handle in the late 1860s and provoked a series of defusing and marginalizing operations in subsequent decades. Consequently, the two halves of Thompsonian burlesque — sexual allure and inversive feminine insubordination — were separated from each other. Either half alone could be controlled and made to please without seriously undermining the position of the male spectator. Fused together in a single performer, however, this combination was much more threatening.[38]

Feminine verbal and physical insubordination were all but eliminated from burlesque with the advent of the cooch dance and the bifurcation of the burlesque show between silent, feminine sexual display and verbal, male-dominated humor. The isolation of feminine sexuality from feminine insubordination can also be seen at work in the forms that made sexual spectacle once again palatable to the middle class: the revue and its first cousin, the cabaret. Florenz Ziegfeld made the chorus girl "respectable" in the 1910s by divesting her image and figure of the markers of working-class culture. The Ziegfeld girl was sexually expressive – principally through the display of her body in revealing costumes – but that body was not the excessively gendered body of the Mastadon Minstrels, but the boyish, nearly androgynous body of the slender, postpubescent girl. Hers was the safe, nonthreatening sexuality of the middle-class girl next door, not the predatory sexuality of the burlesque poster. As Ziegfeld himself put it, "the vampire is not a popular household pet."[39]

And yet the cabaret culture of the teens was also home to another and quite different figuring of feminine sexuality, that represented best, perhaps, by Sophie Tucker. Tucker's persona was the inverse of that of the Ziegfeld girl. Her sexuality was verbal, not visual, expressed through the not-very-subtle double-entendre song. If the chorus girl was white-bread and middle-class, Sophie Tucker was unabashedly ethnic (Jewish) and working-class. Indeed, she first appeared in burlesque in 1908 in blackface as a singer of what were called "coon songs," one subgenre of which was built around the figure of the sexually aggressive black woman. Her theme song, "Some of These Days," was written by a black songwriter, Shelton Brooks. In her cabaret act, she mixed coon songs with those about the Yiddish Momma. She was no wide-eyed ingenue but an earthy, world-wise, independent, aggressive Red Hot Mamma, who sang in only slightly disguised fashion about her sexual appetites. Sophie Tucker's transgressiveness was limited, however, because she was not, at least for most members of the audience, the object of sexual desire. As one of her songwriters told her in 1910, her by-this-time unfashionable girth and lack of sex appeal "made her perfect to sing about sex without offending or enticing anyone." Tucker was the oversexed crone set against the immature sexuality of the chorus girl.[40]

Similarly, the aggressively sexual musical discourse of other women singers of the same period was contained by virtue of their racial otherness. Relegated to traveling tent shows and the "race-record" fringes of the recording industry in the 1920s and 1930s, black women performers such as Ethel Waters, Bessie Smith, and Lizzie Miles belted out blues and ragtime tunes whose direct sexuality is arresting even today. Ethel Waters (long before she launched a second career as a gospel singer) sang about her "Handy Man," who "greases my griddle and strokes my fiddle." Bessie Smith's "You Got to Give Me Some" contained the lyric, "I crave your round steak, you gotta give me some." And in 1930 Lizzie Miles lamented, "My front light's not working / And my double socket's loose / Come look at my meter / I think I need more juice."[41]

In each performer, expressive sexuality was yoked to another, "inappropriate" cultural category, producing what for WASP, bourgeois culture was a grotesque hybrid: sexuality and age; sexuality and (nonwhite) race; sexuality and nonexotic ethnicity; sexuality and the nonfetishized, excessive body. Channeled through these grotesque constructions and consigned to the margins of popular culture (Tucker in the cabaret demiworld; Smith, Waters, and Miles in the ghettos of tent shows and race records), the sexually aggressive songs and jokes of these performers could challenge some aspects of white, patriarchal culture without provoking suppression. Limited as these performers were to the shadows of mainstream culture, they still kept alive something of the insubordinate, inversive spirit of Thompsonian burlesque long after that spirit had been all but drained from burlesque itself.

Eva Tanguay, the only female performer to achieve stardom in big-time vaudeville with an act structured around sexual transgression, succeeded only by virtue of that transgressiveness being channeled through and contained by the grotesque. Tanguay, who entered vaudeville in 1904 after beginning her New York career in musical comedy, became one of vaudeville's highest-paid performers with an "eccentric comedienne" act that combined expressive sexuality with manic energy, bizarre presentation, and self-deprecating humor. Costumed more scantily than any "ordinary" female vaudeville performer dared, Tanguay would explode upon the stage from the wings to a deafening fanfare and launch into her signature song, "I Don't Care," all the while performing a sort of spastic parody of the cooch. Tanguay was never regarded as physically attractive — indeed, for most of her twenty-five-year career she was considerably overweight. She had no singing voice to speak of (a fact rendered academic by her style of shouting the lyrics of her songs), and her dances were singularly graceless. Although her dress and physical movements might have referenced for some spectators the sexuality of burlesque, her sexuality was not so much that of a siren as a mad woman. As such, it could not be taken as "seriously" transgressive but only as comically grotesque.[42]

The vaudeville and Broadway career of Mae West provides an example of a sexually expressive female performer whose image and persona initially were not constructed in terms of the grotesque and who dared to step out of the shadows and into the spotlight of bourgeois culture. Born in Brooklyn in 1893, West first appeared onstage at the age of six, and by 1912, when she put together her first professional vaudeville act, she had more than a decade of acting and performing experience in dramatic stock companies and musical comedy. West's entry into vaudeville was through what was called "small-time" vaudeville: a level of vaudeville that emerged in the wake of the popularity of the movies around 1910. Small-time houses combined films and variety acts in roughly equal proportions, offering as many as five shows per day for prices less than those of "big-time" vaudeville (B. F. Keith and others) and only slightly more than those of storefront movie theaters. Situated somewhere between the all-male, working-class audiences of burlesque and the family, bourgeois audiences of big-time vaudeville, small-time audiences (and managers) were generally more tolerant of double entendres and mildly suggestive material than were the audiences along Keith's "Sunday School circuit."[43]

As West developed her act in the small-time theaters across the country, she created a persona of the glamorous, tough, aggressive, sensual woman. The songs she sang in her act had lyrics whose double-entendre meanings were made transparent by her highly erotic delivery. She also did what was forbidden in Keith theaters: she addressed the audience directly with her songs and patter, closing her act with the tag line that was to become her trademark: "It isn't what you do; it's how you do it!" In effect, she imported the rhetorical directness and the sexuality of burlesque into small-time vaudeville. She even included a version of the cooch in her act, which proved to be too "strong" even for some small-time theaters. In her memoirs, *Goodness Had Nothing To Do with It*, she recalled being fired from the Palace Theater in New Haven, Connecticut (a small-time house on the Poli chain), because of what one newspaper called her "enchanting, seductive, sin-promising wriggle." Although West aspired to the money and fame of big-time vaudeville, the sexual expressiveness of her act and, equally if not more damning, its connections with burlesque precluded her acceptance there – even after five years of trying. In 1916 *Variety* said of her latest tryout in the big time: "Mae West in big-time vaudeville may only be admired for her persistency in believing she is a big-time act and trying to make vaudeville accept her as such. . . . Unless Miss West can tone down her stage presence in every way, she just as well might hop right out of vaudeville into burlesque."[44]

The following year she gave up on vaudeville, accepting a role in a new Broadway revue entitled *Sometime*. In it she claims to have transplanted the shimmy from the black jazz clubs of South Chicago to the New York stage. At the Elite No. 1 Cafe in Chicago, she saw black couples who "stood in one spot, with hardly any movement of the feet, and just shook their shoulders, torsos, breasts and pelvises. We thought it was funny and were terribly amused by it. But there was a naked, aching sensual agony about it too."[45] In *Sometime*, West's sexual expressiveness was reframed in terms of its relation to the theatrical genre of the revue. As such, its ties to the working-class sexuality of burlesque were loosened – even though (West's claims notwithstanding) the shimmy was at that moment updating the cooch dancer's routine in burlesque theaters across the country. West succeeded in revues in the 1920s where she had failed in big-time vaudeville in the 1910s. The audiences for the two forms, although drawn from overlapping economic strata, expected very different types of entertainment. By the 1920s, sensuality was tolerated in revues to a degree that would have been unthinkable in big-time vaudeville and would have been suppressed in burlesque.

Although she enjoyed a successful career in revues in the 1920s, West had higher ambitions. As she recalled in her memoirs,

I had a proper understanding which grew stronger; that behind the symbol I was becoming, there was much good material for drama, satire and some kind of ironic comment on the war of sexes and the eternal engagement and grappling between men and women in a battle that never ends. I did not perhaps treat the subject as seriously as Havelock Ellis, or as deeply as Sigmund Freud, Adler,

Jung or Dr. Kinsey, but I think if we all could have sat down and discussed the subject fully, my ideas would have been listened to with some sense of awe. They may have been the generals, but I was in the front lines — out in an emotional No Man's Land, engaged in dangerous hand-to-hand, lip-to-lip raiding parties. I have always found it's personal experience that counts, not making fever charts.[46]

By 1926 West had already written two unproduced plays, each of which concerned a woman's use of her sexual charms to dominate men.[47] Her first dramatic effort to be seen by an audience was in-spired — as she remembered it — by the sight of gaudily dressed pros-titutes parading arm-in-arm with sailors along the New York water-front. Set initially in a Montreal brothel, the play revolves around the character of Margie Lamont, a prostitute who longs to leave "the life" and find a sugar daddy to support her. Her pimp, Rocky, who also sells his sexual services to women, warns her that if she attempts to leave, he will kill her. Besides, he says, "There's only one thing about you to hold a guy, and outside of that you're merely nothing." A chance police raid discovers one of Rocky's clients, the ignored wife of a Connecticut businessman, whom he has drugged in order to steal her money. To avoid being connected with the crime, Margie follows the advice of Gregg, one of her sailor-clients, and follows him and the fleet to Trin-idad, where she meets and falls in love with Jimmy Stanton, the son of a wealthy absentee plantation owner. Jimmy is not aware of Margie's past and asks her to marry him. She tells Gregg: "Why ever since I've been old enough to know sex I've looked at men as hunters. They're filled with sex. In the past few years I've been a chattel to that sex. All the bad that's in me has been put there by men. I began to hate every one of them — hated them, used them for what I could get out of them, and then laughed at them — and then, then he came along." When Jimmy takes Margie home to Connecticut to meet his parents, she discovers that his mother is none other than the victim of her former pimp, who has kept her liaison and its unfortunate outcome a secret. Margie confronts her: "The things I've done, I had to do for a living. I know it was wrong. I'm not trying to alibi myself. But you've done those same things for other reasons." Both Rocky and Gregg turn up at the Stanton home while Margie is visiting. Rocky has been blackmailing Jimmy's mother; Gregg is a friend of Jimmy from his Trinidad days. Margie calls the police and tells them to come and arrest Rocky; even the officer who arrives turns out to be one of her former clients. In the play's final scene, Margie reveals her past to Jimmy, then leaves with Gregg for Australia.[48]

After the Shubert organization refused to produce the play, West undertook the production herself, arranging financing (part of which she provided) and hiring her own producer and director. Just before its tryout run in New London, Connecticut, she changed the working title of the play from *The Albatross* to *Sex*, and it was as *Sex* that it opened at Daly's Theater on Sixty-third Street in the spring of 1926. Despite the fact that some newspapers refused to run the play's title in advertisements, it was a box office success, running for eleven months.

Not surprisingly, it also attracted the attention of civic authorities. In February 1927, on orders from Acting Mayor Joseph McKee, police raided the theater and arrested twenty members of the cast and two backers for violating Section 1140a of the penal code. At their trial in April, the prosecutor made a particular point of the belly dance West's character performed early in the second act. This, along with the suggestiveness of West's delivery, gestures, and mannerisms, was enough to secure a jury conviction against the entire cast and West's two coproducers. Despite the recommendation of eight jurors that all defendants be given suspended sentences, the judge sentenced West and the two producers, James A. Timony and Clarence Morgenstern, to ten days in jail and a fine of five hundred dollars each. The harsh sentences were justified, he said, by the fact that the evidence clearly showed *Sex* to be an "obscene, immoral, and indecent" play. In his opinion, West "seemed to go to extremes in order to make the play as obscene and immoral as possible." West served her time at the Women's Workhouse on Welfare Island, where she performed "light housework." On her release, she presented a check for one thousand dollars to the prison warden to start the Mae West Memorial Prison Library. Her only complaint about her jail stay concerned the rough cotton underwear she had been issued.[49]

West's experience did not deter her from making sexual transgression the subject of her next play. *The Drag* was, as West later described it, a "clinical and serious" treatment of male homosexuality. The play's attitude toward homosexuality is ambivalent. It opens with a gay man (David) appealing to his doctor for help in dealing with his attraction to a "normal" man. "I'm one of those damned creatures who are called degenerates and moral lepers for a thing they cannot help – a thing that has made us suffer," he says. "There is not one of us who would not be like other men." The doctor suggests that he take up sports. Later in the same act, however, when a judge consults the doctor regarding a case of possible insanity, the doctor argues that notions of abnormality are inherently relative. He gives the example of David, who was born with "inverted sexual desires." As a result, he is "neither male nor female, but something of both – physically a male with feminine instincts." What straight society would regard as "abnormal" desires he feels as normal.[50]

The characters who suffer most in the play are those who deny their true nature or attempt to conceal it. One gay character describes visiting David:

> Well, I goes over and there was the poor queen ready to jump out the window. Of course I knew what was the matter. She needed a jab. She's been taking heroin and morphine by the barrels. The trouble with her is she's sensitive of what she is. Now, I don't give a damn who knows it. Of course, I don't go flouncing my hips up and down Broadway picking up trade or with a sign on my back advertising it. But of course I don't pass anything up either, dearie.

Acknowledgment of one's sexuality, however, is liberating. The entire third act of the play is a "drag," a party attended by forty gay men in drag, who poke fun at themselves and at heterosexual relations in songs, dances, and jokes. In a line that might in another play have been spoken by Mae West herself, one character at the party brags: "I'm just the type that men crave. The type that burns 'em up. Why, when I walk up Tenth Avenue, you can smell the meat sizzling in Hell's Kitchen." The raucous revelry is shattered when the party's host, the son of the judge in the first act who has hidden his "condition" from his wife and family, is shot by David. Rather than have his son's aberration revealed in a trial, his father reports his death as a suicide. *The Drag* opened in Paterson, New Jersey, and played to full houses for two weeks. New York City officials warned West that she faced almost certain prosecution if she moved the play to Broadway, and she closed the show after recouping her investment in the Paterson run.[51]

Despite the subject matter of *The Drag* and the fact that her later films have attracted a cult following among some gay men, West was hardly a champion of gay rights. In her autobiography, she called homosexuality "a danger to the entire social system of western civilization." She did not object to homosexuality as "a cult of jaded inverts or special groups of craftsmen," but if it spread into the culture in general, it had the potential to "rot away" society from the inside.[52] To West, both prostitution and homosexuality were forms of sexual transgression that could be used to point out contradictions in bourgeois society's ordering of sexual categories. *Sex* contrasts the social acceptability of commodified sexuality in marriage with its criminalization as prostitution. In *The Drag*, the judge's refusal to deal with his own son's homosexuality becomes emblematic of polite society's reticence to acknowledge sexuality at all.

In *The Pleasure Man*, which was closed by police on opening night in 1928,[53] West used gay characters as foils for the barbaric masculinity of Rodney Terrill, an actor who seduces, then abandons ingenues. Having seen him roughly treat a jilted lover backstage at the vaudeville theater they are both playing, a gay female impersonator tells Terrill: "If you're a man, thank God I'm a female impersonator." One of the reasons for police intervention was the play's climax, in which Terrill is castrated (offstage) by Ted Arnold, the brother of one of his victims. Arnold unapologetically admits to the murder and, in the play's closing speech, responds to the charge that the manner by which Terrill was dispatched was obscene: "Obscene – obscene . . . when I was in college – in the laboratory, we experimented with vermin . . . we worked on them so that they could never propagate their own kind. The life I took from Terrill was no higher or better than that of a poisonous beast."[54]

Diamond Lil, the most successful of West's Broadway productions and the basis for her second picture, *She Done Him Wrong*, is an evocation of tenderloin life in the 1890s. In the stage version, West played Diamond Lil, an underworld queen who, in addition to performing in a dance hall, trains shoplifters, gives cocaine to friends in need of it, and helps her boyfriend Gus recruit poor women for the brothels of Rio. The representative of the establishment's social and moral order in the play is Captain Cummings, a police detective masquerading as a Salvation Army officer. When he and a confederate arrest Gus for white slavery, Lil angrily rebukes them, in a speech conspicuously absent from the film version:

> You two, emblems of the law, say, what chance would your law have given these poor things that went to Rio, anyway? Would you have given them a helping hand? A square deal? . . . Like hell you would have. You'd have planted them as vagrants, prostitutes, or drunks in your jails where they could have worked out their bodies scrubbing floors so that you folks could walk around all dressed up and see how well the warden ran his prison. Just because Gus sent them out of your clutches where they could sing and dance and get a square meal once in a while, you folks have to sneak around like a snake in the grass and sink your fangs into him.[55]

West's Broadway successes and national tours had brought her to the attention of Paramount executives, who lured her to the West Coast in the summer of 1932 in an effort to rejuvenate business hard hit by the depression. In *Night after Night*, *She Done Him Wrong*, *I'm No Angel*, and *Belle of the Nineties*, she brought to the screen the persona she had developed in more than a decade of characters played in revues and plays: the brash, tough hedonist and "awarish," statuesque vamp whose philosophy was (in the words of Diamond Lil): "Men is all alike. Married or single, it's the same game. *Their game*. I happen to be wise enough to play it their own way." Unlike anything that had been seen and heard since the recent advent of the talking motion picture (1927), West's persona played on the margins of bourgeois tolerance and tested its limits. *She Done Him Wrong* broke box office records in many cities and, some claim, enabled Paramount to avert bankruptcy. The film also spurred to action a coalition of religious and civic pressure groups, whose members were convinced that "constant exposure to screen stories of successful gangsters . . . and of flaming.passion and high power emotionalism may easily nullify every standard of life and conduct set up at home and at school."[56]

Always fearful of externally imposed censorship, Hollywood redoubled its self-censorship in 1934 as a result of a threatened boycott of theaters showing "immoral" films. With West the announced principal target of the Catholic Legion of Decency's "anti-smut" campaign, the release of *Belle of the Nineties* (originally titled *It Ain't No Sin*) was held up at the last moment so that portions of it could be deleted or reshot. West continued to play variations on the Diamond Lil character at Paramount for four more years, in such films as *Klondike Annie* (1936) and *Go West Young Man* (1936), but her sexual impudence was significantly toned down in these roles. In 1938, weary of dealing with the negative publicity her still-profitable pictures generated, Paramount declined to renew her contract. She made only two more pictures before returning to live theater.

Although she does not put it in quite these terms, Marjorie Rosen has in effect argued that, the hysterical reaction of the Legion of Decency notwithstanding, the transgressiveness of West's film roles was blunted by the fact that by the time of her first screen appearance in 1932, her persona had already begun to take on strong undertones of the grotesque. Had they come from the mouth of one of the movies' reigning female sex symbols, the suggestive lines spoken by West's characters would have shocked more than just overly zealous religious watchdog groups. But, as Rosen says, "There stood Mae, age forty in 1933, boned and corseted and looking uncomfortably like a turn-of-the-century sausage, barely able to move because her skirt was too tight and heels too high; posturing with pouting mouth and radiating allure with a burlesque of rolling eyes."[57] West's persona became less and less threatening as it became more and more difficult to take her expressive sexuality seriously. Her sex appeal was no longer obvious; rather, West had to convince her audiences that "goodness had nothing to do with it." We know she is the object of men's fondest erotic desires because she constantly (indeed, obsessively) reminds us that she is. By the time her film career took off, Mae West had come to resemble nothing so much as a female impersonator, parodying rather than exuding the vamp's controlling sexuality.

○ ○ ○   **The Meanings of Burlesque**

The history of burlesque since 1869 demonstrates the transgressive power of the union of charismatic female sexuality and inversive insubordination, as well as the strategies employed by patriarchal culture to disengage, marginalize, and/or contain these two aspects of public, commercial gender representation. For the bourgeois culture at the end of the 1860s, the "horrible prettiness" of Lydia Thompson and her troupe evoked both the threat of gender revolution and the fear of working-class contamination. In the discourse about it, burlesque was constructed in such a way that it became unsupportable as an instance of bourgeois culture. Opposition stopped short of outright suppression. Instead, the threat was contained by driving burlesque out of bourgeois culture and into the less visible and more easily policed realm of working-class commercial culture. There, along with her fellow low-other figures in nineteenth-century popular culture, the minstrel and the freak, the burlesque performer was reconstructed through other discourses and repositioned in terms of her relationship with her new working-class, unisex audience. Her power and the threat that power represented were deflected away from burlesque's audience and dis-placed onto a reassuring reordination of fantasy class relations, in which she figured as the instrument of upper-class humiliation. With the advent of the cooch and the striptease, and with the separation of visual and verbal appeals of burlesque through the male colonization of burlesque humor, the links between expressive sexuality and inversive insubordination were effectively broken. Except as the talking-woman object of lubricious humor, the burlesque performer was silenced, and thus her power to point to the system in which she was inscribed became even more limited. In the Ziegfeld girl, the sexually expressive female was reconstituted through the excorporation (literally and figuratively) of what was left of the burlesque performer's threatening qualities. She might have been an icon of sexual modernity for her male and female spectators, but there was nothing daunting or troublesome about the Ziegfeld girl's wholesome, doll-like, decorative sexuality. The final strategy that emerges from this history was that of tolerating "unruly" female performers so long as their transgressive power was channeled and defused through their construction as grotesque figures. Such fig-ures were authorized to be transgressive because, by their fusing of incongruent cultural categories, they had been "disqualified" as objects of erotic desire.

It would be possible, on the one hand, to interpret the history of burlesque nostalgically – as the eruption of a new, woman-centered form of theatrical expression with strong progressive, antipatriarchal leanings, which was quickly drained of most (or all) of its sexual-political force in order that it could be recuperated within patriarchal hegemony, but whose spirit has infused the work of female performers from Sophie Tucker and Mae West to Bette Midler and Roseanne Barr. On the other hand, one could refuse to see Thompsonian burlesque as a rupture in the history of gender representation, regarding it instead merely as a point in a historical continuum of the cultural exploitation of the female form. *The Black Crook* begets *Ixion*, which begets Madame Rentz's Female Minstrels, which begets the cooch dance, which begets the striptease, which begets *Deep Throat*. Viewed in this way, the insubordination of the burlesque performer merely made the display of her body more titillating and pleasurable. The male spectator found her pretense of control unproblematic and even arousing because it was just that: a pretense.

Neither interpretation alone captures the irreducible complexity of burlesque and of the response it provoked, however, although each points to one side of burlesque's paradoxical nature.[58] In transgressing the norms of sexual expressiveness through performance and display, the burlesque performer pointed to the system of power relations within which she was figured. By 1869 bourgeois standards, Lydia Thompson did more than point to this system; she used it as a framework for her self-presentation and impudent humor. By the same token, the burlesque performer (at whatever historical moment) is constructed within that system and functions within it not to satisfy her own need for self-expression but rather to produce pleasure for male spectators. The language (verbal and bodily) she uses is not entirely of her own choosing; the codes she deploys are those of a system not structured by her or for her benefit. The pleasure the burlesque performer provokes may be alloyed by a temporary fear of losing control. On occasion the spectator's laugh may be the nervous laughter of the bald-headed man with a lipstick-imprinted kiss on his pate whose role in this system of display and gaze has been made all too evident. Nevertheless, the history of burlesque is the history of an otherwise unintelligible system of gender representation driven by male pleasure. Now we may argue over who has the upper hand at particular moments in particular cases, with respect to particular performers and audiences – whether burlesque represents the capture of feminine assertiveness within male specularity or the potential for undermining patriarchal control. But the historical evidence suggests the need to recognize both burlesque's capacity for insubordination and even reordination and concomitantly the simultaneous circumscription, at times even the subversion, of that capacity by the same system that provides the performer a platform on which to act, speak, and show off. This is the inescapable cultural and political paradox of burlesque.

This study has tried to avoid ascribing to burlesque performers either a sense of empowerment that might have resulted from their transgressiveness or the intention to upset the patriarchal order through their insubordination. Furthermore, it does not address the important question of what might have been the effect on *female* spectators of the inversive humor of Thompsonian burlesque, the image of the dominating amazon in the 1880s, the manipulating chorus girl of the 1890s, the frenzied cooch dancer, or the elegant stripper. In part, this reluctance to make these ascriptions stems from an absence of evidence that they are warranted. Although intention is hardly a prerequisite for effect, few burlesque performers have left accounts of their motives, goals, or attitudes toward their roles in burlesque. Lydia Thompson's handwritten notes for a memoir, penned in the 1890s, reveal principally the degree to which she had become a bourgeois matron. Thus, she plays down the insubordination of her early roles. It is also important to recognize that at no point in the history of burlesque were performers totally in control of the form. Lydia Thompson was probably the most powerful and independent female figure in burlesque, and yet her career was managed by her husband and her lines (at least those not improvised by her in performance) were written by men. On the reception side, surviving instances of audience commentary on popular entertainment are rare – except for that discourse generated by critics, reformers, and a few avid theatergoers whose social station made their diaries worth preserving for other reasons. As far as female spectators of burlesque are concerned, we have only Olive Logan's diatribes.

As difficult as it is to speculate regarding the resonance of burlesque among either its female performers or its auditors, the possibility that *some* women found the charismatic, expressive sexuality of burlesque empowering as a means of using an oppressive system against itself must be noted. The evidence for this possibility comes largely from outside the realm of burlesque; however, the systemic connections between burlesque and other sites of gender representation make extrapolation reasonable.

Kathy Peiss has argued that for some urban, working-class young women of the late nineteenth century, commercial leisure constituted an arena within which sexuality could be used to make patriarchy literally pay for its social and economic exploitation of women. For these women there was no bourgeois Manichaean duality about sexual expression, but rather a pragmatic instrumentality. Peiss cites a journalist who overheard two women at Coney Island discuss their dates the previous evening. "What sort of time did you have?" the first asks. "Great. He blew $5 on the blow-out," the other replies. "You beat me again," the first admits, "My chump only spent $2.50."[59] Peiss is quick to point out that the strategy of "treating," by which a woman traded degrees of sexual familiarity for access to the pleasures offered by commercial leisure, was a fundamentally problematic way of negotiating patriarchy:

> This is not to claim that the social and sexual freedom expressed in working women's leisure constituted a form of liberation [for] . . . without economic independence, such freedoms were ultimately hollow. Indeed, one could argue that this culture was primarily a product of the leisure industry's efforts to market entertainment and consumption to working-class women, who were lulled into a state of false consciousness. Without denying the importance of these points, I think it is necessary to understand how women pushed at the boundaries of constrained lives and shaped cultural forms for their own purposes. In essence, understanding working women's culture calls for a doubled vision, to see that women's embrace of style, fashion, romance, and mixed-sex fun could be a source of autonomy and pleasure as well as a cause of their continuing oppression.[60]

It is the double bind Peiss describes, which characterizes the expressive sexuality of burlesque as well, that requires the uncomfortable double view of it. To see it as unproblematically liberatory is naive. To see it as a hegemonic scam in all cases for all women is to make women into mere dupes and to underestimate the resourcefulness of oppressed groups in manipulating the system of their oppression. This resourcefulness can be found even in the most exploitative situations. In the early 1980s former stripper Seph Weene wrote of the complex dynamics of her interaction with male spectators. For some of them, the show was a masochistic ritual of unsatisfied arousal; for others, it was an enactment of sadistic fantasy. But for the performers, she argues, the specifics of the nature of male scopic pleasure were irrelevant. "We wanted control." "The thrill I got from stripping," she says, "was power. I was seen as powerful; more important, I felt powerful." Weene was also aware of the paradoxical nature of that power: "Ordinary restrictions on women's behavior did not apply on that stage. And there was the flaw: it was such relative power. If we were free in the real world, the stage freedom would not matter. I thought I was crazy because both the conventional, male-dominated outlook and feminist doctrine defined what I did as bad. I was having forbidden fun." For Weene, stripping was a means of confronting directly the commodification of female sexuality, not just as it was manifested in her relations with spectators but in the cool commercialism of managers and agents as well. "According to their rules, my sexuality was a product. It was a harsh realization, but liberating. I knew the mind of my enemy. And I knew that, since this dehumanizing view of women was so central to our culture, that it had been in my mind, too. I became conscious of that part of me that saw myself as less than human, and began to resist the self-hatred that has crippled women for so long."[61]

Put another way, within the liminoid setting of commercial popular entertainment sexual transgressiveness can become the basis for a reordination of power relations. It is, to be sure, a reordination bounded by liminality's "set-apartness" from the realm of external social relations and one that need not even be acknowledged by those atop the hierarchy that is being rearranged. We are talking here about how the low other comes to view her own relationship with the system in which she is defined as low other. Nevertheless, the liminality of the site and the transgressive nature of the performance allows for competing ordinations, for asymmetrical constructions of meaning by the actors involved.

A December 1986 feature article in the *Washington Post* describes the latest barroom entertainment craze in suburban Chicago: a variation on female mud wrestling, in which four bikini-clad women, calling themselves the "Chicago Dolls," wrestle each other and (in the last round) male patrons in a plastic pit full of strawberry Jell-O to the delight of predominantly male audiences. In the article, the Dolls acknowledge that Jell-O wrestling takes on very different meanings for them than for their audience:

Sure, you can view it as a sex symbol. But I don't see it that way. I do what I damn well want to. . . . Women view it as aggressive, a thing they've never done, whereas men are going to think it's just something sexy. It took me two years to get aggressive enough to be a good wrestler. I'd never hit anybody before. I had to learn to be aggressive and that's hard for a woman because we were taught to be sweet and nice and cute. . . . We do it for the high. That adrenaline pumping, that forcefulness. The men, they think we're out there to make love to all of them. . . . A lot of them go home very disappointed. . . . It's not exactly what your typical housewife's doing. And we're not stuck at a desk indoors eight hours a day.[62]

Here, empowerment of the low other is facilitated by the fact that the form itself operates through transgression and inversion. The traditionally male and culturally "masculine" sport of wrestling is undertaken and thereby undercut by women. However, the execution of movements that constitute wrestling as an athletic activity are rendered comically grotesque, if not impossible, by the slippery medium in which they must occur. The medium itself, Jell-O, the epitome of wholesome food, is wallowed in by the participants. Furthermore, by replacing mud as the medium in which the performance occurs, Jell-O is linked with filth and with feces. This inversion did not go unnoticed by General Foods, the manufacturers of Jell-O. The article quotes a company spokesman, who complains: "Our trademark attorneys go into conniption fits. . . . It's disgusting to have people swimming around in food." To make this culinary inversion work in another way, the Dolls use only red (strawberry) Jell-O: food becomes symbolic of blood. And the special symbolic connection of blood with women is not missed by either the performers or their audiences. One of the Dolls explains: "We started with cherry, of course, but we got too many comments."

Seph Weene speaks of the disdain the performer feels for her spectatorial adversaries, an attitude shared by others constructed as low others. The turn-of-the-century "charity girls" Kathy Peiss writes about referred to their dates as "chumps." In Morton Minsky's glossary of burlesque jargon, a "jerk" is a member of the audience. Arthur Lewis, in preparation for an interview with William Durks, the three-eyed, two-nosed star of Slim Kelley's carnival sideshow, asked Kelley how he should approach his subject. Kelley's advice was to regard Durks as a show business professional whose opinion of his audiences was not particularly high: "Remember, when people are staring up at them on the platform, they're staring right back. Whatever contempt marks feel for freaks, freaks return *their* own opinions double. Sometimes I wonder which side of the stage is right." Durks explained that when he left the carnival lot, he wore a cap pulled down to his chin to conceal his deformities. But when a store clerk gave him a difficult time or remarked on his cap, he struck back: "I think to myself, 'All right, you marks. I'm not ashamed of nothin'.' So I pull off the cap and shove my face right next to theirs and stare at 'em with all my eyes. They take one look and get white. Many's the time I seen 'em faint dead away and hit their damned heads on the floor. I seen great big men turn around and puke. Serves 'em right!" The tightly knit and self-contained world of carnival performers, who are frequently ostracized by straight society, encourages a reordination of social relations, whereby everyone outside of "the life" is constructed as an object of contempt. "Carnies don't like the marks, seldom associate with them, and look on them with scorn," observes Lewis. "To 'take' a mark whenever and wherever he can be taken is their way of life."[63]

It is difficult to celebrate Weene's reordination of her relationship with the world of stripping or the Jell-O wrestler's empowerment through barroom spectacle as instances of cultural resistance. Such "internal" reordination does not subvert the system; it merely reorders its terms for some of its actors. It is more negotiation than resistance: making the system work perversely – not so much against its own interests as unintentionally in addition to them. But in both cases, experiencing gender power relations from the position of the low other enabled these women to make connections between the dynamics of sexuality in popular entertainment and those dynamics in the outside world. Weene discovered that her attraction to stripping "had less to do with any personal kinks than with the distortion of female sexuality in our culture."[64]

Despite their problematic political nature, or rather because of it, instances of cultural transgression and inversion – such as those found throughout the history of American popular entertainment – demand our attention if we are to better understand the complex operations of cultural power and the equally complex relations among hierarchies of power (race, gender, class) in American society. At work in these instances are the messy dialectics of ordination and subordination, transgression and containment of transgression, inversion and displaced abjection, threat and pleasure, meaning and countermeaning, sense and nonsense. Unequivocal demonstrations of top-down cultural power and examples of outright resistance to this power do not adequately capture the dynamics of cultural power relations in America. We see neither in the history of burlesque. In burlesque's irreducible complexity, we can glimpse something of the larger complexities of the ways we construct meaning and pleasure from our engagements with cultural forms and, in the process, are constructed by them.

Notes

○   ○   ○   ○   ○   ○   ○   ○   ○   ○   ○   ○

CHAPTER ONE

1   Unless otherwise indicated, information on Lydia Thompson's New York debut is taken from various issues of the *New York Clipper*, 1866–68. See especially August 18, 1866, p. 150; February 8, 1868, p. 347; July 18, 1868, p. 118; August 8, 1868, p. 142; September 5, 1868, p. 174; September 19, 1868, p. 190; September 26, 1868, p. 214; October 3, 1868, p. 214; October 17, 1868, cover. Unless otherwise indicated, information on Thompson's London career prior to 1868 is taken from Moses, "Lydia Thompson," pp. 25–46.

2   Betts, "P. T. Barnum"; "Barnum's American Museum" (playbill). Barnum's own museum had burned earlier in the year; hence, his availability as adviser to Wood.

3   Moses, "Lydia Thompson," pp. 87–115.

4   *The Season*, August 29, 1868, clipping, file MWEZ.n.c. 19,546, New York Public Library Performing Arts Collection (hereafter cited as NYPL).

5   Ibid. See also *Spirit of the Times*, September 12, 1868.

6   Poster, "Lydia Thompson in *Ixion*," NYPL; Moses, "Lydia Thompson," p. 37 (quotation); *New York Clipper*, September 26, 1868.

7   *The Season*, August 29, 1868, clipping, file MWEZ.n.c. 19,546, NYPL.

8   Burnham, "Stage Degeneracy," p. 34; *New York Clipper*, October 10, 1868, p. 214; March 6, 1869, p. 382.

9   Hagan, *Records of the New York Stage*, 11:99–11; Croghan, "New York Burlesque," pp. 171–75; Moses, "Lydia Thompson," pp. 43–45; *New York Clipper*, October 3, 1868, p. 214 (poem); advertisement for Wood's Museum, *New York Times*, September 28, 1868, p. 9.

10 Burnand, *Ixion*. The Greek myth of Ixion is recounted in Graves's *Greek Myths*, pp. 208–10. For whatever one would want to make of it, Graves notes that "as an oak-king with mistletoe genitals . . . [Ixion], representing the thunder-god . . . ritually married the rain-making Moon-goddess; and was then scourged, so that his blood and sperm would fructify the earth. . . , beheaded with an axe, emasculated, spread-eagle to a tree, and roasted; after which his kinsmen ate him sacramentally" (p. 209).

11 Quoted in Ewen, *Songs of America*, pp. 156–57.
12 *New York Times*, September 29, 1868, p. 4; *Spirit of the Times*, October 3, 1868, p. 29; *New York Clipper*, November 28, 1868, p. 270; *New York Times*, November 15, 1868, p. 5.
13 *New York Clipper*, October 10, 1868, p. 214.
14 Markham, *The Life of Pauline Markham*, pp. 20–21.
15 *New York Times*, October 1, 1868, p. 6.
16 *Spirit of the Times*, October 3, 1868, p. 29.
17 *New York Times*, December 26, 1868, p. 5; *New York Clipper*, December 26, 1868, p. 302; January 31, 1868, p. 342; Gintautiene, "*The Black Crook*," p. 52. Several secondary sources claim that the reason for the change in venue from Wood's to Niblo's was that Thompson and her troupe were offended by the smell from Wood's menagerie (see Moses, "Lydia Thompson," p. 52). I can find no contemporaneous substantiation for this story. As Moses notes, the reason for the move probably was that Niblo's would provide a more prestigious site and could accommodate more elaborate scenic effects. In her memoirs, Pauline Markham claims the move was hastened by a disagreement between Alexander Henderson and Samuel Colville, manager of Wood's Theater. See Markham, *The Life of Pauline Markham*, p. 24.
18 Logan, *Apropos of Women and Theatres*, p. 138.
19 Brough, *The Field of the Cloth of Gold*. The printed English version of the play is also in the NYPL collection. It notes that Thompson played the role of Darnley in the Strand production.
20 For song lyrics, see Ewen, *Songs of America*, pp. 150–52. On Holt's performance, see *New York Clipper*, February 20, 1869, p. 366; February 27, 1869, p. 374; January 29, 1870, p. 342.
21 Playbill, "Tony Pastor's Opera House, Monday, March 29, 1869," in Hagan, *Records of the New York Stage*, 11:171. As if to demonstrate that burlesque could feed on any topic of public interest or controversy, critics' harping on the artificial blondeness of burlesque performers was written into two burlesques the following season. Lisa Weber and Ada Harland returned to Wood's in the fall of 1869 with *Dora Bella, the Mill, the Mystery, the Mission, the Miss, the Minstrel, and the Dyed Hair*. That spring, Lydia Thompson made her return appearance at Niblo's following her cross-country tour in *Pippin; or, The King of the Gold Mine*. In it, Eliza Weatherby sang, "The Blonde That Never Dyes":

> As I strolled out the other day,
> In fashion's best arrayed,
> I passed and looked and list'd to gents,
> As compliments they paid,
> And one that pleased me most of all,
> Was spoken with such sighs;
> A nice young man says there she goes,

The Blonde that never dyes.
The Blonde that never dyes,
The Blonde that never dyes;
Both far and near I'm sure to hear,
The Blonde that never dyes.

See Banner, *American Beauty*, p. 124; *New York Clipper*, April 24, 1869, p. 414. See also Moses, "Lydia Thompson," pp. 49–50. On *Dora Bella*, see *New York Clipper*, December 25, 1869, p. 302. Music and lyrics for "The Blonde That Never Dyes" are from Levy, *Flashes of Merriment*, p. 90.

22 *New York Clipper*, May 15, 1869, p. 46.
23 Ibid., June 19, 1869, p. 86; June 7, 1869, p. 70 (quotation).
24 Ibid., July 24, 1869, p. 126; September 4, 1869, p. 182; October 2, 1869, p. 206; October 16, 1869, p. 222; November 6, 1869, p. 246; November 13, 1869, p. 254; December 4, 1869, p. 278. See also excerpts from local newspapers reprinted in "The Play of the Period" (broadside).
25 *New York Clipper*, November 6, 1869, p. 246.
26 Ibid., December 4, 1869, p. 278; *Chicago Evening Post*, November 23, 1869, reprinted in "The Play of the Period" (broadside).
27 Quotations reprinted in "The Play of the Period" (broadside).
28 The following account of the Storey incident was taken from "The Play of the Period" (broadside). Thompson might have taken her cue in the horse-whipping incident from the example of a fellow burlesquer, Elise Holt. As will be discussed in a later chapter, Holt's appearance in San Francisco the previous summer had provoked a remarkably similar outpouring of vitriol from several newspapers, especially the *San Francisco News Letter*. Holt is reported to have confronted the editor of the paper in office armed with a cowhide. The outcome is not reported. See Ettore Rella, *A History of Burlesque*, pp. 114–15.

CHAPTER TWO

1 Richard Grant White, "The Age of Burlesque," p. 256.
2 Howells, "The New Taste in Theatricals," pp. 642–43.
3 Stallybrass and White, *The Politics and Poetics of Transgression*, p. 5.
4 On the British cultural studies movement, see Stuart Hall, "Encoding/Decoding" and "Recent Developments in the Theories of Language and Ideology"; Grossberg, "Cultural Studies Revisited and Revised"; and Wren-Lewis, "The Encoding-Decoding Model."
5 Le Roy Ladurie, *Carnival in Romans*.
6 Davis, "Theatre of the Streets," pp. 145–55.
7 Davies, "Stupidity and Rationality," pp. 1, 5.
8 Bakhtin, *Rabelais and His World*.

9 Eagleton, *Walter Benjamin*. See also Balandier, *Political Anthropology*.
10 Turner, "Comments and Conclusions."
11 Ibid., p. 282.
12 Bristol, *Carnival and Theatre*, p. 121.
13 Interestingly, when in 1988 the play's authors organized a concert of the music from *Hair* to celebrate its twentieth anniversary and to benefit AIDS research, they omitted the very songs that had given the play its notoriety.
14 Bristol, *Carnival and Theatre*, pp. 44–45.
15 Cousins and Hussain, *Michel Foucault*, pp. 3–6.

CHAPTER THREE

1 See Rankin, *The Theatre in Colonial America*, pp. 92–93; Brackett, *Theatrical Law*, p. 25; Clapp, "The Drama in Boston"; *Boston Herald*, November 25, 1883, p. 12.
2 Dye, "Pennsylvania versus the Theatre" (quotation, p. 337); Rankin, *The Theatre in Colonial America*, pp. 4–7. See also McNamara, *The American Playhouse in the Eighteenth Century*. Legal prohibitions against the performance of plays in Philadelphia were not repealed until 1789, but the same law that repealed the absolute prohibition instituted civic control over and municipal licensing of theaters (Dye, pp. 367–69). Even in Charleston, South Carolina, a city considerably more hospitable to theater than Philadelphia, a vagrancy law passed in 1783 contained a prohibition against theatrical performance. The law was not repealed until 1792. (See Sodders, "The Theatre Management of Alexandre Placide," p. 331.)
3 Barish, *The Antitheatrical Prejudice*, pp. 82–83.
4 In her study of antebellum street festivals in Philadelphia, for example, Davis ("Theatre of the Streets," pp. 47–54) points out that July Fourth celebrations were occasions on which white, male, middle- and upper-class groups reaffirmed through parades, banners, and street dramas their vision of nation and community. When blacks attempted to use public holidays to publicly express their communal solidarity in the same ways, however, they were verbally and physically attacked. In August 1842, when blacks paraded to commemorate the abolition of slavery in the West Indies, they were set upon by a white mob. Working-class women who participated in public parades risked being regarded as "public women" and "women of the streets" by doing so. Christmas celebrations in Philadelphia were a time for licensed disguise and role-playing. Even so, when in 1846 three young men participated in a New Year's parade dressed as women, they were promptly arrested. The judge hearing their case fined them three hundred dollars each – nearly a year's wages – arguing that "nothing is more offensive in the eye of the law . . . than the assumption of that which by nature we are not, and cannot be" (p. 148). The 1846 case is but one instance of attempts to

suppress cross-dressing in Philadelphia. The first such case occurred only a few years after the founding of the colony. A John Smith was arrested on the day after Christmas for "being maskt or disguised in women's aparell; walking openly through the streets of the citty from house to house . . . it being against the Law of God, the law of this province and the law of nature, etc." (quoted in Dye, "Pennsylvania versus the Theatre," pp. 343–44).

5 Shank, "The Bowery Theater," pp. 224–28 (quotation, p. 226); *New York Clipper*, January 24, 1857, p. 314. Two years earlier (1855) a Philadelphia "dancing room" attempted to reintroduce masquerade balls there, only to have the state legislature pass a law banning masquerades even before the first could be held. (Dye, "Pennsylvania versus the Theatre," p. 344.)

6 Barish, *The Antitheatrical Prejudice*, p. 117.

7 Johnson, "That Guilty Third Tier," p. 577.

8 Stowe quoted in Grimsted, *Melodrama Unveiled*, p. 24; Palmer, "American Theaters," p. 165, cited in Johnson, "That Guilty Third Tier," p. 582.

9 Lawrence Levine (*Highbrow/Lowbrow*) views the first half of the nineteenth century as a time when "Americans, in addition to whatever specific cultures they were part of, shared a public culture less hierarchically organized, less fragmented into relatively rigid adjectival boxes than their descendants were to experience a century later" (p. 9). As evidence of this sense of shared culture, he recounts the enormous popularity of Shakespeare (both as dramatic text and as theatrical performance) during this period, as well as the heterogeneity of the theater audience – an audience, he claims, that was in its diversity not unlike that of Shakespeare's own time.

The prevailing explanation for Shakespeare's popularity among flatboatmen and prospectors, says Levine, is that they were intrigued by nonessential performance elements: the histrionic style of popular actors, ribaldry, and sensationalism, among others. This account assumes that the more substantial pleasures and meanings of Shakespeare's works were lost upon popular audiences. Such a view, he maintains, derives from the literary elitism of its proponents, who can account for Shakespeare's popularity among the unlettered only by devaluing their ability to appreciate his work.

Levine counters this view by arguing that Shakespeare's appeals transcended social and economic categories, reverberating throughout American culture. Shakespeare was popular, in Levine's words, "because he was integrated into the culture and presented within its context. . . . Because so many of his values and tastes were, or at least appeared to be, close to their own, and were presented through figures that seemed real and came to matter to the audience." Shakespeare was, in short, "in tune with much of nineteenth-century American consciousness" (p. 41). This sense of a shared, nonhierarchical culture begins to dissipate by mid-century, Levine continues, and, insofar as entertainment is concerned, is replaced by a structure of hierarchical, fragmented cultures, each with its own venues, audiences, and modes of performance.

Levine's case for a heterogeneous theater audience and performance tradition in the antebellum period is not a new one, and evidence is ample that at theaters across the country theatergoers of different social and class positions attended the same performances at the same theaters. But in attempting to rescue popular culture from the elitists, Levine quite unnecessarily seeks refuge in the notion of a transcendent unitary culture and a national "consciousness." In the first place, as we shall see, the social contract that allowed monied dandies and butchers' apprentices to share the same theater was always a fragile one and maintained in large measure out of economic necessity: especially in smaller cities that could support but a single theater, a theater's survival depended on its ability to draw a diverse audience. Secondly, as I will argue below, what Levine minimizes is the very real contestation that occurred among audience groups within the theater over its control. Finally, Levine erroneously assumes that because different groups of people witnessed the performance of the same plays, they thereby "shared" the same culture. They shared the same space (although, already hierarchically arranged) and saw the same dramas, but whether or not they shared the same cultural experience depends – as I argued in the previous chapter – on what each group made out of that experience. What they made out of it depended in part on the cultural capital each group possessed. By the same logic, it could be argued that since two-thirds of all American women living in homes with television sets consider themselves viewers of daytime soap operas, American women "share" a common culture, and that soap operas succeed because they tap into the "feminine" consciousness. Studies of the audiences for soap operas and for other popular media texts suggest that their appeals are multiple and various rather than unitary, and that the "popular" audience is in fact an aggregate of any number of subaudiences, each of which generates multiple meanings and pleasures from the "same" texts.

Levine presents a wealth of evidence regarding how particular audience members made sense and pleasure out of Shakespeare, but this evidence is inevitably drawn primarily from those social groups with access to public organs of expression or whose letters and memoirs were deemed worthy of preservation (if not publication). What we lack, of course, are the articulated responses of the flatboatmen and apprentices. In the absence of evidence to the contrary, it seems just as logical to assume that widely divergent groups in the theater differed in what they made out of their experience there as to assume that somehow by sharing the same physical space they were divested of all the social, cultural, political, and economic differences they brought with them to the theater. On the audiences for popular television, see Fiske, *Television Culture*, and Allen, *Speaking of Soap Operas*.

10 Hone, *Diary*, quoted in Shank, "The Bowery Theatre," p. 12. Shank notes that Hone's address does not appear in published versions of Hone's diaries, whose earliest entries are from 1828. Hone's address is also notable in that it

marks quasi-official recognition of the theater's social legitimacy. Despite Hone's cautious endorsement of the theater as a potential agent of moral uplift, giving his imprimatur to a theatrical enterprise was still controversial. Viewing with ironic amusement the Democrats' nomination of actor Edwin Forrest for Congress in 1838, Hone recalled "how I was berated by some of my political friends when, as Mayor, I assisted in the ceremony of laying the cornerstone of the Bowery Theatre. . . . No act of my public life cost me so many friends." (Hone, *Diary*, quoted in Shank, p. 15. See also Grimsted, *Melodrama Unveiled*, pp. 33–39; Henneke, "The Playgoer in America," pp. 99–100.)

11 *Spirit of the Times*, October 26, 1861, p. 28, quoted in Henneke, "The Playgoer in America," p. 94.

12 "The Perambulator," *The Rambler's Magazine and New York Theatrical Register*, 1:14.

13 Johnson, "That Guilty Third Tier," pp. 578–79. See also Henneke, "The Playgoer in America," pp. 83–85.

14 *New York Mirror*, June 19, 1824, p. 371, quoted in Shank, "The Bowery Theatre," p. 22; "The Perambulator," *The Rambler's Magazine and New York Theatrical Register*, p. 12.

15 Henneke, "The Playgoer in America," pp. 136–40; Preston, "Reminiscences," p. 146. See also Levine, "William Shakespeare and the American People."

16 Trollope, *Domestic Manners of the Americans*, pp. 116–17.

17 Northall, *Before and behind the Curtain*, p. 177; Preston, "Reminiscences," p. 146.

18 *Spirit of the Times*, October 24, 1846, p. 408, quoted in Grimsted, *Melodrama Unveiled*, p. 64.

19 Coke, *A Subaltern's Furlough*, p. 129, quoted in Henneke, "The Playgoer in America," p. 147. In the same year English visitor and diarist Frances Trollope noted with disdain similar tendencies among Cincinnati audiences: "when a patriotic fit seized them, and 'Yankee Doodle' was called for, every man seemed to think his reputation as a citizen depended on the noise he made" (*Domestic Manners of the Americans*, pp. 87–88, 116 [quotation], 194–95). On the behavior of early nineteenth-century American theater audiences, see also Levine, *Highbrow/Lowbrow*, pp. 24–30.

20 *Sacramento Union* as quoted in Levine, "William Shakespeare and the American People," p. 45.

21 Grimsted, "Rioting in Its Jacksonian Setting." On theater riots, see Moses, "When Audiences Get Angry," and Buckley, "To the Opera House," pp. 162–91.

22 Wilentz, *Chants Democratic*, pp. 256–66; Montgomery, "The Working Classes of the Pre-industrial American City."

23 Tocqueville, *Democracy in America*, 3:80.

24 Meserve, *Heralds of Promise*, pp. 30–31. He argues that the ideology of the

upper classes was in direct conflict with the Jacksonian views that informed attempts to craft a distinctively American drama. Hence, the more popular houses gave rise to the first successful American theatrical phenomena – among them, Ben Baker's *Glance at New York* and its Mose the Fireman character and Thomas Rice's "Jim Crow," which helped to start the minstrel craze. The one exception might be Anna Cora Mowatt's enormously popular *Fashion*, which opened at the Park Theater in 1845.

25 Ireland, *Records of the New York Stage*, 2:16.

26 The causes, contexts, and consequences of the riot are skillfully and thoroughly detailed in Buckley, "To the Opera House." See also Moody, *The Astor Place Riot*. Unless otherwise indicated, my summary of the riot draws upon Buckley's account.

27 Buckley, "To the Opera House," p. 76; Grimsted, *Melodrama Unveiled*, pp. 74–75; Levine, *Highbrow/Lowbrow*, pp. 63–69.

28 See Buckley, "To the Opera House," pp. 249–68; Levine, *Highbrow/Lowbrow*, chap. 2, "The Sacralization of Culture."

29 McGlinchee, *The First Decade of the Boston Museum*, p. 29.

30 *Boston Daily Evening Transcript*, September 2, 1843, p. 2, quoted in McGlinchee, *The First Decade of the Boston Museum*, p. 22.

31 The Boston Museum's reputation for presenting wholesome, family entertainment would last a half century. A guidebook to the city noted in 1860 that "the visitor here has no rowdyism to fear, and nothing ever occurs, either in the audience portion or on the stage, to offend the most fastidious." (*Sketches and Business Directory of Boston*, p. 129. See also *King's How to See Boston*, pp. 11, 83, and Field, "The Boston Museum.")

32 "Barnum's American Museum" (playbill), quoted in Ireland, *Records of the New York Stage*, 2:163.

33 *Barnum's American Museum Illustrated* (1850), quoted in McNamara, " 'A Congress of Wonders,' " pp. 218–19. See also Harris, *Humbug*, pp. 42–53, 104; T. Allston Brown, "The Theater in America," *New York Clipper*, April 28, 1888, p. 104.

34 The cheapest seats in the lecture room were twenty-five cents; seats cost twelve-and-one-half cents more in the parquette (a more commodious version of the pit) and first balcony. ("Barnum's American Museum" [playbill].)

35 Ryan, *Cradle of the Middle Class*, pp. 14, 79–81, 146–53.

36 Barnum not only removed the bar from the theater, but he also advertised the absence of alcohol from his premises as a further reassurance that his patrons "may visit this museum with their families, their wives, and their children, and apprehend nothing calculated to shock the most susceptible moral sensibility." ("Barnum's American Museum" [playbill].)

37 *New York Clipper*, September 22, 1860, p. 182.

38 Wilentz, *Chants Democratic*, p. 113. See also Gutman, "Work, Culture, and Society."

39 Dorson, "Mose the Far-Famed." On the Bowery b'hoy street culture, see Buckley, "To the Opera House," pp. 295–396.

40 Northall, *Before and behind the Curtain*, pp. 91–92.

41 On Barnum's role in the Jenny Lind tour, see Ware and Lockard, *P. T. Barnum Presents Jenny Lind*, and Buckley, "To the Opera House," pp. 498–540.

42 *New York Commercial Advertiser*, February 29, 1850, quoted in Ware and Lockard, *P. T. Barnum Presents Jenny Lind*, pp. 4–5.

43 *Albany Weekly Argus*, September 21, 1850, cited in Ware and Lockard, *P. T. Barnum Presents Jenny Lind*, p. 19.

44 Northall, *Before and behind the Curtain*, p. 177. The Broadway Theater, constructed in 1847 and intended as a successor to the Park, featured a parquette and dress circle (one dollar), family circle and third tier (fifty cents), gallery and "colored" gallery (twenty-five cents), and a few private boxes seating eight persons each (ten dollars). (Ireland, *Records of the New York Stage*, 2:136.) The trend toward the parquette was well enough established by 1848 for one observer to comment on a renovated theater that bucked the trend and retained its pit. When the Park Theater reopened after a summer hiatus for renovation, a newspaper noted that the pit was retained "and was not transformed into that modern absurdity, a 'parquette,' which being a sort of adjunct to the dress circle, is too genteel a place to allow visitors to laugh or applaud in." The Park did replace its pit benches with cushioned seats, however. (Unidentified clipping in Ireland, 2:95.)

45 A visitor to the Bowery Theater in 1876 reported that he saw two thousand theatergoers, one-third of them in shirtsleeves, who would have "hissed [the leading actor] into silence and rushed him off the stage if he had slurred his part or neglected his business." (Clipping, October 15, 1876, in Ireland, *Records of the New York Stage*, 2:163.)

46 *Spirit of the Times*, September 26, 1863, p. 64, cited in Henneke, "The Playgoer in America," p. 178; Henneke, "The Playgoer in America," pp. 139–40.

47 The British case is *Wood v. Leadbitter* (1845). Key U.S. cases are *McCrea v. Marsh* (1858) and *Burton v. Scherpf* (1861). See also "Law of the Theatre."

48 *Pearce v. Spalding* (1882). See also *Clifford v. Brandon* (1809).

49 *Commonwealth v. Porter* (1854). See also *Rex v. Forbes* (1823); *Gregory v. Brunswick* (1843).

50 *Wallack v. City of New York* (1875).

51 *New York Clipper*, February 12, 1859, p. 342; March 5, 1859, p. 364. The presence of large numbers of minors in the Bowery pit was a direct result of their becoming part of the urban economy in the 1840s and 1850s. Successive waves of immigrants into New York's poorest neighborhoods, the absence of a factory economy in the city to absorb children as laborers, and the destruction of the apprentice system all meant that more and more "children" were on the streets in the 1850s, scavenging, scrounging, and ped-

dling. New York's first police chief, George Matsell, had first warned in 1849 of the dangers of "incredible" numbers of urchins, unsupervised by their parents, spreading crime and disease through the streets of New York. Subsequent inquiries and investigations into the "problem" of the streets in the 1850s reinforced the view that poor children in the streets represented a criminal threat to bourgeois order. (Stansell, *City of Women*, pp. 94–205.)

52 Brackett, *Theatrical Law*, pp. 232–33.

53 Stallybrass and White, *The Politics and Poetics of Transgression*, p. 193.

54 Although I have not researched the matter, it might be possible to make a similar case for the emergence of the English music hall and its immediate predecessors, the singing saloon and the pleasure garden, in the first half of the nineteenth century. See Cheshire, *Music Hall in Britain*, pp. 18–24; Bailey, *Leisure and Class in Victorian England*.

55 *New York Clipper*, March 26, 1859, p. 390; May 21, 1859, p. 38; July 30, 1859, p. 118; September 24, 1859, p. 182; December 3, 1859, p. 262; October 20, 1860, p. 214; February 23, 1860, p. 358; July 6, 1861, p. 94; September 21, 1861, p. 182; November 23, 1861, p. 254; November 30, 1861, p. 262.

56 Ibid., September 21, 1861, p. 182; *New York Evening Post*, January 2, 1862, clipping, Harvard Theatre Collection (hereafter cited as HTC).

57 *New York Evening Post*, January 2, 1862, clipping, HTC. The *Clipper* reported on July 6, 1861: "There are several places on Broadway now giving such beastly entertainments both on and off the stage that we understand the authorities have been requested to take cognizance of them, and close them up. Those very places are doing more injury to the morals of young men than the veriest houses of ill repute to be found in this city" (p. 94). The *Clipper* also speculated that calls for state sanctions against concert saloons were coming from managers of legitimate theaters, whose business was being hurt by them (December 28, 1861, p. 294).

58 *New York Clipper*, December 28, 1861, p. 294.

59 *New York Tribune*, April 25, 1862, p. 7; April 28, 1862, p. 3; April 26, 1862, p. 3; *New York Clipper*, March 22, 1862, p. 390; May 3, 1862, p. 22; May 31, 1862, p. 55; November 21, 1863, p. 251; January 16, 1864, p. 315; November 26, 1864, p. 262; May 6, 1865, p. 30. See also Zellers, "The Cradle of Variety"; Hill, "A History of Variety-Vaudeville in Minneapolis," pp. 9–41. In 1863 Tony Pastor, who is generally credited with severing the connection between alcohol and variety, performed at the American Music Hall, one of the first successful nondrinking variety theaters. Thus, Pastor had an opportunity to observe such an operation for two years before he leased his own theater for variety in 1865. (*New York Clipper*, November 14, 1863, p. 243.) On Tony Pastor, see Zellers, "Tony Pastor."

It is unclear exactly how successful the 1862 concert saloon law was in suppressing the concert saloon. Henderson (*The City and the Theatre*, p.

108) claims that the law merely closed those in which a curtain separated performers from the audience. Two years after the passage of the law, however, the *Clipper* (November 26, 1864, p. 262) proclaimed that the era of the "pretty waiter girl" was over in New York and that the only concert saloon remaining from the presuppression days was now a theater.

60 Stansell, *City of Women*, pp. 90–127 (quotation, p. 98); Ruth Rosen, *The Lost Sisterhood*, pp. 40–44. See also Banner, *American Beauty*, pp. 74–75.

61 *New York Clipper*, February 21, 1857, p. 350 (quotation); April 8, 1865, p. 414.

62 Ibid., November 30, 1861, p. 262.

CHAPTER FOUR

1 Grimsted, *Melodrama Unveiled*, particularly chap. 6; Meserve, *Heralds of Promise*, pp. 33–36. On the popularity of Shakespeare on the nineteenth-century American stage, see Levine, "William Shakespeare and the American People."

2 Grimsted, *Melodrama Unveiled*, chap. 9.

3 Ibid., p. 172.

4 On the cult of true womanhood, see Cott, *The Roots of Bitterness*; Degler, *Against the Odds*; Ann Douglas, *The Feminization of American Culture*; and Welter, "The Cult of True Womanhood." On the representation of this ideal in literature, see Brown, *The Sentimental Novel*; Papashvily, *All the Happy Endings*; Baym, *Woman's Fiction*; and Kelley, "The Sentimentalists."

5 Unless otherwise indicated, information on fashion in this period is taken from Halttunen, *Confidence Men and Painted Women*, and Banner, *American Beauty*.

6 Halttunen, *Confidence Men and Painted Women*, pp. 83–89; Banner, *American Beauty*, pp. 45–46, 63 (quotation).

7 See Grimsted, *Melodrama Unveiled*, especially chap. 5.

8 Ireland, *Records of the New York Stage*, 1:528, quoted in Swift, *Belles and Beaux on Their Toes*, pp. 21–22. Charles Gilfert, who was manager of the Bowery from its opening in the fall of 1826 through the 1828–29 season, attempted to position the Bowery between the aristocratic Park and the more working-class Chatham. His strategy did not work, however, and he left the Bowery nearly bankrupt. It was Thomas Hamblin, succeeding Gilfert, who made the Bowery home to artisanal republicans. See Shank, "The Bowery Theatre," p. 233.

9 Morse and Tappan are quoted in Swift, *Belles and Beaux on Their Toes*, pp. 24–25. On Hutin's costume, see Emily Burrell Hoffman to Bridget Wickham, March 14, 1827, Villers-Hatton Collection, New-York Historical Society, quoted in Swift, p. 26.

10 Hiram Fuller, quoted in Banner, *American Beauty*, p. 63.

11 See Marie Taglioni File, Ballet Engravings Collection, Harvard Theatre Collection (hereafter cited as HTC).

12 Swift, *Belles and Beaux on Their Toes*, pp. 89–104. See also Madame Celeste File, Ballet Engravings Collection, HTC.

13 Ruyter, *Reformers and Visionaries*, p. 6; Guest, *Fanny Elssler*; Fanny Elssler File, Ballet Engravings Collection, HTC; Swift, *Belles and Beaux on Their Toes*, pp. 214–24 (quotations, pp. 211, 224).

14 Walter Kendrick, in *The Secret Museum*, discusses what happened when Victorians discovered that even the mantle of art could not cover the explicit sexuality of artifacts uncovered in the excavations at Pompeii. Their strategy was to limit access to these paintings, statues, and household objects to upper-class males. Furthermore, in the nineteenth century, the circulation of works intended to transgress norms regarding the representation of sexuality (pornography) originated with upper-class males. Kendrick writes: "It is clear that the kind of 'hard-core' pornography we now would place at the bottom of the social scale belonged at the top a century ago. Its quality was no higher than what we are familiar with today, but its circulation was confined to that class of 'safe' readers who were granted easy admission to the age's other Secret Museums. It therefore figured hardly at all in public controversies; there was, literally, no harm in it" (p. 78).

15 Unless otherwise indicated, the following discussion of living pictures is based on McCullough, *Living Pictures*. On living pictures as predecessor to burlesque, see Sobel, *A Pictorial History of Burlesque*, p. 109.

16 *New York Herald*, September 25, 1847, p. 2, quoted in McCullough, *Living Pictures*, p. 20.

17 *New York Herald*, March 5, 1848, p. 2, cited in McCullough, *Living Pictures*, p. 28.

18 *New York Herald*, February 2, 1848, p. 2, quoted in McCullough, *Living Pictures*, p. 26.

19 George L. Aiken, *Uncle Tom's Cabin*, 1852, Promptbook, quoted in Moody, *Dramas of the American Theatre*, p. 396.

20 *New York Clipper*, July 30, 1864, p. 126.

21 Ibid., May 14, 1859, p. 25.

22 Ibid., December 8, 1860, p. 270.

23 See, for example, Sobel, *A Pictorial History of Burlesque*, p. 5; Zeidman, *The American Burlesque Show*, p. 21; Corio, *Burlesque*, p. 10.

24 Mankowitz, *Mazeppa*, pp. 16–17. Unless otherwise indicated, information on Menken is taken from Mankowitz. The other contemporary biography of Menken, Noel Gerson's *Queen of the Plaza* (written under the pseudonym of Paul Lewis), must, as Mankowitz discovered, be seriously discounted. Gerson claimed as his principal primary source Menken's diary, which, he admitted in correspondence to Mankowitz, he had fabricated (Mankowitz, pp. 188–89).

25 Mankowitz, *Mazeppa*, pp. 53–55, 11–13, 173.

26 Before the curtain rose at her *Mazeppa* debut in New York City, barely two months after the attack on Fort Sumter, ushers distributed flyers denouncing attacks on Menken's patriotism. The reverse side bore a poem written by Menken for the occasion entitled "Pro Patria – America, 1861." Although Menken was born in New Orleans, there had been no charges of her disloyalty to the Union. It was she who created the false issue in order to publicize her poetic abilities in its refutation. (See Mankowitz, *Mazeppa*, pp. 24, 125–27.)

27 *New York Clipper*, February 3, 1866, p. 342.

28 The one major exception to this seems to have been *Three Fast Women*, a "protean" musical that Menken largely wrote herself and in which she played two female and four male roles. In the piece, which burlesqued San Francisco's Barbary Coast reputation, Menken played a young dandy, a minstrel, and a sailor, among other characters. Mankowitz notes that this "rude" play was well received by San Franciscans and showed Menken at her musical comedy best. However, it does not appear that Menken added the piece to her post-tour repertoire. (See Mankowitz, *Mazeppa*, pp. 105–6.)

29 Rourke, *American Humor*, p. 129; Clinton Baddeley, *The Burlesque Tradition*, p. 109.

30 On burlesque in general during the period, see – in addition to Rourke, *American Humor*; Croghan, "New York Burlesque"; Northall (who was himself the author of numerous burlesques), *Before and behind the Curtain*; and Hutton, *Curiosities of the American Stage*. On pantomime, see Senelick, *The Age and Stage of George L. Fox*.

31 Hutton, *Curiosities of the American Stage*, p. 160.

32 Croghan, "New York Burlesque," pp. 52–69.

33 Lester Wallack, quoted in Hutton, *Curiosities of the American Stage*, p. 162.

34 Hutton, *Curiosities of the American Stage*, p. 164.

35 *Spirit of the Times*, September 20, 1857, quoted in Plotnicki, "John Brougham," p. 424.

36 Brougham, *Met-a-mora*, quoted in Plotnicki, "John Brougham," p. 423.

37 Rourke, *American Humor*, p. 104.

38 Hawes, "Much Ado about John Brougham."

39 All quotes from *Much Ado about a Merchant of Venice* are from the manuscript copy in the Performing Arts Collection, New York Public Library.

40 In emendations made on the promptscript, Brougham added some of the targets of his attack by name: "the ducats Tilden failed to wring / from the rich 'Lords' of the Canal job ring" and "the pennies from what Boss Tweed stole / with which he purchased Dudley Field's great soul!"

41 In his 1850 production of *The Female Guard*, manager A. H. Purdy added to the fairy spectacle the convention of the amazonian march: a corp of women in mock-military costume performing some semblance of close-order drill.

Purdy followed this production with an even more elaborately staged "Grand Fairy Spectacle," a revival of *The Naiad Queen*, which featured a parade of "female warriors," underwater scenes, and a cast of over one hundred performers. What one theater historian calls the first "burlesque spectacle," Planche's *King Charming* was produced at New York's Broadway Theater in 1855. A burlesque of the serious themes then being dealt with in melodramas of that season, it also included a "fairy guard" of forty women. See Oliver, "Changing Pattern of Spectacle," pp. 12, 15, 61–62.

42 Oliver, "Changing Pattern of Spectacle," p. 83; playbill, "Laura Keene's New Theatre," May 15, 1856, quoted in Ireland, *Records of the New York Stage*, 2:72–73.

43 *New York Clipper*, December 8, 1860, p. 270.

44 Ibid., February 26, 1861, p. 350; March 30, 1861, p. 398; Oliver, "Changing Pattern of Spectacle," pp. 100–108.

45 *New York Clipper*, June 21, 1862, p. 78. Even Barnum could not resist the prospect of profits to be made from spectacle. In the summer of 1865, temporarily displaced after the destruction by fire of his American Museum, Barnum took a short lease on the Winter Garden, where he mounted a production of a fairy spectacle entitled *The Witch of the Black Caverns*. It included ballet, stilt dancers, aerialists, and some of his dispossessed human curiosities, among them the "Fat Woman" and the "Giant Girl." One presumes, however, that Barnum's brand of spectacle did not include much in the way of burlesque humor or the displays of "nether limbs" that characterized burlesque spectacle elsewhere in New York. (See Oliver, "Changing Pattern of Spectacle," p. 109.)

46 Rella, *A History of Burlesque*, p. 79.

47 Croghan, "New York Burlesque," pp. 344–45; Hutton, *Curiosities of the American Stage*, p. 164. *Uncle Tom's Cabin* was the object of minstrel show parodies, however.

48 On the production circumstances of *The Black Crook*, see Gintautiene, "*The Black Crook*," pp. 47–64; Odom, "*The Black Crook* at Niblo's Garden"; Mates, "*The Black Crook* Myth"; and Freedley, "*The Black Crook* and *The White Fawn*." On the expenses connected with mounting the production, see also *New York Clipper*, September 1, 1866, p. 166.

49 The first act, for example, calls for a "garland dance by principals and full ballet interspersed with poses or tableaux during which the males gather around the table to eat and drink." An amazonian procession is called for as a part of the final elaborate transformation scene.

50 Whitton, *The Naked Truth*, p. 3.

51 *New York Tribune*, September 17, 1866, and *New York Times*, September 13, 1866, both quoted in Freedley, "*The Black Crook* and *The White Fawn*," pp. 6–10; *New York Clipper*, September 22, 1866, p. 190. The only play to run longer, George L. Fox's *Humpty Dumpty*, opened on March 10, 1867, at the Olympic Theater (formerly Laura Keene's Varieties) and ran for sixty-

two weeks, chalking up 483 performances, 9 more than *The Black Crook*. See Senelick, *The Age and Stage of George L. Fox*, pp. 138–53.

52 *New York Tribune*, October 22, 1867, quoted in Freedley, "*The Black Crook* and *The White Fawn*," p. 14.

53 *New York Clipper*, September 22, 1866, p. 190.

54 *New York Dramatic Mirror*, July 17, 1909, quoted in Gintautiene, "*The Black Crook*," p. 103. See also her discussion of Bonfanti's background, p. 111.

55 *New York Clipper*, September 22, 1866, p. 190; September 29, 1866, p. 198; *New York Times*, September 13, 1866, quoted in Freedley, "*The Black Crook* and *The White Fawn*," p. 10; *New York Clipper*, September 29, 1866, p. 198.

56 *New York Clipper*, October 27, 1866, p. 230.

57 Quoted in Whitton, *The Naked Truth*, p. 23.

58 As Whitton relates the story, the previous year, Bennett had approached Barnum regarding the use of the site of the recently fire-destroyed American Museum for a new *Herald* building. Barnum did not own the land itself, but his ground lease still had a year to run. Barnum exacted an extortionate price, and Bennett responded by barring Barnum from advertising any of his ventures in the *Herald*. Outraged, Barnum appealed to the city's theater managers' organization to withdraw all its advertising from the paper, an action supported by all save William Wheatley and Lester Wallack. Although neither Bennett nor Wheatley ever acknowledged it as such, Whitton claims Bennett's regular excoriations of *The Black Crook* constituted "gold-edged abuse," intentionally calling attention to the dazzlingly demoralizing nature of the production in order to increase patronage among those who, Bennett knew, would have to see for themselves if it was as shockingly indecent as he claimed. (See Whitton, *The Naked Truth*, pp. 20–23.)

59 Quoted in *New York Clipper*, December 1, 1866, p. 268. See also Gintautiene, "*The Black Crook*," p. 97.

60 *New York Clipper*, January 18, 1866, p. 326; Gintautiene, "*The Black Crook*," p. 98.

61 Gintautiene, "*The Black Crook*," pp. 80–82; *New York Clipper*, October 27, 1866, p. 230. Word of its alleged salaciousness preceded *The Black Crook*'s first national tour in the spring of 1867, the first of twenty consecutive seasons during which *The Black Crook* was mounted in American theaters. In March two San Francisco theaters claimed to have secured rights to the play. When the case was taken to court, the judge, never having seen the object of the suit, nevertheless ruled that as an immoral work it fell outside the bounds of copyright protection. The two houses mounted competing productions, one called *The Black Crook*, the other *The Black Rook*. A third theater, in best burlesque tradition, lampooned the whole situation in *The Black Rook with a Crook*. Despite the judge's denunciation, the more handsomely staged of the two serious versions, *The Black Rook*, ran for several months, drawing, as one newspaper put it, "large and fashionable au-

diences." They found "nothing to which the most fastidious can object." A touring company arrived at the Varieties Theater in St. Louis on April 24, 1867, and was a "huge success" there. It attracted all classes of men, women, and children: "the public having discovered," as one local paper put it, "that there was nothing to bring a blush to the cheeks of youth." (Rella, *A History of Burlesque*, pp. 82–88 [quotations], and David, "The Genesis of the Variety Theatre.")

The enormous success of the production "on the road" helped to effect a transformation in the American theatrical industrial structure from the stock company to the "combination system." Prior to this time, a manager's success was due in large measure to his or her ability to establish and keep a resident company of players at the theater he or she had leased. Especially when, as was the case with Laura Keene, William Mitchell, Edwin Booth, and Dion Boucicault, the manager was also his or her company's leading actor, the public came to associate a given theater with a given manager's and stock company's style and repertoire. *The Black Crook* demonstrated the profitability of separating the production from the playhouse and, consequently, contributed to the demise of both the actor/manager and the stock company. Increasingly, theater managers became custodians of real estate holdings and theaters empty vessels waiting to hold whatever entertainment packages were shipped from New York. Actors, previously resident at a particular theater in a particular community, once again became peripatetic, following routes devised along railway lines from one city to another for months at a time. (See Henderson, *The City and the Theatre*, pp. 134–37.)

62 Quoted in Oliver, "Changing Pattern of Spectacle," p. 119, and Freedley, "*The Black Crook* and *The White Fawn*," p. 8.

63 Hornblow, *History of Theatre in America*, p. 101, quoted in Oliver, "Changing Pattern of Spectacle," p. 119.

64 Banner, *American Beauty*, pp. 86–96 (quotation, p. 96).

CHAPTER FIVE

1 *New York Herald*, December 18, 1866, p. 7, quoted in Oliver, "Changing Pattern of Spectacle," p. 124; *New York Clipper*, February 13, 1869, p. 358.

2 Logan, *Apropos of Women and Theatres*, p. 138. See also Wills, "Olive Logan vs. the Nude."

3 *New York Times*, May 15, 1869, p. 5.

4 Logan, *Apropos of Women and Theatres*, p. 135.

5 Ibid., p. 132.

6 Logan, "The Nude Woman Question," reprinted with a new introduction as a chapter of Logan, *Apropos of Women and Theatres*, pp. 123–53.

7 Logan, *Apropos of Women and Theatres*, p. 153.

8 Ibid., p. 21.

9 Ibid., pp. 7–22.

10 Leach, *True Love and Perfect Union*, pp. 88–93 (quotation, p. 91).

11 *New York Times*, November 8, 1868, p. 4.

12 Ibid., February 5, 1869, p. 5.

13 *New York Herald*, October 6, 1867, quoted in Croghan, "New York Burlesque," p. 311.

14 *New York Clipper*, May 22, 1869, p. 54; *New York World*, June 1, 1869, clipping, New York Library Performing Arts Collection (hereafter cited as NYPL); *Spirit of the Times*, May 22, 1869, clipping, NYPL.

15 *Spirit of the Times*, May 22, 1869, clipping, NYPL.

16 Ibid.

17 Ibid., May 29, 1869; *New York World*, June 1, 1869, clipping, NYPL. The following evening, the audience at Niblo's was as large as ever, and, according to the *World*, "no one, not even Lydia Thompson, appeared to care a fig about the recent imbroglio." Apparently, Henderson did not charge Butler with assault; however, he did bring a libel suit against him. Butler was arrested in November but released on $5,000 bail. (*New York Clipper*, November 27, 1869, p. 270.)

18 *New York Times*, June 14, 1869, p. 4.

19 Ibid., June 13, 1869, p. 5.

20 *New York Clipper*, May 15, 1869, p. 46; April 16, 1870, p. 14.

21 Clipping, n.p, n.d, NYPL. Banner (*American Beauty*, p. 122) also contends that the audiences for burlesque at Niblo's were "respectable" and included many women. One of her sources, however, must be held at arm's length in this regard. Richard White's frequently cited essay on burlesque, which appeared in the August 1869 issue of *Galaxy*, describes the audience at Niblo's: "comfortable, middle-aged women from the suburbs, and from the remoter country, their daughters, groups of children, a few professional men, bearing their quality in their faces, some sober, farmer-looking folk, a clergyman or two, apparently, the usual proportion of nondescripts, among which were not many very young men, composed an audience less fashionable than that I had seen in Fourteenth street, but at least as respectable." But far from being an essay in praise of burlesque – which it is almost invariably regarded as being – it is, as the *Times* noted then, mock elegiac and ironic rather than sincere. When he says that he found Thompson's performance in *Sinbad* better than Edwin Forrest's in *Hamlet*, White is saying that he found the former to be more enjoyable than the actor whose work he most detested. His stance is revealed at the end of the piece, when he says that burlesque is merely symptomatic of an age when audiences seek to be amused rather than provoked to think. The legitimate drama, he says, is dead. Thus, it is difficult to assess what White is saying about the audience for burlesque. (See Richard Grant White, "The Age of Burlesque," p. 266, and *New York Times*, July 26, 1869, p. 5.)

22 Howells, "The New Taste in Theatricals."

23 Ibid., p. 639.

24 Ibid., pp. 639–40.

25 Ibid., pp. 640–41.

26 Ibid., p. 642.

27 Ibid., pp. 642–43.

28 Ibid., p. 642. Peter Buckley's analysis of the critical discourse on Thompsonian burlesque ("The Culture of Leg Work") parallels my own in many respects. I am grateful to him for sharing this unpublished paper with me.

29 Prioleau, *The Circle of Eros*, pp. 4–8 (quotation, p. 7). See also Crowley, *The Black Heart's Truth*, p. 72; Wassenstrom, "William Dean Howells," p. 491.

30 *Appleton's Journal of Popular Literature, Science, and Art*, July 3, 1869, p. 440.

31 Richard Grant White, "The Age of Burlesque," p. 256.

32 Banner, *American Beauty*, pp. 106–21; Stansell, *City of Women*, pp. 90–94.

33 Stansell, *City of Women*, p. 171. See Foucault, *The History of Sexuality*. On the simultaneous "explosion" of discourse on prostitution in Great Britain, see Nead, *Myths of Sexuality*, pp. 2–21.

34 Nead, *Myths of Sexuality*, p. 31.

35 *New York Evening Post*, January 2, 1862, clipping, Harvard Theatre Collection; *New York Clipper*, May 14, 1859, p. 25.

36 Nead, *Myths of Sexuality*, pp. 110–14 (quotation, p. 114); Stansell, *City of Women*, pp. 173–75.

37 Linton, *Modern Women*; James, Review of *Modern Women*.

38 *New York Clipper*, February 18, 1865, p. 358.

39 Banner, *American Beauty*, p. 119.

40 Lyrics for "The Girl with the Grecian Bend," quoted in Levy, *Grace Notes in American History*, p. 77.

41 *Banner, American Beauty*, p. 119–20; *New York Times*, November 22, 1868, p. 3; March 28, 1869, p. 4; October 18, 1868, p. 3.

42 Baker-Benfield, *The Horrors of the Half-Known Life*, pp. 84–87. Because the medical profession believed women to be controlled by physiology to a much greater degree than men, they regarded this rebelliousness as having an organic cause and, not surprisingly, a medical – specifically surgical – cure. As Baker-Benfield puts it: "Above all . . . [a woman] was supposed to be entirely predictable. It was a role geared to man's behavior in, and apprehensions of, the ceaseless strife of the world outside home. The overriding importance attached to physiological identity entailed a rigid asserveration of the sexual distinction. Hence any attempt by women to break out of their circumscription signified to men that such disorderly women wanted to become men. Female castration was designed to take care of such a threat. Accordingly, cure was pronounced if a woman was successfully stuffed back into her appropriate slot." He then follows this logic to its extreme: "If women were only sex organs, and female sex organs were by nature a menace to health unless run to earth by pregnancy, then women

were by nature sick; and if women's sickness was construed as intolerable social disorder, then to be a woman was a crime" (pp. 122–23).

43 See Natalie Zemon Davis, "Women on Top." "Evidence" for this theory was found in the experience of doctors who began to use chloroform in obstetrical cases around 1850. Much to their embarrassment, they discovered that some women as they began to succumb to the anesthesia shouted out obscenities and seemed to become sexually excited. In 1866 Dr. Isaac Ray warned that such episodes were not limited to the effects of chloroform and that many women teetered on the brink of hysteria and insanity as a natural consequence of their physiology: "In the sexual evolution, in pregnancy, in the parturient period, in lactation, strange thoughts, extraordinary feelings, unseasonable appetites, criminal impulses, may haunt a mind at other times innocent and pure" (quoted in Poovey, " 'Scenes of an Indelicate Character,' " p. 146.).

44 Ruth Rosen, *The Lost Sisterhood*, pp. 120–21.

45 As Bourdieu (*Outline of a Theory of Practice*, pp. 94–95) argues, sexual order can be maintained only through the vigilant policing of public behavior and conduct. But this policing rarely involves the actual suppression of overt sexual transgression. Rather, it achieves the goal of a stable sexual order through the inculcation and monitoring of norms of dress, manners, and demeanor. Societies place such importance on the seemingly insignificant details of dress, bearing, and the social presentation of self because in doing so they entrust to the body itself "in abbreviated and practical, i.e. mnemonic, form the fundamental principles of the arbitrary content of the culture. . . . The whole trick of pedagogic reason lies precisely in the way it extorts the essential while seeming to demand the insignificant. . . . The concession of *politeness* always contain *political* concessions."

46 Stallybrass and White, *The Politics and Poetics of Transgression*, pp. 191–93.

47 Ibid., pp. 193, 5.

48 *New York Clipper*, March 14, 1868, p. 388.

49 Stallybrass and White, *The Politics and Poetics of Transgression*, p. 2.

50 Howells, "The New Taste in Theatricals," p. 639; *Spirit of the Times*, June 1, 1869, p. 13; *Chicago Times*, February 22, 1870, quoted in *New York Clipper*, March 5, 1870, p. 382.

51 Mary Douglas, *Purity and Danger*, p. 4; *New York Times*, February 5, 1869, p. 5; *New York Tribune* quoted in *Spirit of the Times*, June 12, 1869, p. 272; *Spirit of the Times*, June 1, 1869, p. 14.

52 Logan, "The Leg Business," p. 44.

53 *New York Clipper*, April 24, 1869, p. 22.

54 Moses, "Lydia Thompson," pp. 49–50.

55 See *New York Clipper*, June 7, 1869, p. 70.

56 Howells, "The New Taste in Theatricals," pp. 642–43; Richard Grant White, "The Age of Burlesque," p. 256.

CHAPTER SIX

1 *New York Times*, July 2, 1869, p. 4; *New York Clipper*, June 26, 1869, p. 94. Mary Henderson (*The City and the Theatre*, p. 114) calls Wallack's theater, which between 1861 and 1869 occupied the northeastern corner of Broadway and Thirteenth Street, "the most renowned legitimate theater of its era."

2 See *New York Clipper*, April 16, 1870, p. 14; November 19, 1870, p. 262; January 17, 1871, p. 318; August 26, 1871, p. 166; November 23, 1872, p. 270; *New York Times*, August 26, 1873, p. 5; November 22, 1877, p. 5; Lydia Thompson, handwritten manuscript, n.d., Harvard Theatre Collection (hereafter cited as HTC); Sobel, *A Pictorial History of Burlesque*, p. 30. I am grateful to Peter Buckley for allowing me access to his copy of the Thompson manuscript, a fragment of what appears to be notes for an unfinished memoir.

3 *New York Clipper*, April 16, 1870, p. 14; April 23, 1870, p. 22.

4 Ibid., February 27, 1869, p. 374. The same month Elise Holt's burlesque troupe appeared opposite Thompson at the Waverly Theater in a burlesque of *Lucretia Borgia*, which featured *Black Crook* dancers Betty and Emily Rigl in the cancan. (See *New York Clipper*, February 20, 1869, p. 366.)

5 *New York Clipper*, June 26, 1869, p. 94. One paper, which called Holt "an offense to every modest woman in the audience," suggested that if the theater could not operate without resorting to such "equivocational attractions," it should be closed. Another followed the by-now-familiar strategy of consigning Holt, her troupe, and their audience to the lowest social and moral stratum. Holt was the creation, it said, of a "foul public taste," and as such was "beneath criticism, contempt, or punishment." Her audience had come to see her in the kind of "indecent and nasty" exhibition that previously had been offered only at San Francisco's most notorious concert saloons. The only penalty the paper could suggest for her unspeakable immorality was social ostracism, and a few weeks later it smugly reported that at the California Theater, where Holt appeared in a burlesque afterpiece following a longer dramatic offering, "the respectable circle is pretty thoroughly emptied at the close of the respectable drama; the people who stay are a low lot." (Rella, *A History of Burlesque*, pp. 109–15.)

6 Rella, *A History of Burlesque*, pp. 123–29.

7 *New York Clipper*, September 3, 1870, p. 174.

8 Zeidman, *The American Burlesque Show*, pp. 33–34; Leavitt, *Fifty Years in Theatrical Management*, pp. 308–10. See also Sobel, *A Pictorial History of Burlesque*, pp. 31–41, and Corio, *Burlesque*, p. 30.

9 While Leavitt was still playing with a touring minstrel show, working his way back from San Francisco to New York in the summer of 1870, the *Clipper* began to run notices for touring "female minstrel" companies, buried in its regular weekly column of national show business news culled

from stringers and press notices: Elwood's Female Minstrels appearing in Milwaukee the week of July 16, Barnard's Female Minstrels organized in New York in August, and Ada Tesman's Female Minstrels and Olio Troupe performing in Newark in September. (*New York Clipper*, July 9, 1870, p. 110; July 16, 1870, p. 119; August 20, 1870, p. 159; September 17, 1870, p. 191.) The September 24 issue announced the organization of Madame Rentz's Female Minstrels, under the management not of Leavitt but of Rufus Somersby, and the commencement of a New England tour. The following issue listed among the cast Hattie Forrest, Clara Burton, Sallie Eldridge, Jennie Weston, Madame Rentz, *and* M. B. Leavitt as stage manager. (*New York Clipper*, September 24, 1870, p. 199; October 1, 1870, p. 207.)

10 In his biography of the early minstrel performer Dan Emmett, Hans Nathan suggests that the idea of using whiteface women in a minstrel show format dates back to at least 1854. In that year Emmett was musical director and performer at the Franklin Museum for an ensemble called Lea's Female Opera Troupe. "It presented young ladies in dances and tableaux and in a minstrel band, though in white face. They were assisted by two blackface end men, a bone player and a tamourinist." (*Dan Emmett*, p. 219.)

11 *New York Clipper*, November 19, 1870, p. 262. Indeed, Leavitt's troupe followed the Ada Tesman combination later in the month at Masonic Hall, and their performance was even less enthusiastically reviewed: "With the exception of Clara Burton's jig dancing, there was no merit in the entertainments presented. The singing was bad, and all the acts on the programme were old and badly played. If some enterprising manager were to bring a good troupe of female minstrels to Pittsburgh, he would put money in his pocket" (November 26, 1870, p. 270).

12 The most comprehensive, scholarly account of the minstrel show is Toll, *Blacking Up*. On the format of the minstrel show, see pp. 51–57.

13 *New York Clipper*, January 7, 1871, p. 318.

14 It is difficult (and, frankly, not very important) to determine whether, as Zeidman suggests, Leavitt was the first to effect the all-female first part – he almost certainly was not the first to mount a female minstrel show. From the *New York Clipper*'s minstrel column, it does not appear that Leavitt assumed management of the Madame Rentz company until January 1871, when Somersby left the troupe in Galesburg, Illinois (January 14, 1871, p. 327). The company is listed the following month as a consolidation of the Elwood and Madame Rentz companies, with Leavitt sharing proprietor status with two partners (February 25, 1871, p. 371). The two companies split that spring, with Leavitt listed as manager of Madame Rentz's Female Minstrels in April (April 15, 1871, p. 6).

15 Saxton, "Blackface Minstrelsy," p. 3.

16 Toll, *Blacking Up*, pp. 31–38.

17 On March 4, 1871, the *New York Clipper* commented that "the variety

business has become so popular during the past few years as to induce capitalists to invest large sums of money in the erection of theatres as well as in the formation of [traveling] companies. . . . Some of the prettiest theaters in the country are now devoted to variety performances and thousands of persons find employment therein" (p. 378).

18 Toll, *Blacking Up*, pp. 134–35; *New York Clipper*, February 18, 1871, p. 366.

19 Premiere in his craft was Francis Leon, who in the late 1860s starred in elaborately staged, blackface burlesque operas at the theater in New York he and his partner managed. Such was his success and that of his imitators that by 1873, nearly every minstrel troupe featured a serious female impersonator. Toll (*Blacking Up*, p. 144) captures their probable multiple appeals to the minstrel show audience: "Men in the audience probably were titillated by the alluring stage characters whom they were momentarily drawn to, and they probably got equal pleasure from mocking and laughing at them. Women were probably intrigued by the impeccable grace and femininity of the beautiful illusionists who, unlike the female minstrels, posed no real sexual challenges. . . . As a model of properly 'giddy' femininity, he could reassure men that women were in their places while at the same time showing women how to behave without competing with them. Thus, in some ways, he functioned like the blackface 'fool' who educated audiences while also reassuring them that he was their inferior. Neither man nor woman, the female impersonator threatened no one."

20 Toll, *Blacking Up*, pp. 146–47.

21 Booth, *Prefaces to English Nineteenth-Century Theatre*, p. 186.; Logan, "The Nude Woman Question"; *New York Clipper*, May 15, 1869, p. 46; Zanger, "The Minstrel Show as Theater of Misrule"; Levine, *Highbrow/Lowbrow*, pp. 13–15; Haywood, "Negro Minstrelsy and Shakespearean Burlesque"; Browne, "Shakespeare in America."

22 While playing Washington's National Theater in October 1869, Thompson added an allusion to "the disappointed ex-president [Andrew Johnson] and a most disgraceful scene followed. A portion of the audience hissed violently and the remainder applauded in a boisterous manner. . . . On the following night, the gag was omitted." (*New York Clipper*, November 6, 1869, p. 246.)

23 Toll, *Blacking Up*, p. 53. Minstrel show songs and stump speeches frequently were topical in nature. In 1864 one popular minstrel song even advocated the presidential candidacy of General George B. McClellan, a Democrat:

> We're willing, Father Abram, ten hundred thousand more
> Should help our Uncle Samuel to prosecute the war;
> But then we want a chieftain true, one who can lead the van,
> George B. McClellan you all know, he is the very man.

(Quoted in Saxton, "Blackface Minstrelsy," p. 22.)

24 Zanger, "The Minstrel Show as Theater of Misrule," p. 34. A similar point is made by Saxton, "Blackface Minstrelsy," p. 11.
25 Zanger, "The Minstrel Show as Theater of Misrule," p. 33.
26 White, *The Virginny Mummy*, pp. 3, 12.
27 The most famous of the plantation types was Jim Crow, the character created by Thomas D. Rice, whose Jim Crow dance performed at the Bowery Theater in the early 1830s helped to launch minstrelsy as an entertainment form. (See Dorman, "The Strange Career of Jim Crow Rice.")
28 Toll, *Blacking Up*, pp. 68–69; Nathan, *Dan Emmett*, p. 57–59.
29 Zanger, "The Minstrel Show as Theater of Misrule," p. 37; Saxton, "Blackface Minstrelsy," p. 4.
30 Bakhtin, *Rabelais and His World*, pp. 28–29, 316–18.
31 Ibid., pp. 316–17.
32 The minstrel character's love of liquor was the basis for a parody of the ballad, "Woodman Spare That Tree," which Saxton ("Blackface Minstrelsy," p. 12) contends also suggests auto- or homoeroticism:

> I kiss him two three time,
> And den I suck him dry
> Dat jug, he's none but mine
> So dar you luff him lie.

33 In the words of one minstrel song, "My Susy" is

> handsome
> My Susy she is young . . .
> My Susy looms it bery tall
> Wid udder like a cow
> She'd give nine quarts easy
> But white gals don't know how.

(Quoted in Saxton, "Blackface Minstrelsy," p. 21; see also Toll, *Blacking Up*, p. 67.)
34 Toll, *Blacking Up*, p. 36.
35 Bakhtin, *Rabelais and His World*, p. 30.
36 Sobel, *A Pictorial History of Burlesque*, pp. 67, 124.
37 Phillips, *Susan Lenox*, 1:223.
38 Zeidman, *The American Burlesque Show*, p. 34.
39 Zellers, "The Cradle of Variety," p. 581.
40 Henderson, *The City and the Theatre*, pp. 131–41; Robert William Snyder, "The Voice of the City," pp. 29–35. I am grateful to Professor Snyder for sharing his dissertation with me prior to its publication. See also Zellers, "Tony Pastor."
41 McLean, *American Vaudeville as Ritual*, pp. 41–42.
42 Relatively little is known about the life of B. F. Keith prior to his move to

Boston in 1882 at age thirty-six except through his own accounts and those produced much later by the Keith-Albee organization for public consumption. In his introduction to two autobiographical letters discovered in 1960, McLean ("Genesis of Vaudeville") notes that Keith's version of his early life, like those written by P. T. Barnum, is made to conform to the criteria of the American success story: the Yankee farm boy seeks his fortune, is initiated into the real mercantile world, learns show business by joining the circus, and finally, as McLean puts it, "brings the world to his door by contriving the 'better mousetrap' of American entertainment" (p. 83).

The youngest of eight children, Keith, at age five, was sent from his family's home in Hillsborough, New Hampshire, to live with relatives in western Massachusetts. It was there, Keith recalls, that he became "imbued with the likes and dislikes of a class of people who afterwards became our leaders in the business and professional world and who are the bone and sinew of every community" (ibid.). The inculcation of the values and tastes of land-holding farmers and small-town merchants occurred through Keith's aspirations to join the middle class rather than his membership in it. Around 1865 he left the small town in which he was raised and his job as a clerk in a grocery store to become an itinerant peddler of cheap portraits of Abraham Lincoln. Eventually, Keith's wandering brought him into contact with the John B. Doris circus, which he attached himself to as a "grifter," one who contracts with a circus to sell various gimcracks on the grounds outside the tent.

Keith's experience with the circus (1870–76) introduced him to a complex amusement enterprise, and one that, decades before it became common in other entertainment forms, already had started down the road toward monopoly. By the 1830s menagerie companies had discovered the public's fascination with "wild" animals, but also the difficulty and expense of securing beasts native only to Africa, South America, and Asia. In 1835 a number of such companies formed a joint stock company, known as the Zoological Institute, as a means of dividing the cost of expensive big-game expeditions. Investors discovered the profits to be made from both supplying animals for exhibitions and operating traveling menageries, and soon a few powerful speculators and managers, through the Zoological Institute, virtually controlled American circus. These "flatfoots," as they were called, operated like a classic oligopoly, conspiring among themselves to keep competition to a minimum and new concerns from entering the market. (On the circus, see Murray, *Circus!* pp. 133–225.)

43 Harris, *Humbug*, p. 34. In Cincinnati, for example, a museum was founded by Daniel Drake, the medical doctor and scientist who was connected with "every major cultural, scientific, and education institution in Cincinnati in the 1820–1840 period" (Tucker, "Ohio Show-Shop," p. 77).

44 Chronicler of the New York stage, George Odell, speaks of "the gaudy pictures of 'freaks' that lured from the entrance, and the 'barkers' who

invoked pedestrians to invest their dimes. . . . One passed from these congregated museum-pieces to a 'theater' on the stage of which a wild, half-amateurish 'variety' aggregation entertained auditors who may never have heard of Edwin Booth or Miss Cushman." The first dime museum in the Minneapolis–St. Paul area opened in August 1869 and featured a stuffed two-headed calf with eight legs and two tails. (Odell, *Annals of the New York Stage*, 10:484. See also Staples, "Dime Museums in St. Paul," and Gray, "The Good Old Days of the Dime Museum.")

45 *Boston Herald*, January 7, 1883, p. 11; January 14, 1883, p. 3; January 28, 1883, p. 11; February 11, 1883, p. 7; February 25, 1883, p. 9; April 1, 1883, p. 7; May 20, 1883, p. 11. See also Allen, "B. F. Keith," and Moorehouse, "Benjamin Franklin Keith," p. 25.

46 *Boston Herald*, September 16, 1883, p. 11; June 1, 1884, p. 10; June 15, 1884, p. 10; December 28, 1884, p. 10; April 18, 1885, p. 10; April 26, 1885, p. 10; May 10, 1885, p. 10; *New York Clipper*, December 29, 1883, p. 697; June 7, 1884, p. 187; July 26, 1884, p. 198; " Keith and Batchellor's Mammoth Museum" (handbill); McLean, "Genesis of Vaudeville," pp. 85–86.

47 *King's How to See Boston*, pp. 104–8; Duis, "The Saloon and the Public City," pp. 164, 488–89; McGlinchee, *The First Decade of the Boston Museum*, pp. 29–30, 45 (quotation). Interestingly, for a few years Keith mixed variety with condensed versions of light opera offered at bargain-basement ticket prices. In 1885 light opera was riding the crest of a wave of popularity begun with the huge American success of Gilbert and Sullivan's *H.M.S. Pinafore* in 1879, an event theater historian Gerald Bordman calls "the pivotal landmark" in the history of American lyric theater. Within six months of its New York opening in November 1879, *Pinafore* had been presented in twelve New York theaters – a proliferation caused in large measure by its lack of copyright protection in the United States. Some indication of the opera craze of the mid-1880s is provided by the fact that between 1866 (the year of *The Black Crook*'s introduction) and 1879, New York theater seasons averaged only eight musical productions, but during the 1879–80 season alone there were thirty musical productions, and by 1882–83, forty.

During the 1885–86 season Keith's Gaiety Opera Company alternated with a variety bill, enabling Keith to continue to advertise his stage show as "continuous performance." The company mounted productions of Gilbert and Sullivan, comic operas by Audran, Benjamin Woolf's *The Doctor of Alcantara* (a favorite with Bostonians), and other light operas in "pocket editions," all for the museum's normal admission price of ten cents. (See Bordman, *American Musical Theatre*, pp. 43–46, 67; *Boston Herald*, March 21, 1886, p. 10; *New York Clipper*, May 29, 1886, p. 168.)

48 *New York Clipper*, March 24, 1888, p. 27; "Catalogue of the Gaiety Musee and Bijou Theater" (brochure).

49 Among the Bijou's more unusual features were a painting-lined lobby, an

auditorium embellished with Moorish touches, and one of the first electrically illuminated stages in the country. (See *Boston Herald*, December 10, 1882, clipping, HTC; *Boston Home Journal*, January 31, 1891, clipping, HTC.)

50 McLean, "Genesis of Vaudeville," p. 93. When Keith fired one performer after the first show for violating his strict code of appropriate language, the performer sued for his full week's wages. After losing his suit, the performer's attorney quipped: "I expect one day to see a museum in the clouds, B. F. Keith proprietor, and, written in letters of gold above the door, I read 'None but the angels admitted.' " ("The Profits in Clean Vaudeville," p. 603. See also *Boston Herald*, December 1904, clipping HTC.)

51 Keith, "The Vogue of Vaudeville," quoted in Levine, *Highbrow/Lowbrow*, p. 196.

52 Tucci, *The Boston Rialto*, p. 7.

53 Birkmire, *The Planning and Construction of American Theatres*, pp. 48–56; "B. F. Keith's New Theater" (brochure); "The Model Playhouse of the Country" (brochure) (quotations).

54 The brochure describing Keith's New Theater in Boston pointed out: "[I]t will be seen that the impossibility of the accumulation of dirt is apparent. . . . Indeed it may be said literally, that the cleaning never stops here but is continued uninterruptedly day and night." ("B. F. Keith's New Theater" [brochure]. See also Gilbert, *American Vaudeville*, pp. 204–5.)

55 At the same time that Keith was planning and building his New Theater in Boston, in New York Frederick F. Proctor was announcing the construction of an even more extravagant entertainment complex in Manhattan's upper East Side shopping district, which would be dedicated to continuous performance vaudeville.

Proctor and Keith were remarkably similar in background. Four years Keith's junior, Proctor was also a New Englander (born in 1852 in Dexter, Maine), and he also apprenticed with circuses before opening a dime museum in Albany in 1880. On the basis of its success, Proctor acquired a small circuit of theaters not for variety but for what was called "10–20–30" drama. He and his partner would lease large-capacity theaters and present road shows of recent New York hits or established favorites in melodrama, comedy, or operetta at an admission charge more on the order of a variety theater (hence the name 10–20–30) than a first-rate legitimate theater. In 1888 he built the Twenty-third Street Theater in New York, and after running cheap dramatic productions there for several years, he adopted Keith's continuous performance vaudeville policy in January 1893.

Proctor's Pleasure Palace, which opened on Labor Day 1895, was unlike anything New Yorkers had ever seen. Its romanesque facade extended for two hundred feet along Fifty-eighth Street between Third and Lexington. Inside there was not only a main auditorium but also a roof garden, German café, and smaller auditorium called the Garden of Palms. In the basement was a "library," barbershop, Turkish bath, and stands for the sale of flowers, books, and Turkish coffee. Once a patron had paid his admission fee, she or he could enjoy any of the Pleasure Palace's facilities.

But even the opulence of Proctor's Pleasure Palace was eclipsed by Oscar Hammerstein's Olympia Theater, which opened a few months later (November 25, 1895). The Olympia was for years the final word in vaudeville grandiloquence. Actually four theaters in one, it occupied the entire block of Broadway between Forty-fourth and Forty-fifth streets, just north of Times Square. Contained within the massive complex were two large auditoriums, a concert hall café, and, covering the entire area of the huge building, a roof garden. Below street level were more cafés, billiard rooms, a bowling alley, and Turkish baths. In all, four to five thousand people could be accommodated within the Olympia during the warm months, and nearly three thousand in the interior theaters and facilities alone. It was, as one historian of the city put it, "a structure of superlatives." (Marcuse, *This Was New York*, p. 199. On Proctor, see also *New York Clipper*, April 18, 1885, p. 74; January 7, 1888, p. 686; January 21, 1888, p. 718; April 10, 1890, p. 87; December 17, 1892, p. 657; January 7, 1893, p. 706; December 17, 1892, p. 657; and Marston and Feller, *F. F. Proctor*.)

56 Frederick F. Snyder, "American Vaudeville," p. 26.

57 *New York Clipper*, May 19, 1894, p. 166; June 16, 1894, p. 230; June 20, 1896, p. 262; April 20, 1895, p. 102. On the relationship between vaudeville and the cinema, see Allen, *Vaudeville and Film*. Perhaps the best example of the full incorporation of other performance media into vaudeville is provided by the case of puppetry. Itinerant English puppet troupes toured the United States with their elaborate shows as early as the 1870s. Puppeteers fashioned their complex, multiact performances from pantomime and spectacle theater, often going so far as to close with a transformation scene.

Originally, the puppet troupes played in rented halls or "opera houses" and were completely dependent on local managers. This arrangement frequently left the troupes stranded in the American hinterlands. In the 1880s puppeteers increasingly used variety theaters as venues, so that as variety grew and became as economically stabilized as vaudeville, the economic viability of puppetry increased accordingly. The price puppetry paid for this new economic prosperity was a considerable alteration of its form in order to conform to the demands of the vaudeville bill. Obviously, the first formal change puppetry had to make was a condensation of its performances to fit the temporal limits of a standard vaudeville act: ten to twenty minutes. Further, it was discovered that a puppet act could be more effectively used as an opening or closing "dumb" act — one that was performed as the audience was getting settled or beginning to leave the theater and thus could not rely primarily on sound to carry its meaning. Hence, puppetry in vaudeville dispensed with much of its auditory component. Dialogue was pared away drastically, and even songs disappeared from the routines of some puppet acts.

Walter Deaves, a master puppeteer who toured the Keith circuit in the 1890s and early 1900s, saw more clearly than his contemporaries the intimate bond that had grown between puppetry and vaudeville. He abandoned the old puppetry format based on pantomime and had his puppets perform a miniature vaudeville bill, complete with tiny proscenium set, puppet pit orchestra, and puppet audience. Deaves's miniature vaudeville act became the standard puppetry format. In less than thirty years, puppetry had been transformed from an autonomous entertainment form, audiovisual in nature, to one absolutely dependent economically and aesthetically on vaudeville. (See McPharlin, *The Puppet Theater in America*, pp. 271–88.)

58 Tucci, *The Puritan Muse*, p. 97.

59 *Providence News*, August 21, 1900, clipping. That some theaters saw children as an important part of their audience is indicated by the inclusion in Keith's Providence theater's house organ, the *Keith News*, of a column "for the little people," listing acts booked especially for younger patrons. By 1907 the theater's manager put the value of juvenile patronage there at $10,000 per year. (See *Providence News*, April 21, 1900, clipping, Providence Clipping Book, 1900–1901; *Pawtucket Times*, November 26, 1903, clipping, Providence Clipping Book, 1903–4; *Keith News*, September 5, 1904, clipping, Providence Clipping Book, 1904–5; *Providence Tribune*, April 18, 1907, and *Providence Bulletin*, April 18, 1907, clippings, Providence Clipping Book, 1906–7 – all in the Keith/Albee Collection, University of Iowa Library.)

The dollar value placed upon children's patronage came to light as a result of an attempt by the state of Rhode Island to prohibit unaccompanied juvenile attendance at theaters, roller rinks, and dance halls. These amusements, some legislators felt, encouraged truancy. Keith's Providence manager, Charles Lovenburg, appeared before the legislative committee drafting the bill to urge a counterproposal: ban children from dance halls, shooting galleries, and pool halls, but allow them to frequent vaudeville theaters between the hour of school closing and 6:00 p.m. Lovenburg undiplomatically stated that if the bill were passed he would find "a thousand ways" to beat it, and that he was determined not "to be defrauded out of legitimate earnings amounting to $10,000" per year (*Providence News*, April 18, 1907, clipping). Nevertheless, the bill passed. I am unable to determine its effects or whether Lovenburg made good on this threat to circumvent it.

60 Bell, "A Little Journey to the B. F. Keith Palace."

61 Gilbert, *American Vaudeville*, p. 202.

62 McLean, "Genesis of Vaudeville," p. 88.

63 In 1916 George A. Gottlieb, booking agent for New York's Palace Theater,

the most prestigious vaudeville venue in the country, provided an intuitive functional analysis of the standard vaudeville program. The opening act on a nine-act program was a dumb act, one that did not need to be heard to be enjoyed since it often had to compete with the noise of late-arriving patrons. Dumb acts included acrobats, animal acts, magicians, and dancers. The function of the next number on the bill was to settle the audience down and was usually fulfilled by a duet. The third act had to deliver the first "big punch" of the program and might have been a playlet: a brief one-act dramatic or comic sketch. The fourth spot on the bill was reserved for a "personality act," a comedy team or vocalist. Because it was the last act before intermission, the fifth position was regarded as the second most important spot on the program. The sixth act had to regain the audience's interest and attention, but because the entire second half of the bill built toward the star turn, it could not be "bigger" than any of the succeeding acts. It was often a specialty or comic dumb act. The seventh spot might have been filled by another playlet. The spot reserved for the headliner, a "performer of celebrity status," was eighth – next to closing. The program ended with another dumb act, one that could be enjoyed over the noise of departing patrons and send them home "pleased . . . to the very last minute." (Gottlieb, "Psychology of the American Vaudeville Show," pp. 257–58.)

64 The trend toward monopoly in the legitimate theater began in the 1880s and culminated in 1896 with the formation of a theatrical syndicate, headed by Marc Klaw and A. L. Erlanger, which controlled the booking of more than five hundred theaters on the most important routes from coast to coast. The syndicate solidified its position by forcing both theater circuits and producers into exclusive contracts with it. Within a very short time it was exerting virtually complete control over the entire industry. Although an "independent" movement was mounted in opposition to the trust in 1898 and again in 1902, the syndicate's corner on the theatrical market was not effectively challenged until the emergence of the Shuberts as major forces in theater management around 1905. (See *New York Dramatic Mirror*, February 22, 1896, p. 17; March 26, 1898, pp. 3–4.) The formation of the syndicate and the "independent" challenges to it are chronicled in several articles by Monroe Lippman: "Battle for Bookings," "Death of the Salesmen's Monopoly," "The Effect of the Theatrical Syndicate on Theatrical Art in America," and "The First Revolt against the Theatrical Syndicate."

The growth of vaudeville as a national industry roughly parallels, both chronologically and structurally, that of the legitimate theater. The key period in vaudeville's growth and industrial consolidation was 1894–98, when a surge in vaudeville theater building and the expansion of existing circuits brought vaudeville to the attention of citizens in every major city in the United States. The emergence of vaudeville as the country's premiere popular entertainment form during these years is directly related to the economic depression of 1894 and, as a consequence of it, to a serious slump in business within the legitimate sector. The depression of 1894 cut deep into the national economy, not only bringing to an end a period of sustained industrial growth but also creating serious dislocations within American society. The 1895–96 legitimate season was one of the worst on record. Vaudeville actually profited by the economic downturn and at the expense of the legitimate theater. With tickets at legitimate houses going for $1.50 or more and the vaudeville price ranging from 15¢ to $1.00, middle-class patrons saw in vaudeville a way to stretch their entertainment budgets. Furthermore, the economic downturn drove many dramatic stars into vaudeville when they found themselves "at liberty." (See *New York Dramatic Mirror*, May 2, 1896, p. 14; July 28, 1894, p. 2; July 16, 1898, p. 13; March 21, 1896, p. 14; June 6, 1896, p. 12; November 9, 1895, p. 12; *New York Clipper*, July 7, 1894, p. 278.)

65 *New York Dramatic Mirror*, January 6, 1900, p. 18; Kirkland, *Industry Comes of Age*, p. 237; Frederick F. Snyder, "American Vaudeville," p. 34; McLean, *American Vaudeville as Ritual*, p. 44.

66 Frederick F. Proctor must have been one of the first East Coast managers to attempt such a combination. In the summer of 1895 he contracted with a booking agent, Vaudeville Exchange Co., to control the entire time of ten to twelve acts, guaranteeing them a full season's work at Proctor's four theaters and at other theaters with which Proctor negotiated exclusive contracts. (See *New York Dramatic Mirror*, July 6, 1895, p. 14.)

67 This trust still constituted an uneasy marriage between its western faction (headed by Orpheum president Martin Beck) and its eastern contingent (presided over by Keith and Albee), which for the next decade frequently teetered on the edge of divorce. However, the parties' common monopolistic interests always eventually overrode their competitive impulses. (See *New York Dramatic Mirror*, January 12, 1901, p. 20; *Billboard*, January 5, 1901, p. 10.)

68 "It is a strange thing," one of their union organizers noted in February 1901, "that performers are the only class of professional people who are forced to pay for being allowed to work" (*New York Dramatic Mirror*, February 16, 1901, p. 20). The performers' union, the White Rats, struck VMA member theaters in February 1901, demanding abolition of the booking fee. Keith blamed the strike on "agitators, irresponsible persons who are unable to get good work to do themselves, and who have stirred the others up" (ibid., March 1, 1901, p. 18). Another manager all too bluntly stated his view of the relationship between management and performer in vaudeville's new industrial age: "Where would the actors be if there were not men of brains, shrewdness and discernment to discover them, to put them forward, and push them to success? The sculptor takes a mass of clay and molds it into a work of art. Is it the sculptor or the clay that deserves the credit for the accomplishment?" (ibid., March 9, 1901, p. 18). Although the strike won temporary concessions from VMA, within three months the prestrike status

quo had been restored and the union's power completely undermined. The only legacy of the strike was the blacklisting of some of the principal "agitators." (See *New York Dramatic Mirror*, February 16, 1901, p. 20; February 23, 1901, p. 18; March 1, 1901, p. 18; March 9, 1901, p. 18; *Variety*, February 24, 1906, p. 4.)

In 1906 the booking arm of the VMA was formally organized as the United Booking Office (UBO), and its control over the professional lives of vaudeville performers became nearly absolute. A new standard contract drafted in 1908 made UBO the "sole and exclusive agent" for an act, giving it power of attorney to enter into contracts with theaters and circuits on the act's behalf. Any act that dared to play a non-VMA house was simply barred from VMA theaters, which generally meant that its career in "big time" vaudeville was finished. (See *Variety*, March 21, 1908, p. 1; May 9, 1908, p. 1.)

69 Zeidman, *The American Burlesque Show*, pp. 52–56; Sobel, *A Pictorial History of Burlesque*, pp. 80–81; *New York Times*, April 3, 1900, p. 12; November 30, 1901, p. 9; March 10, 1902, p. 9.

70 *Billboard*, February 10, 1906, pp. 8–9; Zeidman, *The American Burlesque Show*, pp. 62–66.

CHAPTER SEVEN

1 *National Police Gazette*, December 1, 1866, p. 2.
2 Ibid., November 30, 1878, p. 1; December 7, 1878, p. 7; February 1, 1897, p. 3.
3 Ibid., July 31, 1880, p. 6.
4 Ibid., March 18, 1899, p. 3.
5 *New York Clipper*, March 4, 1871, p. 378.
6 *National Police Gazette*, June 26, 1880, p. 6.
7 Dijkstra, *Idols of Perversity*, pp. 237–66, 380 (quotations, pp. 252, 241, 351, 334).
8 Leavitt, *Fifty Years in Theatrical Management*, pp. 329–33. The first pictorial theatrical poster in Great Britain was designed in 1871 by Frederick Walker to advertise a London stage adaptation of Wilkie Collins's *Woman in White*. It was a woodblock print rather than a lithograph, however. (See Hillier, *One Hundred Years of the Poster*, p. iii.)
9 Erenberg, *Stepping Out*, pp. 33–34. A Fannie Hurst short story that appeared in the *Saturday Evening Post* in 1912 has a manicurist choose a genuine working-class suitor over his nouveau-riche rival who has taken rooms in the "lobster palace" hotel in which she works. "I guess, if the truth was known," she tells the ordinary joe, "the crawfish stand better with me than the lobsters." (*Saturday Evening Post*, July 6, 1912, p. 6.) I am grateful to Kristin Thompson for passing along to me this bit of lobster lore.

10 The burlesques produced by Weber and Fields are among the very few that survive in script form. Several can be found in the Harvard Theatre Collection. Information on the career of Weber and Fields is taken from the clipping files in the New York Public Library Performing Arts Collection (hereafter cited as NYPL); "Weber and Fields"; Distler, "The Rise and Fall of Racial Comics in American Vaudeville," pp. 73–77; Zeidman, *The American Burlesque Show*, pp. 44–45; and Sobel, *A Pictorial History of Burlesque*, pp. 42–49.

11 Isman, *Weber and Fields*, p. 83.

12 Morell, *Lillian Russell*, pp. 188–93.

13 Isman, *Weber and Fields*, p. 209.

14 Herbert, *The Geezer*.

15 Ibid.; Isman, *Weber and Fields*, pp. 203–7.

16 *New York Times*, September 6, 1901, p. 2; December 3, 1897, p. 7.

17 *New York Herald*, quoted in Isman, *Weber and Fields*, p. 305; Zeidman, *The American Burlesque Show*, pp. 45–46.

18 Information on the Chicago World's Columbian Exposition is taken from Rydell, *All the World's a Fair*, and Badger, *The Great American Fair*.

19 The fair's anthropological focus provided the impetus for the establishment of Chicago's Field Museum.

20 Rydell, *All the World's a Fair*, p. 40.

21 *Frank Leslie's Popular Monthly* 36 (October 1893): 415, quoted in Rydell, *All the World's a Fair*, p. 66.

22 Bloom, *Autobiography*, p. 135, quoted in Badger, *The Great American Fair*, p. 107; *New York Times*, August 2, 1893, p. 5.

23 Beer, *Hanna, Crane, and the Mauve Decade*, p. 32, quoted in Badger, *The Great American Fair*, p. 121.

24 Darwin, *The Descent of Man*, pp. 643–65, quoted in Dijkstra, *Idols of Perversity*, p. 166.

25 Dijkstra, *Idols of Perversity*, p. 240.

26 Ellis, *Man and Woman*, p. 355, quoted in Dijkstra, *Idols of Perversity*, p. 243.

27 Dijkstra, *Idols of Perversity*, p. 246.

28 *New York Times*, December 3, 1893, p. 2.

29 *New York Times*, December 5, 1893, p. 8; December 7, 1893, p. 3. Ann Corio (*Burlesque*, p. 36) erroneously claims that belly dancing was introduced to American audiences at the Columbian Exposition in 1904 and entered burlesque thereafter.

30 The fair of 1896 was not the Louisiana Purchase Exposition of "Meet Me in St. Louis, Louis," however, which took place in 1904.

31 *National Police Gazette*, October 31, 1896, p. 2 (quotation); Minsky and Machlin, *Minsky's Burlesque*, p. 75.

32 Minsky and Machlin, *Minsky's Burlesque*, pp. 33–34.

33 Zeidman, *The American Burlesque Show*, p. 110.

34 Lewis, *Carnival*, p. 19.

35 Bogdan, *Freak Show*, pp. 35–60; *Amusement World*, cited in Lewis, *Carnival*, p. 16. See also Gray, "The Good Old Days of the Dime Museum," pp. 98–99.

36 Bogdan, *Freak Show*, p. 2.

37 Fiedler, *Freaks*, p. 24.

38 Ibid., pp. 18, 170–77 (quotation, p. 177).

39 Quoted in Lewis, *Carnival*, p. 47.

40 Ibid., pp. 267–68.

41 See various burlesque theater programs, NYPL – among them: London Theater (New York City), November 3, 1891; Star Theater (Cleveland), 1901; Waldman's Opera House (Newark, N.J.), 1893, 1908; Empire Theater (Toledo), 1916.

42 Lydia Thompson (handwritten manuscript).

43 Minsky and Machlin, *Minsky's Burlesque*, pp. 306–7.

44 Corio, *Burlesque*, pp. 168–69.

45 Jean-Paul Debax, "Et voilà pourquoi votre femme est muette," quoted in Brooke-Rose, "Woman as Semiotic Object," p. 310.

CHAPTER EIGHT

1 *National Police Gazette*, October 31, 1896, p. 2; February 25, 1899, p. 2.

2 Leach, "Transformations in a Culture of Consumption," p. 325.

3 On the career of Florenz Ziegfeld, see Carter, *The World of Flo Ziegfeld*. Ziegfeld's innovative mode of feminine sexual display is discussed in Erenberg, *Stepping Out*, pp. 206–21.

4 Erenberg, *Stepping Out*, p. 219.

5 Zeidman, *The American Burlesque Show*, pp. 121–27.

6 *Billboard*, September 27, 1930, p. 25; *New York Times*, November 29, 1933, p. 22.

7 Minsky and Machlin, *Minsky's Burlesque*, pp. 32–35 (quotation, p. 35).

8 Unless otherwise noted, information on the burlesque industry in the 1920s is taken from Zeidman, *The American Burlesque Show*.

9 *New York Herald Tribune*, April 20, 1930, 1931, clippings, NYPL.

10 Cited in Zeidman, *The American Burlesque Show*, p. 142.

11 Henderson, *The City and the Theatre*, pp. 196–97.

12 Zeidman, *The American Burlesque Show*, pp. 168–71.

13 Quoted in Minsky and Machlin, *Minsky's Burlesque*, p. 77.

14 Ibid., pp. 77–85.

15 *New York Times*, March 25, 1932, p. 22; April 7, 1932, p. 29.

16 Ibid., May 5, 1932, p. 13; April 26, 1932, p. 23.

17 Ibid., April 26, 1932, p. 23; April 27, 1932, p. 19; May 3, 1932, p. 23; May 5, 1932, p. 13; May 7, 1932, p. 11.

18 Ibid., May 12, 1932, p. 23; September 18, 1932, p. 1; September 20, 1932,

pp. 1–2; September 21, 1932, p. 20; September 22, 1932, p. 24; May 17, 1933, p. 15.

19 Ibid., October 12, 1932, p. 25; March 16, 1933, p. 19.

20 Ibid., April 9, 1937, p. 23.

21 Ibid., April 16, 1937, p. 27; April 29, 1937, p. 16; May 1, 1937, p. 1.

22 Ibid., April 9, 1937, p. 23; April 16, 1937, p. 27; April 17, 1937, p. 15; April 29, 1937, pp. 1, 16; April 30, 1937, pp. 1, 16; May 1, 1937, p. 1; May 2, 1937, pp. 1, 16; May 3, 1937, p. 1; May 4, 1937, p. 28 (quotation). See also Minsky and Machlin, *Minsky's Burlesque*, pp. 273–79.

23 Zeidman, *The American Burlesque Show*, pp. 174–75.

24 *New York Times*, May 9, 1937, sec. 11, p. 1.

25 Minsky and Machlin, *Minsky's Burlesque*, p. 240.

26 Darrah, *The World of Stereographs*, pp. 1–19, 65.

27 A large collection of stereographs is held in the Division of Prints and Photographs of the Library of Congress, acquired as a part of the copyright deposit system. In some instances, full series are available; in others, only a few images were submitted with the copyright application.

28 Williams, *Hard Core*, pp. 34–48.

29 Ibid., p. 41.

30 Ibid., p. 43.

31 See Allen, *Vaudeville and Film*, pp. 75–115.

32 Bordwell, Staiger, and Thompson, *The Classical Hollywood Cinema*, pp. 113–15.

33 Allen, *Vaudeville and Film*, pp. 109–12.

34 Graham et al., *D. W. Griffith and the Biograph Company*, p. 313; Niver, *Biograph Bulletins*, p. 61.

35 *Biograph Bulletin*, July 6, 1903.

36 Ibid., August 29, 1903.

37 Williams, *Hard Core*, pp. 73–75.

38 Jacqueline Dowd Hall ("Disorderly Women") discusses the calculated use of transgressive behavior and dress as a strategy employed by women in another social sphere: that of labor action. During a strike against the American Bemberg rayon factory in Elizabethton, Tennessee, in 1929, some women taunted and cursed National Guard troops called in to "protect" the mill. When brought to trial, one woman wore a dress sewed from red, white, and blue bunting and a cap made from an American flag. The episode also demonstrates the immediate connection made between women's transgressive social behavior and criminal sexuality. To combat what it saw as the community's moral deterioration brought about by these unruly women, the town council passed an ordinance against "lewdness" aimed exclusively at the female strikers. Hall concludes: "There is nothing extraordinary about this association between sexual misbehavior and women's labor militancy. Since strikers are often young single women who

violate gender conventions by invading public space customarily reserved for men (and sometimes frequented by prostitutes) – and since female aggressiveness stirs up fears of women's sexual power – opponents have often undercut union organizing drives by insinuations of prostitution or promiscuity" (p. 375).

39 Erenberg, *Stepping Out*, pp. 196–222 (quotation, p. 219).

40 Ibid., pp. 193–99 (quotation, p. 197).

41 MacDonald, "Black Women on Stage."

42 Hamilton, "Mae West in Vaudeville."

43 For an account of the rise of small-time vaudeville, see Allen, *Vaudeville and Film*, pp. 230–59.

44 Hamilton, "Mae West in Vaudeville," pp. 2–13; West, *Goodness Had Nothing to Do with It*, pp. 43–51 (quotation, p. 41); *Variety*, July 7, 1916, quoted in Hamilton, "Mae West in Vaudeville," p. 6.

45 West, *Goodness Had Nothing to Do with It*, p. 64.

46 Ibid., p. 73.

47 See West, *The Ruby Ring* and *The Hussy*.

48 West, *Sex*.

49 *New York Times*, April 1, 1927, p. 13; April 5, 1927, p. 10; April 6, 1927, p. 1; April 7, 1927, p. 27; April 20, 1927, p. 1 (quotation); April 21, 1927, p. 29; April 28, 1927, p. 27; West, *Goodness Had Nothing to Do with It*, pp. 98–100.

50 West, *The Drag*.

51 West, *Goodness Had Nothing to Do with It*, p. 95.

52 Ibid., p. 94.

53 Although eventually West was able to get the charges against the play dropped, it was not until after all money for advance ticket sales had been refunded. West decided not to reopen the play, in which she did not appear.

54 West, *The Pleasure Man*.

55 West, *Diamond Lil*.

56 Mary G. Hawks, president, National Council of Catholic Women, quoted in Jowett, *Film*, p. 206.

57 Marjorie Rosen, *Popcorn Venus*, p. 161.

58 Natalie Zemon Davis ("Women on Top") finds a similar complexity and ambiguity in symbolic sexual inversion in early modern Europe. Most anthropologists, she says, contend that sexual reversal serves to reinforce social structures and provides a release for pent-up social tensions. In the sixteenth and seventeenth centuries, however, sexual role inversions did not necessarily work to keep women "in their place." Rather, the image of the disorderly woman "was a multivalent image and could operate to widen behavioral options for women within and even outside marriage, and to sanction riot and political disobedience for both men and women in a society that allowed the lower orders few formal means of protest" (p. 153).

59 Peiss, "'Charity Girls' and City Pleasures," p. 82.

60 Peiss, *Cheap Amusements*, p. 6.
61 Weene, "Venus."
62 Mahany, "No Molds Barred!" p. C8.
63 Minsky and Machlin, *Minsky's Burlesque*, p. 290; Lewis, *Carnival*, pp. 42, 73–75.
64 Weene, "Venus," p. 36.

Bibliography

O   O   O   O   O   O   O   O   O   O   O   O

This bibliography is organized as follows:

Books
Articles and Book Chapters
Theses and Dissertations
Newspapers
Manuscripts and Unpublished Papers
Films, Posters, and Miscellaneous Materials
Legal Cases Cited
Manuscript Collections

BOOKS

Adams, Abigail. *Letters of Mrs. Adams, the Wife of John Adams, with an Introductory Memoir by Her Grandson, Charles Francis Adams.* Boston, 1840.

Allen, Robert C. *Speaking of Soap Operas.* Chapel Hill: University of North Carolina Press, 1985.

———. *Vaudeville and Film, 1895–1915: A Study in Media Interaction.* New York: Arno Press, 1980.

Arthur, Timothy S. *The Maiden: A Story of My Young Countrywoman.* Philadelphia, 1845.

Babcock, Barbara A., ed. *The Reversible World: Symbolic Inversion in Art and Society.* Ithaca: Cornell University Press, 1978.

Baddeley, V. C. Clinton. *The Burlesque Tradition in the English Theatre after 1660.* London: Methuen, 1952.

Badger, Reid. *The Great American Fair: The World's Columbian Exposition and American Culture.* Chicago: Nelson Hall, 1979.

Bailey, Peter. *Leisure and Class in Victorian England: Rational Recreation and the Contest for Control, 1830–1885.* London: Routledge, 1978.

Baker-Benfield, G. J. *The Horrors of the Half-Known Life: Male Attitudes toward Women and Sexuality in Nineteenth-Century America.* New York: Harper and Row, 1976.

Bakhtin, Mikhail. *Rabelais and His World.* Translated by Helene Iswolsky. Cambridge: MIT Press, 1968.

Balandier, Georges. *Political Anthropology.* London: Allen Lane, 1970.

Banner, Lois. *American Beauty.* New York: Knopf, 1983.

Barish, Jonas. *The Antitheatrical Prejudice.* Berkeley: University of California Press, 1981.

Baym, Nina. *Woman's Fiction: A Guide to Novels by and about Women in America, 1820–1870.* Ithaca: Cornell University Press, 1978.

Beer, Thomas. *Hanna, Crane, and the Mauve Decade.* New York: Knopf, 1941.

Bennett, Tony, and Woolacott, Janet. *Bond and Beyond.* London: Methuen, 1987.

Birkmire, William H. *The Planning and Construction of American Theatres.* New York: Wiley, 1896.

Bloom, Sol. *The Autobiography of Sol Bloom.* New York: Putnam, 1948.

Bogdan, Robert. *Freak Show: Presenting Human Oddities for Amusement and Profit.* Chicago: University of Chicago Press, 1988.

Booth, Michael. *Prefaces to English Nineteenth-Century Theatre.* Manchester: Manchester University Press, 1980.

Bordman, Gerald. *American Musical Theatre: A Chronicle.* New York: Oxford University Press, 1978.

Bordwell, David; Staiger, Janet; and Thompson, Kristin. *The Classical Hollywood Cinema: Film Style and Mode of Production to 1960.* New York: Columbia University Press, 1985.

Bourdieu, Pierre. *Outline of a Theory of Practice.* Cambridge: Cambridge University Press, 1977.

Brackett, J. Albert. *Theatrical Law.* Boston: C. M. Clark Publishing Co., 1907.

Bristol, Michael. *Carnival and Theatre: Plebeian Culture and the Structure of Authority in Renaissance England.* New York: Methuen, 1985.

Brougham, John. *Met-a-mora; or, The Last of the Pollywogs.* New York: Samuel French, n.d.

Brown, Herbert Ross. *The Sentimental Novel in America, 1789–1860.* Durham: Duke University Press, 1940.

Carter, Randolph. *The World of Flo Ziegfeld.* New York: Praeger, 1974.

Castle, Terry. *Masquerade and Civilization: The Carnivalesque in Eighteenth-Century English Culture and Fiction.* Stanford: Stanford University Press, 1986.

Cheshire, David F. *Music Hall in Britain.* London: Newton Abbott, David, and Charles, 1974.

Coke, E. T. *A Subaltern's Furlough.* New York: J. and J. Harper, 1833.

Corio, Ann, with Dimona, Joseph. *Burlesque.* New York: Grosset and Dunlap, 1968.

Cott, Nancy, ed. *The Roots of Bitterness: Documents of the Social History of American Women*. New York: Dutton, 1972.

Cousins, Mark, and Hussain, Athar. *Michel Foucault*. London: Macmillan, 1984.

Crowley, John W. *The Black Heart's Truth: The Early Career of W. D. Howells*. Chapel Hill: University of North Carolina Press, 1985.

Darrah, William C. *Cartes de Visite in Nineteenth-Century Photography*. Gettysburg, Pa.: W. C. Darrah, 1981.

———. *The World of Stereographs*. Gettysburg, Pa.: W. C. Darrah, 1977.

Darwin, Charles. *The Descent of Man*. London: J. Murray, 1871.

Degler, Carl. *Against the Odds: Women and the Family in America from the Revolution to the Present*. New York: Oxford University Press, 1980.

Dijkstra, Bram. *Idols of Perversity: Fantasies of Feminine Evil in Fin-de-Siècle Culture*. New York: Oxford University Press, 1986.

Douglas, Ann. *The Feminization of American Culture*. New York: Knopf, 1977.

Douglas, Mary. *Purity and Danger*. New York: Praeger, 1966.

Eagleton, Terry. *Walter Benjamin: Towards a Revolutionary Criticism*. London: Verso, 1981.

Ellis, Havelock. *Man and Woman*. London: W. Scott, 1894.

Erenberg, Lewis. *Stepping Out: New York Nightlife and the Transformation of American Culture, 1890–1930*. Westport, Conn.: Greenwood Press, 1981.

Ewen, David, ed. *Songs of America*. Chicago: Ziff-Davis, 1947.

Faulkner, Harold. *The Decline of Laissez-Faire*. New York: Harper and Row, 1951.

Fiedler, Leslie. *Freaks: Myths and Images of the Secret Self*. New York: Simon and Schuster, 1978.

Fiske, John. *Television Culture*. London: Methuen, 1987.

Foucault, Michel. *The History of Sexuality*. Vol. 1, *An Introduction*. New York: Random House, 1980.

Gallagher, Catherine, and Laqueur, Thomas, eds. *The Making of the Modern Body: Sexuality and Society in the Nineteenth Century*. Berkeley: University of California Press, 1987.

Gerson, Noel [Paul Lewis]. *Queen of the Plaza: A Biography of Adah Isaacs Menken*. New York: Funk and Wagnalls, 1964.

Gilbert, Douglas. *American Vaudeville: Its Life and Times*. New York: Dover Books, 1940.

Ginger, Ray. *The Age of Excess*. New York: Macmillan, 1965.

Graham, Cooper; Higgens, Steve; Mancini, Elaine; and Vieira, Joao Luiz. *D. W. Griffith and the Biograph Company*. Metuchen, N.J.: Scarecrow Press, 1988.

Graves, Robert. *The Greek Myths*. London: Penguin Books, 1960.

Grimsted, David. *Melodrama Unveiled: American Theater and Culture, 1800–1850*. Chicago: University of Chicago Press, 1968.

Guest, Ivor. *Fanny Elssler*. Middletown, Conn.: Wesleyan University Press, 1970.

Hagan, John S. *Records of the New York Stage, 1860–70*. Extra-Illustrated and Extended by Augustus Toedenberg. New York: *New York Dispatch*, n.d.

Halttunen, Karen. *Confidence Men and Painted Women*. New Haven: Yale University Press, 1982.

Harris, Neil. *Humbug: The Art of P. T. Barnum*. Boston: Little, Brown, 1973.

Henderson, Mary. *The City and the Theatre: New York Playhouses from Bowling Green to Times Square*. Clifton, N.J.: James T. White, 1973.

Hillier, Bevis. *One Hundred Years of the Poster*. London: Pall Mall, 1972.

Hone, Philip. *The Diary of Philip Hone, 1828–1851*. Edited by Allan Nevins. New York: Dodd, Mead, 1927.

Hornblow, Arthur. *History of Theatre in America*. New York: Lippincott, 1919.

Hutton, Laurence. *Curiosities of the American Stage*. New York: Harper, 1891.

Ireland, Joseph. *Records of the New York Stage*. 2 vols. New York: T. H. Morrell, 1866–67.

Isman, Felix. *Weber and Fields: Their Tribulations, Triumphs, and Their Associates*. New York: Boni, 1924.

Jauss, Hans Robert. *Toward an Aesthetic of Reception*. Minneapolis: University of Minnesota Press, 1982.

Jowett, Garth. *Film: The Democratic Art*. Boston: Little, Brown, 1976.

Kendrick, Walter. *The Secret Museum: Pornography in Modern Culture*. New York: Viking, 1987.

King's How to See Boston: A Trustworthy Guide Book. Boston: Maculler, Parker, 1895.

Kirkland, Edward C. *Industry Comes of Age: Business, Labor, and Public Policy, 1860–1897*. New York: Holt, Rinehart, and Winston, 1961.

Lansing's Pictorial Diagrams of the Leading Opera Houses, Theatres, etc., in the United States. Boston: Lansing, 1880.

Laurie, Bruce. *Working People of Philadelphia, 1800–1850*. Philadelphia: Temple University Press, 1980.

Laurie, Joe, Jr. *Vaudeville: From the Honky-Tonks to the Palace*. New York: Henry Holt, 1953.

Leach, William. *True Love and Perfect Union: The Feminist Reform of Sex and Society*. New York: Basic Books, 1980.

Leavitt, Michael B. *Fifty Years in Theatrical Management*. New York: Broadway Publishing Co., 1912.

Le Roy Ladurie, Emmanuel. *Carnival in Romans*. Translated by Mary Feeney. New York: G. Braziller, 1979.

Levine, Lawrence W. *Highbrow/Lowbrow: The Emergence of Cultural Hierarchy in America*. Cambridge: Harvard University Press, 1988.

Levy, Lester. *Flashes of Merriment: A Century of Humorous Songs, 1805–1905*. Norman: University of Oklahoma Press, 1971.

————. *Grace Notes in American History*. Norman: University of Oklahoma Press, 1967.

Lewis, Arthur H. *Carnival*. New York: Trident Press, 1970.

Linton, Elizabeth Lynn. *Modern Women and What Is Said of Them*. New York: R. R. Redfield, 1868.

Logan, Olive. *Apropos of Women and Theatres*. New York: Carleton, 1869.

McCullough, Jack M. *Living Pictures on the New York Stage*. Ann Arbor, Mich.: UMI Research Press, 1981.

McGlinchee, Claire. *The First Decade of the Boston Museum*. Boston: Humphries, 1941.

McLean, Albert F., Jr. *American Vaudeville as Ritual*. Lexington: University of Kentucky Press, 1965.

McNamara, Brooks. *The American Playhouse in the Eighteenth Century*. Cambridge: Harvard University Press, 1969.

McPharlin, Paul. *The Puppet Theatre in America*. Boston: Plays, Inc., 1969.

Mankowitz, Wolf. *Mazeppa: The Lives, Loves, and Legends of Adah Isaacs Menken*. New York: Stein and Day, 1982.

Marcuse, Maxwell F. *This Was New York*. New York: Carlton Press, 1965.

Markham, Pauline. *The Life of Pauline Markham, Written by Herself*. New York, 1871.

Marston, William, and Feller, John H. *F. F. Proctor: Vaudeville Pioneer*. New York: Richard R. Smith, 1943.

Meserve, Walter J. *Heralds of Promise: The Drama of the American People during the Age of Jackson, 1829–1849*. New York: Greenwood Press, 1986.

Miller, Tice. *Bohemians and Critics: American Theatre Criticism in the Nineteenth Century*. Metuchen, N.J.: Scarecrow Press, 1981.

Minsky, Morton, and Machlin, Milt. *Minsky's Burlesque*. New York: Arbor House, 1986.

Moody, Richard. *America Takes the Stage: Romanticism in American Drama and Theatre, 1750–1900*. Bloomington: Indiana University Press, 1955.

————. *The Astor Place Riot*. Bloomington: Indiana University Press, 1958.

————, ed. *Dramas of the American Theatre, 1762–1909*. Boston: Houghton Mifflin, 1966.

Morell, Parker. *Lillian Russell: The Era of Plush*. Garden City, N.Y.: Garden City Publishing Co., 1943.

Murray, Marian. *Circus! From Rome to Ringling*. Westport, Conn.: Greenwood Press, 1956.

Nathan, Hans. *Dan Emmett and the Rise of Early Negro Minstrelsy*. Norman: University of Oklahoma Press, 1962.

Nead, Lydia. *Myths of Sexuality: Representations of Women in Victorian Britain*. London: Basil Blackwell, 1988.

Niver, Kemp R. *Biograph Bulletins, 1896–1908*. Los Angeles: Locare Research Group, 1971.

Northall, William Knight. *Before and behind the Curtain; or, Fifteen Years'
    Observations among the Theatres of New York*. New York: W. F. Burgess,
    1851.
Odell, George C. D. *Annals of the New York Stage*. 15 vols. New York: Co-
    lumbia University Press, 1949.
Papashvily, Helen. *All the Happy Endings: A Study of the Domestic Novel in
    America, the Women Who Wrote It, the Women Who Read It, in the Nine-
    teenth Century*. New York: Harper and Row, 1956.
Peiss, Kathy. *Cheap Amusements: Leisure in Turn-of-the-Century New York*.
    Philadelphia: Temple University Press, 1986.
Phillips, David Graham. *Susan Lenox: Her Fall and Rise*. 2 vols. New York: D.
    Appleton, 1917.
Poggi, Jack. *Theater in America: The Impact of Economic Forces, 1870–1967*.
    Ithaca: Cornell University Press, 1966.
Prioleau, Elizabeth Stevens. *The Circle of Eros: Sexuality in the Work of
    William Dean Howells*. Durham: Duke University Press, 1983.
Rankin, Hugh R. *The Theatre in Colonial America*. Chapel Hill: University of
    North Carolina Press, 1965.
Rella, Ettore. *A History of Burlesque*. San Francisco Theatre Research Series,
    no. 14. San Francisco: Works Projects Administration, 1940.
Rosen, Marjorie. *Popcorn Venus*. New York: Avon Books, 1973.
Rosen, Ruth. *The Lost Sisterhood: Prostitution in America, 1900–1918*. Bal-
    timore: Johns Hopkins University Press, 1982.
Rourke, Constance. *American Humor*. New York: Harcourt, Brace, 1931.
Ruyter, Nancy Lee Chalfa. *Reformers and Visionaries: The Americanization of
    the Art of Dance*. New York: Dance Horizons, 1979.
Ryan, Mary P. *Cradle of the Middle Class: The Family in Oneida County, New
    York, 1790–1865*. Cambridge: Cambridge University Press, 1981.
Rydell, Robert W. *All the World's a Fair: Visions of Empire at American Inter-
    national Expositions, 1876–1916*. Chicago: University of Chicago Press,
    1984.
Senelick, Laurence. *The Age and Stage of George L. Fox, 1825–1877*. Han-
    over, N.H.: University Press of New England, 1988.
Shaw, Peter. *American Patriots and the Rituals of Revolution*. Cambridge:
    Harvard University Press, 1981.
Sketches and Business Directory of Boston and Its Vicinity for 1860–61. Boston:
    Damrell and Moore and George Collidge, 1860.
Smith, Bill. *The Vaudevillians*. New York: Macmillan, 1976.
Smith-Rosenberg, Carroll. *Disorderly Conduct: Visions of Gender in Victorian
    America*. New York: Knopf, 1985.
Snitow, Ann; Stansell, Christine; and Thompson, Sharon, eds. *Powers of De-
    sire: The Politics of Sexuality*. New York: Monthly Review Press, 1983.
Sobel, Bernard. *A Pictorial History of Burlesque*. New York: Putnam, 1956.

Stallybrass, Peter, and White, Allon. *The Politics and Poetics of Transgression.* Ithaca: Cornell University Press, 1986.

Stansell, Christine. *City of Women: Sex and Class and New York, 1789–1865.* New York: Knopf, 1986.

Suleiman, Susan, ed. *The Female Body in Western Culture: Contemporary Perspectives.* Cambridge: Harvard University Press, 1986.

Swift, Mary Grace. *Belles and Beaux on Their Toes: Dancing Stars in Young America.* Washington, D.C.: University Press of America, 1980.

Tocqueville, Alexis de. *Democracy in America.* 3 vols. Edited by Phillips Bradley. New York: Knopf, 1985.

Toll, Robert C. *Blacking Up: The Minstrel Show in Nineteenth-Century America.* New York: Oxford University Press, 1974.

Trollope, Frances. *Domestic Manners of the Americans.* London: Whittaker, Treacher, 1832.

Turner, Victor. *Dramas, Fields, and Metaphors: Symbolic Action in Human Society.* Ithaca: Cornell University Press, 1974.

———. *The Ritual Process: Structure and Anti-Structure.* Ithaca: Cornell University Press, 1977.

Ware, W. Porter, and Lockard, Thaddeus C., Jr. *P. T. Barnum Presents Jenny Lind: The American Tour of the Swedish Nightingale.* Baton Rouge: Louisiana State University Press, 1980.

West, Mae. *Goodness Had Nothing to Do with It.* Englewood Cliffs, N.J.: Prentice-Hall, 1959.

White, Charles. *The Virginny Mummy.* New York: Samuel French, 1864.

Whitton, Joseph. *The Naked Truth: An Inside History of "The Black Crook."* Philadelphia: H. W. Shaw, 1897.

Wilentz, Sean. *Chants Democratic: New York City and the Rise of the American Working Class, 1788–1850.* New York: Oxford University Press, 1984.

Williams, Linda. *Hard Core: Power, Pleasure, and the "Frenzy of the Visible."* Berkeley: University of California Press, 1990.

Zeidman, Irving. *The American Burlesque Show.* New York: Hawthorn Books, 1967.

Zellers, Parker. *Tony Pastor: Dean of the Vaudeville Stage.* Ypsilanti, Mich.: Eastern Michigan University Press, 1971.

ARTICLES AND BOOK CHAPTERS

Allen, Robert C. "B. F. Keith and the Origins of American Vaudeville." *Theatre Survey* 21 (1980): 105–15.

Appleton's Journal of Popular Literature, Science, and Art, July 3, 1869, p. 440.

Bennett, Tony. "Marxism and Popular Fiction." *Literature and History* 7 (1981): 138–65.

————. "Text and Social Process: The Case of James Bond." *Screen Education* 41 (1982): 3–14.

Betts, John Rickards. "P. T. Barnum and the Popularization of Natural History." *Journal of the History of Ideas* 20 (1959): 353–68.

Brooke-Rose, Christine. "Woman as Semiotic Object." In *The Female Body in Western Culture: Contemporary Perspectives*, edited by Susan Suleiman, pp. 3–21. Cambridge: Harvard University Press, 1986.

Brown, T. Allston. "The Theater in America." *New York Clipper*, April 28, 1888, p. 104.

Browne, Ray B. "Shakespeare in America: Vaudeville and Negro Minstrelsy." *American Quarterly* 12 (1960): 374–91.

Burnham, Charles. "Stage Degeneracy: An Old Cry." *Theatre Magazine* 26 (July 1917): 34, 52.

Clapp, William W. "The Drama in Boston." In *The Memorial History of Boston, 1630–1880*, edited by Justin Winsor, 4:358–65. Boston: James R. Osgood, 1883.

David, John Russell. "The Genesis of the Variety Theatre: *The Black Crook* Comes to St. Louis." *Missouri Historical Review* 64 (1970): 133–49.

Davies, Christie. "Stupidity and Rationality: Jokes from the Iron Cage." In *Humour in Society: Resistance and Control*, edited by Chris Powell and George E. C. Paton, pp. 1–32. New York: St. Martin's, 1988.

Davis, Natalie Zemon. "Women on Top: Symbolic Sexual Inversion and Political Disorder in Early Modern Europe." In *The Reversible World: Symbolic Inversion in Art and Society*, edited by Barbara A. Babcock, pp. 147–90. Ithaca: Cornell University Press, 1978.

Davis, Susan Gray. "The Career of Colonel Pluck: Folk Drama and Popular Protest in Early Nineteenth-Century Philadelphia." *Pennsylvania Magazine of History and Biography* 109 (1985): 179–202.

Dorman, James. "The Strange Career of Jim Crow Rice." *Journal of Social History* 3 (1969–70): 109–22.

Dorson, Richard. "Mose the Far-Famed and World Renown." *American Literature* 15 (1943): 288–300.

Douglas, Mary. "The Social Control of Cognition." *Man* 3 (1968): 361–76.

Dye, William. "Pennsylvania versus the Theatre." *Pennsylvania Magazine of History and Biography* 55 (1931): 333–72.

Freedley, George. "*The Black Crook* and *The White Fawn*." *Dance Index* 4 (1945): 4–16.

Gottlieb, George A. "Psychology of the American Vaudeville Show from the Manager's Point of View." *Current Opinion*, April 1916, pp. 257–58.

Gray, Barry. "The Good Old Days of the Dime Museum." *Billboard*, December 8, 1928, pp. 98–99.

Grimsted, David. "Rioting in Its Jacksonian Setting." *American Historical Review* 77 (1972): 361–97.

Grossberg, Lawrence. "Cultural Studies Revisited and Revised." In *Com-*

munications in Transition, edited by Mary S. Mander, pp. 39–70. New York: Praeger, 1983.

Gutman, Herbert. "Work, Culture, and Society in Industrializing America." *American Historical Review* 78 (1973): 531–87.

Hall, Jacqueline Dowd. "Disorderly Women: Gender and Labor Militancy in the Appalachian South." *Journal of American History* 73, no. 2 (1986): 354–82.

Hall, Stuart. "Encoding/Decoding." In *Culture, Media, Language*, edited by Stuart Hall, Dorothy Hobson, Andrew Lowe, and Paul Willis, pp. 128–39. London: Hutchinson, 1980.

———. "Recent Developments in the Theories of Language and Ideology." In *Culture, Media, Language*, edited by Stuart Hall, Dorothy Hobson, Andrew Lowe, and Paul Willis, pp. 157–62. London: Hutchinson, 1980.

Hawes, David. "Much Ado about John Brougham and Jim Fisk." *Midcontinent American Studies Journal* 8 (1967): 73–89.

Haywood, Charles. "Negro Minstrelsy and Shakespearean Burlesque." In *Folklore and Society: Essays in Honor of Benjamin A. Botkin*, edited by Bruce Jackson, pp. 77–92. Hatboro, Pa.: Folklore Association, 1966.

Herskowitz, Richard. "P. T. Barnum's Double Bind." *Social Text* 2 (Summer 1979): 133–41.

Howells, William Dean. "The New Taste in Theatricals." *Atlantic Monthly*, May 1869, pp. 635–44.

Hurst, Fanny. "Power and Horse Power." *Saturday Evening Post*, July 6, 1912, p. 6.

Irving, Henry. "The American Audience." *The Fortnightly* 43 (1885): 197–201.

James, Henry. Review of *Modern Women and What Is Said of Them*, by Elizabeth Lynn Linton. *Nation*, October 22, 1868. In *Henry James: Literary Criticism*, edited by Leon Edel, 1:19–25. New York: Literary Classics of the United States, 1984.

Jerome, William. "Vaudeville Epitaphs." *Variety*, May 11, 1912, p. 17.

Johnson, Claudia. "Burlesques of Shakespeare." *Theatre Survey* 21 (May 1980): 49–62.

———. "That Guilty Third Tier: Prostitution in Nineteenth-Century American Theaters." *American Quarterly* 27 (1975): 575–84.

Kaye, Joseph. "The Last Legs of Burlesque." *Theatre*, February 1930, pp. 36–37.

Keith, B. F. "The Vogue of Vaudeville." *National Magazine*, November 1898, pp. 146–53.

Kelley, Mary. "The Sentimentalists: Promise and Betrayal in the Home." *Signs* 4 (1979): 434–46.

Kennedy, John P. "Revised Version." *Colliers*, November 12, 1932, pp. 14, 45–48.

Krutch, Joseph Wood. "Burlesque." *Nation*, June 8, 1932, p. 642.

"Law of the Theatre." 12 *Central Law Journal* 390–92 (n.d.).

Leach, William. "Transformations in a Culture of Consumption." *Journal of American History* 71 (1984): 319–42.

Levine, Lawrence. "William Shakespeare and the American People." *American Historical Review* 89 (February 1984): 34–67.

Lippman, Monroe. "Battle for Bookings: Independents Battle the Trust." *Tulane Drama Review* 2 (1958): 38–45.

———. "Death of the Salesmen's Monopoly." *Theatre Survey* 1 (1960): 65–81.

———. "The Effect of the Theatrical Syndicate on Theatrical Art in America." *Quarterly Journal of Speech* 26 (1940): 275–82.

———. "The First Revolt against the Theatrical Syndicate." *Quarterly Journal of Speech* 41 (1955): 343–51.

Logan, Olive. "The Leg Business." *Galaxy*, August 1867, pp. 40–44.

———. "The Nude Woman Question." *Packard's Monthly*, July 1869, pp. 193–98.

McLean, Albert. "Genesis of Vaudeville: Two Letters from B. F. Keith." *Theatre Survey* 1 (1960): 82–95.

McNamara, Brooks. "'A Congress of Wonders': The Rise and Fall of the Dime Museum." *Emerson Society Quarterly* 20 (1974): 218–19.

Mahany, Barbara. "No Molds Barred!" *Washington Post*, December 27, 1986, C1, 8.

Mates, Julian. "*The Black Crook* Myth." *Theatre Survey* 7 (1966): 31–43.

Mattfield, Julius. "A Hundred Years of Grand Opera in New York, 1825–1925." *Bulletin of the New York Public Library* 29 (October 1925): 695–702.

Montgomery, David. "The Working Classes of the Pre-industrial American City." *Labor History* 9 (1968): 3–22.

Moses, Montrose J. "When Audiences Get Angry." *Theatre Magazine* 131 (January 1912): 28–32.

Odom, Leigh George. "'The Black Crook' at Niblo's Garden." *Drama Review* 26 (Spring 1982): 21–37.

Palmer, Albert M. "American Theatres." In *1795–1895, One Hundred Years of American Commerce*, edited by Chauncey Depew, pp. 167–70. New York: Haynes Pub. Co., 1895.

Peiss, Kathy. "'Charity Girls' and City Pleasures: Historical Notes on Working-Class Sexuality, 1880–1920." In *Powers of Desire: The Politics of Sexuality*, edited by Ann Snitow, Christine Stansell, and Sharon Thompson, pp. 75–87. New York: Monthly Review Press, 1983.

"The Perambulator." *The Rambler's Magazine and New York Theatrical Register*, 1809, 1:12, 14, 77.

Plotnicki, Rita. "John Brougham: The Aristophanes of American Burlesque." *Journal of Popular Culture* 12 (1978): 422–31.

Poovey, Mary. "'Scenes of an Indelicate Character': The Medical 'Treatment' of Victorian Women." In *The Making of the Modern Body: Sexuality and Society in the Nineteenth Century*, edited by Catherine Gallagher and Thomas Laqueur, pp. 146–55. Berkeley: University of California Press, 1987.

Preston, Paul. "Reminiscences of a Man About Town." In *Records of the New York Stage*, edited by Joseph Ireland, 2:146. New York: T. H. Morrell, 1866–67.

"The Profits in Clean Vaudeville." *Literary Digest*, October 7, 1911, pp. 603–5.

Saxton, Alexander. "Blackface Minstrelsy and Jacksonian Ideology." *American Quarterly* 27 (1975): 3–28.

Senelick, Lawrence. "Variety into Vaudeville: The Process Observed in Two Manuscript Gagbooks." *Theatre Survey* 19 (1978): 1–15.

Stansell, Christine. "Women, Children, and the Uses of the Street: Class and Gender Conflict in New York City, 1850–1860." *Feminist Studies* 8 (Summer 1982): 309–35.

Stedman, Jane. "From Dame to Women: W. S. Gilbert and Theatrical Transvestism." *Victorian Studies*, September 1970, pp. 27–46.

Sterling, Philip. "Burlesque." *New Theatre*, June 1936, pp. 18–19, 36–37.

"The Theatre." *Hopkinsian Magazine*, February 1829, p. 326.

Tucker, Louis L. "Ohio Show-Shop: The Western Museum of Cincinnati, 1820–1867." In *A Cabinet of Curiosities*, edited by Whitfield J. Bell, Jr., pp. 75–85. Charlottesville: University Press of Virginia, 1967.

Turner, Victor. "Comments and Conclusions." In *The Reversible World: Symbolic Inversion in Art and Society*, edited by Barbara A. Babcock, pp. 276–96. Ithaca: Cornell University Press, 1978.

Wassenstrom, William. "William Dean Howells: The Indelible Stain." *New England Quarterly* 32 (December 1959): 491–518.

"Weber and Fields." *Bulletin of the New York Public Library* 36 (1932): 802–3.

Weene, Seph. "Venus." *Heresies* 3 (1981): 36–38.

Welter, Barbara. "The Cult of True Womanhood, 1820–1860." *American Quarterly* 18 (Summer 1966): 151–74.

White, Allon. "Pigs and Pierrots: The Politics of Transgression in Modern Fiction." *Raritan* 2 (1982): 35–51.

White, Richard Grant. "The Age of Burlesque." *Galaxy*, August 1869, pp. 256–66.

Wills, Robert J. "Olive Logan vs. the Nude Woman." *Players* 47 (October–November 1971): 37–43.

Wren-Lewis, Justin. "The Encoding-Decoding Model: Criticisms and Redevelopments for Research on Decoding." *Media, Culture, and Society* 5 (1983): 179–97.

Zanger, Jules. "The Minstrel Show as Theater of Misrule." *Quarterly Journal of Speech* 60 (1974): 33–38.

Zellers, Parker. "The Cradle of Variety: The Concert Saloon." *Educational Theatre Journal* 20 (1968): 578–85.

THESES AND DISSERTATIONS

Buckley, Peter. "To the Opera House: Culture and Society in New York City, 1820–1860." Ph.D. dissertation, State University of New York at Stony Brook, 1984.

Croghan, Leland A. "New York Burlesque, 1840–1870: A Study in Theatrical Self-Criticism." Ph.D. dissertation, New York University, 1967.

Crossett, David Alan. "One Night Stand: A History of Live and Recorded Entertainment in Warren, Pennsylvania, from 1795 to the Present." Ph.D. dissertation, New York University, 1983.

Davidson, Frank Costellow. "The Rise, Development, Decline, and Influence of the American Minstrel Show." Ph.D. dissertation, New York University, 1952.

Davis, Susan Gray. "Theatre of the Streets: Parades and Ceremonies in Philadelphia, 1800–1850." Ph.D. dissertation, University of Pennsylvania, 1983.

Distler, Paul Antonie. "The Rise and Fall of Racial Comics in American Vaudeville." Ph.D. dissertation, Tulane University, 1963.

Duis, Perry R. "The Saloon and the Public City: Chicago and Boston, 1880–1970." Ph.D. dissertation, University of Chicago, 1975.

Garrett, Thomas M. "A History of Pleasure Gardens in New York City, 1700–1865." Ph.D. dissertation, New York University, 1978.

Gintautiene, Kristina. "*The Black Crook*: Ballet in the Gilded Age (1866–1876)." Ph.D. dissertation, New York University, 1984.

Henneke, Ben Graf. "The Playgoer in America, 1752–1952." Ph.D. dissertation, University of Illinois, 1956.

Hill, Lawrence James. "A History of Variety-Vaudeville in Minneapolis, Minnesota, from Its Beginnings to 1900." Ph.D. dissertation, University of Minnesota, 1979.

Kelley, Paul B. "Portrait of a Playhouse: The 'Troc' of Philadelphia, 1870–1978." Ph.D. dissertation, New York University, 1982.

Kroger, Alicia Kae. "A Critical Analysis of Edward Harrigan's Comedy." Ph.D. dissertation, University of Michigan, 1984.

Moorehouse, Vera. "Benjamin Franklin Keith: Vaudeville Magnate, the First Fifty Years, 1846–1896." M.A. thesis, Eastern Michigan University, 1975.

Moses, Marilyn A. Stolzman. "Lydia Thompson and the 'British Blondes' in the United States." Ph.D. dissertation, University of Oregon, 1978.

Oliver, George B. "Changing Pattern of Spectacle on the New York Stage (1850–1890)." Ph.D. dissertation, Pennsylvania State University, 1956.

Shank, Theodore Junior. "The Bowery Theatre, 1826–1836." Ph.D. dissertation, Stanford University, 1956.

Snyder, Frederick F. "American Vaudeville – Theatre in a Package: The Origins of Mass Entertainment." Ph.D. dissertation, Yale University, 1970.

Snyder, Robert William. "The Voice of the City: Vaudeville and the Formation of Mass Culture in New York Neighborhoods, 1880–1930." Ph.D. dissertation, New York University, 1986.

Sodders, Richard P. "The Theatre Management of Alexandre Placide in Charleston, 1794–1812." Ph.D. dissertation, Louisiana State University, 1983.

Stevens, Gary L. "Gold Rush Theater in the Alaska-Yukon Frontier." Ph.D. dissertation, University of Oregon, 1984.

Zellers, Parker. "Tony Pastor: Manager and Impressario of the American Variety Stage." Ph.D. dissertation, University of Iowa, 1964.

NEWSPAPERS

Billboard, 1900–1905.
Boston Herald, 1883–90.
National Police Gazette, 1876–1910.
New York Clipper, 1853–90.
New York Dramatic Mirror, 1895–1900.
New York Times, 1868–1938.
New York Tribune, 1862.
Philadelphia Inquirer, 1889.
Spirit of the Times, 1860–90.
Variety, 1905–15.

MANUSCRIPTS AND UNPUBLISHED PAPERS

Barras, Charles. *The Black Crook*. Original manuscript, 1862. Harvard Theatre Collection.

Brough, William. *The Field of the Cloth of Gold* [1868?]. Printed script, n.p. Performing Arts Collection, New York Public Library.

Brougham, John. *Much Ado about a Merchant of Venice* (1868). Printed script with handwritten emendations. Performing Arts Collection, New York Public Library.

Buckley, Peter. "The Culture of Leg Work: The Transformation of Burlesque after the Civil War." Paper presented at the American Historical Association Conference, December 1986.

Burnand, F. C. *Ixion; or, The Man at the Wheel.* Typescript, 1863. Performing
 Arts Collection, New York Public Library.
Byron, Henry J. *La! Sonnambula.* Printed script, n.d. Performing Arts Collec-
 tion, New York Public Library.
———; Gilbert, W. S.; Hood, T.; Leigh, H. S.; and Sketchley, Arthur. *Robin-
 son Crusoe.* Typescript, ca. 1867. British Museum, London.
Dumont, Frank. *Fun on the Twentieth-Century Limited.* Typescript, 1902. Li-
 brary of Congress.
Field, R. M. "The Boston Museum: An Interesting Retrospect." Typescript,
 n.d. Boston Public Library.
Hamilton, Marybeth. "Mae West in Vaudeville." Paper, 1987.
Herbert, Joseph. *The Geezer.* Typescript, n.d. Harvard Theatre Collection.
MacDonald, J. Fred. "Black Women on Stage: Bessie Smith to Millie Jack-
 son." Paper presented at the American Studies Association Conference,
 1988.
"The Model Playhouse of the Country." Brochure, 1894. Harvard Theatre
 Collection.
Poole, John. *Faust* (1867). Printed script, n.p. Performing Arts Collection,
 New York Public Library.
Smith, Edgar. *Fiddle-dee-dee.* Typescript, n.d. Harvard Theatre Collection.
———. *Higgledy-Piggledy.* Typescript, n.d. Harvard Theatre Collection.
———. *Hoity-Toity.* Typescript, n.d. Performing Arts Collection, New York
 Public Library.
———. *Hurly-Burly.* Typescript, n.d. Harvard Theatre Collection.
———. *Whirligig.* Typescript, n.d. Performing Arts Collection, New York
 Public Library.
———. *Whoop-Dee-Doo.* Typescript, n.d. Performing Arts Collection, New
 York Public Library.
Staples, L. S. "Dime Museums in St. Paul." Manuscript, n.d. Minnesota His-
 torical Society., Minneapolis.
Thompson, Lydia. Handwritten manuscript, [1890s]. Harvard Theatre Col-
 lection.
West, Mae. *Diamond Lil.* Typescript, 1928. Manuscripts Division, Library of
 Congress.
———. *The Drag.* Typescript, 1927. Manuscripts Division, Library of Con-
 gress.
———. *The Hussy.* Typescript, 1922. Manuscripts Division, Library of Con-
 gress.
———. *The Pleasure Man.* Typescript, 1928. Manuscripts Division, Library of
 Congress.
———. *The Ruby Ring.* Typescript, 1921. Manuscripts Division, Library of
 Congress.
———. *Sex.* Typescript, 1922. Manuscripts Division, Library of Congress.

————. *The Wicked Age*. Typescript, 1927. Manuscripts Division, Library of Congress.

FILMS, POSTERS, AND MISCELLANEOUS MATERIALS

"Barnum's American Museum." Playbill, [1851?]. Harvard Theatre Collection.

"Beautiful Indian Maidens." Poster, n.d. Prints and Photographs Division, Library of Congress.

Bell, Archie. "A Little Journey to the B. F. Keith Palace, Cleveland." Booklet, [1913?]. Harvard Theatre Collection.

"B. F. Keith's New Theatre." Brochure, 1894. Harvard Theatre Collection.

"Bon Ton Burlesquers: 365 Days Ahead of Them All." Poster, 1897. Prints and Photographs Division, Library of Congress.

"Bon Ton Burlesquers: A Warm Reception." Poster, 1898. Prints and Photographs Division, Library of Congress.

"Bon Ton Burlesquers: On the String." Poster, 1898. Prints and Photographs Division, Library of Congress.

"British Blondes Burlesque Troupe." Poster, 1870. Prints and Photographs Division, Library of Congress.

"Catalogue of the Gaiety Musee and Bijou Theatre." Brochure, 1891. Harvard Theatre Collection.

"A Dance in Pajamas." Film. American Mutoscope and Biograph Co., ca. 1903. Motion Pictures Division, Library of Congress.

"Developing Muscles of the Back and Chest." Film. Winthrop Motion Picture Co., ca. 1906. Motion Pictures Division, Library of Congress.

"Devere's High Roller's Burlesque Co.: Dining a High Roller Girl after the Show." Poster, 1898. Prints and Photographs Division, Library of Congress.

"Devere's High Roller's Burlesque Co.: How the High Roller Girls Do It." Poster, 1898. Prints and Photographs Division, Library of Congress.

"Foxy Grandpa and Polly in a Little Hilirity [sic]." Film. American Mutoscope and Biograph Co., ca. 1902. Motion Pictures Division, Library of Congress.

"Girls Swinging." Film. American Mutoscope and Biograph Co., ca. 1902. Motion Pictures Division, Library of Congress.

"High Rollers Extravaganza Co.: Initiating a High Roller." Poster, 1899. Prints and Photographs Division, Library of Congress.

"High Rollers Extravaganza Co.: Mamie Lamb." Poster, 1899. Prints and Photographs Division, Library of Congress.

"High Rollers Extravaganza Co.: A Ten Strike." Poster, 1899. Prints and Photographs Division, Library of Congress.

"The High Rollers: The Great Chariot Race in Bend Her." Poster, 1900. Prints and Photographs Division, Library of Congress.

"How Biddy Served the Potatoes Undressed." Stereograph, 1890. Prints and Photographs Division, Library of Congress.

"A Hustling Soubrette." Film. American Mutoscope and Biograph Co., ca. 1904. Motion Pictures Division, Library of Congress.

"Imperial Burlesquers: Imperials Always to the Front." Poster, 1901. Prints and Photographs Division, Library of Congress.

"Keith and Batchellor's Mammoth Museum." Handbill, September 27, 1884. Rare Book Room, Boston Public Library.

"Merry Maidens Burlesquers." Poster, 1898. Prints and Photographs Division, Library of Congress.

"The Model Playhouse of the Country." Brochure, 1894. Harvard Theatre Collection.

"Pajama Girl." Film. American Mutoscope and Biograph Co., ca. 1903. Motion Pictures Division, Library of Congress.

"Pajama Statue Girls." Film. American Mutoscope and Biograph Co., ca. 1903. Motion Pictures Division, Library of Congress.

"Phil Sheridan's New City Sports Co." Poster, n.d. Prints and Photographs Division, Library of Congress.

"The Play of the Period: The Blondes and Their Abusers." Broadside, n.d. Performing Arts Collection, New York Public Library.

"Poor Girls: It Was a Hot Night and the Mosquitoes Were Thick." Film. American Mutoscope and Biograph Co., ca. 1903. Motion Pictures Division, Library of Congress.

"The Pouting Model." Film. American Mutoscope and Biograph Co., ca. 1902. Motion Pictures Division, Library of Congress.

"Rice and Barton's Big Gaiety Spectacular Extravaganza Co." Poster, 1899. Prints and Photographs Division, Library of Congress.

"Rice and Barton's Big Gaiety Spectacular Extravaganza Co.: Hotel Jolly or Satan's Inn." Poster, 1899. Prints and Photographs Division, Library of Congress.

"Rose Hill English Folly Co." Poster, 1899. Prints and Photographs Division, Library of Congress.

"Rose Hill English Folly Co." Poster, ca. 1900. Prints and Photographs Division, Library of Congress.

"She Meets with Wife's Approval." Film. American Mutoscope and Biograph Co., ca. 1902. Motion Pictures Division, Library of Congress.

"Three Girls in a Hammock." Film. American Mutoscope and Biograph Co., ca. 1903. Motion Pictures Division, Library of Congress.

"Trapeze Disrobing Act." Film. Edison, ca. 1901. Motion Pictures Division, Library of Congress.

Tucci, Douglas Shand. *The Boston Rialto: Playhouses, Concert Halls, and*

Movie Palaces. Booklet published by author, 1977. Harvard Theatre Collection.

———. *The Puritan Muse*. N.p., n.d. Boston Public Library.

"Victoria Loftus British Blondes." Poster, 1878. Prints and Photographs Division, Library of Congress.

"Wine, Women, and Song." Film. American Mutoscope and Biograph Co., ca. 1906. Motion Pictures Division, Library of Congress.

LEGAL CASES CITED

Burton v. Scherpf, 1 Allen 133 (1861).
Clifford v. Brandon, 2 Camp. 358–68 (1809).
Commonwealth v. Porter, 1 Gray 476 (1854).
Gregory v. Brunswick, 1 C. & K. 24 (1843).
McCrea v. Marsh, 12 Gray 211 (1858).
Pearce v. Spalding, 12 Mo. App. 141 (1882).
Rex v. Forbes, 1 Craw. & D. 157 (1823).
Wallack v. City of New York, 3 Hun. 84 (1875).
Wood v. Leadbitter, 13 M. & W. 838 (1845).

MANUSCRIPT COLLECTIONS

Boston, Mass.
  Boston Public Library
Cambridge, Mass.
  Harvard University
    Harvard Theatre Collection
      Ballet Engravings Collection
Iowa City, Iowa
  Keith/Albee Collection, University of Iowa Library
New York, New York
  Performing Arts Collection, New York Public Library
Washington, D.C.
  Library of Congress
    Manuscripts Division
      Charlotte Cushman Papers
      Laura Keene Papers
      Mae West Papers
    Motion Pictures Division
    Prints and Photographs Division

Index

○ ○ ○ ○ ○ ○   ○ ○ ○ ○ ○ ○